A BOOK

OF

NEW ENGLAND LEGENDS

AND

FOLK LORE

In Prose and Poetry

BY

SAMUEL ADAMS DRAKE

AUTHOR OF "NOOKS AND CORNERS OF THE NEW ENGLAND COAST,"
"OLD LANDMARKS OF BOSTON," ETC.

ILLUSTRATED BY F. T. MERRILL

CASTLE BOOKS

INTRODUCTION.

———◆———

THE recovery of many scattered legendary waifs that not only have a really important bearing upon the early history of our country, but that also shed much light upon the spirit of its ancient laws and upon the domestic lives of its people, has seemed to me a laudable undertaking. This purpose has now taken form in the following collection of New-England Legends.

As in a majority of instances these tales go far beyond the time when the interior was settled, they naturally cluster about the seaboard; and it would scarcely be overstepping the limit separating exaggeration from truth to say that every league of the New-England coast has its story or its legend.

Disowned in an age of scepticism, there was once — and the time is not so far remote — no part of the body politic over which what we now vaguely term the legendary did not exercise the strongest influence; so that, far from being merely a record of amusing fables, these tales, which are largely founded on fact, disclose the secret springs by which society was moved and history made. One looks beneath every mechanical contrivance for the true origin of power. That is to assume that the beliefs of a people are the key to its social and political movements, and that history, taken in its broadest sense, cannot be truly written without having regard to such beliefs. Had the conviction that witches existed not been universal, public sentiment would never have countenanced the executions that took place in New England.

It may be said, then, that while History has its truth, the Legend has its own ; both taking for their end the portrayal of Man as he has existed in every age, — a creature in whom the imagination is supreme, and who performs deeds terrible or heroic according as it may be aroused into action.

No apology need be made for the prevalence of superstition among our ancestors. Our century is not the judge of its predecessors. It was a superstitious age. King Charles I. inherited all the popular beliefs. He kept, as an *attaché* of his court, an astrologer, whom he was accustomed to consult before entering upon any important or hazardous undertaking. Laud, the highest prelate in England, the implacable persecutor of our Puritan ancestors, was a man haunted by the fear of omens. Indeed the most exalted personages in Church and State yielded full credence to all those marvels, the bare mention of which now calls up a smile of incredulity or of pity. New England was the child of a superstitious mother.

Since the assertion is so often made that this is a practical age, owing no allegiance whatever to the degrading thraldom of ancient superstition, but coldly rejecting everything that cannot be fully accounted for upon rational grounds, I have thought it worth while to cite a few of those popular beliefs which neither the sceptical tendencies of the age we live in, nor its wonder-working achievements, have been able to eradicate. They belong exclusively to no class, and have been transmitted from generation to generation through the medium of an unwritten language, to which the natural impulse of the human mind toward the supernatural is the common interpreter. While religion itself works through this mysterious channel of the Unknown and the Unseen, one need not stop to argue a fact that has such high sanction. So long as these beliefs shall continue to exert a control over the every-day actions of men, it would be useless to deny to them a place in the movements regulating society ; and so long as the twin mysteries of life and death confront us with their unsolved problems, it is certain that where reason cannot pass beyond, the imagination will still strive to penetrate within, the barrier separating us from the invisible world. This invisible world is the realm of the supernatural.

You will seldom see a man so much in a hurry that he will not stop to pick up a horseshoe. One sees this ancient charm against evil spirits in every household. In fact this piece of bent iron has become the popular symbol for good luck. Throwing an old shoe after a departing friend is as common a practice to-day as it ever was. Very few maidens neglect the opportunity to get a peep at the new moon over the right shoulder; and the old couplet, —

> See the moon through the glass,
> You'll have trouble while it lasts, —

is still extant. I know people who could not be induced to sit with thirteen at the table, who consider spilling the salt as unlucky, and who put faith in dreams!

With Catholics the belief in the efficacy of charms and of relics is a part of their religion. It is not long since a person advertised in a public journal for a caul; while among ignorant people charms against sickness, or drowning, or evil spirits are still much worn. But their use is not wholly confined to this class; for I have myself known intelligent men who were in the habit of carrying a potato in their pocket, or of wearing a horse-chestnut suspended from the neck, as a cure for the rheumatism.

Sailors retain unimpaired most of their old superstitions concerning things lucky or unlucky. Farmers are invariably a superstitious folk, — at least in those places where they have lived from generation to generation. The pretty and touching custom of telling the bees of a death in the family is, as I have reason to know, a practice still adhered to in some parts of the country. The familiar legend of the hedgehog remains a trusted indication of an early or a late spring. Farmers have many superstitions that have been domesticated among them for centuries. For instance, it is a common belief that if a creature loses its cud the animal will die unless one is obtained for it by dividing the cud of another beast. A sick cow will recover by having a live frog pass through her; but the frog must be living, or the charm will not work. If a dog is seen eating grass, it is a sign of wet weather; so it is if the grass is spotted with what is vulgarly called frogs' spittle. The girls believe that if you can form a wish while a meteor is falling, the wish will be fulfilled; they will not pluck the common red field-lily, for fear it will make them become freckled. In the country there are still found persons plying the trade of fortune-telling, while the number of haunted houses is notably increasing. The "lucky-bone" of a codfish and the "wishing-bone" of a chicken are things of wide repute.

Plants and flowers — those beautiful emblems of immortality — have from immemorial time possessed their peculiar attributes or virtues. There are the mystic plants, and there are the symbolical ones, like the evergreens used in church-decoration and in cemeteries. Where is the maiden who has not diligently searched up and down the fields for the bashful four-leaved clover? How many books enclose within their leaves this little token of some unspoken wish! The oracle of the Marguerite in Goethe's "Faust," —

> Il m'aime;
> Il m'aime beaucoup;
> A la folie;
> Pas du tout, —

may oftener be consulted to-day than many a fair questioner of Fate would be willing to admit. Let those who will, say that all this is less than nothing; yet I much doubt if the saying will bring conviction to the heart of womankind.

Precious stones continue to hold in the popular mind something of their old power to work good or evil to the wearer. A dealer in gems tells me that the sale of certain stones is materially affected by the superstitions concerning them. It will be seen that some of these superstitions attach to the most important concerns of life. My friend the dealer, who is quite as well versed in his calling as Mr. Isaacs was, says that the opal is the gem that is most frequently spoken of as unlucky, and that the sale of the opal of late years has been very slow on that account. "It seems," he continues, "as if many ladies really believed that it would bring them misfortune to wear or even to own an opal; and we frequently hear ladies say that they would not accept one as a gift." Some writers attribute this unpopularity to Scott's "Anne of Geierstein." This, at least, is a modern superstition; for the opal was once considered a talisman of rare virtue.

An old jeweller tells me that he frequently sells a moonstone as a "lucky stone." It is of little pecuniary value, but he says that it is worn in rings and charms as bringing good luck. The moonstone has furnished Wilkie Collins with the theme for one of his weird tales.

My informant goes on to say that "a fine turquoise is of a beautiful blue, — about the color of a robin's egg. For some reason not perfectly understood it changes from blue to green, and sometimes to white. I own a turquoise myself, which I am sure changes color, sometimes looking green, and sometimes blue. This change of color gave rise to the belief that the color of a turquoise varied with the health of the wearer, being blue when the wearer was in good health, and white or green in case of ill-health. The emerald is said to be the symbol of jealousy, — 'the green-eyed monster.' For this reason it is not considered as being suitable for an engagement-ring. I don't know that I ever heard of one being offered as an engagement-gift; and if a young gentleman should ask my advice in regard to buying an emerald ring for this purpose, I should dissuade him, on the ground that the young lady might look upon it as a bad omen." This feeling or superstition is used in Black's story of "The Three Feathers," in which a marriage is prevented by the gift of an emerald ring; "for," says the novelist, "how could any two people marry who had engaged themselves with an emerald ring?" A sapphire, on the contrary, given by another admirer, brings matters to a happy conclusion; once more fulfilling the prophecy of an old rhyme, —

Oh, green 's forsaken,
And yellow 's forsworn,
And blue 's the sweetest
Color that 's worn !

There certainly is a difference in the way that all these beliefs are received, — some people subscribing to them fully and
frankly, while others, who do not like to be laughed at by
their sceptical neighbors, speaking of them as trifles.   But such
doubters may be better judged by their acts than by their pro-
fessions, — at least so long as they are willing to try the potency
of this or that charm, "just to see how it will come out."

To return to the legendary pieces that compose this volume,
it is proper to state that only certain poetic versions have hitherto been accessible to the public, and that consequently impressions have been formed that these versions were good and valid
narratives ; while the fact is that the poems are not so much
designed to teach history or its truth, as to illustrate its spirit
in an effective and picturesque manner.   Yet in most cases they
do deal with real personages and events, and they stand for
faithful relations.

It was this fact that first gave me the idea of bringing the
prose and poetic versions together, in order that those interested,
more especially teachers, might have as ready access to the truth,
as hitherto they have had to the romance, of history.   •

For enabling me to carry out this idea my thanks are especially due to Messrs. Houghton, Mifflin & Co., who promptly
granted me their permission to use the several extracts taken
from the poems of Longfellow, Whittier, and Holmes ; and
I beg all those literary friends who have extended the like
courtesy to accept the like acknowledgment.

S. A. D.

MELROSE, Mass., Oct. 1883.

Contents

Part First.

BOSTON LEGENDS.

	PAGE
The Solitary of Shawmut. — *J. L. Motley*	3
Boston Common. — *O. W. Holmes*	10
Mistress Anne Hutchinson	11
The Death of Rainsborough	22
The Case of Mistress Ann Hibbins	28
Mary Dyer	36
The King's Missive	46
The Quaker Prophetess	56
In the Old South Church. — *J. G. Whittier*	59
More Wonders of the Invisible World	60
Calef in Boston. — *J. G. Whittier*	65
Nix's Mate	66
The Duel on the Common	69
Duc d'Anville's Descent	71
A Ballad of the French Fleet. — *H. W. Longfellow*	75

PAGE

Christ Church. — *Edwin B. Russell* 77
Paul Revere's Ride 78
Peter Rugg. — *William Austin* 90
A Legend of the Old Elm. — *Isaac McLellan, Jr.* 105
Roxbury Pudding-Stone 111
The Dorchester Giant. — *O. W. Holmes* 111

Part Second.

CAMBRIDGE LEGENDS.

The Washington Elm 115
The Last of the Highwaymen 119
The Eliot Oak 121

Part Third.

LYNN AND NAHANT LEGENDS.

The Bridal of Pennacook 128
The Pirate's Glen 132
Moll Pitcher 137
High Rock. — *Elizabeth F. Merrill* 141
Nahant 148
The Sea-Serpent 156
The Floure of Souvenance 159
Swampscott Beach 162

Part Fourth.

SALEM LEGENDS.

Salem 167
The Escape of Philip English 176
Endicott and the Red Cross 180
Cassandra Southwick 183
The Witchcraft Tragedy 188
Giles Corey the Wizard 194
The Bell Tavern Mystery 196

Part Fifth.

MARBLEHEAD LEGENDS.

PAGE

Marblehead : The Town 205
The Shrieking Woman 211
The Strange Adventures of Philip Ashton 212
Agnes, the Maid of the Inn 221
Skipper Ireson's Ride 227
A Plea for Flood Ireson. — *Charles T. Brooks* 232

Part Sixth.

CAPE-ANN LEGENDS.

Cape Ann 237
Captain John Smith 243
Thacher's Island 244
Anthony Thacher's Shipwreck 245
The Swan Song of Parson Avery. — *J. G. Whittier* 252
The Spectre Leaguers 253
The Garrison of Cape Ann. — *J. G. Whittier* 258
Old Meg, the Witch 259
An Escape from Pirates 261
Norman's Woe 263
Hannah binding Shoes. — *Lucy Larcom* 267

Part Seventh.

IPSWICH AND NEWBURY LEGENDS.

Ipswich 273
Old Ipswich Town. — *Appleton Morgan* 277
Heartbreak Hill 279
Newburyport 284
Lord Timothy Dexter 292
The Old Elm of Newbury 301
The Prophecy of Samuel Sewall 304
The Double-Headed Snake 307
Thomas Macy, the Exile 310
Telling the Bees 314

Part Eighth.

HAMPTON AND PORTSMOUTH LEGENDS.

PAGE

Hampton 319
Jonathan Moulton and the Devil 322
Goody Cole 328
The Wreck of Rivermouth. — *J. G. Whittier* 329
Portsmouth 331
The Stone-throwing Devil 333
Lady Wentworth 337

Part Ninth.

YORK, ISLES-OF-SHOALS, AND BOON-ISLAND LEGENDS.

Isles of Shoals 345
On Star Island. — *Sarah O. Jewett* 348
A Legend of Blackbeard 350
The Spanish Wreck 352
The Spaniards' Graves. — *Celia Thaxter* 354
Boon Island 355
The Watch of Boon Island. — *Celia Thaxter* 356
The Grave of Champernowne 357
Agamenticus (York, Maine) 358
Mount Agamenticus 359
Saint Aspenquid. — *John Albee* 360

Part Tenth.

OLD-COLONY LEGENDS.

Hanging by Proxy 365
The Old Oaken Bucket. — *Samuel Woodworth.* 370
Destruction of Minot's Light 375
Minot's Ledge. — *Fitz-James O'Brien* 377
Legends of Plymouth Rock 378
Mary Chilton. — *George Bancroft Griffith* 380
The Courtship of Myles Standish 383
The Pilgrim Fathers. — *Percival, Pierpont, Hemans, Sprague* . . . 389

Part Eleventh.

RHODE-ISLAND LEGENDS.

PAGE

The Skeleton in Armor 393
The Newport Tower. — *J. G. Brainard, L. H. Sigourney* 401
Block Island 403
The Buccaneer 409
The Palatine. — *J. G. Whittier* 413
The Last of the Wampanoags 414

Part Twelfth.

CONNECTICUT LEGENDS.

The Phantom Ship 417
The Charter Oak 421
The Charter Oak (*poem*). — *L. H. Sigourney* 426
The Place of Noises 427
Matchit Moodus. — *J. G. Brainard* 429
The Spanish Galleon 431
The Money-Diggers. — *J. G. Brainard* 435
The Norwich Elms. — *L. H. Sigourney* 436

Part Thirteenth.

NANTUCKET AND OTHER LEGENDS.

Nantucket Legends 441
The Alarmed Skipper. — *James T. Fields* 447
The Unknown Champion 449

Authors cited in Prose.

SIR WALTER SCOTT.
JOHN L. MOTLEY.
WILLIAM AUSTIN.
ISAAC McLELLAN, JR.
NATHANIEL HAWTHORNE.
JOSEPH BESSE.
CHARLES LAMB.
JOSEPH STORY.

BAYARD TAYLOR.
ANTHONY THACHER.
COTTON MATHER.
OLIVER CROMWELL.
THOMAS MORTON.
ALONZO LEWIS.
BENJAMIN TRUMBULL.
RICHARD HAKLUYT.

———◇———

Authors cited in Poetry.

O. W. HOLMES.
H. W. LONGFELLOW.
JAMES R. LOWELL.
LUCY LARCOM.
J. G. WHITTIER.
J. G. BRAINARD.
SAMUEL BUTLER.
CHARLES T. BROOKS.
EDWIN B. RUSSELL.
LYDIA H. SIGOURNEY.
ELIZABETH F. MERRILL.
W. W. STORY.
R. H. DANA.
CELIA THAXTER.
JONATHAN PLUMMER.

APPLETON MORGAN.
HANNAH F. GOULD.
SARAH O. JEWETT.
HARRIET P. SPOFFORD.
JOHN ELWYN.
JOHN ALBEE.
SAMUEL WOODWORTH.
FITZ-JAMES O'BRIEN.
GEORGE BANCROFT GRIFFITH.
JOHN PIERPONT.
CHARLES SPRAGUE.
JAMES G. PERCIVAL.
FELICIA HEMANS.
JAMES T. FIELDS.
ROBERT SOUTHEY.

LIST OF ILLUSTRATIONS.

	PAGE
Robinson, Stevenson, and Mary Dyer going to Execution, *Frontispiece*	
Vignette, Puritan Hats	3
The Solitary of Shawmut	6
Hanging-Lamp	11
Site of Mrs. Hutchinson's House	15
Trial of Mrs. Hutchinson	19
The Death of Rainsborough	26
Night-Watchman	28
Execution of Mrs. Hibbins	32
The Old Elm	34
Scourging a Quaker	37
Hand-Reel	42
Endicott receiving the King's Order	48
Liberty Tree	50
Ancient Houses, North End	58
Candlestick, Bible, and Spectacles	62
Tomb of the Mathers	64
Nix's Mate	66
The Duel on the Common	70
Old South Church	71
Christ Church	77
Boston, from Breed's Hill	80
Sign of the Green Dragon	81
Grenadier, 1775	83
Revere arousing the Minute-Man	86
Peter Rugg and the Thunder-Storm	92
Equestrians	94
Hackney-Coach	95
Market-Woman	100

	PAGE
Boston Truck	103
Chaise, 1776	107
The Money-Digger	109
Old Milestone, Dorchester	111
Old Fire-Dogs	112
Vignette, Wine and Hour Glasses	115
The Washington Elm	116
The Eliot Oak, Brighton	122
Milestone, Cambridge	124
Vignette, Symbols of Witchcraft	127
An Indian Princess	129
Moll Pitcher	138
Moll Pitcher's Cottage	143
Egg Rock and the Sea-Serpent	157
Forget-me-nots	159
A Spring Carol	164
Vignette, The Witches' Ride	167
Philip English's House, Salem	177
Cutting out the Cross	181
Soldier of 1630	182
Condemned to be sold	184
The Parsonage, Salem Village	191
Staffs used by Jacobs when going to Execution	192
The Bell from an Old Print	199
Tailpiece	201
Endicott's Sun-Dial; Designs from Old Money	205
Low's Pirate Flag	212
Alone on the Desert Island	217
Love at First Sight	222
Skipper Ireson's Ride	229
Tailpiece	233

	PAGE
Vignette, Pewter Dishes	237
The Magnolia	237
The Shipwreck	246
A Sortie upon the Demons	255
Norman's Woe Rock	264
Poor lone Hannah	268
Tailpiece, Bats	269
Vignette, The Cabalistic Nine	273
Padlock and Key, Ipswich Jail	275
Ipswich Heads	278
Men of Mark	280
The Maiden's Watch	281
Beacon, Salisbury Point	285
Whitefield's Monument	290
Lord Timothy Dexter's Mansion	293
Warming-Pan	298
Lord Timothy Dexter	299
The Old Elm of Newbury	302
Ye Double-Headed Snake	308
Escape of Goodman Macy	312
Beehive	315
Tailpiece	316
Vignette, Bats	319
Boar's Head	319
Jonathan Moulton and ye Devil	323
"I shall ride in my Chariot yet, Ma'am!"	340
Tailpiece, Umbrella	342
Captain Teach, or Blackbeard	351

	PAGE
Vignette, Mayflowers	365
The Old Oaken Bucket	372
The First Minot's Lighthouse	375
Mary Chilton's Leap	379
Ancient Gravestone, Burial Hill	381
Monument over Forefathers' Rock, Plymouth	382
Standish House, Duxbury	384
"Prithee, John, why don't you speak for yourself?"	387
Tailpiece, Candlestick, Bible, and Spectacles	390
Helmet, Puritan Time	393
Old Windmill, Newport	394
The Skeleton in Armor	397
Ancient Windmill	405
Lee on the Spectre Horse	411
Vignette, Hairdresser's Shop	417
The Phantom Ship	419
The Charter Oak	423
Old Warehouses, New London	432
Ancient Mill, New London	433
Vignette, Quaker Heads	441
Bass Rocks, Gay Head, Cuttyhunk	442
Goffe rallying the Settlers	453
Graves of the Regicides, New Haven	456
Tailpiece, Blacksmith's Arms	457

Part First.

BOSTON LEGENDS.

THE SOLITARY OF SHAWMUT.

BY J. L. MOTLEY.

1628.

A SOLITARY figure sat upon the summit of Shawmut. He was a man of about thirty years of age, somewhat above the middle height, slender in form, with a pale, thoughtful face. He wore a confused dark-colored, half-canonical dress, with a gray broad-leaved hat strung with shells, like an ancient palmer's, and slouched back from his pensive brow, around which his prematurely gray hair fell in heavy curls far down upon his neck. He had a wallet at his side, a hammer in his girdle, and a long staff in his hand. The hermit of Shawmut looked out upon a scene of winning beauty. The promontory resembled rather two islands than a peninsula, although it was anchored to the continent by a long slender thread of land which seemed hardly to restrain it from floating out to join its sister islands, which were thickly strewn about the bay. The peak upon which the hermit sat was the highest of the three cliffs of the peninsula : upon the southeast, and very near him, rose another hill of lesser height and more rounded form ; and upon the other side, and toward the north, a third craggy peak presented its bold and elevated front to the ocean. Thus the whole peninsula was made up of three lofty crags. It was from this triple conformation of the promontory of Shawmut that was derived the appellation of Trimountain, or Tremont, which it soon afterwards received.

The vast conical shadows were projected eastwardly, as the hermit, with his back to the declining sun, looked out upon the sea.

The bay was spread out at his feet in a broad semicircle, with its extreme headlands vanishing in the hazy distance, while beyond rolled the vast expanse of ocean, with no spot of habitable earth beyond those outermost barriers and that far distant fatherland which the exile had left forever. Not a solitary sail whitened those purple waves, and saving the wing of the sea-gull, which now and then flashed in the sunshine or gleamed across the dimness of the eastern horizon, the solitude was at the moment unbroken by a single movement of animated nature. An intense and breathless silence enwrapped the scene with a vast and mystic veil. The bay presented a spectacle of great beauty. It was not that the outlines of the coast around it were broken into those jagged and cloud-like masses,— that picturesque and startling scenery where precipitous crag, infinite abyss, and roaring surge unite to awaken stern and sublime emotions ; on the contrary, the gentle loveliness of this transatlantic scene inspired a soothing melancholy more congenial to the contemplative character of its solitary occupant. The bay, secluded within its forest-crowned hills, decorated with its necklace of emerald islands, with its dark-blue waters gilded with the rays of the western sun, and its shadowy forests of unknown antiquity expanding into infinite depths around, was an image of fresh and virgin beauty, a fitting type of a new world unadorned by art, unploughed by industry, unscathed by war, wearing none of the thousand priceless jewels of civilization, and unpolluted by its thousand crimes, — springing, as it were, from the bosom of the ocean, cool, dripping, sparkling, and fresh from the hand of its Creator.

On the left, as the pilgrim sat with his face to the east, the outlines of the coast were comparatively low, but broken into gentle and pleasing forms. Immediately at his feet lay a larger island, in extent nearly equal to the peninsula of Shawmut, covered with mighty forest-trees, and at that day untenanted by a human being, although but a short time afterwards it became the residence of a distinguished pioneer. Outside this bulwark a chain of thickly wooded islets stretched across from shore to shore, with but one or two narrow channels between, presenting a picturesque and effectual barrier to the boisterous storms of ocean. They seemed like naiads, those islets lifting above the billows their gentle heads, crowned with the budding garlands of the spring, and circling hand in hand, like protective deities, about the scene.

On the south, beyond the narrow tongue of land which bound the peninsula to the main, and which was so slender that the spray from the eastern side was often dashed across it into the calmer cove of the west, rose in the immediate distance that long, boldly broken purple-colored ridge called the Massachusetts, or Mount Arrow Head, by the natives, and by the first English discoverer baptized the Cheviot Hills. On their left, and within the deep curve of the coast, were the slightly elevated heights of Passanogessit, or Merry Mount, and on their right stretched the broad forest, hill beyond hill, away. Towards the west and northwest, the eye wandered over a vast undulating panorama of gently rolling heights, upon whose summits the gigantic pine-forests, with their towering tops piercing the clouds, were darkly shadowed upon the western sky, while in the dim distance, far above and beyond the whole, visible only through a cloudless atmosphere, rose the airy summits of the Wachusett, Watatick, and Monadnock Mountains. Upon the inland 'side, at the base of the hill, the Quinobequin River, which Smith had already christened with the royal name of his unhappy patron, Charles, might be seen writhing in its slow and tortuous course, like a wounded serpent, till it lost itself in the blue and beautiful cove which spread around the whole western edge of the peninsula; and within the same basin, directly opposite the northern peak of Shawmut, advanced the bold and craggy promontory of Mishawum, where Walford, the solitary smith, had built his thatched and palisaded house. The blue thread of the River Mystic, which here mingled its

THE SOLITARY OF SHAWMUT.

waters with the Charles, gleamed for a moment beyond the heights of Mishawum, and then vanished into the frowning forest.

Such was the scene, upon a bright afternoon of spring, which spread before the eyes of the solitary, William Blaxton, the hermit of Shawmut. It was a simple but sublime image, that gentle exile in his silvan solitude. It was a simple but sublime thought, which placed him and sustained him in his lone retreat. In all ages there seem to exist men who have no appointed place in the world. They are before their age in their aspirations, above it in their contemplation, but behind it in their capacity for action. Keen to detect the follies and the inconsistencies which surround them, shrinking from the contact and the friction of the rough and boisterous world without, and building within the solitude of their meditations the airy fabric of a regenerated and purified existence, they pass their nights in unproductive study, and their days in dreams. With intelligence bright and copious enough to illuminate and to warm the chill atmosphere of the surrounding world, if the scattered rays were concentrated, but with an inability or disinclination to impress themselves upon other minds, they pass their lives without obtaining a result, and their characters, dwarfed by their distance from the actual universe, acquire an apparent indistinctness and feebleness which in reality does not belong to them.

The impending revolution in Church and State which hung like a gathering thunder-cloud above England's devoted head, was exciting to the stronger spirits, whether of mischief or of virtue, who rejoiced to mingle in the elemental war and to plunge into the rolling surge of the world's events ; while to the timid, the hesitating, and the languid, it rose like a dark and threatening phantom, scaring them into solitude, or urging them to seek repose and safety in obscurity. Thus there may be men whose spirits are in advance of their age, while still the current of the world flows rapidly past them.

Of such men, and of such instincts, was the solitary who sat on the cliffs of Shawmut. Forswearing the country of his birth and early manhood, where there seemed, in the present state of her affairs, no possibility that minds like his could develop or sustain themselves, — dropping, as it were, like a premature and unripened fruit from the bough where its blossoms had first unfolded, — he had wandered into voluntary exile with hardly a regret. Debarred from ministering at the altar to which he had consecrated his youth, because unable to comply with mummery at which his soul revolted, he had become a high priest of nature, and had reared a pure and solitary altar in the wilderness. He had dwelt in this solitude for three or four years, and had found in the contemplation of nature, in the liberty of conscience, in solitary study and self-communing, a solace for the ills he had suffered, and a recompense for the world he had turned his back upon forever.

His spirit was a prophetic spirit, and his virtues belonged not to his times. In an age which regarded toleration as a crime, he had the courage to cultivate it as a virtue. In an age in which liberty of conscience was considered fearful licentiousness, he left his fatherland to obtain it, and was as ready to rebuke the intolerant tyranny of the nonconformist of the wilderness, as he had been to resist the bigotry and persecution of the prelacy at home. In short, the soul of the gentle hermit flew upon pure white wings before its age, but it flew, like the dove, to the wilderness. Wanting both power and inclination to act upon others, he became not a reformer, but a recluse. Having enjoyed and improved a classical education at the University of Cambridge, he was a thorough and an elegant scholar. He was likewise a profound observer, and a student of nature in all her external manifestations, and loved to theorize and to dream in the various walks of science. The botanical and mineralogical wonders of the New World were to him the objects of unceasing speculation, and he loved to proceed from the known to the unknown, and to weave fine chains of thought, which to his soaring fancy served to bind the actual to the unseen and the spiritual, and upon which, as upon the celestial ladder in the patriarch's vision, he could dream that the angels of the Lord were descending to earth from heaven.

The day was fast declining as the solitary still sat upon the peak and mused. He arose as the sun was sinking below the forest-crowned hills which girt his silvan hermitage, and gazed steadfastly towards the west.

"Another day," he said, "hath shone upon my lonely path; another day hath joined the buried ages which have folded their wings beneath yon glowing west, leaving in their noiseless flight across this virgin world no trace nor relic of their passage. 'T is strange, 't is fearful, this eternal and unbroken silence. Upon what fitful and checkered scenes hath yonder sun looked down in other lands, even in the course of this single day's career! Events as thickly studded as the stars of heaven have clustered and shone forth beneath his rays, even as his glowing chariot-wheels performed their daily course; and here, in this mysterious and speechless world, as if a spell of enchantment lay upon it, the silence is unbroken, the whole face of nature still dewy and fresh. The step of civilization hath not adorned nor polluted the surface of this wilderness. No stately temples gleam in yonder valleys, no storied monument nor aspiring shaft pierces yonder floating clouds; no mighty cities, swarming with life, filled to bursting with the ten thousand attendants of civilized humanity, luxury and want, pampered sloth, struggling industry, disease, crime, riot, pestilence, death, all hotly pent within their narrow precincts, encumber yon sweeping plains; no peaceful villages, clinging to ancient, ivy-mantled churches; no teeming fields, spreading their vast and nourishing bosoms to the toiling thousands, meet this wandering gaze. No cheerful chime of vesper-bell, no peaceful low of the returning kine, no watch-dog's bark, no merry shout of children's innocent voices, no floating music from the shepherd's pipe, no old familiar sounds of humanity, break on this listening ear. No snowy sail shines on yon eternal ocean, its blue expanse unruffled and unmarred as the azure heaven; and ah! no crimson banners flout the sky, and no embattled hosts shake with their martial tread this silent earth. 'T is silence and mystery all. Shall it be ever thus? Shall this green and beautiful world, which so long hath slept invisibly at the side of its ancient sister, still weave its virgin wreath unsoiled by passion and pollution? Shall this new, vast page in the broad history of man remain unsullied, or shall it soon flutter in the storm-winds of fate, and be stamped with the same iron record, the same dreary catalogue of misery and crime, which fills the chronicle of the elder world? 'T is passing strange, this sudden apocalypse! Lo! is it not as if the universe, the narrow universe which bounded men's thoughts in ages past, had swung open, as if by an almighty fiat, and spread wide its eastern and western wings at once, to shelter the myriads of the human race?"

The hermit arose, slowly collected a few simples which he had culled from the wilderness, a few roots of early spring flowers which he destined for his garden, and stored them in his wallet, and then, grasping his long staff, began slowly to descend the hill.

BOSTON COMMON, — FIRST PICTURE.

BY O. W. HOLMES.

[The first of the poet Holmes's "Three Pictures" depicts the same person and scene that we have considered the most fitting introduction to our Legends, — the solitary inhabitant and the solitude that his presence rendered still more lonely. But preferring this to the companionship of the "Lord's brethren," as he is said to have called the Puritan settlers of Boston, Blackstone removed into the heart of the outlying wilderness, where savages were his only neighbors. Here he died. The spot where his lonely cottage stood in Shawmut, and the place where he is buried, are equally unknown.]

> ALL overgrown with bush and fern,
>   And straggling clumps of tangled trees,
> With trunks that lean and boughs that turn,
>   Bent eastward by the mastering breeze, —
> With spongy bogs that drip and fill
>   A yellow pond with muddy rain,
> Beneath the shaggy southern hill,
>   Lies, wet and low, the Shawmut plain.

And hark ! the trodden branches crack ;
  A crow flaps off with startled scream ;
A straying woodchuck canters back ;
  A bittern rises from the stream ;
Leaps from his lair a frightened deer ;
  An otter plunges in the pool ; —
Here comes old Shawmut's pioneer,
  The parson on his brindled bull !

MISTRESS ANNE HUTCHINSON.

1634.

THE biographies of Mrs. Anne Hutchinson have, so to speak, been written by her enemies. Modern authors, in writing of her, have rehearsed her story from the point of view of the seventeenth century, and we live in the nineteenth. But History accepts no verdict that is not founded in impartial justice, and impartial justice was the one thing that Anne Hutchinson could expect neither from her accusers nor her judges. All the errors imputed to her — and they were sufficiently venial of themselves — mere quibbles, in fact — might and should, we think, have been settled within the church of which she was a member ; but the voice of the community in which she lived, which knew and respected her most for her Christian virtues and her shining talents, was silenced in the general outcry raised from without, "Crucify her, crucify her !" and, weakly yielding to it, the civil arm struck her down as relentlessly as it would have done the worst

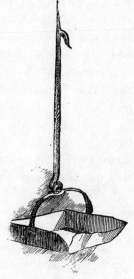

LAMP.

of criminals or the most dangerous enemy to public order. Mrs. Hutchinson was driven with ignominy from her home into exile, for maintaining in her own house that a mere profession of faith could not evidence salvation unless the Spirit first revealed itself from within. Her appeal is to be heard. It is too late to blot out the record, but there is yet time to reverse the attainder.

We begin our sketch with a simple introduction.

Anne Marbury was a daughter of Francis Marbury, who was first a minister in Lincolnshire, and afterwards in London. This fact should be borne in mind when following her after career. She was the daughter of a scholar and a theologian. Naturally, therefore, much of her unmarried as well as her married life had been passed in the society of ministers, whom she learned to esteem more for what they knew than for what they preached. The same fact, too, her intellectual gifts being considered, reasonably accounts for her pondering deeply the truths of Christianity and her fondness for theological discussion both for its own sake and as involving the great problem of her own life. It was the atmosphere in which she had lived and moved and had her being. It aroused and quickened her intellectual faculties and perceptions. She lived, too, in a time of great religious excitement, soon to become one of active warfare, the period of the great Puritan revolt, so that it is easily seen how that movement, which had enlisted some of the noblest women in England, should absorb such a one as Anne, who was intellectually an enthusiast and morally an agitator, who had been accustomed to breathe the atmosphere of adulation, and who was ambitious, capable, and adroit. While still young, she married William Hutchinson, a country gentleman of good character and estate, also of Lincolnshire. We know very little of him, and that little comes from Winthrop, the bitter enemy and persecutor of his wife, who indeed speaks of the husband in terms approaching contempt. But this is also an unconscious tribute to the superior talents of Anne. Were it all true, we simply discover once more the mutual yet unaccountable sympathy existing between a strong woman and a weak man which it is the custom of the world to satirize or to sneer at. There is, however, little doubt that the attachment of one for the other was mutually lasting and sincere, in spite of the sore trials to which their married life was exposed. But allowing that he was eclipsed by the superior brilliancy of his wife, there is quite enough evidence to prove that William Hutchinson was a man of sterling character and worth. He played a secondary, but no ignoble, part in the events we have to narrate.

It happened that the Hutchinsons were parishioners of the Rev. John Cotton when that celebrated divine was minister of the Church of Boston, in Lincolnshire. For him and his abilities Mrs. Hutchinson had the highest respect and esteem. And when Cotton fled to New England, as he like so many others was at length compelled to do, in order to escape from the tyranny of the bishops, the Hutchinsons also resolved to emigrate thither, and presently the whole family did so. It is proper to be mentioned here that Mr. Hutchinson's sister had married the Rev. John Wheelwright, another minister of Lincolnshire, who was also deprived for nonconformity, and who also came to New England in consequence of the persecutions of Archbishop Laud.

The long interval that elapsed between the date of her marriage and that of her removal to America is very imperfectly filled out in the notices we have of Mrs. Hutchinson's life. We are not made acquainted with any of those formative processes by which she became so well equipped for the mental and spiritual conflict that she was soon to enter upon with an adversary who could neither learn nor forget. A family had now grown up around her. The oldest children were now young men and young women ; so that it was no young, sentimental, or unbalanced novice, but a middle-aged, matured, and experienced woman of the world who embarked in the autumn of 1634 for New England, looking eagerly there to obtain and enjoy liberty of conscience among those who might be supposed, if any people on the earth could, to know its value.

During the voyage she entered into discussions with some Puritan ministers who were also going out to New England, upon such abstruse points as what were the evidences of justification, and she broadly hinted that when they should arrive at their destination they might expect to hear more from her. From these things, trivial in themselves, it is clear that Mrs. Hutchinson considered herself to have a mission to deliver to the people and churches of New England. She avowed her entire belief in direct revelations made to the elect, moreover declaring that never had anything of importance happened to her which had not been revealed to her beforehand.

The vessel made her port on the 18th of September, 1634. Its appearance was so mean and so uninviting, that one of her fellow passengers, supposing it to have depressed her spirits, commented upon it, in order, as it appeared, to draw her out. But she denied that the meanness of the place had in any way affected her, because, as she said, "she knew that the bounds of her habitation were already determined."

Upon their arrival, Mr. and Mrs. Hutchinson made their application to be received as members of the church. This step was indispensable to admit them into Christian fellowship and him to the privileges of a citizen. He was admitted in October, but in consequence of the reports already spread concerning her extravagant opinions, Mrs. Hutchinson was subjected to a searching examination before her request was granted. She, however, passed through the ordeal safely, the examining ministers, one of whom was her old and beloved pastor, Mr. Cotton, declaring themselves satisfied with her answers. She entered the Boston church in November.

For some time onward we hear very little of Mrs. Hutchinson, except that she was treated with particular respect and attention by Mr. Cotton and others. The getting settled in a new home probably occupied her to the exclusion of everything else. Her husband took a house in Boston, and being duly admitted a freeman of the Colony, he was immediately called upon to bear his part in business of public concern, which he did willingly

and faithfully.   He received a grant of lands in Braintree from
the General Court.   He was elected to, and served for several
terms as a deputy in, this body, it being, singularly enough, his
fortune to sit as a member when Roger Williams was brought
to the bar, tried for his heretical opinions, and banished by it
out of the Colony.

The year 1636 was destined to witness one of the greatest
religious commotions that have ever puzzled the unlearned or seriously called in question the wisdom of the founders of the Colony.
The more it is studied the more inexplicable it appears.

SITE OF MRS. HUTCHINSON'S HOUSE.

A young man of liberal views, who had not been hardened
by persecution, was then governor of the Colony, and, for the
moment, the popular idol.   This was Harry Vane, who afterwards died on the scaffold.   He with Mr. Cotton took much
notice of Mrs. Hutchinson, and their example was quickly followed by the leading and influential people of the town, who
treated her with much consideration and respect.   Already her
benevolence toward the suffering or the needy had won for her

many friends, while her intrepidity of soul and her capacity for dealing with those interesting questions from the discussion of which they were excluded, led many of her own sex to look up to her not only as a person whose opinions were worth regarding, but also with admiration amounting to homage.

Adopting an established custom of the town, Mrs. Hutchinson held in her own house two weekly meetings, — one for men and women, and one exclusively for women, — at which she was the oracle. These meetings were for no other purpose than to hear read and to discuss the sermons of the previous Sabbath, and for general religious conversation and edification. They were what would be called in our own day a club. The bringing women together in any way for independent thought and action was a most bold and novel innovation, requiring much moral courage on the part of the mover. Her manner and address, her ready wit, her thorough mastery of her subject, the strong purpose she displayed, established her ascendency in these discussions, and were fast gaining for her a popularity that, spreading from her house as a centre, alarmed the ministers for their own hold upon the public mind, and so determined them to call her and her doctrines seriously to account.

That Mrs. Hutchinson's conversations were not at first considered to be dangerous either in themselves or in their effects, is clear from the fact that the most eminent ministers and magistrates, attracted by her fame, came from all quarters to hear and dispute with her. Such was her ready command of Scripture authorities and her skill in using all the weapons of argument, that the strongest heads in the colony found themselves unable to cope with her successfully upon her chosen ground. She was impassioned, she was adroit; she was an enthusiast, and yet she was subtle, logical, and deep; she was a woman who believed herself inspired to do a certain work, and who had the courage of her convictions. Could any other have brought such men as Cotton, Vane, Wheelwright, Coddington, completely to embrace her views, or have sent one like Winthrop to his closet, wrestling with himself, yet more than half persuaded? To call such a woman an adventuress, a termagant, or a "Jezebel," is a grave reflection upon the understanding of some of the best minds in the Colony.

Anne Hutchinson's doctrines were, in plain English, these: She held and advocated as the highest truth that a person could be justified only by an actual and manifest revelation of the spirit to him personally. There could be, she said, no other evidence of grace. She repudiated a doctrine of works, and she denied that holiness of living alone could be received as evidence of regeneration, since hypocrites might live outwardly as pure lives as the saints do. The Puritan churches held that sanctification by the will was evidence of justification.

For a time people of every condition were drawn into the dispute about these subtleties. The Boston church divided upon it, the greater number, however, siding with Mr. Cotton, whose views were understood to agree with those maintained by Mrs. Hutchinson. From Boston it rapidly spread into the country, but there, removed from the potent personal magnetism of Mrs. Hutchinson, the clergy were better able to withstand the movement that it may be truly said had carried Boston by storm.

In announcing these opinions of hers, Mrs. Hutchinson freely criticised those ministers who preached a covenant of works. This embittered them toward her. Emboldened by the increasing number of her followers, she became more and more aggressive, so that the number of her enemies was increasing in proportion to that of her proselytes. The breach that coolness and moderation might easily have bridged soon widened into a gulf that could not be crossed. Unsuspicious of any danger, or that what was said in the privacy of her own house was being carefully treasured up against her, poor Mrs. Hutchinson was led into speaking her mind more freely as to doctrines and persons than was consistent with prudence or foresight, so that before she was aware of it what had so far been a harmless war of words, now becoming an unreconcilable feud, burst forth into a war of factions. Events then marched rapidly on.

Governor Winthrop and Mr. Wilson, the pastor of the church,

led the opposition in Boston. The matter was first brought before the General Court upon a sermon preached by Mr. Wheelwright, and in this body the country was able to make head against the town. A personal struggle ensued between Winthrop and Vane, in which the former was victorious. Vane then left the country in disgust.

The party having as it were lost its head, made no difference with Mrs. Hutchinson. She continued her lectures, undisturbed by the signs of the approaching storm, until all the churches could be summoned to a general synod, which assembled in great solemnity at Cambridge, to sit in judgment upon the new and startling Familistic doctrines. This was the first synod held in the western hemisphere. Its deliberations were preceded by a day of fasting and prayer throughout the Colony. What it decreed would be sustained by the civil power.

The convocation was a stormy one. Three weeks were spent in discussing the errors that were formulated in the indictment presented to it. Perceiving the drift toward persecution, some of the members for Boston withdrew in disgust. The Synod finished by condemning as heresies all of the eighty odd points covering the new opinions, thus bringing them within the pale of the law. Mr. Cotton was either too weak or too politic to withstand the pressure brought to bear upon him, and he gave a qualified adhesion to the proceedings.

Being thus backed by the whole spiritual power of the Colony, the Winthrop party no longer hesitated to use severe measures. Mr. Wheelwright was first called before the Court, to be summarily sentenced to disfranchisement and banishment. No one pretends that he was not an able, pure, and upright man. Others of Mrs. Hutchinson's adherents received various sentences. Then the priestess and prophetess herself was arraigned at the bar as a criminal of the most dangerous kind.

The proceedings at this trial are preserved in the "History of Massachusetts under the Colony and Province," of which Governor Hutchinson, the descendant of the persecuted Anne, is the author. They are voluminous. Winthrop, who presided, first catechised her. She answered him boldly, but with dignity. Then Bradstreet, and then Dudley, the deputy-governor, took turns in trying to extort from her some damaging admission.

TRIAL OF MRS. HUTCHINSON.

Neither succeeded. Governor Winthrop allows as much when using this extraordinary language toward the prisoner who is defending herself single-handed against a multitude of prosecutors:

"It is well discerned to the Court that Mrs. Hutchinson can tell when to speak and when to hold her tongue. Upon the answering of a question which we desire her to tell her thoughts of, she desires to be pardoned."

Anne Hutchinson did not fall into the snare. She replied: "It is one thing for me to come before a public magistracy and there to speak what they would have me to speak, and another when a man comes to me in a way of friendship, privately; there is difference in that."

Six of the foremost ministers in the Colony, among whom were the Apostle Eliot and the subsequently famous Hugh Peters, then gave evidence that she had told them they were not able ministers of the New Testament, and that they preached a covenant of works. Only Mr. Shepard, of the Cambridge church, spoke of her considerately; the rest had steeled themselves against her.

Mrs. Hutchinson gave a plump denial to some things that these ministers had alleged, and then she prudently asked that they might be required to give their evidence under oath, in a case touching her personal liberty as this did. To this the Governor strongly demurred; but Mrs. Hutchinson stoutly maintaining her right, she finally prevailed. From a score or more of accusers, the number of ministers who were willing to swear was thus reduced to three.

The only persons who spoke for her were silenced by being browbeaten. Her fate was determined when the Court assembled. Mr. Cotton defended her weakly and equivocally. Mr. Coddington most valiantly, but to as little purpose. Seeing how the case was going against her, he spoke up hotly while smarting under a rebuke just administered by the President:

"I beseech you do not speak so to force things along, for I do not, for my own part, see any equity in all your proceedings. Here is no law of God that she hath broken, nor any law of the country, and therefore deserves no censure. And if she say that the elders preach as the apostles did (before the Ascension), why they preached a covenant of grace, and what wrong is that to them?"

Governor Winthrop then pronounced sentence of banishment

against the woman who, as Coddington truly said, "had broken no law either of God or of man."

This mockery of a trial, in which the judges expounded theology instead of law, and in which no rule of evidence was respected until the prosecutors were shamed into allowing the prisoner's demand that her accusers should be sworn, was now ended. Pending the further order of the Court, Mrs. Hutchinson was delivered into the custody of Mr. Joseph Weld, of Roxbury. She had still another, probably a harder, trial to go through with, when the Boston church of which she was a member, and which had so lately applauded and caressed her, sat in judgment upon her and excommunicated her. Her husband then sold all his property, and removed with his family to the Island of Aquidneck, as did many others whose opinions had brought them under the censure of the governing powers. Mr. Hutchinson nobly stood by his wife to the last. When a committee of the Boston church went to Rhode Island for the purpose of endeavoring to bring these lost sheep back into the fold, he told them that he accounted his wife "a dear saint and servant of God."

The triumphant opposition now carried matters with a heavy hand. Winthrop strenuously exerted himself to crush Mrs. Hutchinson's followers. In consequence of this a great number of the principal inhabitants of Boston who had become involved in these troubles, and who were now deprived of their political privileges as a punishment therefor, also removed to Rhode Island. Of these Coddington and Dummer had been assistants or counsellors; Hutchinson, Coggeshall, and Aspinwall were representatives. Rainsford, Sanford, Savage, Eliot, Easton, Bendall, and Denison, were all persons of distinction. About sixty others were disarmed. These exiles, having purchased the island of the Indians, were the first to found a civil government there. And thus did the stone which the builders rejected become the head of the corner.

The rest of Mrs. Hutchinson's history is briefly told. After the death of her husband, which happened five years later, she again removed with her family into the Dutch territory of New Netherlands, settling near what is now New Rochelle. During the following year her house was suddenly assaulted by hostile Indians, who, in their revengeful fury, murdered the whole family, excepting only one daughter, who was carried away into captivity.

Mrs. Hutchinson's offence consisted in using the great intellectual powers with which she was undeniably gifted for solving the problem of her own life. Her enemies vanquished, but they could not convince, her. It is not denied that she was a pure woman, an affectionate wife and mother, to the poor a benefactor, and to her convictions of Christian duty conscientious and faithful to the last. To succeeding generations she is an amazing example of the intolerance existing in her day.

THE DEATH OF RAINSBOROUGH.

1648.

THE civil wars in England preceding the dethronement and death of Charles I. opened an alluring field for reaping individual renown which many adventurous New Englanders hastened to enter. It was there in New England, if anywhere, that the revolt against the crushing tyranny from which thousands had fled should find its legitimate echo. Moreover, an appeal to arms had become the dream of many of the enthusiastic young men of this martial age. No sooner, therefore, had the sword been drawn, than these men of New England, taking their Geneva Bibles and their Spanish rapiers in their hands, enrolled themselves under the banners of the Parliament, and some of them carved with their good blades an enduring record upon the history of the time.

Foremost among these volunteers for the Puritan cause was William Rainsborough, who lived here in 1639, and was, with

Robert Sedgwick and Israel Stoughton, then a member of the Honorable Artillery Company of Boston. Rainsborough had speedily risen to be colonel of a regiment in the Parliamentary army, in which this Stoughton was lieutenant-colonel, Nehemiah Bourne, a Boston shipwright, major, and John Leverett, afterwards governor, a captain ; William Hudson, supposed to be also of Boston, was ensign. A son of Governor Winthrop also served with credit in these same wars, and in New England the having furnished one of Oliver's soldiers was long one of the most valued of family traditions.

Rainsborough owed his rapid advancement to the distinguished gallantry that he displayed in the field, as well as to his zeal for the cause, both of which qualifications, so essential in the Puritan soldier, earned for him the warm friendship of Cromwell, with whom he was thoroughly one in spirit. Indeed he appears to have held political sentiments quite as advanced as those of his great leader. We find him sustaining positions of high trust both in camp and council, always with ability, and always with credit to himself and his patron.

In the memorable storming of Bristol, then held by Prince Rupert, Rainsborough commanded a brigade which was posted in front of the strongest part of the enemy's line of defence. The duty of assaulting this position fell to him. Cromwell tells how it was performed, in an official letter written from Bristol immediately after the surrender of the place.

"Colonel Rainsborough's post was near to Durham Down, whereof the dragoons and three regiments of horse made good a post upon the Down, between him and the River Avon, on his right hand. And from Colonel Rainsborough's quarters to Froom River, on his left, a part of Colonel Birch's and the whole of General Skippon's regiment were to maintain that post."

The signal for storming being given, the Parliamentary troops advanced with great resolution against the enemy's whole line, and were suddenly in possession of the greater portion of it.

"During this," says the General, "Colonel Rainsborough and Colonel Hammond attempted Pryor's Hill Fort and the line downward towards Froom; and the major-general's regiment being to storm towards Froom River, Colonel Hammond possessed the line immediately, and beating the enemy from it, made way for the horse to enter. Colonel Rainsborough, who had the hardest task of all at Pryor's Hill Fort, attempted it, and fought near three hours for it. And indeed there was great despair of carrying the place,. it being exceedingly high, a ladder of thirty rounds scarcely reaching the top thereof; but his resolution was such that, notwithstanding the inaccessibleness and difficulty, he would not give it over. The enemy had four pieces of cannon upon it, which they plied with round and case shot upon our men; his lieutenant, Colonel Bowen (Bourne), and others were two hours at push of pike, standing upon the palisades, but could not enter. But now Colonel Hammond being entered the line . . . by means of this entrance of Colonel Hammond, they did storm the fort on that part which was inward; and so Colonel Rainsborough's and Colonel Hammond's men entered the fort, and immediately put almost all the men in it to the sword."

For his resolute bravery on this occasion Rainsborough was one of the officers deputed by Fairfax to receive the surrender of the place.

Rainsborough subsequently acted as one of the commissioners from the Army, with Ireton and Hammond, to treat with the King, and he was also one of the officers who stirred up in the Army that spirit of discontent with the half measures of Parliament which, bursting out into open revolt, paved the way to its final and humiliating downfall.

When the insurrection immediately preceding the second civil war broke out, Rainsborough was in command and on board of the English fleet, and he is then called Admiral Rainsborough. It is well known that the sailors embraced, almost to a man, the Royalist side. They put their Admiral on shore, and then hoisted sail for Holland and the young Prince of Wales. Rainsborough then went up to London, presently receiving orders to go upon his last service, into Yorkshire.

It was in the year 1648 that the Yorkshire Royalists, who had been living in quiet since the first war, were again excited by intelligence of Duke Hamilton's intended invasion. A plan was laid and successfully carried out by them to surprise Pomfret Castle (sometimes called Pontefract), the greatest and strongest castle in all England, then held by Colonel Cotterel as governor for the Parliament. It was then victualled to withstand a long siege. The Castle was soon besieged by Sir Edward Rhodes and Sir Henry Cholmondley with five thousand regular troops, but the royal garrison stubbornly held out for the King.

It being likely to prove a tedious affair, General Rainsborough was sent from London by the Parliament to put a speedy end to it. He pitched his headquarters for the moment at Doncaster, twelve miles from Pomfret, with twelve hundred foot and two regiments of horse.

The Castle garrison having in some way learned of Hamilton's disastrous defeat at Preston, that he was in full retreat for Scotland, and that Sir Marmaduke Langdale, who commanded the English in that battle, was a prisoner, formed the bold design of seizing General Rainsborough in his camp and holding him as a hostage for Sir Marmaduke; for it was clear enough that the principal actors in this unlucky rising would now be in great peril of losing their heads on the charge of high treason. The scheme seemed all the more feasible because the General and his men were under no apprehension of any surprise; the Castle being twelve miles distant, closely besieged, and being moreover now the only garrison held for the King in all England.

The plan was shrewdly laid, favored by circumstances, and was completely successful, except that instead of bringing the General off as a prisoner, they killed him. With twenty-two picked men, all bold riders and well mounted, Captain William Paulden penetrated through the besiegers' lines into Doncaster undiscovered. The guards were immediately assaulted and

THE DEATH OF RAINSBOROUGH.

dispersed, while a party of four troopers made direct for the General's lodgings. At the door they were met by his lieutenant, who, upon their announcing that they had come with despatches from General Cromwell, conducted them to the chamber where Rainsborough was in bed. While the General was opening the false despatch, which contained nothing but blank paper, the King's men told him that he was their prisoner, but that not a hair of his head should be touched if he went quietly along with them. They then disarmed his lieutenant, who had so innocently facilitated their design, and brought both the General and him out of the house. A horse stood ready saddled, which Rainsborough was directed to mount. He at first seemed willing to do so, and put his foot in the stirrup; but upon looking about him and seeing only four enemies, while his lieutenant and a sentinel (whom they had not disarmed) were standing by him, he suddenly pulled his foot out of the stirrup and cried out, "*Arms! Arms!*"

Upon this, one of his enemies, letting fall his sword and pistol, — for the object was to take the General alive, — caught hold of Rainsborough, who grappled fiercely with him, and both fell struggling to the ground. The General's lieutenant then picked up the trooper's pistol, but was instantly run through the body by Paulden's lieutenant while he was in the act of cocking it. A third then stabbed Rainsborough in the neck; yet the General gained his feet with the trooper's sword, with whom he had been struggling, in his hand. Seeing him determined to die rather than be taken, the lieutenant of the party then passed his sword through his body, when the brave but ill-fated Rainsborough fell dead upon the pavement of the courtyard.

THE CASE OF MISTRESS ANN HIBBINS.

1656.

"THE devil is in it!" Is not this pithy expression, we inquire, a surviving memento of the dark day of superstition, when everything that was strange or inexplicable was by common consent referred to the devices of the Evil One?

It would be both interesting and instructive further to ask

if there are still people who regard spilling the salt, beginning a journey on Friday, breaking a looking-glass, or sitting with thirteen at the table, as things of evil omen, to be scrupulously avoided; or whether they would be willing to admit that hanging a charm about a child's neck, setting a hen on an odd number of eggs, putting trust in a rusty horseshoe, or seeing the moon over a particular shoulder, — to say nothing of dreams, signs, or haunted houses, — are neither more nor less than so many indications of the proneness of our nature to admit

NIGHT WATCHMAN.

the supernatural. Nor is it so long ago since people were living in the rural towns of New England who could remember reputed witches, and what dread they inspired in the minds of the ignorant or the timid. Upon looking back over the ground that the enlightenment of the age has conquered, one is half inclined to say that, in some form or other, superstition will be about the last thing eradicated from the human mind. It is in order to enable the reader fairly to make the comparison of his own with a remote time that we offer him these hints before beginning our story about Mrs. Hibbins.

The little that can be recovered concerning this most unfortunate woman, of whom we would gladly know more than we do, puts any connected account of her out of the question. Our curiosity is strongly piqued, only to be unsatisfied at last by a perusal of the few meagre scraps that have the seal of authenticity upon them. Nor is it at all probable that it ever will be satisfied.

We simply know that Mrs. Ann Hibbins, the aged widow of a merchant of note, the reputed sister of the Deputy-Governor of the Colony, was tried, convicted, and suffered death at Boston in the year 1656 for being a witch. This relationship by blood and marriage announces a person of superior condition in life, and not some wretched and friendless hag such as is associated with the popular idea of a witch. It supposes her to have had connections powerful enough to protect her in such an extremity as that of life or death in which she was placed. But in her case it is clear that they were powerless to stay the final execution of the horrid sentence, which was carried into effect, with all its revolting details, according to the decree of the Court.

To be censorious is easy here. Such a tale of horror is in fact a shock to all our preconceived notions of the solid wisdom and well-balanced judgments characterizing our ancient lawgivers. Still, when kings wrote learned treatises, ministers preached, and poets rhymed about it, — when the penal statutes of all civilized States recognized and punished it as a crime, — people of every condition may well be pardoned for putting full faith in witchcraft as a thing belonging to the category of incontestable facts, admitted by the wisest and holiest men, and punished as such by the ordinances of God and man. What is the wonder, then, that they dealt with it as a fact? For our own part, in order that we may understand this deplorable tragedy, and that full justice may be done to the actors therein, it is indispensable first candidly to admit all that this strange belief in witchcraft implied from their point of view. We may lament their ignorance, but we should be slow to condemn them for being no wiser than their own generation.

Such a state of things being imagined, one easily sees why the men who were wisest and strongest in every other emergency simply lost their heads when confronting this terrible bugbear that kept the imagination continually upon the stretch, that was a lurking terror in every household, and that by exposing them, as they fully believed, to all the crafts and assaults of the Devil (their own friends and neighbors being the instruments), held their intellect in abject bondage. Against such insidious attacks as these there was no good defence. Hence the notion of a witch was like that of a serpent in the house whose sting is mortal. No wonder it was the one thing capable of chasing the color

> From cheeks that never changed in woe,
> And never blanched in fear.

This case of Mrs. Hibbins is further interesting as being the second one that the lamentable annals of witchcraft record, that of Margaret Jones, in 1648, being the first. The simple statement should suffice to correct the belief, more or less prevalent to-day, that the Salem outbreak was the beginning, instead of being the tragical end, of the delusion in New England. Mrs. Hibbins's cause is also memorable as the first known instance of the General Court of the Colony sitting in trial in a case of life and death. The tragedy, therefore, lacked no element of solemnity to render it deeply impressive.

Mrs. Ann Hibbins was the wife of William Hibbins, a wealthy and influential merchant of Boston. Hutchinson says that he was one of the principal merchants in all the Colony. At this early day in its history he had served the Colony with credit, first as its agent in England, and again as one of the assistants, or chief magistrates. These important trusts denote the high esteem in which he was held, and they confirm his admitted capacity for public affairs. A series of unlucky events, however, brought such heavy losses upon him in his old age as seriously to impair his estate; but what was perhaps worse to bear, the sudden change from affluence to a more straitened way of living is alleged not only to have soured his wife's naturally unstable temper, but to have so far unsettled her mind that she became in turn so morose and so quarrelsome as to render her odious to all her neighbors. Instead of being softened by misfortune, she was hardened and embittered by it. And it is thought that some of these neighbors were led to denounce her as a witch, as presently they did, through motives of spite, or in revenge for her malice toward, or her abusive treatment of, them.

. It was a credulous age, when the spirit of persecution was easily aroused. The eye of the whole town was presently turned upon Mrs. Hibbins. There is little room to doubt that she was the unfortunate possessor of a sharp tongue and of a crabbed temper, neither of which was under proper restraint. Most unfortunately for her, as it fell out, a superior intelligence and penetration enabled her to make shrewd guesses about her neighbors and their affairs, which the old wives and gossips believed and declared no one else but the Devil or his imps could have known or told her of. From dislike they advanced to hatred, then to fear, and then it no doubt began to be freely whispered about that she was a witch. Such a reputation would naturally cast a fatal blight over her life. No wife or mother believed herself or her infant for one moment safe from the witch's detestable arts, since she might take any form she pleased to afflict them. Presently, the idle gossip of a neighborhood grew into a formal accusation. How much could be made in those days of a little, or how dangerous it then was to exercise any gift like that of clairvoyance or mind-reading, the following fragment will make clear to the reader's mind. Upon this point Mr. Beach, a minister in Jamaica, writes to Dr. Increase Mather as follows: —

"You may remember what I have sometimes told you your famous Mr. Norton once said at his own table, before Mr. Wilson the pastor, Elder Penn, and myself and wife, etc., who had the honour to be his guests, — that one of your magistrates' wives, as I remember, was

EXECUTION OF MRS. HIBBINS.

hanged for a witch, only for having more wit than her neighbours. It was his very expression, she having, as he explained it, unhappily guessed that two of her persecutors, whom she saw talking in the street, were talking of her ; which, proving true, cost her her life, notwithstanding all he could do to the contrary, as he himself told us."

One can hardly read this fragment without shuddering.

The increasing feeling of detestation and fear having now broken out into a popular clamor for justice upon the witch, Mrs. Hibbins was first publicly expelled from the communion of her church, and then publicly accused and thrown into prison. When the prison door closed behind her, her doom was sealed.

Fortunately, perhaps, for him, for he died a year before this bitter disgrace sullied his good name, the husband was not alive to meet the terrible accusation or to stem the tide setting so strongly and so pitilessly against the wife whom he had sworn at the altar to love, cherish, and protect.   If her brother, Richard Bellingham, then holding the second place in the Colony, made any effort to save her, that fact nowhere appears.   Her three sons, whom she seems to have loved with the affectionate tenderness of a fond mother, were all absent from the Colony.   Alone, friendless, an object of hatred to her own neighbors, her heart may well have sunk within her.

Under such distressing circumstances was poor old Dame Hibbins, who once held her head so high, dragged from her dungeon before the Court which was to try her as the worst of criminals known to the law.   The jury, however, failed to convict her of any overt act of witchcraft.   But she could not escape thus. The people, it is said, demanded her blood, and nothing short of this would satisfy them.   So the magistrates, having the power to set aside the verdict, obeying the popular voice, brought her before the bar of the General Court, where, in presence of the assembled wisdom of the Colony, she was again required to plead guilty or not guilty to being a witch.   She answered with firmness and spirit that she was not guilty, and said she was willing to be tried by God and the Court.   The evidence already taken against her was then read, witnesses were heard, and her

answers considered ; and the whole case being then submitted for
its decision, the Court by its vote this time found her guilty
of witchcraft according to the tenor of the bill of indictment.
Governor Endicott, rising in his place, then pronounced in open
court the awful sentence of death upon the doomed woman for
a crime which had no existence save in the imagination of her
accusers.   The warrant for her execution was made out in due
form, the fatal day was fixed, and the marshal-general was

THE OLD ELM.

therein directed to take with him "a sufficient guard."   Then
the poor, infirm, superannuated old woman, as innocent as the
babe unborn, was led back to prison a condemned felon.   Then
the members of the Great and General Court, satisfied that they
had done God's work in hanging a witch, dispersed in peace
to their homes, made more secure, as they believed, by this act
of justice.

As the sentence was not carried into effect for a whole year, it is probable that the intercession of friends may have procured for the condemned woman this reprieve. But it could not avert her final doom, however it might delay it. That was sealed. On the day that she was to suffer she made and executed in prison a codicil to her will, clearly disposing of all her property. She was then taken to the usual place of execution, and there, hanged.

The "usual place of execution" being the Common, it is a tradition that Mrs. Hibbins, as well as others who suffered at the hands of the public executioner, was launched into eternity from the branch of the Great Elm Tree that stood, until within a few years, a commanding and venerated relic of the past, near the centre of this beautiful park. Her remains were shamefully violated. A search was immediately made upon the dead body of the poor woman for the distinguishing marks that all witches were supposed to have on their persons. Her chests and boxes were also ransacked for the puppets or images by which their victims were afflicted, but none were found. The remains were then probably thrust into some obscure hole, for the sufferer, being excommunicated and a condemned witch, would not be entitled to Christian burial, although she earnestly begged this poor boon in her will. Hubbard, who writes nearest to the event, says that they who were most forward to condemn Mrs. Hibbins were afterward observed to be special marks for the judgments of Divine Providence.

And all this really happened in the good town of Boston in the year 1656 !

MARY DYER.

1659.

IT is a matter of history that in 1656 a people who wore their hair long, kept their hats on in the public assemblies, and who said "thee" and "thou," instead of "you," when addressing another person, made their unwelcome appearance in New England. They were forthwith attacked with all the energy of a bitter persecution.

When called upon to speak out in defence of their cruel proceedings, the Puritan authorities declared their creed to be this : They having established themselves in a wilderness in order to enjoy undisturbed their own religious convictions, held it right to exclude all others who might seek to introduce different opinions, and therefore discord, among them. From this it is plain to see that the idea of toleration had not yet been born. The further fact that to this cruel and selfish policy, sternly persevered in to the last, the Colony owed the loss of most of the political privileges that it had hitherto enjoyed, renders it one of the stepping-stones of history. Nor have the most zealous apologists for these acts of the Puritan fathers ever been able to erase the stain of blood from their otherwise fair escutcheon.

Let us recount a single startling episode of this lugubrious history. Two words will explain the situation.

On both sides of the ocean the Puritan cry was "freedom to worship God as we do." The persecution of Quakers had already begun in England under the austere rule of the Puritan Commonwealth. They were treated as weak fanatics who needed wholesome correction, rather than as persons dangerous to the public weal. After this had been some time in progress, some of the persecuted Friends came over to New England for an asylum, or out of the frying-pan into the fire. The local authorities, urged on by the whole body of Orthodox ministers, resolved to strangle this new heresy in its cradle. But they had forgotten the story of the dragon's teeth. For every Quaker they banished, ten arose in his place.

SCOURGING A QUAKER.

Among the first Quakers to arrive in the Colony were two women. And it should be observed that the women all along took as active a part in disseminating the new doctrines as the men did. As was inevitable, such an abrupt innovation upon the settled convictions of the time respecting woman's place in the churches and in society, was a moral shock to the community which quickly recoiled upon the heads of the offenders.

These intruding Quakers, having announced themselves as confessors and missionaries of the true faith of Christ, were all presently put under lock and key as persons guilty of promulgating rank heresies, and as blasphemers, and their sectarian books were also seized and committed to the flames by the common hangman. The Quakers then became violent and aggressive in their turn. They retaliated with prophesies of evil. They freely denounced the judgments of Heaven upon their oppressors. One woman, seeing Governor Endicott pass by the prison, vociferated from her grated window, —

"Woe unto thee! thou art an oppressor!"

The first comers were all banished, with a stern admonition not to return to the Colony. They were put on shipboard and ordered to depart. And this, it was hoped, would be the last of them. This was, in fact, the easiest way of ridding the country of them and their errors, had these not already taken root in the soil itself. Then, as no such law existed, one was made, punishing any Quaker who might afterward come into the jurisdiction. This law imposed severe penalties. Yet, though cruelly enforced, it was soon found inadequate, the number of Quakers increasing; and so, the authorities being now at their wits' end, another law, decreeing death to any of that sect who should presume to return after banishment, was enacted, against strong opposition. There was, in fact, a conscience in the Colonial body. But the rulers could not now retreat without admitting themselves vanquished; and so, pressing the point, the "bloody law" was inscribed upon the statute-book of the Colony.

We have now finished the prologue of the drama, and it is time to introduce the real actors upon the stage.

Mary Dyer, a comely and grave matron, then living in Rhode Island, was one of those rare spirits who are predestined to become martyrs and saints to the faith that they profess.

She and her husband, William Dyer, were originally inhabitants of Boston, and members of the church there, they having emigrated from England to the Colony in the year 1635. From these incidents surrounding Mrs. Dyer's career it is clear that both she and her husband belonged to the better class of emigrants. She is represented by Sewel, the Quaker historian, as being a person of good family and estate, and by Winthrop as a very proper and fair woman, but, as he deprecatingly adds, having a "very proud spirit." In her, therefore, we have the portrait of a comely woman of fine presence, high spirit, a fair share of education, and possessing, moreover, a soul endowed with the purpose of an evangelist or, at need, a martyr. Both Mrs. Dyer and her husband became early converts to the peculiar doctrines held by that priestess of common-sense, Mrs. Anne Hutchinson, to whose untoward fortunes they continued steadfast. There was, in fact, a bond of sympathy between these two women. When Mrs. Hutchinson was excommunicated, young Mrs. Dyer walked out of the church with her in presence of the whole congregation. When she was banished, Mrs. Dyer followed her to Rhode Island. This was in 1637.

During the excitement produced by the rapid spread of Mrs. Hutchinson's opinions, and by her subsequent arrest and trial on the charge of heresy, Mrs. Dyer gave premature birth, it was said, to a monster, which Winthrop describes with nauseating minuteness. Losing sight of Mrs. Dyer for nearly twenty years, we suppose her life to have been an uneventful one, — perhaps one of unconscious preparation and of spiritual growth for the work she was to do and the suffering she was destined to undergo. When we next see her, the comely young wife has become a middle-aged matron, who is blindly obeying the command of destiny. She now presents herself in the garb of a Quakeress, and in company with professing Quakers, to the people of Boston, any one of whom, by harboring her even for a single night, or offering her a crust of bread, became a breaker of the law, and was liable to a heavy penalty for so doing. She was immediately taken up and thrust into the common jail, where she remained in confinement until her husband, being apprised of her arrest, hastened to her relief. His urgent prayer for his wife's release was only granted upon his giving bonds in a large sum to take her away out of the Colony, and even then the authorities further stipulated that she should be permitted to speak with no one during the journey. Upon these conditions she was conducted under guard beyond the settlements.

In September, 1659, in company with William Robinson, Marmaduke Stevenson, and Nicholas Davis, Mary again, and this time with full knowledge of the peril of the act, visited Boston for the purpose of testifying against the iniquitous laws in force there, or, as they declared it themselves, " to look the bloody laws in the face," and to meet the oppressors of her people, as it were, in their own stronghold.

Short was the time allowed them. The whole four were quickly made prisoners, and were brought before the Court, which passed sentence of banishment, to which the certain penalty of death now attached, should they return again. They were then released, and ordered to depart out of the Colony. Not obeying this mandate, Robinson and Stevenson were soon again apprehended, and were again consigned to prison, where they were used like condemned felons, being chained to the floor of their dungeon. Within a month Mary also became, for the second time, an inmate of the same prison, having been recognized and taken while standing in front of it. By thus setting the law at defiance, the trio were regarded as rushing upon a fool's fate.

With Mary came Hope Clifton, also of Rhode Island. The declared purpose of the women was to visit and minister to the Friends then lying in prison. The settled purpose of the prisoners to defy the law being known to their friends, and no mercy being expected for them, several of these came to Boston in order to assist in the last act of the tragedy. One even brought linen for the sufferers' shrouds. All this imparts a highly dramatic character to the acts of the resolute martyrs.

The three prisoners who had thus forfeited their lives to the law were, on the 20th of October, brought before the Court of

Magistrates. The incorruptible but implacable Endicott presided. The men keeping their hats on, Endicott ordered the officer to pull them off. He then addressed the prisoners in the language of stern remonstrance and reproof. He told them that neither he nor the other magistrates then present desired their death, but that the laws must be enforced. All three were condemned to be hanged.

Mrs. Dyer heard her doom pronounced with serene composure, simply saying, —

" The Lord's will be done ! "

" Take her away, marshal," commanded Endicott, impatiently.

" I joyfully return to my prison," she rejoined.

On her way back to prison, filled with the exaltation of the Spirit, she said to the marshal, or high-sheriff, who was conducting her, " Indeed, you might let me alone, for I would go to the prison without you."

" I believe you, Mrs. Dyer," the officer replied ; " but my orders are to take you there, and I must do as I am commanded."

During the interval of a week occurring between the sentence and the day fixed for its execution, Mrs. Dyer wrote an " Appeal to the General Court," in which she compares herself with Queen Esther, and her mission with that of the queen to Ahasuerus. It is pervaded throughout by a simple and touching dignity. There is not one craven word in it, or one entreating pardon or expressing a doubt of the righteousness of her own acts. Calmly she rehearses the history of her case, and then concludes her appeal, " in love and the spirit of meekness," to the justice and magnanimity of the Court which was able to set her free. But if it was heeded, her prayer was unanswered. The renewed and earnest intercession of Mrs. Dyer's husband and son were alike ineffectual ; the magistrates remained unmoved. But it is said that the son, in the hope of yet saving her, passed the last night in his mother's cell, beseeching her to abjure, or at least so far to retract her mistaken opinions as to give some chance for hope that the judges might yet relent, and so commute her sentence of death to banishment. History has kindly drawn the veil over this scene. All we know is that the mother preferred death to dishonor.

HAND REEL.

Nor were other efforts wanting to save the condemned prisoners. Suitors who were able to make themselves heard in the council-chamber and in the Governor's closet earnestly labored to prevent the consummation of the crime.

On Thursday, the 27th of October, in the morning, according to an ancient custom, the drummers of the trained bands beat their drums up and down the streets, to notify the soldiers to get under arms. This being the time-honored lecture-day, which was also the one usually appointed for holding public executions, as soon as the public worship was over, the drums were again heard, the trained bands assembled and formed in order, and were then marched to the prison, where they halted. Then the high-sheriff, exhibiting his warrant, called for the bodies of the prisoners by name, their irons were knocked off by the jailer, and, after tenderly embracing each other, they were led forth to take their places in the ranks of the guard, Mary being placed between the two men who were to suffer with her. A great multitude had assembled to witness these solemn proceedings. The procession then moved, the prisoners on foot, the people pressing closely around them, in order not to lose a word of what they might say; but whenever the condemned attempted to speak, as now and then they did, the drummers were ordered to beat their drums, and so drowned the voices in the uproar. One sees here, as always, that every tyranny is afraid of its victims. Hemmed in by armed men, and surrounded by a surging and excited throng, the prisoners walked hand in hand all the way to the scaffold, supporting and comforting each other in this most trying moment with a sublime fortitude. The brutal marshal, seeing this, said sneeringly to Mary : " Are you not ashamed, you, to walk thus hand in hand between two young men ? "

Unmoved by the taunt, she replied : " No ; this is to me an hour of the greatest joy I could have in this world."

The *cortége* having at length reached the place of execution, it having marched by a roundabout way, — for fear, it is said, that a rescue might be attempted, — Mary and her fellow sufferers bid each other a last farewell. Robinson first ascended the fatal ladder. While uttering his dying words, predicting a visitation of divine wrath to come upon his slayers, a harsh voice in the crowd cried out : " Hold thy tongue ! Thou art going to die with a lie in thy mouth ! "

Stevenson's last words were these : " Be it known unto all, this day, that we suffer not as evil-doers, but for conscience' sake."

It was now Mary's turn. Her two dear friends were hanging dead before her eyes. Fearlessly she mounted the fatal ladder, and fearlessly she submitted herself to the hangman's hands. She was then pinioned, blindfolded, and the fatal noose placed about her neck. All being then ready, the crowd awaited the last act in breathless suspense, when in the distance a voice was heard crying out, " Stop ! She is reprieved ! "

The agitation of the spectators is something that we can only faintly conceive. But Mary, it is said, remained calm and unmoved through it all. " Her feet being loosed," says Sewel, "they bade her come down.   But she, whose mind was already as it were in heaven, stood still, and said she was there willing to suffer as her brethren did, unless they would annul their wicked law." She was then taken down from the scaffold and re-conducted to prison, where her son, who was anxiously awaiting her return, embraced her as one risen from the dead. Only then she learned that to his importunity with the magistrates she owed her deliverance from the fate of her brethren. The son had saved his mother. The death-sentence had been commuted to banishment; but Mary now received a solemn warning to the effect that the extreme penalty would surely be exacted should she again offend against the majesty of the law. She was then conducted under guard to the Colony frontier, whence she pursued her way home to Rhode Island.

But the old impulse reviving in her in full force, in defiance of the warning thrice repeated, Mary again sought to obtain the crown of martyrdom to which she was foreordained. Burning with fanatical zeal, regardless, too, of the conditions which had procured the remission of her sentence, she deliberately violated the law again. In May, 1660, the unfortunate woman had so little regard for her personal safety as again to come to "the bloody town of Boston." She was soon summoned before the General Court. Swift was the judgment, swift the execution. Endicott, indeed, — respect to his manhood for it ! — offered her a chance of escape ; but her soul was too lofty, her purpose too strongly fixed, to avail herself of a subterfuge to save her life. Endicott conducted her examination. He was as hard as iron, she gentle but undaunted.

"Are you the same Mary Dyer that was here before?" he began.

"I am the same Mary Dyer that was here at the last General Court," she replied.

"Then you own yourself a Quaker, do you not?" said the Governor.

"I own myself to be reproachfully called so."

Then the jailer spoke up and said that Mary was a vagabond.

" I must then repeat the sentence once before pronounced upon you," said Endicott.

Mary quietly rejoined : " That is no more than what thou saidst before."

" True," said Endicott sternly, " but now it is to be executed ; therefore prepare yourself for nine o'clock to-morrow."

Mary then began to speak of her call, when the Governor burst out with, —

" Away with her ! away with her ! "

In great anguish of mind, he being wholly ignorant that she meditated this fatal step, her husband wrote to the General Court of Massachusetts, once more imploring its clemency. His entreaties would have moved a stone to pity. But it was now too late. On the first day of June the solemn ceremonies of the previous October were repeated. The scaffold was erected on Boston Common, a broad area of unoccupied land adjoining the town, then used by the inhabitants in commonage, and on muster-days as a training-field, as well as for the place of public execution.

At the appointed hour the marshal came for her, and entering without ceremony the cell where she was, he roughly bade her make haste. Mary, speaking to him mildly, asked a few moments' delay, saying that she would be ready presently. But he rudely and unfeelingly retorted that it was her place to wait upon him, and not his upon her. Then one of the female prisoners, with the instinct of her sex, ventured to expostulate with this brutal functionary, when he turned upon her fiercely, and with threats and abuse silenced her. In fact, the Quakeresses were treated like vagabonds and outcasts.

The authorities having reason to fear a popular tumult, the prisoner was taken strongly guarded over a circuitous route to the fatal spot, and again her voice was silenced by the rattle of drums before and behind her. With the birds innocently twittering above her head, once more Mary ascended the scaffold with a firm step. Pity was not wholly extinct. Some of the people present made a last effort to save her, but Mary would not agree to leave the country. To the hope some expressed that her life would be again spared, the officer commanding the armed escort roughly retorted that she was guilty of her own blood.

"Nay," she replied, "I came to keep bloodguiltiness from you, desiring you to repeal the unrighteous and unjust law made against the innocent servants of the Lord."

Mr. Wilson, minister of Boston, attended her on the scaffold in her last moments, not to offer consolation, but to exhort her to recant.

"Mary Dyer," he exclaimed, "oh, repent! oh, repent! Be not so deluded and carried away by the deceits of the Devil!"

She answered him in terms of mild reproof: "Nay, man, I am not now to repent."

A colloquy by which her last moments were embittered was kept up on the scaffold. She was reproached for saying that she had been in paradise. She reiterated it. "Yes," said this undaunted woman, "I have been in paradise several days."

The executioner then performed his office.

THE KING'S MISSIVE.

1661.

"CHARLES R.

"Trusty and Wellbeloved, we greet you well. Having been informed that several of our Subjects among you, called Quakers, have been and are imprisoned by you, whereof some have been executed, and others (as hath been represented unto us) are in Danger to undergo the Like: We have thought fit to signify our Pleasure in that Behalf for the future, and do require, that if there be any of those people called Quakers amongst you, now already condemned to suffer Death, or other Corporal Punishment, or that are imprisoned, or obnoxious to the like Condemnation, you are to forbear to proceed any farther, but that you forthwith send the said Persons (whether condemned or imprisoned) over to this our Kingdom of England, together with their respective Crimes or Offences laid to their Charge, to the End such Course may be taken with them here, as shall be agreeable to our Laws and their Demerits. And for so doing, these our Letters shall be your sufficient Warrant and Discharge. Given at our Court at Whitehall, the 9th day of September, 1661, in the thirteenth Year of our Reign.

"Subscribed, To our Trusty and Wellbeloved John Endicot, Esq.; and to all and every other the Governour or Governours of our Plantation of New-England, and of the Colonies thereunto belonging, that now are, or hereafter shall be : And to all and every the Ministers and Officers of our said Plantation and Colonies whatever, within the Continent of New-England.

"By His Majesty's Command.

"WIL. MORRIS."

THIS was no common letter which in November, 1661, fell like a bombshell into the wicked town of Boston. It was certainly an alarming manifesto. . It brought a proud and sensitive people, who had ceased to pay respect to loyalty, and had almost forgotten its forms, once more rudely to their knees. And they were a stern race, fearing God more than they honored the King. But they felt the shock that had just overthrown the Puritan Commonwealth; and the voice which rose from among its ruins, commanding them to obey, sounded at the moment in their ears very much like the voice of God.

Continued encroachment upon the prerogative of the throne had doubtless much to do with ordering their destiny, — possibly as much as had the cruelties practised toward the offending Quakers, to whose prayers for redress the Parliament had paid little attention; but with the return of the old monarchy, its likings and its hatreds, the politic Friends had hopes that the easy-going Charles would lend a more gracious ear to them in the hour of his great triumph over the Puritan cause; nor would he be found unwilling to lower the pride of those haughty Puritan subjects of his on the other side of the Atlantic who were endeavoring to carry on a little commonwealth of their own. The moment was indeed opportune. Floating in adulation, Charles the king was well disposed to clemency toward all except those who had kept him for twelve years Charles the exile. The Quakers were on their part strongly roused to make renewed effort, too, by the news they received of the execution of William Leddra at Boston. Then Edward Burroughs, a leading Friend, and a man of action, entreated and obtained an audience of the King.

ENDICOTT RECEIVING THE KING'S ORDER.

When he was ushered into the presence-chamber his first words were, —

"Sire, there is a vein of innocent blood opened in your Majesty's dominions which, if not stopped, may overrun all."

"I will stop that vein," said the King, shortly.

Burroughs then laid before the King a detailed account of what had been done in New England. After he had listened to the catalogue of scourgings, brandings, cropped ears, banishments upon pain of death, and lastly of the execution of four persons of this sect for presuming to return to the Colony when forbidden to do so, the suitor, turning accuser, then presented the King with the proofs that the New England authorities had refused to allow the Quakers an appeal to England when they had demanded it. His Majesty is reported to have taken great notice of this particular item of the indictment, calling out to the lords who were with him to hear it, and then exclaiming ironically, —

" Lo ! these are my good subjects of New England."

He then inquired when a ship would be ready to sail for New England, and upon being informed, dismissed Burroughs, with the promise that he should presently hear from him through the Lord Chancellor. This promise Charles punctually kept. The mandatory letter which precedes our account was duly prepared, and then — bitterest pill of all for the disloyal colonists to swallow! — whom should the King's minister select to be the bearer of it, but Samuel Shattuck, an exiled Quaker, and one who had given the New England magistrates no end of trouble, he being finally banished by them from the Colony upon pain of death. It will thus be seen that nothing had been omitted that could render the humiliation complete.

The London Friends, immediately this was done, chartered a vessel, of which Ralph Goldsmith, another Quaker, was captain, to carry the King's order and his messenger to Boston. In six weeks the ship arrived at her destination. It being the Sabbath, all the company remained quietly on board.

Seeing a vessel, with an English ensign at her peak, cast anchor in their road, some of the selectmen of the town hastened on board to learn the news, little dreaming it, however, to be of so much personal interest to themselves. They eagerly asked the captain if he had brought any letters ; for, as may be imagined, intelligence of the events then taking place in England was awaited with the utmost anxiety and impatience. The master replied that he had, but he would not deliver them on that day ; and so his visitors got into their boat and went on shore again as wise as they came. But in the meantime some of them having recognized Shattuck and others on board as being Quakers, they spread the report that "Shattuck and the devil and all had come back again."

The next morning, armed with the King's mandate, Shattuck came on shore accompanied by Goldsmith, the master, and they two, after sending their boat back to the ship, went directly through the town to Governor Endicott's house, passing in their

LIBERTY TREE, PLANTED 1646.   BUILDING ERECTED 1666.

way the market-place where so many of their friends had been mercilessly whipped, and the jail in which many were still confined. A few steps more would bring them face to face with their worst enemy. They knew that they were bearding the lion when they knocked at Governor Endicott's door.

The servant who opened it asked what was their business with his master. They bid him say that, being charged with the commands of his Majesty the King, they should deliver their message into none but the Governor's own hands. They were then admitted without further questioning, and presently the redoubted Governor came in to them; but upon perceiving that Shattuck kept his hat on, he commanded it to be taken off, which was done. Then having received the deputation and the papers, the Governor formally acknowledged its official character by removing his own hat, and ordering that of Shattuck to be given to him again. ·Yet the man who now stood before him enjoying his moral degradation while protected by an inviolable safeguard, was the same one whom he had formerly sentenced to stripes and banishment. The draught was a bitter one, but Endicott bore himself with dignity. After this by-play indicating the homage due to royalty and its representative, the Governor read the letter, and bidding Shattuck and Goldsmith to follow him, then went to the Deputy-Governor's house, which stood near his own, and laid the papers before Bellingham. Having held some conference with the Deputy, the nature of which may easily be imagined from the sequel, the Governor turned to the messengers and said briefly and with dignity, —

"We shall obey his Majesty's command."

After this interview was ended, Goldsmith gave liberty to all his passengers to come on shore, which they did, and afterward publicly held a religious meeting with those of their faith in the town, "returning thanks to God for his mercy manifested in this most wonderful deliverance." All such assemblies as this having been unlawful, this act announced the King's active intervention in their affairs to the people. An order soon after issued, releasing all Quakers then in custody.

The scene between Endicott and Bellingham is imagined by Mr. Longfellow in his " New England Tragedies." He there endeavors to depict the characters of the chief actors, and to show the spirit of these extraordinary times. In this particular field he has therefore preceded Mr. Whittier, whose "King's Missive," prepared for the "Memorial History of Boston," deals exclusively with the events surrounding the order of Charles II. The two pieces offer, however, a striking contrast in method as well as in style, one being a consecutive and homogeneous narrative, while the other is made up of separated incidents, selected here and there for their dramatic quality rather than their coherence or historical sequence. Both, however, have the same purpose — eternally to set the seal of condemnation on a great wrong by exhibiting the Quakers in the light of martyrs. To this end Mr. Longfellow takes for his heroine a young girl, Edith Christison by name, who is brutally scourged from town to town, is then released, and driven forth into the wilderness. Such was the law, and such things actually occurred. Singularly enough, this is also the motive of Mr. Whittier's "Cassandra Southwick." In both cases the youth, beauty, constancy, and heroism of the sufferers strongly appeal to our sympathies, and are supposed deeply to move the actual spectators. But with a deeper insight into the human heart Mr. Longfellow makes the son of Governor Endicott himself fall in love with Edith, whose martyrdom he has witnessed, thus bringing straight home to the stern father the consequences of his own evil acts. The King's imperious mandate wounds his pride; his son's conduct strikes at the heart, and this wound is mortal. Thus it is no less strange than true that, under favor of one of the most profligate and irreligious of monarchs, the beneficent era of religious toleration began its unpromising dawning in New England.

It is to be noted that whenever they can do so, Mr. Longfellow's characters speak in the actual language of history. Indeed, the tragedy is not a creation, like "Ernani," but a fragment of sober history, taken from existing records, into which a poetic feeling is infused, and whose episodical parts afford occasional glimpses of the author's genius shining like pure gold in the rough metal.

(From Longfellow's " New England Tragedies.")

SCENE III. *The Governor's Private Room.   Papers upon the table.* ENDICOTT
and BELLINGHAM.

ENDICOTT.

THUS the old tyranny revives again !
Its arm is long enough to reach us here,
As you will see.   For, more insulting still
Than flaunting in our faces dead men's shrouds,
Here is the King's Mandamus, taking from us,
From this day forth, all power to punish Quakers.

BELLINGHAM.

That takes from us all power ; we are but puppets,
And can no longer execute our laws.

.   .   .   .

ENDICOTT.

Opens the Mandamus and hands it to BELLINGHAM ; *and while he is reading,*
ENDICOTT *walks up and down the room.*

Here, read it for yourself ; you see his words
Are pleasant words — considerate — not reproachful —
Nothing could be more gentle — or more royal ;
But then the meaning underneath the words,
Mark that.   He says all people known as Quakers
Among us, now condemned to suffer death
Or any corporal punishment whatever,
Who are imprisoned, or may be obnoxious
To the like condemnation, shall be sent
Forthwith to England, to be dealt with there
In such wise as shall be agreeable
Unto the English law and their demerits.
Is it not so ?

BELLINGHAM (*returning the paper*).

Ay, so the paper says.

.   .   .   .

ENDICOTT.

I tell you, Richard Bellingham, — I tell you,
That this is the beginning of a struggle
Of which no mortal can foresee the end.
I shall not live to fight the battle for you,
I am a man disgraced in every way ;
This order takes from me my self-respect
And the respect of others.   'T is my doom,
Yes, my death-warrant, — but must be obeyed !
Take it, and see that it is executed
So far as this, that all be set at large ;
But see that none of them be sent to England
To bear false witness, and to spread reports
That might be prejudicial to ourselves.   [*Exit* BELLINGHAM.
There 's a dull pain keeps knocking at my heart,
Dolefully saying, " Set thy house in order,
For thou shalt surely die, and shalt not live ! "
For me the shadow on the dial-plate
Goeth not back, but on into the dark !   [*Exit.*

Mr. Whittier's poem presents the events we have recorded
in a harmonious and remarkably picturesque narrative.   He is
conscientiously faithful both to the spirit and letter of the
subject itself, while to the implacable spirit of persecution,
personified here by Endicott, he is a generous and impartial
judge.   We write it, nevertheless, as a fact, that the poem
caused much discussion on its first appearance, — a discussion
fully vindicating the Quaker poet's adherence to the truth of
history.   But the prose and poetic versions are now before the
reader for his decision.

THE KING'S MISSIVE.

UNDER the great hill sloping bare
　　To cove and meadow and Common lot,
In his council chamber and oaken chair
　　Sat the worshipful Governor Endicott, —

A grave, strong man, who knew no peer
In the pilgrim land where he ruled in fear
Of God, not man, and for good or ill
Held his trust with an iron will.

He had shorn with his sword the cross from out
    The flag, and cloven the May-pole down,
Harried the heathen round about,
    And whipped the Quakers from town to town.
Earnest and honest, a man at need
To burn like a torch for his own harsh creed,
He kept with the flaming brand of his zeal
The gate of the holy commonweal.

.   .   .   .

The door swung open, and Rawson the Clerk
    Entered and whispered underbreath :
" There waits below for the hangman's work
    A fellow banished on pain of death, —
Shattuck of Salem, unhealed of the whip,
Brought over in Master Goldsmith's ship,
At anchor here in a Christian port
With freight of the Devil and all his sort ! "

Twice and thrice on his chamber floor
    Striding fiercely from wall to wall,
" The Lord do so to me and more,"
    The Governor cried, " if I hang not all !
Bring hither the Quaker." Calm, sedate,
With the look of a man at ease with fate,
Into that presence grim and dread
Came Samuel Shattuck with hat on head.

" Off with the knave's hat ! " An angry hand
    Smote down the offence ; but the wearer said,
With a quiet smile : " By the King's command
    I bear his message and stand in his stead."
In the Governor's hand a missive he laid
With the Royal arms on its seal displayed,
And the proud man spake as he gazed thereat,
Uncovering, " Give Mr. Shattuck his hat."

He turned to the Quaker, bowing low :
   " The King commandeth your friends' release.
Doubt not he shall be obeyed, although
   To his subjects' sorrow and sin's increase.
What he here enjoineth John Endicott
His loyal servant questioneth not.
You are free ! — God grant the spirit you own
May take you from us to parts unknown."

THE QUAKER PROPHETESS.

1677.

THE Old South Church in Boston — not the present building, but the one first erected upon the same spot — was
the scene of an event without a parallel in the annals of our
Puritan churches, in some of which, nevertheless, remarkable
scenes had occurred.

To the simple and austere Quaker manners, outdoing even
Puritan ideas of moral and physical self-restraint, now and then
comes the unexpected contrast of theatrical climax in its most
bizarre forms. So the early history of the Friends in New
England shows the dominant principle of passive opposition to
persecution occasionally giving way, all at once, to an aggressive
spirit that impelled the actors on through thorny ways toward
the goal for which they strove and struggled. If, now and then,
one half crazed by suffering was betrayed into some act of folly,
it is surely not a matter for astonishment or exultation. Their
annals present the names of no informers and no apostates.

Obeying the command of a hallucination to which she bowed
as if it were a divine behest, the Quakeress Deborah Wilson
had walked naked through the streets of Salem " as a sign of
spiritual nakedness in town and country," and for so doing she
was most uncharitably whipped with thirty stripes. Again,
Lydia Wardwell, who is called " a young and tender chaste

person," for startling the congregation of Newbury by walking
into the meeting-house there, unclothed, in the time of public
worship, was tied up to the fence-post of the tavern where the
court sat, at Ipswich, to undergo a similar punishment.

But the case of Margaret Brewster differs from these others in
that a number of persons took part in carrying out what it was
expected would strike terror to the hearts of the beholders, and
to this end it was conducted with studied attention to dramatic
effect.

One quiet Sabbath morning in July, 1677, accompanied by
several of the most noted persons of her sect, both male and
female, Margaret Brewster presented herself at the door of the
Old South Meeting-house in sermon-time, the strangest visitor
that had ever crossed its consecrated threshold. She first took
off her riding-habit and her shoes and stockings, and then
entered. In his Diary, which perhaps may become as famous
as that of the immortal Pepys, Judge Sewall notes that while
the congregation was listening to the words of the sermon from
the aged pastor's lips, there suddenly was seen the apparition
of a woman walking slowly up the broad aisle between two
men, while two others walked behind. The woman was barefooted, her head was sprinkled with ashes, her loosened hair
straggled wildly down about her neck and shoulders, her face
was besmeared with soot, and she wore a sackcloth gown loosely
gathered around her person. This appearance, says the indignant diarist, "occasioned the greatest and most amazing uproar
that ever I saw."

No one has told us, but we can imagine the congregation
rising in consternation to their feet, the sudden stop in the
sermon, the moment of silence, like the calm before the storm,
during which the dark prophetess delivered her solemn warning
of a grievous calamity shortly to signify to them the displeasure
of God. Then the excited voices of the men, all talking and
gesticulating at once, the women shrieking in terror or dropping
in a dead faint, the surging to and fro of a multitude, all occa-
sioning "the greatest and most amazing uproar" that was ever

heard inside these sacred walls, witnessed to the little central group that they had indeed created a profound sensation. The offenders were all quickly taken into custody and hurried off to prison. When Margaret was arraigned before the court, the constable declared himself wholly unable to identify her as the

ANCIENT HOUSES, NORTH END.

person he had arrested, she being then, as he deposed, "in the shape of a devil." She was sentenced to be whipped up and down the town at the cart's tail, which cruel order was carried into effect a few days later.

This event, as well it might, newly brought the affairs of the Friends to a crisis. The first feeling of exasperation demanded its victims. But this having spent itself, the Quakers, taking courage, assembled in their houses of worship in such formidable numbers that the multitude of offenders became their safe-guard.

IN THE OLD SOUTH CHURCH.

J. G. WHITTIER.

SHE came and stood in the Old South Church,
  A wonder and a sign,
With a look the old-time sibyls wore,
  Half crazed and half divine.

Save the mournful sackcloth about her wound,
  Unclothed as the primal mother,
With limbs that trembled, and eyes that blazed
  With a fire she dare not smother.

Loose on her shoulder fell her hair,
  With sprinkled ashes gray ;
She stood in the broad aisle, strange and weird
  As a soul at the judgment-day.

And the minister paused in his sermon's midst,
  And the people held their breath,
For these were the words the maiden said
  Through lips as pale as death : —

" Thus saith the Lord : ' With equal feet
  All men my courts shall tread,
And priest and ruler no more shall eat
  My people up like bread! '

" Repent ! repent ! ere the Lord shall speak
  In thunder and breaking seals !
Let all souls worship him in the way
  His light within reveals ! "

She shook the dust from her naked feet,
  And her sackcloth closely drew,
And into the porch of the awe-hushed church
  She passed like a ghost from view.

"MORE WONDERS OF THE INVISIBLE WORLD."

1693.

TO one who is not familiar with all the phases which the history of witchcraft in New England takes, Mr. Whittier's poem entitled "Calef in Boston" would doubtless be an enigma, although its foundation is fact and its purpose distinct. For such a champion of common-sense as Robert Calef proved himself to be when he entered the lists against this monstrous superstition, the poet has a natural and unstinted sympathy, and, using the privilege of genius, he has conferred upon the humble tradesman a patent of nobility. Our own generation, applauding the act, hastens to inscribe the name of Calef among the benefactors of his age.

The general subject of witchcraft, including the settled beliefs touching it, is set forth in another place in all its deformity. The active agency of Satan in human affairs being a thing admitted, it became the bounden duty of the godly ministers to meet his insidious attacks upon the churches, and they, as men deeply learned in such things, were naturally appealed to by magistrates and judges for help and guidance. They at once put on all the armor of righteousness. Solemn fasting and prayer were resorted to as things most efficacious in the emergency. It was declared from the pulpit that the Devil was making a most determined effort to root out the Christian religion in New England, and the Government was advised vigorously to prosecute the cases of witchcraft before it. In all the subsequent proceedings the ministers took a prominent part. They assisted in framing the questions to be put in such a way as to entrap the supposed witches, and they attended and took minutes of the examinations. They visited the accused persons in prison who were believed to be in league with Satan, thus putting in practice the principle that, —

> The godly may allege
> For anything their privilege,
> And to the Devil himself may go,
> If they have motives thereunto ;
> For as there is a war between
> The Dev'l and them, it is no sin
> If they, by subtle stratagem,
> Make use of him as he does them.

Cotton Mather was the foremost clergyman of that dark day. He directed all his great abilities and learning energetically to exterminate the "devils" who, as he tells us in his "Wonders," were walking about the streets "with lengthened chains, making a dreadful noise ; and brimstone (even without a metaphor) was making a horrid and hellish stench" in men's nostrils. Learned, eloquent, and persuasive, a man of great personal magnetism and large following, his influence was sure to be potential on which-ever side it might be cast. It was now thrown with all its force, not to avert, but to strengthen, the delusion, thereby aggra-vating its calamitous consequences. Some writers, indeed, have found it easy to doubt his sincerity. Mr. Whittier, it will be seen, writes in full accord with this feeling. But the same charge might with equal fairness include all the Christian ministers of Mather's time.

Against Mather, the neighbor, adviser, and bosom friend of Governor Sir William Phips, the acknowledged head of the New England clergy in its highest spiritual estate, a man having ancient and modern lore at his tongue's end, and withal gifted with a fluency, vivacity, and readiness in composing and writing that might make a bolder man hesitate to attack him, now entered the lists, like another David, Robert Calef, a simple clothier, unknown outside of his own obscure neighborhood. The controversy began in this wise. Calef addressed some let-ters to Dr. Mather, in which he arraigned not only the witchcraft proceedings, but the delusion itself, the occasion being one Margaret Rule, a young woman of Mather's own congregation, whose singular afflictions had just been published to the world by him under the startling caption of "Another Brand pluckt from the Burning."

According to Mather, this young woman was haunted by no fewer than eight malignant spectres, led on by a principal demon, who upon her refusal to enter into a bond with him, continually put her in excruciating bodily torture by pinching, scorching, and sticking pins into her flesh, throwing her into convulsions, lifting her bodily off the bed, and the like, wherein,

CANDLESTICK, BIBLE, AND SPECTACLES.

says Mather, she languished "for just six weeks together." And we are also told that at times the spectators of her miseries would be nearly choked with the fumes of brimstone rising in the chamber.

Taking the alarm, which many no doubt equally shared, dreading a new outbreak of the delusion whose embers, unquenched by blood, were still smouldering, Calef also seems to have distrusted either the integrity or the wisdom of his learned adversary, whom he now opposed in behalf of religion and of public policy, not only with ability and vigor, but with a surprisingly well-equipped arsenal of scriptural learning. In vain Mather sneeringly spoke of him as "the weaver turned minister," Calef only plied him the more pointedly. At the end of the controversy the despised clothier turned out to be one of those men whose reason is never overthrown by panic, and who do not recede a single inch. Mather began with the mistake of underrating him as an antagonist.

After Mather's story of Margaret Rule had been made public, Calef also drew up and circulated one, taken from the mouths of other eye-witnesses, which is a protest against the methods used by Mather to draw out extravagant and incoherent statements from the afflicted girl. This proceeding gave great offence to the reverend author of "The Wonders." He retorted with abusive epithets, and threatened Calef with an action for slander. Calef was, in fact, arrested on a warrant for uttering "scandalous libels," and was bound over for trial; but no prosecutor appearing, the case was dismissed.

Instead of being silenced, Calef pursued with unremitting pertinacity his purpose to prevent a new access of the dismal frenzy of the preceding year, which he terms, with strong feeling, "the sorest affliction and greatest blemish to religion that ever befell this country." Later on Mather condescended to reply; but it is evident that the reaction had now set in, and that those who had been the most forward in abetting the witchcraft proceedings were anxiously considering how best to exculpate themselves both to their own and to the newly awakened public conscience. Mather was no exception. Favored by this reaction, Calef continued to press him hard. Cotton Mather's story of Margaret Rule is, in fact, a plea and an apology for the past. In it he asks, "Why, after all my unwearied cares and pains to rescue the miserable from the lions and bears of hell, which had seized them, and after all my studies to disappoint the devils in their designs to confound my neighborhood, must I be driven to the necessity of an apology?" This language shows how hard a thing it was for him to be forced to descend from his high pedestal.

And again he naively says: "And now I suppose that some of our learned witlings of the coffee-house, for fear lest these proofs

of an Invisible World should spoil some of their sport, will
endeavor to turn them all into sport; for which buffoonery
their only pretence will be : ' They can't understand how such
things as these could be done.' " He has become exquisitely
sensitive to ridicule.

But witchcraft had now indeed got to the length of its blood-
corroded chain, and while the belief still prevailed almost as
strongly as ever, few men could be found bold enough openly
to advocate it. The sickening reflection that the judges had
decreed the death of a score of innocent persons upon a mistake paralyzed men's tongues, unless, like Calef, they spoke
in obedience to the command of conscience. In 1700 he
collected and had printed in London all the pieces relating
to his controversy with Cotton Mather, to which were added
an " Impartial Account " of the Salem outbreak, and a review

TOMB OF THE MATHERS,
COPP'S HILL.

of Mather's life of Sir William Phips. To this he gave
the title of " More Wonders of
the Invisible World." No printer could be found in Boston
or in the Colony willing to
undertake the publication, or
expose it for sale. It was
publicly burned in the College-
yard at Cambridge by order of
the president, whom its exposures reached through his near relative. To break its force, a vindication was prepared and
printed ; but there were no more denunciations made for witchcraft, or courts assembled to hang innocent people. Calef indeed felt the resentment of the Mathers, but he had saved the
cause.

This is the subject to which Mr. Whittier addresses his verses
entitled " Calef in Boston." The allusion to puppet-play is
drawn from the account of the Rule case, wherein it is related
by Mather that the demons who tormented the girl had puppets
into which they would thrust pins whenever they wished to

hurt her. This was a piece of olden superstition which assumed that by making an image in wax or clay of the person she might hold a grudge against, a witch could put that person to the same torture that she did, in a mimic way, the image.

CALEF IN BOSTON.

J. G. WHITTIER.

IN the solemn days of old
   Two men met in Boston town,
One a tradesman frank and bold,
   One a preacher of renown.

Cried the last, in bitter tone:
   " Poisoner of the wells of truth !
Satan's hireling, thou hast sown·
   With his tares the heart of youth !"

Spake the simple tradesman then ;
   " God be judge 'twixt thou and I ;
All thou knowest of truth hath been
   Unto men like thee a lie.

.   .   .   .   .

" Of your spectral puppet play
   I have traced the cunning wires ;
Come what will, I needs must say,
   God is true, and ye are liars."

When the thought of man is free,
   Error fears its lightest tones ;
So the priest cried, " Sadducee ! "
   And the people took up stones.

In the ancient burying-ground,
   Side by side, the twain now lie, —
One with humble grassy mound,
   One with marbles pale and high.

5

NIX'S MATE.

THERE are two local legends, one of disaster and one of piracy, which, most unfortunately for the completeness of our collection, come either in whole or in part under the head of lost legends. The first is the account of the drowning

NIX'S MATE.

of Captain George Worthylake, the keeper of the first lighthouse that was erected at the entrance to Boston Harbor.

This sufficiently simple incident derives its chief interest from the curious fact that it was the subject of Franklin's earliest, and if we are to believe him, misdirected, effort to court the Muses in a ballad. He says of it that his brother James, whose apprentice he then was, thinking that he might find his account in printing them, had encouraged him to write two ballads, one called the " Lighthouse Tragedy," containing an account of the loss of Captain Worthylake and his two daughters, the other a sailor's song on the capture of the noted pirate, Blackbeard. " They were," he ingenuously remarks, " wretched verses in point of style, mere blind-men's ditties." When they were struck off, his brother despatched him to hawk them about the town. The first he assures us had a prodigious run, because the event was recent and had made a great noise. No copy of this ballad is known to exist, nor has tradition transmitted to us a single line of its verses.

It is easily learned from contemporary records that Captain George Worthylake, who lived upon Lovell's Island, while on his way up the harbor, " took heaven by the way," as one writer piously puts it. His wife Ann and his daughter Ruth, who accompanied him, also perished with him by drowning, and the three unfortunates were all buried in one grave in the ancient cemetery of Copp's Hill. The gravestone records the fact that they died November 3, 1718; but it is exasperatingly silent concerning any incident that was likely to produce a commemorative ballad.

The other legend is the true story of the origin of the name long ago given to the submerged islet called Nix's Mate, over which a lonely obelisk rises out of the flowing tides, not for a memorial of dark and bloody deeds, as some people suppose, but as a guiding landmark to warn ships to steer clear of the dangerous reef beneath. No spot within a wide range of the coast is the subject of more eager curiosity to sailors or landsmen, or of more exaggerated conjecture, precisely because to this day its true history remains an enigma. But such as it is the legend is given for what it may be worth.

Following the repulsive custom of erecting the public gibbet at the entrance to a town or a village, where the stark bodies of condemned malefactors were the first objects seen by all who passed in or out, it was usual to hang in chains condemned pirates at the entrance to a port, to signal a like warning to those who followed the sea as their highway. Long custom had sanctioned this *post-mortem* sentence. The laws allowed it and the people approved it. It followed that the stranger who passed underneath one of these ensigns of terror could have no doubt that he had entered a Christian land, since the administration of justice according to its most civilized forms confronted him upon its very threshold.

The sunken reef now known as Nix's Mate was once an islet containing several acres of land, and it was at a very early day the property of a certain John Gallup, from whom the adjacent island is named. The sea has destroyed every vestige of it, excepting only the blackened boulders that lie exposed at low tide, over which the monument stands guard. Yet not more certainly has the islet perished through the action of destroying currents than has the memory of Nix or his Mate been swept

away into oblivion by the tides of time. Still the name is a
fact entered upon the public records of the Colony as a thing
of general knowledge; and we therefore continue to call the
reef Nix's Mate without in the least knowing why we do so.

The only other fact giving authority to the tradition connected
with the islet is the certainty that it was more or less used in
times past as a place of execution for condemned pirates, several
of whom finished here a career of crime, the bare recital of which
makes one's blood run cold. The name of Nix only is wanted
to complete the black calendar. Every trace of the soil to which
the bones of the victims were consigned has disappeared, and
only the solitary monument indicates this graveyard of the sea,
which the waves have kindly levelled and blotted out forever.

It has, however, been handed down from generation to generation, — and we have yet to find the individual bold enough to
dispute it, — that one of these freebooters persisted to the last
in declaring his innocence of the crimes for which he was to
suffer death at the hangman's hands; and he protested with his
latest breath, before giving up the ghost, that in proof of the
truth of his dying assertion the island would be destroyed. In
effect, the waves having done their work unhindered by any
artificial obstruction, the superstitious have always seen in this
a decree of Fate, and Nix's Mate is supposed by them to have
suffered unjustly. But knowing as we do that the disappearance of the island is due to natural causes, we are unable satis-
factorily to establish the connection between the prediction and
its fulfilment. In any case, the verification of innocence, if such
it shall be accounted, came too late by a century to save Nix's
Mate from the halter.

THE DUEL ON THE COMMON.

1728.

ASSOCIATED with the vicinity of the Great Elm, is an episode not only of deepest tragical interest, but one still further remarkable as disproving for the thousandth time the popular fallacy that "murder will out." In New England there had been no need of edicts against duelling. The practice was universally looked upon as being no whit better than murder, and that feeling was voiced by Franklin, truly, though in language more pungent than polite, in his memorable reply to a demand for satisfaction *à la mode*. A combat of words began. After two or three passes, the philosopher easily disarmed his adversary with his usual weapon, hard logic, of which he was a consummate master. Our story is a brief one.

On the morning of July 4, 1728, at daybreak, the body of Benjamin Woodbridge, a young merchant of the town, was found lying in a pool of blood in a deserted part of the Common. He had been dead some hours of a sword-thrust. In fact, the weapon had passed completely through the unfortunate young man.

No one can begin to imagine the consternation excited by the discovery ; and the feeling was not allayed when it transpired that Woodbridge had fallen in a duel with another young gentleman of the town named Phillips. Both of the principals were of the highest respectability. The affair was conducted without seconds, and the victor, after seeing his adversary fall, had fled. It was evidently a duel to the death.

This has proved one of the best-kept family secrets that ever baffled a scandal-loving generation. To this day the real cause of the singular and fatal nocturnal combat remains shrouded in mystery. It is indeed alleged that the quarrel originated over a game of cards at the public-house ; but this supposition is hardly consistent with the secrecy, the absence of all witnesses, and the deadly purpose with which the duel was conducted. The parties had met early on the previous evening at the Royal Exchange, arranged the meeting, and immediately repaired to the rendezvous which one of them was destined never to leave alive.

Positively nothing, then, is known of the origin of the affair. Still, it is evident that no common and vulgar quarrel over dice or cards, when one or both had made too free with "the Tuscan grape," could have so eternally sealed the lips of those to whom the real cause of this singular affair of honor must have been revealed. Phillips was hurried away on board a ship by

THE DUEL ON THE COMMON.

his friends, and died miserably in exile. The inquest elicited nothing of moment beyond the barren facts here narrated. Justice was completely baffled. The headstone in the old Granary, where, in the language of the day, poor Woodbridge was "decently and handsomely interred," is silent. Satan, who had the arranging of this lugubrious combat, thrust home with young Phillips. Ignorant as we are of the real cause, we are yet irresistibly led to conclude that these misguided youths crossed swords not in a moment of passion, but at the instigation of some offence over which the grave itself must close. The grave has closed over it.

DUC D'ANVILLE'S DESCENT.

1746.

HAVING regard, possibly, to the maxim that a danger escaped is a danger no longer, the historians have in general treated the descent of Admiral d'Anville with easy indifference. Yet the startling fact remains that so long as his fleet rode the seas in safety, the fate of New England trembled in the balance. We beg the reader's consideration of the story from this point of view.

OLD SOUTH CHURCH, 1872.

The taking of Louisburg in 1745, a piece of audacity at which France first stood aghast, and then went into a towering rage over it, came near being the prelude to a struggle involving nothing less than the destinies of England's American colonies. By opening new and alluring vistas of conquest to British statesmen, it set them upon fresh schemes for the conquest of Canada which they were secretly preparing to put in execution. In fact, by this mettled achievement, New England had driven the entering wedge into the very heart

of the French colonial empire.   England was now gathering her
strength to force it home.

On the other hand, it so incensed the French Court, then fresh
from its brilliant victories in the Low Countries, that orders
were given for the immediate equipping, at Brest, of a formidable land and sea armament, which it was meant should not
only recover what had been lost, but carry the war energetically
to the enemy's own doors.   To guarantee the security of your
possessions by recalling your enemy to the defence of his own,
is a military maxim so old that the Cabinet of Versailles could
not be safely assumed to be ignorant of it.

This double-shotted idea promised results highly important to
the colonial schemes, as well as to the waning prestige, of France.
So also did it give good promise of success ; for at Paris, thanks
to British parsimony, it was well known that the British American seaports were no Louisburgs.   Since, therefore, to ravage the
New England sea-coast was a thing perfectly feasible to do, Count
Maurepas resolved to do it.   And he meant to do it effectually.
The preparations at Brest being quickly known in London, the
two ancient gladiators began once more to strip for the approaching combat.

Pursuing its own plans, the English Ministry was at the
same time collecting ships, men, and materials of war at Portsmouth, for the invasion of Canada.   Orders were sent out to
the Colonies to hasten the raising of troops for the same purpose.   Then, the destination of the French fleet not being quite
clear, the Ministry sent a squadron to blockade it in Brest ; but
the French Admiral, eluding the vigilance of the British cruisers,
slipped out and got to sea notwithstanding.   Such was the situation in the midsummer of 1746.

The fleet now on the sea numbered eleven ships of the line
and twenty frigates, carrying 814 guns and 7000 sailors, to
which were joined thirty-four transports having on board five
battalions of the veteran troops of France.   The fleet was commanded by M. de la Rochefoucauld, Duc d'Anville, a man of
illustrious descent, in the prime of life, to whom the fortunes of

the expedition had been committed with fullest confidence in his
ability to execute his orders to the letter. Those orders were to
retake Louisburg and dismantle its fortifications, recapture Annapolis and garrison it, and then to burn and destroy Boston, and
lay waste with fire and sword the whole coast as far as Florida.

Boston, the place where the plans for capturing Louisburg
had originated, the brain and heart of the English Colonies, the
centre of English aggression, the perpetual menace to French
dominion in Canada, was to be especially distinguished by
the vengeance of the Cabinet of Versailles. Boston was to be
destroyed. Indeed, her defenceless condition invited an attack.
Her only fortress had been stripped of its cannon to enable
Pepperell to batter down Louisburg. There was no British
squadron to defend it, and there was not a single British soldier in the whole province.

All these circumstances being appreciated, it is impossible to
exaggerate the consternation with which the certain intelligence
of the escape of D'Anville was received at Boston. People stood
aghast. The danger was indeed imminent. He might at any
moment be expected to announce his arrival upon the coast
with his cannon. England, says Hutchinson, was not more
alarmed with the Spanish Armada, than were Boston and the
other North American seaports by the hourly expectation of this
truly formidable flotilla. Brave man that he was, Governor
Shirley prepared to meet the emergency with such means as he
had. But there was not a moment to lose. He instantly called
out a levy *en masse*. The scenes preceding the Louisburg expedition were repeated on a larger scale. Couriers spurred in every
direction bearing the summons to arms, and everywhere the
brave yeomanry responded with eager promptitude to the call.
At night the hills blazed with bonfires. By day the roads
swarmed with armed men hastening toward Boston. The Common became a camp. All business except that of repelling the
invader was at an end, and nothing else was talked of. In this
activity the people a little recovered from the panic into which
they had at first been thrown.

While the people were awaiting in feverish anxiety further news of the fleet, a fisherman came in from sea, who said that he had been brought to on the Nova Scotia coast by four heavy ships of war. They required him to pilot them into Chebucto, which was the designated rendezvous for D'Anville's fleet. While lying to under the guns of one of these ships, he read on her stern the name " Le Terrible." Then, a fog having suddenly shut them in, he had succeeded in making good his escape, and had steered directly for Boston with the news.

But the splendid fleet of D'Anville was destined to encounter a series of disasters hardly paralleled in the naval annals of France. An evil destiny pursued it. When it was off Cape Sable, it experienced violent storms that scattered and dispersed it beyond the power of reassembling. Conflans with four ships made sail for France ; others steered for the West Indies ; and still others were drifting, disabled wrecks, at the mercy of the winds and waves. Finally the Duke succeeded in getting to the rendezvous with two or three ships only of all the magnificent squadron that had sailed from Brest. Within a week he died, it is hinted from the effect of poison administered by himself, he choosing death rather than to survive the disgrace which had so suddenly overwhelmed him. The Vice-Admiral then proposed that the remains of the fleet should return to France. La Jonquière, Governor-General of Canada, being present at the Council, warmly opposed this, urging that the fleet, now augmented by the arrival of three more ships, and strengthened by the recovery of the sick, ought to strike one blow for the honor of France. He begged the Vice-Admiral to attempt at least the carrying out of a part of his instructions. These arguments prevailing with the Council, D'Estournelles, the Vice-Admiral, finding himself opposed and thwarted, lost his head, became delirious, and presently put an end to his life by falling on his own sword. The command then devolved on La Jonquière. The troops that had been landed were re-embarked, and the fleet sailed to attack Annapolis; but it again meeting with a disabling storm, this enterprise was also abandoned, and the shat-

tered remnant of D'Anville's armada steered for France.   Upon
this the French Canadian forces then invading Nova Scotia
broke up their camps and retreated.   The hopes of the French
Ministry had thus been everywhere wrecked.

When these events became known in Boston, the great weight
that had oppressed the minds of the people was so suddenly
lifted off, that at first they could scarcely realize the change.
When they did, the universal joy showed itself, not in noisy
demonstrations, but, in the true Puritan spirit, in prayer and
thanksgiving.   Prayers of gratitude went up from all the pul-
pits ; for in the utter destruction of D'Anville's proud fleet by
the winds and waves alone was seen, on every side, the hand
of God once more manifesting itself, as in the old days, to his
people.

In this spirit, and taking these truly picturesque incidents
for his theme, Longfellow supposes the Rev. Thomas Prince,
then pastor of the Old South Church in Boston, to be recounting
them to his congregation, ascribing to the power of prayer the
destruction that overtook the fleet of France.

A BALLAD OF THE FRENCH FLEET.

OCTOBER, 1746.

MR. THOMAS PRINCE (*loquitur*).

A FLEET with flags arrayed
  Sailed from the port of Brest,
And the Admiral's ship displayed
  The signal, " Steer southwest."
For this Admiral d'Anville
  Had sworn by cross and crown
To ravage with fire and steel
  Our helpless Boston town.

There were rumors in the street,
  In the houses there was fear
Of the coming of the fleet,
  And the danger hovering near;

And while from mouth to mouth
  Spread the tidings of dismay,
I stood in the Old South,
  Saying humbly, " Let us pray !

" O Lord ! we would not advise ;
  But if in thy providence
A tempest should arise
  To drive the French fleet hence,
And scatter it far and wide,
  Or sink it in the sea,
We should be satisfied,
  And thine the glory be."

This was the prayer I made,
  For my soul was all on flame ;
And even as I prayed,
  The answering tempest came, —
It came with a mighty power,
  Shaking the windows and walls,
And tolling the bell in the tower
  As it tolls at funerals.

        .   .   .   .   .   .

The fleet it overtook,
  And the broad sails in the van
Like the tents of Cushan shook,
  Or the curtains of Midian.
Down on the reeling decks
  Crashed the o'erwhelming seas ;
Ah ! never were there wrecks
  So pitiful as these !

Like a potter's vessel broke
  The great ships of the line ;
They were carried away as a smoke,
  Or sank like lead in the brine.
O Lord ! before thy path
  They vanished, and ceased to be,
When thou didst walk in wrath
  With thine horses through the sea !

CHRIST CHURCH.

EDWIN B. RUSSELL.

GRAY spire, that from the ancient street
The eyes of reverent pilgrims greet,
   As by thy bells their steps are led,

CHRIST CHURCH.

Thou liftest up thy voice to-day,
Silvery and sweet, yet strong as aye,
   Above the living and the dead.

Beneath thy tower, how vast the throng
That moved through porch and aisle along
    The holy fane, the galleried height;
As years came in, and years went out,
With sob of woe, or joyful shout,
    With requiem rest, or anthem bright.

Old faces haunt the ancient pew,
And in the organ-loft renew
    The sacred strain of earlier times,
When knight and dame in worship bent,
And from their lips the homage sent
    That mingled with the answering chimes.

And here the patriot hung his light,
Which shone through all that anxious night,
    To eager eyes of Paul Revere.
There, in the dark churchyard below,
The dead Past wakened not, to know
    How changed the world, that night of fear.

The angels on thy gallery soar,
The Saviour's face thine altar o'er
    Is there, as in the elder day.
The royal silver yet doth shine,
And holds the pledge of love divine,
    That cannot change, nor pass away.

PAUL REVERE'S RIDE.

1775.

IN Boston the first inquiry that every stranger makes is for
Bunker Hill; the next is to be directed to the old church
where the lanterns were hung out on the night before the battles
of Lexington and Concord.

At nearly every hour of the day some one may be seen in the
now unfrequented street looking up at the lofty spire with an

expression of deep satisfaction, as if some long-cherished wish had at last been accomplished.

While he is endeavoring to impress the appearance of the venerable structure upon his memory, the pilgrim to historic shrines sees that a tablet, with an inscription cut upon it, is imbedded in the old, but still solid, masonry of the tower front. Salem Street is so narrow that he has no difficulty whatever in reading it from the curbstone across the way, which he does slowly and attentively. Bostonians all know it by heart. Thus it runs : —

THE SIGNAL LANTERNS OF
PAUL REVERE,
DISPLAYED IN THE STEEPLE OF THIS CHURCH,
APRIL 18, 1775,
WARNED THE COUNTRY OF THE MARCH
OF THE BRITISH TROOPS
TO LEXINGTON AND CONCORD.

This inscription, then, has constituted Christ Church, in effect, a monument to Paul Revere and his famous exploit. The poet Longfellow has given him another.

No stranger enters this neighborhood who does not get the impression that he has somewhere, unknown to himself, walked out of the Nineteenth Century into the Eighteenth.

The whole neighborhood is in a languishing state, though quite in keeping with the softened feeling that always comes over one in such retired corners. For here he has full liberty to lose himself, undisturbed either by noise or bustle, and he can quietly enjoy the seclusion needful for getting into a frame of mind proper to the associations of the spot. Yet, strange as it now seems, this was once a fashionable quarter of the town, although that was long ago, and traces of the old-time gentility are still apparent here and there to the eye of the wanderer up and down the deserted thoroughfares. In point of fact, notwithstanding it is one of the oldest divisions of the old city, the whole North End has lagged full half a century behind the other sections, — so far, indeed, that it is doubtful whether it will ever overtake them. This old church, with its venerable chimes, the armorial tombstones on Copp's Hill above it, and sundry antiquated mansions in antiquated lanes, are the silent witnesses to the fact that the neighborhood has really seen better days.

We have devoted so much space to the locality because it was the birthplace and home of Paul Revere.

At the time of his memorable ride, Paul Revere was forty years old, and was living in the neighborhood where he was born. Though he was brought up to the trade of a goldsmith, Revere was one of those skilful mechanics who can turn their hands to many things, and having already learned to engrave on silver, he took up and soon began to be known as an engraver

BOSTON FROM BREED'S HILL, 1791.

on copper-plate, in which art he acquired a rude proficiency. Revere, like most of his class, went heart and soul with the Whigs when the troubles with the mother country drew men to one or the other side ; and he very soon became one of the most active and daring spirits of a secret organization, composed of men like himself, who had sworn on the Bible not to betray each other, and whose purpose was to spy out and defeat the measures of the British Governor-General, cost what it might. These men knew nothing and cared nothing about the tricks of diplomacy. They were simply anxious to decide all outstanding questions by blows, the sooner the better.

Their meetings were held and their plans concerted at the

Green Dragon Tavern in Union Street. They were directed
how to act for the interests of the common cause by Adams,
Hancock, Warren, and one or two others of the acknowledged
leaders. Between Warren and Revere there grew up a sympathy so especially close and intimate, that when Adams and
Hancock left it, and Warren alone remained to observe and
direct events in the town, Revere became his chosen lieutenant.
This brings us to the event recorded in the inscription.

The Province of Massachusetts was on the verge of open revolt. It had formed an army, commissioned its officers, and pro-

SIGN OF THE GREEN DRAGON.

mulgated orders as if there were no such person as George III. It
was collecting stores, cannon, and muskets, in anticipation of the
moment when this army should take the field. It had, moreover,
given due notice to the British general-in-chief, as well as the
rest of mankind, that the first movement into the country made
by the royal troops in force would be considered as an act of hos-
tility and treated as such. If this was not raising the standard
of open rebellion, it certainly was something very like it.

The King had sent General Gage to Boston to put down the
rebellion there, and he had promised to do it with four battalions. He was now in Boston with a small army. Yet he

hesitated to act. Neither party would recede an inch, yet on both sides the commission of an overt act which any moment might precipitate war was awaited in the utmost suspense and dread.

At length General Gage resolved to strike a crippling blow, and if possible to do it without bloodshed.

The principal depot of the patriots was forming at Concord, in the County of Middlesex, about twenty miles from Boston, where it was considered quite safe from any sudden dash by the royal troops. General Gage was kept thoroughly informed by his spies of what was going on, and he determined to send a secret expedition to destroy those stores. The patriots, on their side, knew that something was in agitation, and it was no difficult matter for them to guess what was its real purport and aim. Still, so long as these remained in doubt, they were anxious and fearful and restless. They, however, redoubled their vigilance. All the landing-places of the town, the soldiers' barracks, and even the Province House itself, were closely watched, while guards were regularly kept in all the surrounding towns, promptly to give the alarm whenever the head of a British column should appear. General Gage held the capital of the province, but outside of its gates his orders could be executed only at the point of the bayonet.

Fully appreciating the importance of secrecy, General Gage quietly got ready eight hundred picked troops, which he meant to convey under cover of the night across the west bay, and to land on the Cambridge side, thus baffling the vigilance of the townspeople, and at the same time considerably shortening the distance his troops would have to march. So much pains was taken to keep their actual destination a profound secret, that even the officer who was selected for the command only received an order notifying him to hold himself in readiness. The guards in the town were doubled, and, in order to intercept any couriers who might slip through them, at the proper moment mounted patrols were sent out on the roads leading to Concord. Having done what he could to prevent intelligence from reaching the

country, and to keep the town quiet, the British General gave
his orders for the embarkation;
and at between ten and eleven
of the night of April 18th the
troops destined for this service
were taken across the bay in
boats to the Cambridge side
of the river.   At this hour his
pickets were guarding the deserted roads leading into the
country, and up to this moment
no patriot courier had gone out.
The General had thus got a long
start of the patriots.   But their
vigilance detected the movement as soon as it was made.
As Lord Percy was returning
from an interview with General Gage, he met groups of the
townspeople talking excitedly
together, and upon going near
enough to overhear the subject
of conversation, one of them
said to him defiantly: "The
British troops have marched,
but they will miss their aim."

"What aim?" asked the
Earl.

"The cannon at Concord,"
was the reply.

Percy instantly retraced his
steps to the Province House.
After listening in silence to his

GRENADIER, 1775.

report, the General broke out with, "Then I have been betrayed!"

It is now believed that a member of the General's own household was the medium through which his secret had become

known to the rebels. Their difficulty now was to transmit the news seasonably, to prevent the loss of the provincial magazines. There were only two modes of egress from the town, one being by the old ferry to Charlestown, the other by the neck connecting Boston with the mainland, which was only wide enough for a single road. The ferry-landing was kept by a subaltern's guard, and it was commanded by the batteries of a frigate anchored off in the stream. The road was blocked by a fortress extending across it, the gates of which were shut at a certain hour, after which no one could pass in or out except by order of the General himself.

To provide against this, Revere, only a day or two earlier, had concerted signals which should apprise his friends in Charlestown whenever a movement of troops was actually taking place. When these signals should be displayed, the watchful patriots there knew what they had to do.

The signals agreed upon were lights to be shown from the belfry of the North Church: two if the troops went out by water, and one if by land. The redcoats had scarcely got into their boats, when Warren sent in great haste for Paul Revere and William Dawes. He knew that the crisis had now come. Telling them in two words that the soldiers had started, and that he feared they meant to seize the patriot leaders, Hancock and Adams, he despatched Revere by the way of Charlestown, and Dawes by the great high-road over the Neck. In this way, should one be stopped, the other might elude the vigilance of the sentinels and succeed in getting through the lines. With the parting injunction in their ears, not to lose a moment, the two patriots started on the most momentous errand of the century.

Revere first went to a friend and requested him to show the signal, one lantern in the church belfry. He then went home, hurried on his riding-boots and surtout, and having picked up two friends and a boat, the three stealthily rowed across the river, passing unseen under the muzzles of the frigate's guns that guarded the ferry.

Leaping on shore, Revere learned that his signal had been seen and understood. At that very moment its warning beams shone from the distant tower. A fleet horse was quickly saddled and bridled for him to mount. Revere seized the bridle, jumped into the saddle, and spurred off at the top of his speed for Lexington, ten miles away, where Hancock and Adams, unconscious of danger, were then asleep in their beds. Dawes, too, had fortunately succeeded in evading the sentinels, so that the two were now, in the dead of night, galloping on like messengers of fate, not sparing either whip or spur, and each nerved by the imminent peril of the moment to do or dare everything for the salvation of friends and country. Revere had hardly got clear of Charlestown when a horseman suddenly barred his passage. Another rode up, then a third. He had ridden headlong into the midst of the British patrol! They closed in upon him. But Revere was not the man to be thus taken in a trap without a struggle. He quickly pulled up, turned his horse's head, dug the spurs into his flanks, and dashed off into a by-road with the patrol at his heels. Being the better mounted, he soon distanced his pursuers, and in ten minutes more rode into Medford, shouting like a madman at every house he came to, "Up and arm! Up and arm! The regulars are out! The regulars are out!" He awoke the captain of the minute-men, told his startling story in a breath, and before the shrill neighing of the excited steed or the shouts of the rider had grown faint in the distance, the Medford bells began to ring out their wild alarm. When Revere entered it, the town was as still as the grave; he left it in an uproar.

The regulars were indeed out; but where? By this time they should have been well advanced on their march, had not an excess of caution ruined at the outset every chance of surprising the Provincials. Possibly to prevent the expedition's getting wind, instead of furnishing the troops with rations before starting, they had been cooked on board the fleet, and put into the boats furnished by the different ships of war. After landing upon the Cambridge marshes, and after floundering through water up to the knee, to the shore, the royal troops were kept drawn up in a dirty by-road until two o'clock in the morning, waiting for their provisions to be brought from the boats and distributed. To lose hours when minutes counted for hours was fatal. The three thus idled away decided the fate of the expedition. The British grenadiers were still shivering on the spot where they disembarked, when Revere, after raising the country in arms, rode into Lexington. It was just midnight when he dismounted at the door where Hancock and Adams were asleep. He saw that he was in time. A patriot

REVERE AROUSING THE MINUTE-MAN.

guard was stationed outside. The drowsy sergeant sharply admonished Revere to make less noise, or he would disturb the household. " Noise ! " exclaimed the thoroughly excited Revere; " you 'll have noise enough before long. The regulars are out ! " He was then admitted.

In the course of half an hour the other express arrived, and the two rebel leaders being now fully convinced that Concord was the threatened point, after allowing the bold riders the time to swallow a few mouthfuls, hurried them on to Concord. Adams did not believe that Gage would send an army merely to take two men prisoners. To him the true object was very clear.

Revere, Dawes, and young Dr. Prescott of Concord, who had joined them, had got over half the distance, when at a sudden turning they saw in the gray light a group of dusky figures filling the road; at the same instant they heard the sharp command to halt. It was a second patrol, armed to the teeth. Prescott leaped his horse over the roadside wall, and so escaped across the fields to Concord. Revere, seeing the muzzle of a pistol covering him with sure aim, gave himself up, with the better grace now that one of the party had got clear. Dawes did the same thing. An officer then put his cocked pistol to Revere's head, telling him that he would scatter his brains in the road if he did not make true answers. His business on the road at that hour was then demanded. He was told, in return, to listen; when, through the still morning air, coming distinct and threatening, the distant booming of the alarm-bells, peal upon peal, was borne to their ears. Revere then boldly avowed his errand to be what it was, significantly adding that the country below was up in arms. Another prisoner told the patrol that they were all dead men. It was the Britons who were now uneasy. One of the rebel couriers had escaped them; the country below them was up; and there was no news of the troops. Ordering the prisoners to follow them, the troop rode off at a gallop toward Lexington, and when they were at the edge of the village Revere was told to dismount, and was then left to shift for himself. He ran as fast as his legs could carry him across the pastures, back to the parsonage, to report his misadventure, while the patrol galloped off toward Boston to announce theirs.

By this time the minute-men of Lexington had rallied to oppose the march of the troops. At this hour the alarm had spread throughout the surrounding country; and it was still resounding, still extending on every side, and multiplying itself like a destroying conflagration swept onward by the winds. In two hours more the whole Province was in flames. Thanks to the intrepidity of Paul Revere the goldsmith, instead of surprising the rebels in their beds, the redcoats found them marshalled on Lexington Green, at Concord Bridge, in front, flank, and rear, armed and ready to dispute their march to the bitter end.

At five in the morning his Majesty's troops by command fired upon and killed a number of the citizen soldiers at Lexington; they then gave three loud and triumphant cheers for the victory. At five in the evening General Gage knew that this volley had been discharged over the grave of his master's American empire, which he had promised to preserve with four battalions; the yeomanry of one county only had chased six of them back to their quarters.

From this narration it appears that it was not the signal, but Revere himself who "warned the country of the march of the British troops." Yet had he failed, the result would probably have been the same, thanks to his promptitude and his invention in this historic emergency. Mr. Longfellow in his famous ballad so arranges the scene as to make Revere impatiently watching for the signal-light to appear. Revere was the signal.

PAUL REVERE'S RIDE.

LISTEN, my children, and you shall hear
Of the midnight ride of Paul Revere,
On the eighteenth of April, in Seventy-five;
Hardly a man is now alive
Who remembers that famous day and year.

He said to his friend, "If the British march
By land or sea from the town to-night,

Hang a lantern aloft in the belfry arch
Of the North Church tower as a signal light, —
One, if by land, and two, if by sea ;
And I on the opposite shore will be,
Ready to ride and spread the alarm
Through every Middlesex village and farm,
For the country folk to be up and to arm."
Then he said " Good night ! " and with muffled oar
Silently rowed to the Charlestown shore,
Just as the moon rose over the bay,
Where swinging wide at her moorings lay
The " Somerset," British man-of-war ;
A phantom ship, with each mast and spar
Across the moon like a prison bar,
And a huge black hulk, that was magnified
By its own reflection in the tide.

.   .   .   .

Meanwhile, impatient to mount and ride,
Booted and spurred, with a heavy stride
On the opposite shore walked Paul Revere.
Now he patted his horse's side,
Now gazed at the landscape far and near,
Then, impetuous, stamped the earth,
And turned and tightened his saddle-girth ;
But mostly he watched with eager search
The belfry-tower of the Old North Church,
As it rose above the graves on the hill,
Lonely and spectral and sombre and still.
And lo ! as he looks, on the belfry's height
A glimmer, and then a gleam of light !
He springs to the saddle, the bridle he turns,
But lingers and gazes, till full on his sight
A second lamp in the belfry burns !

A hurry of hoofs in a village street,
A shape in the moonlight, a bulk in the dark,
And beneath, from the pebbles, in passing, a spark
Struck out by a steed flying fearless and fleet :
That was all ! And yet, through the gloom and the light,

The fate of a nation was riding that night;
And the spark struck out by that steed, in his flight,
Kindled the land into flame with its heat.

.   .   .   .

It was one by the village clock,
When he galloped into Lexington.
He saw the gilded weathercock
Swim in the moonlight as he passed,
And the meeting-house windows, blank and bare,
Gaze at him with a spectral glare,
As if they already stood aghast
At the bloody work they would look upon.

.   .   .   .

You know the rest. In the books you have read,
How the British Regulars fired and fled, —
How the farmers gave them ball for ball,
From behind each fence and farmyard wall,
Chasing the redcoats down the lane,
Then crossing the fields to emerge again
Under the trees at the turn of the road,
And only pausing to fire and load.

PETER RUGG, THE MISSING MAN.

BY WILLIAM AUSTIN.

(From Jonathan Dunwell of New York to Mr. Herman Krauff.)

SIR, — Agreeably to my promise, I now relate to you all
the particulars of the lost man and child which I have
been able to collect. It is entirely owing to the humane interest you seemed to take in the report that I have pursued the
inquiry to the following result.

You may remember that business called me to Boston in the summer of 1820. I sailed in the packet to Providence; and when I arrived there, I learned that every seat in the stage was engaged. I was thus obliged either to wait a few hours, or accept a seat with the driver, who civilly offered me that accommodation. Accordingly I took my seat by his side, and soon found him intelligent and communicative. When we had travelled about ten miles, the horses suddenly threw their ears on their necks as flat as a hare's. Said the driver, " Have you a surtout with you?"

" No," said I ; " why do you ask ? "

" You will want one soon," said he. " Do you observe the ears of all the horses ? "

" Yes ; " and was just about to ask the reason.

" They see the storm-breeder, and we shall see him soon."

At this moment there was not a cloud visible in the firmament ; soon after a small speck appeared in the road.

" There," said my companion, " comes the storm-breeder ; he always leaves a Scotch mist behind him. By many a wet jacket do I remember him. I suppose the poor fellow suffers much himself — much more than is known to the world."

Presently a man with a child beside him, with a large black horse and a weather-beaten chair, once built for a chaise-body, passed in great haste, apparently at the rate of twelve miles an hour. He seemed to grasp the reins of his horse with firmness, and appeared to anticipate his speed. He seemed dejected, and looked anxiously at the passengers, particularly at the stage-driver and myself. In a moment after he passed us, the horses' ears were up, and bent themselves forward so that they nearly met.

" Who is that man ? " said I ; " he seems in great trouble."

" Nobody knows who he is ; but his person and the child are familiar to me. I have met him more than a hundred times, and have been so often asked the way to Boston by that man, even when he was travelling directly from that town, that of late I have refused any communication with him ; and that is the reason he gave me such a fixed look."

PETER RUGG AND THE THUNDER-STORM.

"But does he never stop anywhere?"

"I have never known him to stop anywhere longer than to inquire the way to Boston. And let him be where he may, he will tell you he cannot stay a moment, for he must reach Boston that night."

We were now ascending a high hill in Walpole; and as we had a fair view of the heavens, I was rather disposed to jeer the driver for thinking of his surtout, as not a cloud as big as a marble could be discerned.

"Do you look," said he, "in the direction whence the man came; that is the place to look. The storm never meets him, it follows him."

We presently approached another hill; and when at the height the driver pointed out in an eastern direction a little black speck about as big as a hat, — "There," said he, "is the seed storm; we may possibly reach Polley's before it reaches us, but the wanderer and his child will go to Providence through rain, thunder, and lightning."

And now the horses, as though taught by instinct, hastened with increased speed. The little black cloud came on rolling over the turnpike, and doubled and trebled itself in all directions. The appearance of this cloud attracted the notice of all the passengers; for after it had spread itself to a great bulk, it suddenly became more limited in circumference, grew more compact, dark, and consolidated. And now the successive flashes of chain lightning caused the whole cloud to appear like a sort of irregular network, and displayed a thousand fantastic images. The driver bespoke my attention to a remarkable configuration in the cloud; he said every flash of lightning near its centre discovered to him distinctly the form of a man sitting in an open carriage drawn by a black horse. But in truth I saw no such thing. The man's fancy was doubtless at fault. It is a very common thing for the imagination to paint for the senses, both in the visible and invisible world.

In the mean time the distant thunder gave notice of a shower at hand; and just as we reached Polley's tavern the rain poured

down in torrents. It was soon over, the cloud passing in the
direction of the turnpike toward Providence. In a few moments
after, a respectable-looking man in a chaise stopped at the door.
The man and child in the chair having excited some little sympathy among the passengers, the gentleman was asked if he
had observed them. He said he had met them; that the man

EQUESTRIANS.

seemed bewildered, and inquired the way to Boston; that he
was driving at great speed, as though he expected to outstrip
the tempest; that the moment he had passed him, a thunder-
clap broke directly over the man's head, and seemed to envelop
both man and child, horse and carriage. "I stopped," said the
gentleman, "supposing the lightning had struck him; but the
horse only seemed to loom up and increase his speed; and as

well as I could judge, he travelled just as fast as the thunder-cloud."

While this man was speaking, a pedlar with a cart of tin merchandise came up all dripping; and on being questioned, he said he had met that man and carriage, within a fortnight, in four different States; that at each time he had inquired the way to Boston, and that a thunder-shower, like the present, had each time deluged his wagon and his wares, setting his tin pots, etc., afloat, so that he had determined to get marine insurance done for the future. But that which excited his surprise most was the strange conduct of his horse; for that long before he could distinguish the man in the chair, his own horse stood still in the road, and flung back his ears. "In short," said the pedlar, " I wish never to see that man and horse again; they do not look to me as though they belonged to this world."

HACKNEY-COACH.

This was all I could learn at that time; and the occurrence soon after would have become with me "like one of those things which had never happened," had I not, as I stood recently on the doorstep of Bennett's Hotel in Hartford, heard a man say, "There goes Peter Rugg and his child! He looks wet and weary, and farther from Boston than ever." I was satisfied it was the same man I had seen more than three years before; for whoever has once seen Peter Rugg can never after be deceived as to his identity.

"Peter Rugg!" said I; "and who is Peter Rugg?"

"That," said the stranger, "is more than any one can tell exactly. He is a famous traveller, held in light esteem by all inn-holders, for he never stops to eat, drink, or sleep. I wonder why the Government does not employ him to carry the mail."

"Ay," said a bystander; "that is a thought bright only on one side. How long would it take in that case to send a letter to Boston ? — for Peter has already, to my knowledge, been more than twenty years travelling to that place."

"But," said I, "does the man never stop anywhere? Does he never converse with any one? I saw the same man more than three years since near Providence, and I heard a strange story about him. Pray, sir, give me some account of this man."

"Sir," said the stranger, "those who know the most respecting that man say the least. I have heard it asserted that Heaven sometimes sets a mark on a man either for judgment or a trial. Under which Peter Rugg now labors, I cannot say; therefore I am rather inclined to pity than to judge."

"You speak like a humane man," said I; "and if you have known him so long, I pray you will give me some account of him. Has his appearance much altered in that time?"

"Why, yes ; he looks as though he never ate, drank, or slept ; and his child looks older than himself; and he looks like time broken off from eternity, and anxious to gain a resting-place."

"And how does his horse look?" said I.

"As for his horse, he looks fatter and gayer, and shows more animation and courage, than he did twenty years ago. The last time Rugg spoke to me he inquired how far it was to Boston. I told him just one hundred miles.

"'Why,' said he, 'how can you deceive me so? It is cruel to mislead a traveller. I have lost my way; pray direct me the nearest way to Boston.'

"I repeated, it was one hundred miles.

"'How can you say so?' said he; 'I was told last evening it was but fifty, and I have travelled all night.'

"'But,' said I, 'you are now travelling from Boston. You must turn back.'

"'Alas!' said he, 'it is all turn back! Boston shifts with the wind, and plays all around the compass. One man tells me it is to the east, another to the west; and the guide-posts, too, they all point the wrong way.'

" 'But will you not stop and rest?' said I; 'you seem wet and weary.'

" ' Yes,' said he ; 'it has been foul weather since I left home.'

" ' Stop, then, and refresh yourself.'

" 'I must not stop; I must reach home to-night, if possible ; though I think you must be mistaken in the distance to Boston.'

" He then gave the reins to his horse, which he restrained with difficulty, and disappeared in a moment. A few days afterward I met the man a little this side of Claremont, winding around the hills in Unity, at the rate, I believe, of twelve miles an hour."

" Is Peter Rugg his real name, or has he accidentally gained that name ? "

" I know not, but presume he will not deny his name ; you can ask him — for see, he has turned his horse, and is passing this way."

In a moment a dark-colored, high-spirited horse approached, and would have passed without stopping ; but I had resolved to speak to Peter Rugg, or whoever the man might be. Accordingly I stepped into the street, and as the horse approached, I made a feint of stopping him. The man immediately reined in his horse. " Sir," said I, "may I be so bold as to inquire if you are not Mr. Rugg ? — for I think I have seen you before."

" My name is Peter Rugg," said he : " I have unfortunately lost my way. I am wet and weary, and will take it kindly of you to direct me to Boston."

" You live in Boston, do you ? — and in what street ? "

" In Middle Street."

" When did you leave Boston ? "

" I cannot tell precisely ; it seems a considerable time."

" But how did you and your child become so wet ? It has not rained here to-day."

" It has just rained a heavy shower up the river. But I shall

7

not reach Boston to-night if I tarry. Would you advise me to take the old road, or the turnpike?"

"Why, the old road is one hundred and seventeen miles, and the turnpike is ninety-seven."

"How can you say so? You impose on me! It is wrong to trifle with a traveller. You know it is but forty miles from Newburyport to Boston."

"But this is not Newburyport; this is Hartford."

"Do not deceive me, sir. Is not this town Newburyport, and the river that I have been following the Merrimac?"

"No, sir; this is Hartford, and the river the Connecticut."

He wrung his hands and looked incredulous.

"Have the rivers, too, changed their courses, as the cities have changed places? But see! the clouds are gathering in the south, and we shall have a rainy night. Ah, that fatal oath!"

He would tarry no longer. His impatient horse leaped off, his hind flanks rising like wings; he seemed to devour all before him, and to scorn all behind.

I had now, as I thought, discovered a clew to the history of Peter Rugg, and I determined, the next time my business called me to Boston, to make a further inquiry. Soon after, I was enabled to collect the following particulars from Mrs. Croft, an aged lady in Middle Street, who has resided in Boston during the last twenty years. Her narration is this:

The last summer, a person, just at twilight, stopped at the door of the late Mrs. Rugg. Mrs. Croft, on coming to the door, perceived a stranger, with a child by his side, in an old weather-beaten carriage, with a black horse. The stranger asked for Mrs. Rugg, and was informed that Mrs. Rugg had died in a good old age more than twenty years before that time.

The stranger replied, "How can you deceive me so? Do ask Mrs. Rugg to step to the door."

"Sir, I assure you Mrs. Rugg has not lived here these nineteen years; no one lives here but myself, and my name is Betsey Croft."

The stranger paused, and looked up and down the street, and

said : "Though the painting is rather faded, this looks like my house."

"Yes," said the child ; "that is the stone before the door that I used to sit on to eat my bread and milk."

"But," said the stranger, "it seems to be on the wrong side of the street. Indeed everything here seems to be misplaced. The streets are all changed, the people are all changed, the town seems changed ; and, what is strangest of all, Catherine Rugg has deserted her husband and child. Pray," continued the stranger, "has John Foy come home from sea ? He went a long voyage ; he is my kinsman. If I could see him, he could give me some account of Mrs. Rugg."

"Sir," said Mrs. Croft, "I never heard of John Foy. Where did he live ?"

"Just above here, in Orange Tree Lane."

"There is no such place in this neighborhood."

"What do you tell me ? Are the streets gone ? Orange Tree Lane is at the head of Hanover Street, near Pemberton's Hill."

"There is no such lane now."

"Madam ! you cannot be serious. But you doubtless know my brother, William Rugg. He lives in Royal Exchange Lane, near King Street."

"I know of no such lane, and I am sure there is no such street as King Street in this town."

"No such street as King Street ! Why, woman, you mock me ! You may as well tell me there is no King George ! However, madam, you see I am wet and weary ; I must find a resting-place. I will go to Hart's tavern, near the market."

"Which market, sir ? — for you seem perplexed ; we have several markets."

"You know there is but one market, — near the Town dock."

"Oh, the old market ; but no such person has kept there these twenty years."

Here the stranger seemed disconcerted, and uttered to himself quite audibly : "Strange mistake ! How much this looks like the town of Boston ! It certainly has a great resemblance to it; but I perceive my mistake now. Some other Mrs. Rugg, some other Middle Street."

"Then," said he, "madam, can you direct me to Boston?"

"Why, this is Boston, the city of Boston. I know of no other Boston."

"City of Boston it may be; but it is not the Boston where I live. I recollect now, I came over a bridge instead of a ferry. Pray what bridge is that I just came over?"

"It is Charles River Bridge."

"I perceive my mistake; there is a ferry between Boston and Charlestown; there is no bridge. Ah, I perceive my mistake.

MARKET-WOMAN.

If I were in Boston my horse would carry me directly to my own door. But my horse shows by his impatience that he is in a strange place. Absurd, that I should have mistaken this place for the old town of Boston! It is a much finer city than the town of Boston. It has been built long since Boston. I fancy it must lie at a distance from this city, as the good woman seems ignorant of it."

At these words his horse began to chafe and strike the pavement with his fore-feet. The stranger seemed a little bewildered, and said, "No home to-night;" and giving the reins to his horse, passed up the street, and I saw no more of him.

It was evident that the generation to which Peter Rugg belonged had passed away.

This was all the account of Peter Rugg I could obtain from Mrs. Croft; but she directed me to an elderly man, Mr. James Felt, who lived near her, and who had kept a record of the principal occurrences for the last fifty years. At my request she sent for him; and after I had related to him the object of my inquiry, Mr. Felt told me he had known Rugg in his youth; that his disappearance had caused some surprise; but as it sometimes happens that men run away, sometimes to be rid of others, and sometimes to be rid of themselves; and Rugg took his child with him, and his own horse and chair; and as it did not appear that any creditors made a stir, — the occurrence soon mingled itself in the stream of oblivion, and Rugg and his child, horse and chair, were soon forgotten.

"It is true," said Mr. Felt, "sundry stories grew out of Rugg's affair, — whether true or false I cannot tell; but stranger things have happened in my day, without even a newspaper notice."

"Sir," said I, "Peter Rugg is now living; I have lately seen Peter Rugg and his child, horse, and chair. Therefore I pray you to relate to me all you know or ever heard of him."

"Why, my friend," said James Felt, "that Peter Rugg is now a living man, I will not deny; but that you have seen Peter Rugg and his child is impossible, if you mean a small child; for Jenny Rugg, if living, must be at least — let me see — Boston Massacre, 1770 — Jenny Rugg was about ten years old. Why, sir, Jenny Rugg, if living, must be more than sixty years of age. That Peter Rugg is living, is highly probable, as he was only ten years older than myself, and I was only eighty last March; and I am as likely to live twenty years longer as any man."

Here I perceived that Mr. Felt was in his dotage; and I despaired of gaining any intelligence from him on which I could depend.

I took my leave of Mrs. Croft, and proceeded to my lodgings at the Marlborough Hotel.

If Peter Rugg, thought I, has been travelling since the Boston Massacre, there is no reason why he should not travel to the end of time. If the present generation know little of him, the next will know less; and Peter and his child will have no hold on this world.

In the course of the evening I related my adventure in Middle Street.

"Ha!" said one of the company, smiling, "do you really think you have seen Peter Rugg? I have heard my grandfather speak of him as though he seriously believed his own story."

"Sir," said I, "pray let us compare your grandfather's story of Mr. Rugg with my own."

"Peter Rugg, sir, if my grandfather was worthy of credit, once lived in Middle Street, in this city. He was a man in comfortable circumstances, had a wife and one daughter, and was generally esteemed for his sober life and manners. But, unhappily, his temper at times was altogether ungovernable; and then his language was terrible. In these fits of passion, if a door stood in his way, he would never do less than kick a panel through. He would sometimes throw his heels over his head and come down on his feet, uttering oaths in a circle; and thus in a rage he was the first who performed a somerset, and did what others have since learned to do for merriment and money. Once Rugg was seen to bite a tenpenny nail in halves. In those days everybody, both men and boys, wore wigs; and Peter, at these moments of violent passion, would become so profane that his wig would rise up from his head. Some said it was on account of his terrible language; others accounted for it in a more philosophical way, and said it was caused by the expansion of his scalp, — as violent passion, we know, will swell the veins and expand the head. While these fits were on him Rugg had no respect for heaven or earth. Except this infirmity, all agreed that Rugg was a good sort of man; for when his fits were over, nobody was so ready to commend a placid temper as Peter.

"It was late in autumn, one morning, that Rugg, in his own

chair, with a fine large bay horse, took his daughter and proceeded to Concord. On his return a violent storm overtook
him. At dark he stopped in Menotomy, now West Cambridge,
at the door of a Mr. Cutter, a friend of his, who urged him
to tarry the night. On Rugg's declining to stop, Mr. Cutter
urged him vehemently. 'Why, Mr. Rugg,' said Cutter, 'the
storm is overwhelming you : the night is exceeding dark : your
little daughter will perish : you are in an open chair, and the
tempest is increasing.' '*Let the storm increase,*' said Rugg, with
a fearful oath ; '*I will see home to-night, in spite of the last tempest, or may I never see home!*' At these words he gave his
whip to his high-spirited horse, and disappeared in a moment.

BOSTON TRUCK.

But Peter Rugg did not reach home that night, or the next ;
nor, when he became a missing man, could he ever be traced
beyond Mr. Cutter's in Menotomy.

   " For a long time after, on every dark and stormy night, the
wife of Peter Rugg would fancy she heard the crack of a whip,
and the fleet tread of a horse, and the rattling of a carriage
passing her door. The neighbors, too, heard the same noises ;
and some said they knew it was Rugg's horse, the tread on
the pavement was perfectly familiar to them. This occurred so
repeatedly, that at length the neighbors watched with lanterns,
and saw the real Peter Rugg, with his own horse and chair,
and child sitting beside him, pass directly before his own door,
his head turned toward his house, and himself making every
effort to stop his horse, but in vain.

"The next day the friends of Mrs. Rugg exerted themselves to find her husband and child. They inquired at every public-house and stable in town; but it did not appear that Rugg made any stay in Boston. No one, after Rugg had passed his own door, could give any account of him; though it was asserted by some that the clatter of Rugg's horse and carriage over the pavements shook the houses on both sides of the streets. And this is credible, if indeed Rugg's horse and carriage did pass on that night. For at this day, in many of the streets, a loaded truck or team in passing will shake the houses like an earth-quake. However, Rugg's neighbors never afterward watched; some of them treated it all as a delusion, and thought no more of it. Others, of a different opinion, shook their heads and said nothing.

"Thus Rugg and his child, horse and chair, were soon for-gotten, and probably many in the neighborhood never heard a word on the subject.

"There was, indeed, a rumor that Rugg afterward was seen in Connecticut, between Suffield and Hartford, passing through the country with headlong speed. This gave occasion to Rugg's friends to make further inquiry. But the more they inquired, the more they were baffled. If they heard of Rugg one day in Connecticut, the next they heard of him winding round the hills in New Hampshire; and soon after, a man in a chair with a small child, exactly answering the description of Peter Rugg, would be seen in Rhode Island inquiring the way to Boston.

"But that which chiefly gave a color of mystery to the story of Peter Rugg was the affair at Charlestown Bridge. The toll-gatherer asserted that sometimes on the darkest and most stormy nights, when no object could be discerned, about the time Rugg was missing, a horse and wheel carriage, with a noise equal to a troop, would at midnight, in utter contempt of the rates of toll, pass over the bridge. This occurred so frequently, that the toll-gatherer resolved to attempt a discovery. Soon after, at the usual time, apparently the same horse and carriage approached the bridge from Charlestown Square. The toll-gatherer, prepared, took his stand as near the middle of the bridge as he dared, with a large three-legged stool in his hand. As the appearance passed, he threw the stool at the horse, but heard nothing, except the noise of the stool skipping across the bridge. The toll-gatherer, on the next day, asserted that the stool went directly through the body of the horse; and he persisted in that belief ever after. Whether Rugg, or whoever the person was, ever passed the bridge again, the toll-gatherer would never tell; and when questioned, seemed anxious to waive the subject. And thus Peter Rugg and his child, horse and carriage, remain a mystery to this day."

This, sir, is all that I could learn of Peter Rugg in Boston.

A LEGEND OF THE OLD ELM.

BY ISAAC McLELLAN, JR.

MIKE WILD was a substantial grocer, and flourished in the good old days of Boston. He has for many years been peacefully gathered to his fathers, as a small gray tablet, very much defaced by the hand of time and the idle schoolboy, will testify. This memorial of Mr. Wild's mortality may be seen by the curious antiquary in the Old Granary Churchyard, bearing a pithy inscription, which denotes the years and days of Mike's mortal career, and is disfigured by the customary cherub and seraph of churchyard sculpture.

Mike was known to be a hard man, miserly and penurious; but it was never clearly proved that he was dishonest. If his crafty and calculating spirit could discriminate nicely between a sure and a doubtful speculation, it could determine with equal accuracy how far to overreach his neighbor, and yet escape the hazard of becoming obnoxious to the charge of fraud. But he valued himself most upon his shrewdness and caution, professing to hold in utter contempt the folly of credulity; and when he read or heard of any imposition practised upon his neighbors, he used to say : " Folks must be up betimes to overreach Mike Wild."

One stormy evening, about the close of the autumn of 1776, Mike was enjoying his customary household comforts, his can and pipe, in the little back parlor of his dwelling, Number —, North End, being the house next to that occupied by Mr. Peter Rugg, famous in story. The night was dark without as the " throat of the black wolf," and as turbulent as that animal when a long snow-storm upon the hills has driven him mad with famine.

This obscure chamber was the theatre of his earthly felicity. It was here that he counted over his accumulating gains, with every returning night ; indulged in the precious remembrance of past success, and rioted in the golden visions of future prosperity. Therefore with this room were associated all the pleasing recollections of his life.

It was the only green spot in his memory, — the refreshing oasis in the barren desert of his affections. It was there alone that the solitary gleam of consolation touched and melted the ice of his soul. It was natural, then, considering his selfish nature, that he should keep it sacred and inviolate. The foot of wife or child was never permitted to invade this sanctum. Such approach on their part would have been deemed high treason, and punished as such without " benefit of clergy." Such intrusion by a neighbor would have been deemed a declaration of hostilities, and would have been warmly repelled. It were, indeed, safer to have bearded the lion in his den or the puissant Douglas in his hall ; for Mike possessed all those physical virtues which can keep the head from harm, if at any time the absence of better qualities provoke assault.

The besom of the thrifty housewife never disturbed the venerable dust and cobwebs that supplied its only tapestry. From generation to generation the spider had reigned unmolested in the corners and crevices of the wall ; and so long had the territory been held and transmitted from sire to son, that if a title by prescription could ever avail against the practical argument of the broom, there was little fear of a process of ejectment.

As the old lamp at the gate creaked dismally, and the crazy shutters of his chamber rattled still more noisily in the wind, the mercury of Mike's spirits rose higher, — a physical phenomenon not easily explained. Perhaps, as the elemental war grew sharper, his own nature grew more benign in the consciousness that a secure shelter was interposed between his own head and the elements.

The last drops of good liquor had disappeared from Mike's silver tankard, the last wavering wreath of smoke had dissolved in the air, and the dull embers of his hearth were fast dying away in the white ashes, when Mike, upon raising his eyes suddenly,

CHAISE, 1776.

was much startled to observe that he had company in his solitude. He rubbed his eyes and shook himself, to ascertain his personal identity ; but still the large, strong figure of a man was seated in the old leather chair directly opposite to him. Whence he came, by what means he had entered, what were his purposes, were mysteries too deep for Mike's faculties at that time to fathom. There *he* sat, however, motionless as a statue, with his arms folded, and a pair of large, lustrous black eyes fastened full upon him. There was a complete fascination in that glance, which sent a thrill through his whole frame, and held him as with an iron chain to his chair.

Mike, like a good general, soon rallied his routed faculties, reanimated his fugitive thoughts, and resolved, though possessing a faint heart, to show a bold front, — a cheat often practised by better tacticians. He thereupon plucked up heroism, and soon ascertained that his visitor was of very affable and benignant bearing.

He communicated his business briefly, in which virtue of brevity we shall condescend to be an imitator. He revealed that he was indeed of unearthly nature, — a disembodied spirit, and that during his earthly sojourn he had secreted a most precious treasure, which had been unlawfully acquired, under the Old Elm Tree in the centre of the Common. He could not rest quietly in the grave until he had imparted the secret to some human being ; and as Mike was a man after his own heart, he had selected him as the object of his bounty. Mike thanked him sincerely for the compliment and kindness, and promised to go forth without delay in search of the treasure. He sallied forth with his " spiritual guide," his mind intoxicated with the thought of the heavy ingots, and the bars of gold, and the rich foreign coin which he believed would be shortly his own. The night was black and rainy ; the scattered sleet swept furiously along the streets, pursued by the screaming wind ; but the wrath of the elements was disarmed by the glorious vision of riches and honor which possessed him.

They arrived at length, after much wading and tribulation, at the Old Elm, now the trysting-place of young people on the days of Election festivity. In those days it was sometimes used as a gallows, for want of a better ; and it is said, at this very day, that on dark and tempestuous nights the ghosts of those who perished on its branches are seen swinging and heard creaking in the wind, still struggling in the last throe and torment of dissolution, in expiation of crimes committed long ago.

When Mike paused at the roots of the old tree, he requested his guide to designate the particular spot that contained the treasure ; but receiving no response to this very natural inquiry, he looked round and saw that his genius had vanished "into the air," probably like Macbeth's witches. He was not to be disheartened or daunted, however ; so he resolutely commenced delving, with the zeal of an ardent money-digger. He turned up many a good rood of soil without meeting the precious ore, when his fears got the better of his discretion, and his fancy busily peopled the obscure tops and limbs of the old tree with all manner of grotesque shapes and gib-

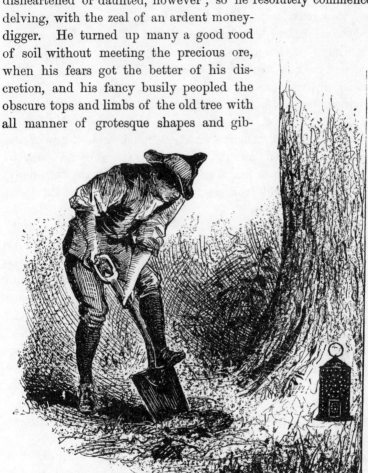

THE MONEY-DIGGER.

bering monsters, and he fancied that the evil spirits of departed malefactors were celebrating their festival orgies, and making merry with their infernal dances around him.

His fear had increased to agony. The spade dropped from his powerless hand, his hair bristled with terror, and his great eyes nearly leaped from his head in his endeavor to penetrate the gloom that surrounded him. Once more his mysterious guide stood before him ; but one glance of his awfully altered face completed the climax of his fright. Those large black, lustrous eyes now kindled like two balls of flame ; and as their fiendish lustre glared upon him, he shrank back as from a scorching flame. A nose, enormous and rubicund as the carbuncle of the East, protruded many a rood from the face of his evil spirit, and immense whiskers, rough and shaggy as the lion's mane, flowed around his visage. The gold-monster continued to frown upon him fearfully, till at length the bewildered eyes of Mike could look no longer, and he fell to the earth utterly senseless.

When Mike awoke, the morning sun was looking cheerfully into his own chamber window, and the birds that make merry in every bright summer morning were singing gayly on the house-eaves above his head. He rubbed his eyes in astonishment, and was in doubt whether he had not lost his senses, or whether the visitor, the money, the walk of midnight, and the horrible goblin, were not all the mere creations of a dream.

While lost in these doubts and difficulties, a neighbor opportunely stepped in, to whom he related the whole scene, adding at the same time suitable embellishments to the appearance of the fiend-like apparition which had haunted him.

His friend heard him for some time expatiate on the miraculous adventure, but at length could preserve his gravity no longer, and burst forth in a loud ha ! ha ! ha ! When he had recovered sufficient breath to articulate, he confessed to the electrified Mike that his visitor was no other than himself, and that he had practised the hoax in order to decide a wager with mine host of the Boar's Head, who had bet a dozen of his choicest bin that no one could get the better of shrewd Mike Wild of the North End.

ROXBURY PUDDING-STONE.

IN those pleasant suburban districts of Boston that were formerly the towns of Roxbury and Dorchester, the rock everywhere seen in the roadside walls and outcropping ledges is the very curious conglomerate familiarly known as pudding-stone; so called, no doubt, on account of the pebbles that are imbedded so solidly within the cooled mass as now to form a part of it. Rejecting all scientific hypotheses in favor of a legend, the genial Dr. Holmes accounts for the geological phenomenon in his own felicitous way in the "Dorchester Giant," thus enabling us to conclude our historical pieces with the customary geological description.

OLD MILE-STONE.

THE DORCHESTER GIANT.

OLIVER WENDELL HOLMES.

THERE was a Giant in time of old,
    A mighty one was he;
He had a wife, but she was a scold,
So he kept her shut in his mammoth fold;
    And he had children three.

   ·   ·   ·   ·   ·   ·   ·

Then the Giant took his children three,
    And fastened them in the pen;
The children roared; quoth the Giant, "Be still!"
And Dorchester Heights and Milton Hill
    Rolled back the sound again.

Then he brought them a pudding stuffed with plums,
   As big as the State-House dome ;
Quoth he, " There 's something for you to eat ;
So stop your mouths with your 'lection treat,
   And wait till your dad comes home."

     .   .   .   .

What are those loved ones doing now,
   The wife and children sad?
Oh, they are in a terrible rout,
Screaming and throwing their pudding about,
   Acting as they were mad.

They flung it over to Roxbury hills,
   They flung it over the plain,
And all over Milton and Dorchester too,
Great lumps of pudding the giants threw,
   They tumbled as thick as rain.

     .   .   .   .

And if, some pleasant afternoon,
   You 'll ask me out to ride,
The whole of the story I will tell,
And you may see where the puddings fell,
   And pay for the punch beside.

Part Second.

CAMBRIDGE LEGENDS.

THE WASHINGTON ELM.

THIS patriarch among trees is one of those perishable historic objects we can still point to with a feeling of satisfaction that it continues in the enjoyment of a vigorous old age. Long live the Washington Elm ! It has survived the renowned Charter Oak, it outlives its venerated neighbor, the Boston Elm ; and, though much shattered " alow and aloft," it bids fair to round the century with head proudly erect, as the living link joining the settlement of the country with the era of its greatest prosperity.

The historic elm-tree stands in the public highway, by the side of the Common, in the city of Cambridge. The Common was the training-field of the first republican army, formed almost as if by magic, in the years '75 and '76, of glorious memory. Beyond the elm of renown, on the other side, are the quaint old College buildings, which then served as barracks for this army ; while scattered round about the neighborhood are many of the residences that the chances of war turned into quarters for the officers when they were vacated in a hurry by their Tory owners. So that many vestiges of those stirring times remain to attract the visitor to one of the most historic places of the Commonwealth.

Many pilgrims wend their way to the spot where the massive old tree-trunk — the Washington Elm — shakes out its annual foliage, that is like the ivy clinging and clustering about a ruin. As a tree, it would be sure to command attention on account of its apparent great age; but it is something more than a tree. Silent witness to all the scenes that have been enacted here since the white men first forced their way through the thickets covering the surrounding plain, it is as much an object of veneration to the citizens as if it were really able to impart what

THE WASHINGTON ELM.

it had seen. May its shadow never be less! It saw the mustering of the raw Provincial levies for the seven years' march to Yorktown; it has been blackened by cannon-smoke, has seen the glittering circle of camp-fires lighting the long line of an investing army steadily tightening its coils about the beleaguered capital. But one thing, above others, invests it with a grandeur inseparable from him who was the noblest Roman of them all.

The inscription placed at the base of the tree tells the whole story ; to this it is unnecessary to add a single word :

UNDER THIS TREE
WASHINGTON
FIRST TOOK COMMAND
OF THE
AMERICAN ARMY,
JULY 3ᴅ, 1775.

THE WASHINGTON ELM.

MRS. L. N. SIGOURNEY.

WORDS ! words, Old Tree !   Thou hast an aspect fair,
   A vigorous heart, a heaven-aspiring crest ;
And sleepless memories of the days that were,
   Lodge in thy branches, like the song-bird's nest.

Words ! give us words !   Methought a gathering blast
   Mid its green leaves began to murmur low,
Shaping its utterance to the mighty Past,
   That backward came, on pinions floating slow :

" The ancient masters of the soil I knew,
   Whose cane-roofed wigwams flecked the forest-brown ;
Their hunter-footsteps swept the early dew,
   And their keen arrow struck the eagle down.

" I heard the bleak December tempest moan
   When the tossed 'Mayflower' moored in Plymouth Bay ;
And watched yon classic walls as, stone by stone,
   The fathers reared them slowly toward the day.

" But lo ! a mighty Chieftain 'neath my shade
   Drew his bright sword and reared his dauntless head ;
And Liberty sprang forth from rock and glade,
   And donned her helmet for the hour of dread :

While in the hero's heart there dwelt a prayer
    That Heaven's protecting arm might never cease
To make his young, endangered land its care,
    Till through the war-cloud looked the angel Peace.

" Be wise, my children," said that ancient Tree,
    In earnest tone, as though a Mentor spake,
" And prize the blood-bought birthright of the free,
    And firmly guard it for your country's sake."

Thanks, thanks, Old Elm ! and for this counsel sage,
    May Heaven thy brow with added beauty grace,
Grant richer emeralds to thy crown of age,
    And changeless honors from a future race.

THE WASHINGTON ELM.

JAMES RUSSELL LOWELL.

BENEATH our consecrated elm
A century ago he stood,
Famed vaguely for that old fight in the wood
Whose red surge sought, but could not overwhelm
The life foredoomed to wield our rough-hewn helm : —
From colleges, where now the gown
To arms had yielded, from the town,
Our rude self-summoned levies flocked to see
The new-come chiefs, and wonder which was he.
No need to question long ; close-lipped and tall,
Long trained in murder-brooding forests lone
To bridle others' clamors and his own,
Firmly erect, he towered above them all,
The incarnate discipline that was to free
With iron curb that armed democracy.

   .   .   .   .   .   .

Musing beneath the legendary tree,
The years between furl off ; I seem to see
The sun-flecks, shaken the stirred foliage through,
Dapple with gold his sober buff and blue,

And weave prophetic aureoles round the head
That shines our beacon now, nor darkens with the dead.
O man of silent mood,
A stranger among strangers then,
How art thou since renowned the Great, the Good,
Familiar as the day in all the homes of men !
The wingéd years, that winnow praise and blame,
Blow many names out ; they but fan to flame
The self-renewing splendors of thy fame.

THE LAST OF THE HIGHWAYMEN.

MICHAEL MARTIN, *alias* Captain Lightfoot, after a checkered career in Ireland, his native country, and in Scotland, as a highway robber, became in 1819 a fugitive to America. He first landed at Salem, where he obtained employment as a farm-laborer. But a life of honest toil not being so congenial to him as that of a bandit, he again took to his old occupation on the road, this time making Canada the scene of his exploits.

After committing many robberies there and in Vermont and New Hampshire, and always eluding capture, Martin at length arrived in Boston. He at once began his bold operations upon the highway; but here his usual good luck deserted him. His first and last victim was Major John Bray, of Boston. Martin had somehow found out that His Excellency Governor Brooks intended giving a dinner-party at his mansion in Medford on a certain afternoon, and he had determined to waylay some of the company on their return, shrewdly guessing that they might be well worth the picking. In fact, as Major Bray was driving leisurely homeward in his chaise over the Medford turnpike, he was suddenly stopped by a masked horseman, who presented a pistol and sternly commanded him to deliver up his valuables.

The place was a lonely one, and well chosen for the robber's purpose. The astounded Major handed over his watch and his purse. Having secured his booty, the highwayman wheeled his horse, gave him the spur, and galloped off; while his frightened and crestfallen victim, lashing his horse to a run, raised a hue-and-cry at the nearest house.

Martin fled. He was hotly pursued, and was taken, after a chase of a hundred miles, asleep in bed at Springfield. The officers brought him back, and lodged him in East Cambridge jail to await his trial. He was tried at the next assizes for highway robbery, was convicted, and sentenced to be hanged. This being the first trial occurring under the statute punishing such an offence, it naturally created a great deal of stir, and when the prisoner was brought to the bar, the court-room was thronged with curious spectators. Throughout the proceedings the prisoner was perfectly cool. As the pupil of the celebrated Thunderbolt, he had a reputation to maintain; and when the judge, putting on the black cap, pronounced the awful sentence of death, he dryly observed: "Well, that's the worst you can do for me."

The doomed man, however, made one desperate effort to escape from prison. He had found some way to procure a file, with which he filed off his irons so that he could remove them whenever he liked; and when the turnkey one morning came into the cell, he being off his guard, the prisoner, using his irons as a weapon, felled him to the ground with a savage blow on the head, and leaving him stunned and bleeding upon the floor of the cell, rushed out of the open door into the prison-yard. The outer walls were too high to be scaled, and free passage into the street was barred by a massive oaken gate. But this did not stop the resolute highwayman, who was a man of herculean strength. Dashing himself repeatedly, with all his force, against it, he at last succeeded in breaking the gate open, and passing quickly through, he emerged into the street beyond; but being exhausted by his frantic efforts to escape, after a short flight his pursuers overtook and secured him. He was loaded with irons and chained to his cell. After this desperate attempt to gain his liberty, he was guarded with greater vigilance until the day appointed for his execution, when the "Last of the Highwaymen" paid the penalty of his crimes upon the scaffold.

THE ELIOT OAK.

IN that part of Boston formerly constituting the town of Brighton, and still farther back forming a precinct of Cambridge, there is a pleasant locality called Oak Square. It was so named on account of the old oak-tree which stood there, and which is probably better known as the Eliot Oak.

This gigantic relic of the primeval forest was in its day the largest and the oldest tree of its species growing within the four boundaries of the old Bay State, and it was officially declared to be so by a scientific commission which was charged with making a botanical survey of the State. The declaration is made that "It had probably passed its prime centuries before the first English voice was heard on the shores of Massachusetts Bay." Its circumference at the ground was given at twenty-five feet and nine inches, or two feet more than that of the Great Elm of Boston. Through decay the trunk became hollow at the base, furnishing a cavity large enough to serve as a hiding-place for the schoolboys who played under the shade of its wide-spreading branches. The enormous weight of these, with their foliage, was at last supported by a mere shell of trunk, and as every gale threatened to lay it low, to the regret of thousands, the brave old oak was through a hard necessity compelled to bite the dust. By an order of the town it was cut down in May, 1855.

A little west of this tree was the former site of the wigwam of Waban, Chief of the Nonantums, and he must often have rested under its generous shade. The old Indian trail extended

THE ELIOT OAK, BRIGHTON.

from this tree northeast to the Charles River, connecting the settlement here with the Colleges at Old Cambridge.

Tradition says that the Apostle Eliot of glorious memory preached to the Indians here under this oak. We are amazed to think of it as then being — near two centuries and a half ago — in its vigorous maturity. This is the incident which the poet Longfellow embalms in his sonnet, the scene being, however, transferred to Natick, Massachusetts, where these Indians, by the advice of Eliot, founded one of their Praying Towns, and adopted the customs of civilized life.

ELIOT'S OAK.

H. W. LONGFELLOW.

THOU ancient oak! whose myriad leaves are loud
   With sounds of unintelligible speech,
   Sounds as of surges on a shingly beach,
   Or multitudinous murmurs of a crowd;
With some mysterious gift of tongues endowed,
   Thou speakest a different dialect to each;
   To me a language that no man can teach,
   Of a lost race, long vanished like a cloud.
For underneath thy shade, in days remote,
   Seated like Abraham at eventide
   Beneath the oaks of Mamre, the unknown
Apostle of the Indians, Eliot, wrote
   His Bible in a language that hath died
   And is forgotten, save by thee alone.

Part Third.

LYNN AND NAHANT LEGENDS.

LYNN AND NAHANT LEGENDS.

THE vivid and life-like description of the coast scenery of
ancient Saugus, borrowed from "The Bridal of Pennacook," is a most fitting introduction to our legends; for nowhere
could a wilder or more romantic region, or one embodying more
striking natural traits, prepare the mind for receiving those weird
tales which so truly present to it the superstitious side of old
New England life.

A wild and broken landscape, spiked with firs,
    Roughening the bleak horizon's northern edge,
Steep, cavernous hillsides, where black hemlock spurs
    And sharp, gray splinters of the wind-swept ledge
Pierced the thin-glazed ice, or bristling rose,
Where the cold rim of the sky sunk down upon the snows.

And eastward cold, wide marshes stretched away,
    Dull dreary flats without a bush or tree,
O'er-crossed by icy creeks, where twice a day
    Gurgled the waters of the moon-struck sea ;
And faint with distance came the stifled roar,
The melancholy lapse of waves on that low shore.

THE BRIDAL OF PENNACOOK.

IN the "Bridal of Pennacook," Mr. Whittier, who is himself at once the product and the poet of this romantic coast, tells us that he chanced upon the motive of the poem while poring over

> An old chronicle of border wars
> And Indian history.

This was undoubtedly Thomas Morton's "New English Canaan," — a book which the Puritans indignantly denominated "scandalous," and for which they imprisoned the author a whole year, then dismissing him with a fine. But aside from its merciless ridicule of them and their ways, its value as "Indian history" is duly certified by most competent judges, one of whom says that Morton's description of the Indians "is superior to that of most authors before his time ; and though he sometimes indulges his imagination, yet this part of his work is of exceeding great value to inquirers about the primitive inhabitants of New England."

The poet goes on to relate, that among the ill-assorted collection of books forming his landlord's library he found this old chronicle, wherein he read, —

> A story of the marriage of the Chief
> Of Saugus to the dusky Weetamoo,
> Daughter of Passaconaway, who dwelt
> In the old time upon the Merrimack.

This is the story as it is related by Morton. Winnepurkit, the son of Nanapashemet, or the New Moon, was the Sagamore of Saugus, Naumkeag, and Massabequash, — now known as Saugus, Lynn, Salem, and Marblehead. When he came to man's estate this young sachem, who was both valiant and of noble blood, made choice for his wife of the daughter of Passaconaway, the great chieftain of the tribes inhabiting the valley of the Merrimack.   Not only was Passaconaway a mighty chief in war or peace, but he was also the greatest powow, or wizard, of whom

AN INDIAN PRINCESS.

we have any account.   Indeed the powers attributed to him by the English colonists would almost surpass belief, were they not fully vouched for by the learned and reverend chroniclers of that day, who gravely assert that so skilled was he in the arts of necromancy, that he could cause a green leaf to grow in winter,

9

trees to dance, water to burn, and the like marvels to appear in the course of his mystical invocations.

With the consent and good liking of this redoubtable saga-more, Winnepurkit wooed and married the daughter of Passa-conaway. Bountiful was the entertainment that he and his attendants received at her father's hands, according to the cus-tom of his people when celebrating an event of this kind, and such as suited the exalted rank of the bride and groom. Feasting and revelry succeeded, or rather they made a part of the marriage solemnities, as with all ancient peoples. The cere-monies being over, Passaconaway caused a select number of his braves to escort his daughter into the territories belonging to her lord and husband, where being safely come, they were, in a like manner, most hospitably entertained by Winnepurkit and his men, and when they were ready to depart, were generously rewarded with gifts for their loving care and service.

Not long afterward the newly wedded princess was seized with a passionate longing to revisit once again her native country, and to behold once more the face of the mighty chief, her father. Her lord listened to her prayer, which seemed reasonable enough, and he therefore, in all love and kindness for her welfare, chose a picked body from among his most trusted warriors to conduct his lady to her father, to whom they with great respect presently brought her safe and sound; and then, after being graciously received and as graciously dismissed, they returned to give an account of their errand, leaving their princess to continue among her friends at her own good will and pleasure. After some stay in her old home by the beautiful mountain river, the lady signi-fied her desire to go back to her husband again, upon which Pas-saconaway sent an embassy to Winnepurkit with order to notify him of this wish on her part, and to request that the Sachem of Saugus, his son-in-law, might at once despatch a suitable guard to escort his wife back through the wilderness to her home. But Winnepurkit, strictly standing for his honor and reputation as a chief, bade the messengers to carry his father-in-law this answer : "That when his wife departed from him, he caused his own men to wait upon her to her father's territories, as did become him; but now that she had an intent to return, it did become her father to send her back with a convoy of his own people; and that it stood not with Winnepurkit's reputation either to make himself or his men so servile as to fetch her again."

Thereupon the old sachem, Passaconaway, was much incensed at having this curt answer returned to him by one whom he considered at most only a petty chief and a vassal; and being moreover sadly nettled to think that his son-in-law should pretend to give him, Passaconaway, a lesson in good-breeding, or did not esteem him more highly than to make this a matter for negotiation, sent back this sharp reply: "That his daughter's blood and birth deserved more respect than to be slighted in such a manner, and therefore if he (Winnepurkit) would have her company, he were best to send or come for her."

The young sachem, not being willing to undervalue himself, and being withal a man of stout spirit, did not hesitate to tell his indignant father-in-law that he must either send his daughter home in charge of his own escort, or else he might keep her; since Winnepurkit was, for his own part, fully determined not to stoop so low.

As neither would yield, the poor princess remained with her father, — at least until Morton, the narrator, left the country; but she is supposed to have finally rejoined her haughty spouse, though in what way does not appear in the later relation before us. She was no true woman, however, if she failed to discover a means to soften the proud heart of Winnepurkit, who after all was perhaps only too ready to accord to her tears and her entreaties what he had so loftily refused at the instigation of a punctiliousness that was worthy of the days of chivalry.

The poet has made a most felicitous use of this story, into which are introduced some descriptions of the scenery of the Merrimack of exceeding beauty and grace. The poem has, however, a more dramatic ending than the prose-tale we have just given. In the poem the heart-broken and deserted bride of

Pennacook at last determines to brave the perils of the swollen
and turbid Merrimack alone, to seek the wigwam of her dusky
husband. Stealing away from her companions, she launches
her frail canoe upon the bosom of the torrent, and is instantly
swept by it, —

> Down the vexed centre of that rushing tide,
> The thick huge ice-blocks threatening either side,
> The foam-white rocks of Amoskeag in view,
> With arrowy swiftness —
>
> .   .   .   .
>
> Down the white rapids like a sere leaf whirled,
> On the sharp rocks and piled-up ices hurled,
> Empty and broken, circled the canoe
> In the vexed pool below — but where was
> Weetamoo ?

———————•———————

THE PIRATES' GLEN.

THE year 1658 was signalized in New England by a great
earthquake, which is mentioned in some of the old chronicles. Connected with this convulsion, which in the olden
time was regarded as a most signal mark of the displeasure of
Heaven, is the following story. There are, it should be said,
two or three circumstances, or rather facts, giving to this legend
a color of authenticity, which are of themselves sufficient to
create a doubt whether, after all, it has not a more substantial
foundation than has generally been conceded to it. We willingly give it the benefit of this doubt; meanwhile contenting
ourselves with the statement that its first appearance in print,
so far as known to the writer, was in Lewis's " History of Lynn."
But here is the legend in all its purity.

Some time previous to the great earthquake, in the twilight of a pleasant evening on the coast, a small bark was seen to approach the shore, furl her sails, and drop her anchor near the mouth of Saugus River. A boat was presently lowered from her side, which four men got into and rowed silently up the river to where it enters the hills, when they landed, and plunged into the woods skirting the banks. These movements had been noticed by only a few individuals; but in those early times, when the people were surrounded by dangers and were easily alarmed, such an incident was well calculated to awaken suspicion, so that in the course of the evening the intelligence had spread from house to house, and many were the conjectures respecting the strangers' business. In the morning all eyes were naturally directed toward the shore, in search of the stranger-vessel; but she was no longer there, and no trace either of her or of her singular crew could be found. It was afterward learned, however, that on the morning of the vessel's disappearance a workman, upon going to his daily task at the Forge, on the river's bank, had found a paper running to the effect that if a certain quantity of shackles, handcuffs, and other articles named were made, and with secrecy deposited in a certain place in the woods, which was particularly described, an amount of silver equal to their full value would be found in their stead. The manacles were duly made and secreted, in conformity with the strange directions. On the following morning they had been taken away, and the money left according to the letter of the promise; but notwithstanding the fact that a strict watch had been kept, no sign of a vessel could be discovered in the offing. Some months later than this event, which had furnished a fruitful theme for the village gossips, the four men returned, and selected one of the most secluded and romantic spots in the woods of Saugus for their abode; and the tale has been further embellished to the effect that the pirate chief brought with him a beautiful woman. The place of their retreat was a deep and narrow valley, shut in on two sides by craggy, precipitous rocks, and screened on the others by a thick growth of pines, hemlocks, and cedars. There was only one small spot to which the rays of the noonday sun could penetrate. Upon climbing the rude and nearly perpendicular steep of the cliff on the eastern side of this glen, the eye commanded a noble expanse of sea stretching far to the south, besides a wide extent of the surrounding country. No spot on the coast could have been better chosen for the double purpose of concealment and observation. Even at this day, when the neighborhood has become thickly peopled, it is still a lonely and desolate place, whose gloomy recesses are comparatively unknown and unvisited. Here the pirates built themselves a small hut, made a garden, and dug a well, of which some traces still remain. It is supposed that they also buried money here, and search has been made for it at various times, but none has ever been found; and to deepen the mystery, it is said that the pirate's mistress, who is described as very pale and beautiful, having sickened and died, was buried here in an unknown grave, under the thick shade of the pines. After a time the retreat of the pirates became noised about. They were traced to their glen. Three of them were taken to England, — there being at that time no law in the Colony to punish piracy, — where it is supposed that they paid the penalty for their crimes upon the gibbet. The third, whose name was Thomas Veale, escaped to a cavern in the woods, which he and his confederates had previously made use of as a place of deposit for their ill-gotten booty. In this lonely place the fugitive fixed his residence, practising the trade of a shoemaker, and occasionally visiting the village to obtain food, until the earthquake which ushered in the legend, splitting to its foundations the rock in which the cavern was situated, forever sealed the entrance, enclosing the doomed corsair in his frightful tomb. This cliff has ever since been known as Dungeon Rock, and the first retreat of the freebooters has always borne the name of The Pirates' Glen.

The sequel to the legend that we have so conscientiously related to the reader, is more striking by its reality, more incredible, one might almost say, than the legend itself is, with all its

dramatic surroundings. The story of Dungeon Rock now leaves
the realm of the legendary for that of active supernatural
agency; and it may be doubted if the whole world can produce
another such example of the absorbing pursuit of an idea which
has become the fixed and dominant impulse of a life. But first
let us introduce the reader to the locality itself.

Two miles out of the city of Lynn, in the heart of the secluded
and romantic region overlooking it, is a hill high and steep, one
side of which is a naked precipice; the other, which the road
ascends, is still covered with a magnificent grove of oak-trees
growing among enormous bowlders, and clad, when I saw them,
in the rags of their autumnal purple. Few wilder or more
picturesque spots can be found among the White Hills; and
here we are not a dozen miles removed from the homes of half
a million people. The rumored existence of treasure shut up in
the heart of this cliff by the earthquake seems to have found
credit in the neighborhood, if one may judge from the evidences
of a heavy explosion in what was supposed to be the ancient
vestibule of the cavern, where a yawning rent in the side of the
ledge is blocked up with tons of massy *débris* and every vestige of what was perhaps an interesting natural curiosity thus
wantonly destroyed.

Under the direction of spirit mediums, the work of piercing
Dungeon Rock was begun by Hiram Marble about thirty years
ago, and has continued, with little intermission, nearly to the
present time. For more than a quarter of a century, — spurred
on, when they were ready to abandon the work in despair, by
some delusive revelation of the spirits, — father and son toiled on
in the vain hope of unlocking its secret. Tons upon tons of
the broken rock have been removed by their hands alone, for
the windings of the gallery make any mechanical contrivance
useless for the purpose. So hard is the natural formation, that
they sometimes advanced only a foot in a month; and the labor
was further increased by the accumulation of water, which is
constantly oozing from fissures of the rock. Death at length
released the elder enthusiast from his infatuation; but the son

pursued the work as the most sacred of trusts, until he too died in the same fatal delusion.

A woman whom I found in the cabin on the summit, and who proved to be the treasure-seeker's sister, conducted me to the entrance of the shaft, which was closed by a grated door, above which I read this eminently practical legend in an unpractical place : "Ye who enter here, leave twenty-five cents behind." She turned the key in the lock, swung back the grating, and we began to descend, first by a series of steps cut in the rock, then by such foothold as the slippery floor afforded. When we arrived at the extreme limit of the excavation, we had come not far from one hundred and fifty feet in a perpendicular descent of only forty ; yet I remarked that the gallery at times almost doubled upon itself, in order to accomplish what might have been reached in half the distance, and, of course, with half the labor, in a direct line, — which would seem to imply that the work might have proceeded more expeditiously under the direction of a competent mining engineer. Nothing in the appearance of the rock indicated that it had been disturbed since the creation. It was as hard as adamant, as firm as marble, as impenetrable as Fate.

My guide pointed out the supposed locality of the ancient entrance. She also showed me, as a thing to which the fee duly entitled even such sceptics as myself, the fragment of a corroded scabbard, which had been found, she said, embedded in a cranny within the excavation. But when I afterward mentioned this circumstance to the poet Longfellow, who was familiar with the locality and its story, he laughed pleasantly, and said that unless his memory was greatly at fault, he had seen, years before, during one of his drives in the neighborhood, this identical thing at a blacksmith's shop where he had stopped on some errand. Such questions as I asked were freely answered ; but she talked in a way that was almost startling in its matter-of-fact assumption of the supernatural as the controlling element in one's life experience. The invisible spirits of Dungeon Rock I found dealt in enigmas which the Delphic oracle could never have surpassed

yet here were believers who staked their lives upon the truth of
utterances equally delusive! Here the problem is suggestively
presented, whether latter-day superstition, acting upon the weak
and impressible nature, is on the whole to be preferred, either in
its manifestations or results, to olden delusion as exemplified in
the witches or wizards of our forefathers. Who shall say? I,
at any rate, found this visit to Dungeon Rock one of the most
singular experiences of a lifetime.

MOLL PITCHER.

IN passing from the boundaries of Saugus into those of Lynn,
a word or two acquaints us with the origin of both places.
Thomas Dudley, Deputy-Governor of "the Massachusetts,"
writing in 1630 to the "Lady Bryget, Countesse of Lincoln,"
says of the Colonists who, like himself, emigrated in that year
from England, "We began to consult of the place of our sitting
down, for Salem, where we landed, pleased us not." Various
causes having led to their dispersion along the coast from Cape
Ann to Nantasket, one of the scattered bands settled "upon the
river of Saugus," as he writes; another founded Boston. The
Indian name Saugus, which still belongs to the river and to a
fragment of the ancient territory, was superseded in 1637 by
that of Lynn, or the King's Lynn, from Lynn Regis, on the
River Ouse, in England. Lynn is therefore one of the oldest
towns in Massachusetts. It is beautifully situated on the shore
of Massachusetts Bay, ten miles north of Boston and five south
of Salem. Swampscot is a rib taken from her side; so is
Nahant, and so is Lynnfield; yet, like the fabled monster, she
seems to grow the faster from successive mutilations.

If one may credit the legend, Veale, the pirate recluse of
Dungeon Rock, was among the first to follow the trade of a
"cordwainer" here; but it may be questioned whether he is

really looked upon as one of the founders of the craft. Be that
as it may, it is certain that one of the earliest settlers, Francis
Ingalls by name, established the first tannery in all the colony,
and he may therefore be considered the originator of that
branch of industry, in the steady pursuit of which Lynn has
grown to be both rich and famous. When shoemaking was a
trade, I suppose that nearly every man in Lynn was a shoe-

MOLL PITCHER.

maker; but now, when no one person makes a whole boot or
a whole shoe, the trade, as a trade, has degenerated. Two of the
noblest men that America has produced have graduated from the
shoemaker's bench. The poet Whittier once followed this humble
calling, until he found his higher vocation; and the philanthropist, William Lloyd Garrison, once worked at the bench here in
Lynn. This ancient handicraft is therefore by no means without some very honorable traditions.

But Lynn is likely to be celebrated throughout all time as having been the residence of the most successful fortune-teller of her

day and generation, — we might also say of whom we have any
account in mystical lore, ancient or modern.   While she lived
she was without a rival in her peculiar art, and the prophetic
words that she let fall were capable of being transmuted into
gold.   She it is that one of our native poets has in mind when
he is singing — too soon, we think, — a requiem over the last
witch of his native land.

> How has New England's romance fled,
>   Even as a vision of the morning !
> Its rites foredone, — its guardians dead, —
> Its priestesses, bereft of dread,
>   Waking the veriest urchin's scorning !
> Gone like the Indian wizard's yell
>   And fire-dance round the magic rock,
> Forgotten like the Druid's spell
>   At moonrise by his holy oak !
> No more along the shadowy glen
> Glide the dim ghosts of murdered men ;
> No more the unquiet churchyard dead
> Glimpse upward from their turfy bed,
>   Startling the traveller, late and lone ;
> As, on some night of starless weather,
> They silently commune together,
>   Each sitting on his own headstone !
> The roofless house, decayed, deserted,
> Its living tenants all departed,
> No longer rings with midnight revel
> Of witch, or ghost, or goblin evil ;
> No pale blue flame sends out its flashes
> Through creviced roof and shattered sashes ! —
> The witch-grass round the hazel spring
> May sharply to the night-air sing,
> But there no more shall withered hags
> Refresh at ease their broomstick nags,
> Or taste those hazel-shadowed waters
> As beverage meet for Satan's daughters ;
> No more their mimic tones be heard, —
> The mew of cat, — the chirp of bird, —

Shrill blending with the hoarser laughter
Of the fell demon following after!

.   .   .   .   .

Even she, our own weird heroine,
Sole Pythoness of ancient Lynn,
    Sleeps calmly where the living laid her;
And the wide realm of sorcery,
Left by its latest mistress free,
    Hath found no gray and skilled invader.

It was once said of Napoleon that he left a family, but no successor. Moll Pitcher left none in her wonderful gift of foretelling the future by practising palmistry, or by simply gazing into the bottom of a teacup. She was therefore no Sidrophel. Yet even the most incredulous were compelled to admit her predictions to be wholly unaccountable; while those who came to laugh went away vanquished, if not fully convinced. What is singular is that her reputation has rather increased than diminished with time. We have no account of her dupes, nor is there any "Exposure" extant. It follows that the spot where for so many years Moll Pitcher so successfully practised her art is the one to which the stranger first asks to be directed.

Should he happen to stray a little way out of the more crowded part of the city, his attention would at once be arrested by a remarkable cliff of dull red porphyry rising high above the house-tops, that has apparently detached itself from the broken hill-range which skirts the coast, and has elbowed its way into the plain, thrusting the houses aside out of its path, until it almost divides the city in twain. High Rock, as it is called, is to Lynn what the Citadel is to Quebec, — you look down, and see at a glance all the out-door life of the place; you look up, and see the blue arch of the sky springing from the rim of the ocean.

The following poetical description of the ravishing view of sea and shore unrolled from the summit of High Rock naturally takes precedence of our own : —

HIGH ROCK.

ELIZABETH F. MERRILL.

OVERLOOKING the town of Lynn,
So far above that the city's din
Mingles and blends with the heavy roar
Of the breakers along the curving shore,
Scarred and furrowed and glacier-seamed,
Back in the ages so long ago,
The boldest philosopher never dreamed
To count the centuries' ebb and flow,
Stands a rock with its gray old face
Eastward, ever turned to the place
Where first the rim of the sun is seen, —
Whenever the morning sky is bright, —
Cleaving the glistening, glancing sheen
Of the sea with disk of insufferable light.
Down in the earth his roots strike deep ;
Up to his breast the houses creep,
Climbing e'en to his rugged face,
Or nestling lovingly at his base.
Stand on his forehead, bare and brown,
Send your gaze o'er the roofs of the town
Away to the line so faint and dim,
Where the sky stoops down to the crystal rim
Of the broad Atlantic, whose billows toss,
Wrestling and weltering and hurrying on
With awful fury whenever across
His broad bright surface, with howl and moan,
The Tempest wheels, with black wing bowed
To the yielding waters which fly to the cloud,
Or hurry along with thunderous shocks
To break on the ragged and riven rocks.

When the tide comes in on a sunny day
You can see the waves beat back in spray
From the splintered spurs of Phillips Head,
Or tripping along with dainty tread,

As of a million glancing feet,
Shake out the light in a quick retreat,
Or along the smooth curve of the beach,
Snowy and curling, in long lines reach.
An islet anchored and held to land
By a glistening, foam-fringed ribbon of sand ;
That is Nahant, and that hoary ledge
To the left is Egg Rock, like a blunted wedge,
Cleaving the restless ocean's breast,
And bearing the lighthouse on its crest.

It was at the foot of this cliff that Moll Pitcher, the fortune-teller of Lynn, dwelt.   Forty years ago there were very few firesides in New England that her fame had not reached, perhaps disturbed ; and her successful predictions, alike astounding to the vulgar or to the enlightened, were the theme of many a midnight watch or forecastle confab.   She was not, if we may credit local report, the withered, decrepit, and toothless crone of Spenser, or Otway's

> " wrinkled hag, with age grown double,
> Picking dry sticks and mumbling to herself,"

but a woman who lived in the full gaze and gossip of a world which only accepted her claim to foreknowledge upon the unequivocal testimony of a thousand witnesses.   Do you contend that her reputation was due solely to the shrewdness, penetration, and ready wit with which she was undoubtedly in a remarkable degree gifted ?   How, then, will you explain revelations of the future made ten and twenty years before the events predicted took place ?

When she was in the meridian of her fame and life the ordinary applicant saw a woman of medium stature, having an unusually large head, a pale, thin, and rather intellectual face, shaded by masses of dark brown hair, who was as thoroughly self-possessed as he was ill at ease, and whose comprehensive glance measured his mental capacity before he could utter a syllable.   People of better discernment, who recollect her, say that her face had none of the wildness of the traditional witch, but was clouded with a habitual sadness, as of a mind over-burdened with being the depository of so many confidences, perhaps crimes. She had a full, capacious forehead, arched eye-brows, eyes that read the secret thoughts of a suitor, a nose "inclined to be long," and thin lips — a physiognomy wholly unlike the popular ideal, but rather that of a modern Egeria, — in short, the witch of the nineteenth century.

During the fifty years that she pursued her trade of fortune-telling, in what was then a lonely and little frequented quarter

MOLL PITCHER'S COTTAGE.

of the town, not only was she consulted by the poor and igno-rant, but also by the rich and intelligent class. Love affairs, legacies, the discovery of crime, lotteries, commercial ventures, and the more common contingencies of fortune, formed, we may well imagine, the staple of her predictions; but her most valued clients came from the opulent seaports that are within sight of High Rock. The common sailor and the master, the cabin-boy and the owner, equally resorted to her humble abode to know the luck of a voyage. It is asserted that many a vessel has been deserted when on the eve of sailing, in consequence of

Moll's unlucky vaticination. She was also much besought by treasure-seekers — a rather numerous class in her day, whose united digging along the coast of New England would, if usefully directed, have reclaimed for cultivation no inconsiderable area of virgin soil. For such applicants the witch had a short and sharp reply. "Fools!" she would say; "if I knew where money was buried, do you think I would part with the secret?"

Moll Pitcher died in 1813, at the age of seventy-five. She was originally of Marblehead, and is said to have inherited the gift of prophecy from her grandfather, John Dimond, who was himself a wizard of no mean reputation in that place. In proof of this it is said that he was in the habit of going to the old burying-ground on the hill whenever a violent gale at sea arose, and in that lonely place, in the midst of the darkness and the storm, to astound and terrify the simple fisherfolk in the following manner. He would direct vessels then at sea how to weather the roughest gale, — pacing up and down among the gravestones, and ever and anon, in a voice distinctly heard above the howling of the tempest, shout his orders to the helmsman or the crew, as if he were actually on the quarter-deck, and the scene all before him. Very few doubted his ability to bring a vessel safely into port. Mary Dimond's father sailed out of Marblehead as master of a small vessel. She married Robert Pitcher, a shoemaker, in 1760. Mr. Lewis, the historian of Lynn, who remembered her, asserts that she was connected with some of the best families in Essex; that, except her fortune-telling pretension, there was nothing disreputable in her life; and that her descendants were living and respected when he wrote. Her life seems rather to mark the line which divides old and new superstition, than any decay of that inextinguishable craving to pry into futurity which has distinguished the human race in all ages and in all climes.

This describes the celebrated fortune-teller as she was known to her contemporaries. We have, however, picked up among the flotsam of literary drift a different portrait, drawn in verse.

In 1832 Whittier published, anonymously, a poem of which
Moll Pitcher is the heroine. The statement made by the author
in an introductory note concerning himself will doubtless be
considered to-day as being even a greater curiosity than the poem
itself is. There he naively says : " I have not enough of the poetical mania in my disposition to dream of converting, by an alchemy
more potent than that of the old philosophers, a limping couplet
into a brace of doubloons, or a rickety stanza into a note of hand.
Moll Pitcher ('there's music in the name') is the offspring of a
few weeks of such leisure as is afforded by indisposition, and is
given to the world in all its original negligence, — the thoughts
fresh as when first originated."

The poem is the story of a maiden, fond and fair, whose sailor
lover had gone on a long voyage to sea, where

> He sought for gold — for yellow gold, —

in order that he might come back a rich man and wed the girl
he had left behind him. The maiden's mind becomes filled with
gloomy forebodings concerning him. Obeying an uncontrollable
impulse, in an evil hour she seeks the well-trodden path leading to Moll Pitcher's abode, in order to know her destiny ; and
while on her way thither she encounters the witch, who is thus
described : —

> She stood upon a bare tall crag
>   Which overlooked her rugged cot —
> A wasted, gray, and meagre hag,
>   In features evil as her lot.
> She had the crooked nose of a witch,
>   And a crooked back and chin;
> And in her gait she had a hitch,
> And in her hand she carried a switch,
>   To aid her work of sin, —
> A twig of wizard hazel, which
> Had grown beside a haunted ditch,
> Where a mother her nameless babe had thrown
> To the running water and merciless stone.

The fortune-teller cherishes a secret enmity towards her trembling visitor, and wickedly determines on revenging herself. She leading the way, —

> The twain passed in — a low dark room,
>   With here and there a crazy chair,
> A broken glass — a dusty loom —
> A spinning-wheel — a birchen broom,
>   The witch's courier of the air,
> As potent as that steed of wings
>   On which the Meccan prophet rode
> Above the wreck of meaner things
>   Unto the Houris' bright abode.
> A low dull fire by flashes shone
> Across the gray and cold hearthstone,
> Flinging at times a trembling glare
> On the low roof and timbers bare.

After this glimpse of her home, the weird woman proceeds to try her art by looking steadfastly into the sorceress's cup, which, we are told, constituted her whole fortune-telling paraphernalia. Presently she speaks.

> Out spoke the witch, — "I know full well
>   Why thou hast sought my humble cot !
> Come, sit thee down, — the tale I tell
>   May not be soon forgot."
> She threw her pale blue cloak aside,
>   And stirred the whitening embers up,
> And long and curiously she eyed
>   The figures of her mystic cup ;
> And low she muttered while the light
> Gave to her lips a ghastlier white,
> And her sunk eyes' unearthly glaring
> Seemed like the taper's latest flaring :
> "Dark hair — eyes black — a goodly form —
>   A maiden weeping — wild dark sea —
> A tall ship tossing in the storm —
>   A black wreck floating -- *where is he ?*

Give me thy hand — how soft, and warm,
 And fair its tapering fingers seem ! —
And who that sees it now would dream
That winter's snow would seem less chill
Ere long than these soft fingers will ?
A lovely palm ! — how delicate
 Its veined and wandering lines are drawn !
Yet each are prophets of thy fate —
 Ha ! — this is sure a fearful one !
That sudden cross — that blank beneath —
 What may these evil signs betoken ?
Passion and sorrow, fear and death —
 A human spirit crushed and broken !
Oh, thine hath been a pleasant dream,
But darker shall its waking seem ! "

 . . . . .

Like a cold hand upon her heart
 The dark words of the sorceress lay,
Something to scare her spirit's rest
 Forever more away.
Each word had seemed so strangely true,
Calling her inmost thoughts in view,
And pointing to the form which came
 Before her in her dreary sleep,
Whose answered love — whose very name,
Though nought of breathing life was near,
 She scarce had given the winds to keep,
Or murmured in a sister's ear.

 . . . . .

Overcome by the terrible revelation, to which her own fears
lend a too ready belief, the poor girl becomes a maniac. She is
always watching for the sail in the offing which never comes;
she wanders up and down the rocky shores of Nahant, gazing
vacantly out to sea, until on one lucky day, in spite of Moll's
fatal prediction, the lover's ship sails gallantly into the bay, and
with it the one thing capable of restoring the maiden's reason
again. The witch, however, does not escape the consequences of
her malevolence, but dies miserably in her wretched hovel,

being tended in her last moments by a little child of the woman she has so cruelly wronged.

The poem being too long for us to reproduce in full, we have thus merely outlined it for the reader.

NAHANT LEGENDS.

ABOUT three miles from where we stand, rising abruptly from the sea, is a castellated gray rock crowned with a lighthouse. Egg Rock, as it is called, is not more than eighty feet from sea to summit, but its isolated and lonely position, its bold outlines cut clean and sharp on the blue background, make it seem higher. This rocky islet, the former eyrie of wild sea-birds, is by far the most picturesque object of this picturesque shore. It is almost always seen encircled with a belt of white surf, while in violent storms the raging seas assail it with such tremendous impetuosity as to give the idea of a fortress beleaguered by the combined powers of sea and air. At such times it cannot be approached with safety. Then the lighthouse keeper, whatever his wants may be, can hold no communication with the shore, but is a prisoner during the pleasure of the gale.

The occasional and distant glimpses of Nahant had from the main shore are certain to excite the desire for a nearer survey, a more intimate acquaintance. We will, therefore, let this choice bit of description, which Mr. Longfellow particularly admired, serve as our introduction. "If," says N. P. Willis, "you can imagine a buried Titan lying along the length of a continent, with one arm stretched out into the midst of the sea, the spot to which I would transport you, reader mine, would be, as it were, in the palm of the giant's hand."

One of Whittier's earliest poetic productions is also addressed to this charming spot :

Nahant, thy beach is beautiful! —
   A dim line through the tossing waves,
Along whose verge the spectre gull
   Her thin and snowy plumage laves —
What time the Summer's greenness lingers
   Within thy sunned and sheltered nooks,
And the green vine with twining fingers
   Creeps up and down thy hanging rocks!
Around — the blue and level main —
   Above — a sunshine rich, as fell,
Bright'ning of old, with golden rain,
   The isle Apollo loved so well! —
And far off, dim and beautiful
The snow-white sail and graceful hull,
   Slow, dipping to the billow's swell.
Bright spot! — the isles of Greece may share
A flowery earth — a gentle air ; —
The orange-bough may blossom well
In warm Bermuda's sunniest dell ; —
But fairer shores and brighter waters,
Gazed on by purer, lovelier daughters,
   Beneath the light of kindlier skies,
The wanderer to the farthest bound
Of peopled Earth hath never found
   Than thine — New England's Paradise!

Mrs. Sigourney follows in the same strain of unstinted praise : —

NAHANT.

RUDE rock-bound coast, where erst the Indian roamed,
The iron shoulders of thy furrowed cliffs,
Made black with smiting, still in stubborn force
Resist the scourging wave.
               Bright summer suns
In all the fervor of their noontide heat
Obtain no power to harm thee, for thou wrapp'st
Thy watery mantle round thee, ever fresh
With ocean's coolness, and defy'st their rage.

The storm-cloud is thy glory.
                           Then, thou deck'st
Thyself with majesty, and to its frown
And voice of thunder, answerest boldly back,
And from thy watch-towers hurl'st the blinding spray,
While every dark and hollow cavern sounds
Its trumpet for the battle.
                        Yet 't is sweet
Amid thy fissured rocks to ruminate,
Marking thy grottos with mosaic paved
Of glittering pebbles, and that balm to breathe
Which gives the elastic nerves a freer play,
And tints the languid cheek with hues of health.

The sand-beach and the sea!
                      Who can divine
Their mystic intercourse, that day and night
Surceaseth not?   On comes the thundering surge,
Lifting its mountain-head, with menace stern,
To whelm the unresisting; but impelled
In all the plenitude of kingly power
To change its purpose of authority,
Breaking its wand of might, doth hurry back;
And then, repenting, with new wrath return.
Yet still that single, silvery line abides,
Lowly, and fearless, and immutable.
God gives it strength.
                    So may he deign to grant
The sand-line of our virtues power to cope
With all temptation.   When some secret snare
Doth weave its meshes round our trembling souls,
That in their frailty turn to him alone,
So may he give us strength.

There is a good road over the Long Beach; but when the tide is nearly down, a broad esplanade of sand beckons us aside from the embankment over which that is now built.   Here is a course such as no Roman charioteer ever drove upon.   Here the heavy farm-carts that are gathering seaweed leave scarcely a print of their broad-tired wheels.   Stamp upon it with the foot, and see how hard and firm it is; or smile at the lightning it emits under the impact, — your childhood's wonder. We pass over half an acre of sand, moulded in the impress of little wavelets that have left their print like cunning chiselling or like masses of sandy hair in crimp. There behind a clump of rocks crouches a sports-man, who is patiently waiting for twilight to come, when the black ducks and coots fly over; those stooping figures among the rocks are not treasure-seekers, but clam-diggers.

Having crossed the Long Beach, we betake ourselves again to the road which winds around the shore of Little Nahant to a second beach, half a mile long. We again leave this behind, to climb the rocky ascent of the greater promontory, then finding ourselves in the long street of the village. Nahant is tempting to artist or antiquary, but especially so to the man of refined literary tastes, who knows no greater enjoyment than to visit the spots consecrated by genius. In Jonathan Johnson's house Longfellow partly wrote "Hiawatha;" and here, at Nahant, was also the birthplace of the "Bells of Lynn," which the poet heard,

> Borne on the evening wind across the crimson twilight.

And we too hear their musical vibrations, softened by the distance, lingering lovingly in the air, and we can see as in our own memories the pictures to which his matchless verse gives life:

> The fisherman in his boat, far out beyond the headland,
> Listens, and leisurely rows ashore, O Bells of Lynn!

> Over the shining sands the wandering cattle homeward
> Follow each other at your call, O Bells of Lynn!

> The distant lighthouse hears, and with his flaming signal
> Answers you, passing the watchword on, O Bells of Lynn!

> And down the darkening coast run the tumultuous surges,
> And clap their hands, and shout to you, O Bells of Lynn!

> Till from the shuddering sea, with your wild incantations,
> Ye summon up the spectral moon, O Bells of Lynn!

> And startled at the sight, like the weird woman of Endor,
> Ye cry aloud, and then are still, O Bells of Lynn!

The "Ladder of St. Augustine" and other of his lyrics in which the actual presence of the sea is felt by the reader were also written here under its influence, for Longfellow is always moved by it to a pitch of high-wrought emotion — to a kind of speechless speech — which only the impressible nature knows. In the "Dedication" to his Seaside verses he gives us the key to this exquisite spiritual sensibility, —

> Therefore I hope to join your seaside walk,
> Saddened, and mostly silent, with emotion ;
> Not interrupting with intrusive talk
> The grand, majestic symphonies of ocean.

And in the opening stanza of "The Secret of the Sea" he frankly confesses to the fascination with which it possesses him : —

> Ah ! what pleasant visions haunt me
> As I gaze upon the sea !
> All the old romantic legends,
> All my dreams, come back to me.

Somewhat farther on we descend into an enticing nook, shaded by two aged and gigantic willows. Here, in the modest cottage of Mrs. Hannah Hood, surrounded by old Dutch folios, Motley began his "Dutch Republic." By ascending the rise of ground beyond the Hollow we may see the roof of the cottage where Prescott, who died, like Petrarch, in his chair, worked at "Ferdinand and Isabella," the "Conquest of Mexico," and "Philip II." On the point beyond us, assisted by his gifted wife, Agassiz produced "Brazil." Willis, Curtis, Mrs. Sigourney, and an admiring host of lesser celebrities who have felt its magnetic influence, celebrate Nahant in prose or verse. The residence of such eminent representatives of American literature could hardly fail to impress itself upon the social character of a place ; but it has also made this little peninsula one of the best remembered spots of American ground to scholars of the Old World who have visited it. And the privilege of traversing her rocky shores, with Longfellow or Agassiz for a guide, was indeed something to be remembered.

The Hollow seems the proper standpoint for a brief glance at the history of Nahant, down to the time when it became the retreat of culture, refinement, and wealth. Nahant (the twins) is a musical Indian name that trips lightly from the tongue. On the map it looks like the wyvern of heraldry, hanging to the coast by its tail. It was sold by Poquanum, a sagamore, in 1630, to the Lynn settlers, who used it in common as a pasture. Being to all intents an island, or rather two islands, at high tide, it was named the Fullerton Isles, in 1614, by Captain Smith. It had been granted in 1622 to Captain Robert Gorges; but his title seems to have lapsed, and not to have been successfully revived. Under the rule of Andros, his favorite, Randolph, tried to steal it. The price originally paid for Nahant was a suit of clothes; it has now a tax-roll of six and a half millions. In the earlier accounts given of them, the two peninsulas appear to have been well wooded; but, in common with all the coast islands, the natural forest long ago disappeared, and Nahant remained almost treeless, until Thomas H. Perkins, a wealthy Boston merchant, planted several thousand shade-trees. His efforts to make Nahant a desirable summer residence were effectively seconded by Frederick Tudor, the ice-king, by Cornelius Coolidge, and other men of wealth and taste. Its name and fame began to resound abroad. A hotel was built in 1819, and a steamboat began to ply in the summer months between Boston and the peninsulas. In 1853 Nahant threw off her allegiance to Lynn, and became a separate town. Her earlier frequenters were, with few exceptions, wealthy Boston or Salem families, and they continue to possess her choicest territories.

Since the great hotel was destroyed by fire in 1861, there is only the modest hostelry of Mr. Whitney for the reception of casual guests. This was one of five houses the peninsula contained seventy odd years ago, and was the former homestead of the Breed family, who, with the Hood and Johnson families, were sole lords of the isles. Though there has been an "invasion," there never has been a "conquest." The Nahantese who are "native here, and to the manner born," cling to what is left of their ancient patrimony with unyielding grasp. Wander where they may, they always come back here to die. One of them, who had refused tempting offers for his land, said to me, "Here I was born, here is my home, and here I mean to abide."

The admirably kept roads lead where the most engaging sea-views are to be had. You lean over a railing and look down eighty feet to the bottom of a cove, where the sea ripples without breaking, and the clean, smooth pebbles chase back the refluent wave with noisy chatter. The tawny rocks wear coats of grass-green velvet; the perfume of sweet-fern and of eglantine is in the air. The cliffs of the eastern headland are very fine. It takes one's breath away to witness the rush and roar of the eternal surges among their iron ribs; yet the effect seems little more than would be produced by a hungry lion licking the bars of his cage. In a few instances, such as Castle Rock and the Devil's Pulpit notably present, the rocks arise in regular castellated masses; but in general they are as much the expression of chaos of form as we might expect to see in the broken arches and colonnades of the earth's foundations. Being pitched about in fantastic yet awful confusion, they present curious accidental formations, or are split from summit to foundation-stone in chasms deep and gloomy, where the seething waters hiss and boil, much as they might have done when these colossal masses were first cooling. Here and there on the shores the sea has neatly hollowed out the natural curiosities locally known as the Natural Bridge, Swallows' Cave, Irene's Grotto, and the Spouting Horn; and in storms the shore is as full of noises as Prospero's Island —

A voice out of the silence of the deep,
A sound mysteriously multiplied,
As of a cataract from the mountain's side,
Or roar of winds upon the wooded steep.

The sea-view from the portico of the chapel, which is situated on the highest point of the headland, is certainly one of the

rarest on the whole coast, embracing, as it does, many miles of
the mainland, from Lynn as far as the extreme point of Cape
Ann ; of the South Shore from Scituate to Boston Light, — a
slender, shapely, and minaret-like tower set on a half-submerged
ledge at the entrance to Boston Harbor.   On a clear day the
dusky gray pillar of Minot's Light, and by night its ruddy flash,
on the south coast, are visible.   One of these towers — probably
the first — inspired Longfellow's poem, " The Lighthouse,"
beginning —

> The rocky ledge runs far into the sea,
> And on its outer point, some miles away,
> The Lighthouse lifts its massive masonry, —
> A pillar of fire by night, of cloud by day.

And ending —

> " Sail on ! " it says, " sail on, ye stately ships !
> And with your floating bridge the ocean span :
> Be mine to guard this light from all eclipse,
> Be yours to bring man nearer unto man ! "

Longfellow's summer residence was upon the southern shore,
which is less precipitous, but more sheltered from the bleak
winds, than the northern shores are.   " It is a house of ample size,
with wide verandas, and is surrounded with such shrubbery as
the unsparing winds that sweep the peninsula allow."   When,
after the appearance of " Nooks and Corners of the New England Coast," the writer called upon him, the poet said, " Ah ! but
why did you leave Nahant out in the cold ? "   And he urged
him to repair the omission without delay.

Prescott also lived on the southern shore, on a rocky point not
far from the Swallows' Cave, named by him " Fitful Head."
Agassiz' cottage, on the contrary, is on the north shore.   It is a
modest, though not unpicturesque building, all upon the ground,
and was probably better suited to the great scientist's simple
tastes than were the handsome villas of his eminent literary neighbors.   Possibly it may have reminded him in some silent way
of his fatherland, — " the beautiful Pays du Vaud."   It is to

Agassiz dead that this touching apostrophe is addressed by his friend Longfellow, who is so rarely a questioner of fate, —

> I stand again on the familiar shore,
>   And hear the waves of the distracted sea
>   Piteously calling and lamenting thee,
>   And waiting restless at thy cottage door.
> The rocks, the sea-weed on the ocean floor,
>   The willows in the meadow, and the free
>   Wild winds of the Atlantic welcome me ;
>   Then why shouldst thou be dead, and come no more ?
> Ah, why shouldst thou be dead when common men
>   Are busy with their trivial affairs,
>   Having and holding ?   Why, when thou hadst read
> Nature's mysterious manuscript, and then
>   Wast ready to reveal the truth it bears,
>   Why art thou silent ?   Why shouldst thou be dead ?

THE SEA–SERPENT.

> Mayhap you all have heard to tell
> Of the wonderful sea-snake. — OLD BALLAD.

THERE is one topic with which the annals of Nahant are inseparably associated that we feel a natural diffidence in approaching, yet cannot in conscience ignore, and that is the sea-serpent.   Words are inadequate to describe the wide-spread consternation which the apparition of such a monster created among the hardy population of our New England seaboard ; for he was soon perceived to possess none of the attributes of a sportive and harmless fish, but to belong strictly to the reptile tribe !   And what a reptile !   The most exaggerated reports of his length prevailed throughout all the fishing towns of Cape Ann, and up and down the length of the coast.   One skipper swore that he was as long as the mainmast of a seventy-four ; another would eat him if the steeple of Gloucester meeting-house could hold a candle to him for length ; still another declared upon his solemn " affidavy " that, having sighted the shaggy head of the snake early in the morning, with a stiff six-knot breeze, and everything full, he had been half a glass in overhauling his snakeship's tail, as he lay motionless along the water.

For a time nothing else was talked of but the wonderful sea-snake, which was repeatedly seen in Gloucester Bay in August, 1817, and occasionally also in the waters of Nahant Bay, by hundreds of curious spectators, who ran to the beaches or pushed off in boats at the first news of his approach. There

EGG ROCK AND THE SEA-SERPENT.

was not a fishwife along thirty miles of coast who did not shake in her shoes when he was reported in the offing. It is needless to say that his snakeship was not molested by any alert customs' officer, but " entered " and " cleared " at each port at his own good will and pleasure. But as time wore on, and the serpent's pacific, even pusillanimous, disposition became evident, courage revived ; and though the fish was a strange one, the fishermen determined, with characteristic boldness, on his capture.

Stimulated, also, by the large reward offered for the serpent, alive or dead, vessels were fitted out, manned by expert whales-men, which cruised in the bay. The revenue vessel then on the station was ordered to keep a vigilant look-out, and she kept her guns double-shotted for action. Nets were also spread in his snakeship's accustomed haunts, and one adventurous fellow, who had approached so near as to see the white of his glittering eye, emptied the contents of a ducking gun into the monster's head. But he seemed to bear a charmed life ; and having easily eluded his pursuers, derisively shook the spray of Nahant Bay from his tail ere he disappeared in the depths of the ocean. Since this time the gigantic ophidian has from time to time revisited Nahant, and strange tidings have lately come of him from other climes. But it is clear that his stuffed skin was never destined to adorn the walls of a museum, and it is doubtful if he will ever know other pickle than his native brine.

The tradition associating the sea-serpent with Nahant is of very early date. John Josselyn, Gent., who was here in 1638, is the first to mention this monster. He says that one was seen " quoiled up on a rock at Cape Ann " by a passing boat, and that when an Englishman would have fired at him, an Indian hastily prevented his doing so, saying that it would bring them ill luck.

It is our privilege to rescue this poetic waif dedicated by the poet Brainard to the wandering monster of the deep : —

SONNET TO THE SEA-SERPENT.

J. G. BRAINARD.

Hugest that swims the ocean stream.

WELTER upon the waters, mighty one,
And stretch thee in the ocean's trough of brine ;
Turn thy wet scales up to the wind and sun,
And toss the billow from thy flashing fin ;
Heave thy deep breathings to the ocean's din,
And bound upon its ridges in thy pride ;
Or dive down to its lowest depths, and in

The caverns where its unknown monsters hide,
Measure thy length beneath the Gulf Stream tide —
Or rest thee on the navel of that sea
Where, floating on the Maelstrom, abide
The krakens sheltering under Norway's lee, —
But go not to Nahant, lest men should swear
You are a great deal bigger than you are.

THE FLOURE OF SOUVENANCE.

WE have already pointed out to the reader the huge hump-backed bowlder rising from the sea called Egg Rock. The story we are about to relate is intimately associated with that picturesque object. Long ago, when Nahant first began to claim attention as a summer resort, two young people met here for the first time. The acquaintance soon ripened into friendship, and from friendship into love. The pair were inseparable. He was devoted to infatuation, she too happy to remember that there was any world outside of that in which they then lived. The lover was in every way worthy of the lady, and she of him; and only one thing stood in the way of

FORGET-ME-NOTS.

their happiness. That one obstacle lay in the fact that the young man was an Italian by adoption, although an American by birth; and Alice, the young girl whose love he had won, when pressed by him to consent to an immediate marriage, had replied: "My dear friend, first go and obtain the sanction of your parents, and then it shall all be as you wish."

Possessed with this purpose, which had now become the sole motive of his life, the young man secured a passage in a vessel which was to sail in two days for Leghorn. He then returned to Nahant in order to spend the few hours remaining to him in the society of his betrothed.

It was the last evening, and the young couple were wandering over the brow of the headland where they had so often walked before, and whence the long leagues of glittering sea had always seemed so beautiful, and the breeze and the billows so invigorating and elevating to them. Both were silent. Unknown to each other, they were musing upon the question that has distracted so many minds, — the serpent in their Eden, — Since we are so happy, why should we be separated? But the sullen dash of the waves at their feet was their only response. They clung to each other and dreamed on.

While standing thus on the edge of the cliff, a strange fancy came into the lover's head. Why it is that in moments of supreme trouble the merest trifles should force themselves uppermost in our minds, we do not pretend to explain. The young man suddenly recollected one of the local traditions, running to the effect that the lady who should receive from her lover's hand the Floure of Souvenance, or Forget-me-not, growing only in one lonely spot on the little island before them, would remain forever constant.

"Let me give you one more proof of my love, dear Alice, before we part, and let it be the flower plucked from the summit of yonder rock that lies there before us," he gayly said, feeling that she would divine his purpose.

"I require no new proof of your affection," she replied; "but do as you will."

Unobserved by the lovers, the sea was steadily rising, and upon the distant coast the rote was growing every moment more ominously distinct. The young man was much too intent, however, upon his object to notice these warning signs; in his present frame of mind he would gladly have braved even greater dangers in order to gratify his mistress. He ran lightly down the rocks to where his boat was anchored, and in a moment more, heedless of the warning voice of a stranger, had seated himself at the helm, and was mounting the incoming waves on his way to Egg Rock.

"Wait for the next tide," shouted the warning voice, "or I will not answer for your safety!"

"The next tide," murmured the young man, "will bear me far from her; it is now or never," waving his hand to Alice on the cliff. Alice watched him in a kind of stupor; she had heard the voice. "My God!" she murmured with white lips, "what have I done?"

The adventurous young man, however, reached the rock in safety, climbed its rugged side, and stood at length on its summit. He was soon seen to come down to the shore again, to loosen his sail, unmoor, and stand boldly for Nahant. All this was seen from the cliff. Alice had not stirred from the spot where he had left her.

But from moment to moment the rising wind and tide, swelling in angry chorus, rendered the passage more and more perilous. In vain the intrepid voyager tried to hold his course; the little boat seemed to lie at their mercy. Now it sank down out of sight, and now it struggled up again to the summit of a billow rolling heavily in and shaking the foam from its mane. It soon became unmanageable, drifting helplessly toward the rocks. The seas drenched it, the darkness closed around it; but as it came nearer and nearer, the lookers-on could see the young man still grasping the helm as if buoyed up by the hope of steering to some opening among the rocks where he might safely land. At one moment it seemed as if he would succeed; but in another the boat was swallowed up by a breaker that crushed it like an egg-shell against the rocks, at the feet of the spectators. The next day the body was recovered; in its clenched and stiffened hand was the fatal Forget-me-not.

SWAMPSCOTT BEACH.

SWAMPSCOTT is a succession of hard sand-beaches and rocky, picturesque headlands, forming with Nahant, Nahant Bay. It was formerly, as we remember, a part of Lynn; and so closely are they united to-day, that it would require a surveyor to tell where the one ends or the other begins. In making a tour of the shores one crosses successively King's Beach, Whale Beach, and Phillips Beach, — all of which are the summer playground of the multitudes who in that season come here for health or recreation, or for both. The high and glittering shore sweeps gracefully around toward the east, far out into the ocean, until it is frittered away in a cluster of foam-crested ledges that lie in treacherous ambuscade at its extreme point. That curving shore is Phillips Point, and the reef is Dread Ledge. There is a handsome villa or cottage for every elevated site along the two miles of shore.

The extremity of Phillips Point is a wicked-looking shore, and Dread Ledge is the synonyme for danger to the mariner. The surrounding waters are thickly sown with half-submerged rocks, which in the delirium of a gale seem rooted in hell itself. Here, in January, 1857, the ill-fated *Tedesco* was swallowed up, with every soul on board; and such was the mastery of the tempest over things terrestrial, that the disaster was not known in the neighboring village until the following day. In that memorable gale the sea inundated the marshes, swept unchecked over its ordinary barriers, and heaped a rampart of frozen surf upon the beaches, in which the broken masts of wrecks were left sticking. Streets and roads were so blocked up by immense snowdrifts, that all travel was suspended for several days. The ponderous anchors of the *Tedesco* were found lying, where the seas had thrown them, upon the top of a rock; and they were all that was left to tell the tale, for not a vestige of the hull remained. Another vessel was afterward wrecked here; but, being driven nearer the land, her crew, one by one, walked to the shore over the bowsprit.

Swampscott was, and still is, a typical New-England fishing-village; that is its true estate. The summer visitors are mere birds of passage; but the men who are native here pursue their hazardous calling the whole year through. Nothing can be more curious than to see the old life of a place thus preserved in the midst of the wealth and fashion that have grown up around it and overshadowed it. But in this fact we think lies one great charm of such a place.

There is no difficulty whatever in placing the scene of Hawthorne's "Village Uncle" here. That sketch is in truth only a series of pictures of the surroundings and of the plain fisherfolk, taken from life, to which, from the snug chimney-corner of a fisherman's humble cottage, the garrulous old "Uncle" adds his own store of gossip and of sea-lore. Hear him: —

"Toss on an armful of those dry oak-chips, — the last relics of the 'Mermaid's' knee-timbers, the bones of your namesake, Susan. Higher yet, and clearer, be the blaze, till our cottage windows glow the ruddiest in the village, and the light of our household mirth flash far across the bay to Nahant.

"Now, Susan, for a sober picture of our village! It was a small collection of dwellings that seemed to have been cast up by the sea, with the rock-weed and marine plants that it vomits after a storm, or to have come ashore among the pipe-staves and other lumber which had been washed from the deck of an Eastern schooner. There was just space for the narrow and sandy street between the beach in front and a precipitous hill that lifted its rocky forehead in the rear, among a waste of juniper-bushes and the wild growth of a broken pasture. The village was picturesque in the variety of its edifices, though all were rude. Here stood a little old hovel, built perhaps of driftwood; there a row of boat-houses; and beyond them a two-story dwelling of dark and weatherbeaten aspect, — the whole intermixed with one or two snug cottages painted white, a sufficiency of pigsties, and a shoemaker's shop."

By the same family resemblance is Philips Beach recognized as the scene of those wayward reveries, " Footprints on the Seashore," in which this author thinks aloud, rather than talks, betraying the old truant impulse which occasionally mastered him to get away from that world in which it is true he lived and moved, but could hardly be said to have had his being. We here find him in one of his own creation.

Part Fourth.

SALEM LEGENDS.

SALEM LEGENDS.

IN New England no town except Plymouth takes precedence of Salem in the order of settlement, — a fact of which her citizens are naturally as proud as an old family is of its pedigree going back to the Conquest, or the Creation. And really, in the creation of the Puritan Commonwealth, one represents the First Day, and the other the Second.

The political and commercial fortunes of Salem have been singularly alike. Roger Conant, the founder, and leader of a forlorn hope, was eclipsed by Endicott, who was in turn overshadowed by Winthrop, — a man quick to see that no place was large enough to contain three governors, two of them deposed, one in authority, and all ambitious to lead the Puritan vanguard in the great crusade of the century. The site was not approved. He therefore sought out a new one, to which the seat of government was presently removed, leaving Salem, by the course of these events, a modest reflection of the Puritan capital, and nothing more. The halls of the Essex Institute contain many interesting relics of the time when Salem played an important part in Colonial history.

In respect to its commercial importance, which at one time was very great, — ships in the Hooghly and the Yang-tse, ships at Ceylon and Madagascar, ships on the Gold Coast, in Polynesia and Vancouver; you can hardly put a thought on the wide seas where there were not ships flying like a swarm of industrious bees to every far sea and clime, — an importance so great, indeed, that its merchants were called King this and King that, while by reason of the frequent intercourse had with those " far countrees," its society took a tone and color almost Oriental ; yet, its greater rival again overshadowing it, most singularly converted Salem from a seaport of the first rank into a modestly flourishing place of manufactures. That side of the city representing its old eminence is paralyzed ; while the other half, although exhibiting a still vigorous life, has no such distinctive traits as when Salem was the recognized mart of the Indies. In the cabinets of the Peabody Museum the interested visitor sees on all sides a thousand evidences of her ancient commercial renown, brought from the four quarters of the globe in her own ships, and the sole proofs to-day that such renown ever existed.

Quite recently an embassy from the Queen of Madagascar arrived in the United States. In the course of their tour they visited Boston, not for the sake of anything that city could offer as a temptation to African curiosity, but because it lay in the route to Salem. They were particularly anxious to see Salem, whch is still supposed by many of the natives of Madagascar to be the only port of much importance in America.

Story, the sculptor-poet, who, like Hawthorne, is Salem-born, commemorates these well-remembered scenes of his youth, —

> Ah me, how many an autumn day
>   We watched, with palpitating breast,
> Some stately ship from India or Cathay,
>   Laden with spicy odors from the East,
>   Come sailing up the Bay !
>
> Unto our youthful hearts elate,
> What wealth beside their real freight
>   Of rich material things they bore!
> Ours were Arabian cargoes fair,
> Mysterious, exquisite, and rare.

And of the old houses, "dark, gloomy, and peculiar," wherein strange things were said to have happened, he says : —

> How oft, half fearfully, we prowled
>   Around those gabled houses quaint and old,
> Whose legends, grim and terrible,
> Of witch and ghost that used in them to dwell,
>   Around the twilight fire were told ;
> While huddled close with anxious ear
> We heard them quivering with fear ;
> And if the daylight half o'ercame the spell,
>   'T was with a lingering dread
> We oped the door and touched the stinging bell.
>
> .   .   .   .   .
>
> For with its sound it seemed to rouse the dead,
> And wake some ghost from out the dusky haunts
>   Where faint the daylight fell.

But it so chances — or mischances, according to the light in which we may view it — that the very things impeding her progress have left Salem all the more interesting for our own purpose, — as, in fact, it must be to him who, receiving his impressions from history, expects to find distinct traces of Endicott and of Roger Williams, or having imbibed them from romance, eagerly looks about him for some authentic memorials of "The Scarlet Letter" or for "The House of the Seven Gables." For here the past not only survives, but it may be said actually to flourish with perennial freshness in old houses, old traditions, old silver, antique portraits, and in all the much treasured heirlooms of other days.

The two most noteworthy things that have happened in Salem are the Witchcraft Persecution — that anomaly among events — and the birth of Nathaniel Hawthorne, — that anomaly among men. Without suspecting it, the traveller who arrives by the usual route is at once ushered upon the scene of a tragedy in which it was the guilty who escaped, and the innocent who were punished.

Just out of the city, on its southern skirt, the Eastern Railway passes within near view of an uncouth heap of steep-sided gray rocks, moderately high, on whose windy summit a few houses make a group of dusky silhouettes. This is a sort of waste place, good neither for planting, grazing, or building, nor likely to serve any more useful purpose than a stone-quarry or a land-mark might, for the region surrounding it. In no way does it vary the monotony of the landscape, being wholly treeless and almost without vegetation. Travellers look listlessly, and turn away. Yet stay a moment !

Long ago, so long that no living man remembers it, one soli-tary tree grew upon that rocky, wind-swept height. But at length a blight fell upon it ; it sickened and died ; its limbs one by one rotted and dropped off; and, after contending a while with the wintry blasts that threatened to uproot it, the withered skeleton of a tree was cut down and cast into the fire. Those cold gray ledges where it stood is Gallows Hill. The tree, tradition says, was that upon which the condemned witches were hung. The houses encroach upon the graves of the victims.

From the moment of passing this fatal place, neither the noise nor the throng will be able to distract the stranger's thoughts, wholly occupied as they are with the sinister memories that the sight has awakened within him.

Let us throw a glance around us.

Upon entering the city, the great high-road running north and south takes the more ambitious and dignified name of street. Upon reaching the heart of the city, it expands into a public square, or, not to mix up two distinct eras, the old town market-place. At one end the street skirts Gallows Hill. As he advances towards the centre, the curious visitor may still see the quaint old house, now an apothecary's, in which Roger Williams lived, and in which tradition says that some of the witchcraft examinations were held ; in the Square he has arrived in the region, half real, half romantic, described in Hawthorne's tales (not twice, but a thousand times, told), " Main Street," " A Rill from the Town-Pump," and " Endicott and the Red Cross," of which latter this is a fragment : —

"The central object in the mirrored picture was an edifice of humble architecture, with neither steeple nor bell to proclaim it — what nevertheless it was — the house of prayer. A token of the perils of the wilderness was seen in the grim head of a wolf which had just been slain within the precincts of the town, and, according to the regular mode of claiming the bounty, was nailed to the porch of the meeting-house. The blood was still plashing on the door-step.

"In close vicinity to the sacred edifice appeared that important engine of Puritanic authority, the whipping-post — with the soil around it well trodden by the feet of evil-doers, who had there been disciplined. At one corner of the meeting-house was the pillory, and at the other the stocks ; and, by a singular good fortune, for our sketch, the head of an Episcopalian and suspected Catholic was grotesquely incased in the former machine ; while a fellow-criminal who had boisterously quaffed a health to the King was confined by the legs in the latter."

But this truly Hudibrastic picture is only the grimly humorous prelude to another of a very different nature, upon which is founded that story of sin, remorse, and shame, "The Scarlet Letter."

In the throng surrounding the culprits just sketched for us, "There was likewise a young woman with no mean share of beauty, whose doom it was to wear the letter 'A' on the breast of her gown, in the eyes of all the world and her own children. And even her own children knew what that initial signified. Sporting with her infamy, the lost and desperate creature had embroidered the fatal token in scarlet cloth with golden thread and the nicest art of needlework ; so that the capital A might have been thought to mean Admirable, or anything rather than Adulteress."

Mr. Hawthorne tells us that he found the missive from which this incident is drawn, and which subsequently formed the groundwork of his novel, in the room occupied by him in the Salem Custom-House while he was serving as surveyor of the port under the veteran General James Miller, — the hero of Lundy's Lane. In one respect, therefore, the distinguished American novelist's life has its analogy to that of Charles Lamb, following whom in his inimitable monologue on the South Sea House, which forms the initial chapter to the "Essays of Elia" our own countryman, though in a different spirit, sketches the Old Custom-House and its corps of superannuated weighers, gaugers, and tide-waiters as the introductory chapter to "The Scarlet Letter."

THE SCARLET LETTER.

This old red-brick edifice, if we except a later renovation of its interior, stands precisely as it did in the novelist's time, — the prominent object in a region which it is only too evident has seen better days, but is gradually growing more and more ruinous as every year the houses grow grayer and more shaky. The same flag waves from the cupola, the same eagle, much tarnished, however, by the weather, extends its gilded wings above the entrance door. The novelist describes it in a grimly satirical way as an asylum for decayed politicians, who dozed and slept in easy tranquillity during the hours nominally devoted to business, there being little to do, except to keep up the appearance of official regularity. The surveyor cuts his portraits with a diamond. His desk, showing the marks of a nervous or an idle hand visible in many lines and gashes upon it, is preserved among the curiosities of Plummer Hall. When we look at it, even the homage due to genius can hardly prevent a feeling of pity rising for the life that was so long overcast by the gloom of unfulfilled aspirations, so embittered by the tardiness of a recognition which came too late.

Not far from the Custom-House, in a narrow by-street, is the ancient wooden tenement in which the novelist was born. We pass, as it were, through a corner of the eighteenth century, of which this house is indubitably a relic. It is an humble dwelling, with humble surroundings. Here he wrote many of the shorter tales, that it is entirely safe to say have now more readers than when they first saw the light, and many more that he tells us were committed to the flames ; here he kept that long and weary vigil while waiting for the slow dawning of his fame ; and here he tells us that it was won.

To these early struggles, ending with repeated disappointment, is doubtless to be ascribed the indifference with which Hawthorne speaks of the city of his birth. He refers his return to it from time to time to a sort of fatality which he passively obeyed. Though indeed he admits a certain languid attraction to it, we can hardly distinguish it from repulsion, so intimately do these opposite feelings mingle in the current. Yet the same hand that penned " The House of the Seven Gables " and the " Old Custom-House " puts the early history of Salem in a nutshell in " Main Street ;" and it also gave us those fascinating chapters of revery, " Sights from a Steeple " and "A Rill from the Town-Pump," — all drawn from the associations of the master's birthplace.

But to speak of things as they are, " The Scarlet Letter " was really one of those ingenious methods of punishment, almost Satanic in their conception, which disgrace the criminal annals of the Colony. For different offences a different letter was prescribed, to be worn as well in private as in public, — the wearer thus being made, perhaps for a lifetime, the living record of his or her own infamy. The drunkard wore a capital letter D, the criminal convicted of incest an I, of heresy an H, and of adultery an A, sewed on the arm or breast ; and this accusing insignia was forbidden to be removed upon pain of a severer penalty, if such a thing were possible. Many a poor sinner thus wore his heart upon his sleeve, " for daws to peck at."

The novelist, by instinct, seized upon one of the most striking episodes of the hard Puritan life. The scene of his tale is laid, not in Salem, but in Boston. As we have said, the sketch of " Endicott and the Red Cross " contains the germ of this story, which afterward became in the author's hands the work generally conceded to be his greatest.

Although Hawthorne makes but slight use of the witchcraft history in constructing his " House of the Seven Gables," the opening chapter of that remarkable story shows him to have been familiar with it. But notwithstanding the apparent adherence to truth there, contrived with such consummate art as to fix the impression in the reader's mind that the legend of the old Pyncheon family is derived from some authentic source, it will be better to regard the author's statement, made in his own characteristic way, "that the reader, according to his own pleasure, may either disregard, or allow it to float imperceptibly about the characters and events for the sake of picturesque effect." Thus by freely availing himself of the names of actual personages whose history is artfully interwoven with occurrences that have really happened, and again by associating these with local descriptions of rare fidelity, the wished-for effect of solid reality is produced, and the story proceeds on a chain of circumstantial evidence whose strength lies solely in the master-hand that fabricated it, link by link, from the materials of his own rich fancy. In the concluding words of his preface, the author, with singular frankness, when his purpose is considered, again disenthralls the minds of his auditors of the effect which he was quick to see that his peculiar method must inevitably produce therein. But as a preface is always the last thing written, so it notoriously is the last to be read ; and thus has the author's apology for introducing names which struck his fancy, and for connecting them with scenes familiar to him from boyhood, so far failed of its purpose, that people still persist in prying into the antecedents of a family, distinguished in the early annals of New England, on whose escutcheon no stain or stigma is known to rest !

After this explanation it will be scarcely necessary to observe that the words which are put into the mouth of Matthew Maule at the moment he is ascending the fatal ladder, a condemned and abhorred wizard, and which form the underlying motive of the "House of the Seven Gables," — the blight of an evil destiny passing from generation to generation, — were as a matter of fact really spoken by Sarah Good, not to Colonel Pyncheon, but to the Reverend Nicholas Noyes, who most cruelly and wickedly embittered her last moments by telling her that she was a miserable witch. And it was to him she made the memorable reply that "if he took away her life, God would give him blood to drink."

There is, however, reason for supposing, since it has been so minutely described, that the house of the seven gables was at least suggested by that of Philip English, who was near becoming a martyr to the witchcraft horror himself. What is clearer still, is that the novelist has laid several of the old Colonial houses, both in Salem and Boston, under contribution for whatever might embellish his description, which is certainly no invention, but is a true picture of the early architecture even in its minutest details. But in such an unreal atmosphere as surrounds it, we are not sure that the house itself may not turn out to be an illusion of the mirage created by an effort of the weird romancer's will. Its appearance is thus portrayed in the opening words of the romance, —

"There it rose, a little withdrawn from the line of the street, but in pride, not modesty. Its whole visible exterior was ornamented with quaint figures, conceived in the grotesqueness of a Gothic fancy, and drawn or stamped in the glittering plaster, composed of lime, pebbles, and bits of glass, with which the woodwork of the walls was overspread. On every side the seven gables pointed sharply towards the sky, and presented the aspect of a whole sisterhood of edifices, breathing through the spiracles of one great chimney. The many lattices, with their small, diamond-shaped panes, admitted the sunlight into hall and chamber, while nevertheless the second story, projecting far over the base, and itself retiring beneath the third, threw a shadowy and thoughtful gloom into the lower rooms. Carved globes of wood were affixed under the jutting stories. Little spiral rods of iron beautified each of the seven peaks. On the triangular portion of the gable, that fronted next the street, was a dial, put up that very morning, and on which the sun was still marking the passage of the first bright hour in a history that was not destined to be all so bright."

THE ESCAPE OF PHILIP ENGLISH.

THE story of Philip English and his wife is quite as well worthy a romance as the house in which they lived. We can moreover, answer for its strict truth.

During the time of the witchcraft delusion at the Village, the victims were in nearly every case people in the humblest walk of life. Philip English of Salem was the first person of superior station to be attainted by this persecution, which, like a wolf that is maddened by the taste of blood, began to grow bolder in pursuit of its victims.

Philip English had emigrated to America from the island of Jersey. Having found a home in the family of Mr. William Hollingsworth, a wealthy inhabitant of Salem, he formed the acquaintance of Mr. Hollingsworth's only child, Susanna, who, as is evident from her history, besides having received from her father an education superior to the usual requirements of that day, possessed rare endowments of mind and person. The acquaintance ripened into mutual affection, and in due time Philip English married the daughter of his friend and patron. He too became in time a rich and eminent merchant.

In April, 1692, the terrible accusation fell like a thunderbolt upon this happy home. The wife and mother was the first victim to the credulity or malignity of her neighbors. In the night the officer entered her bedchamber, read his fatal warrant, and then surrounded the house with guards, intending to carry her to prison in the morning. Mrs. English gave herself up for lost. With supreme heroism, however, she gathered her stricken family together in the morning to its usual devotions, gave directions for the education of her children, clasped them to her bosom, kissed them, and then, commending them and her-

self to God, bade them farewell. She was then taken by the
sheriff before the sitting magistrates, Hathorne and Curwen,
who committed her to Salem jail as a witch. Her firmness is
memorable. A little later her husband was also accused by a
poor bedridden creature. He concealed himself for a time; but
at length he came forward, gave himself up, and demanded the

PHILIP ENGLISH'S HOUSE, SALEM.

privilege of sharing his wife's fate. The two were immured in
the same dungeon to await the solemn farce of a trial. The
prison being crowded to overflowing, English and his wife
were, through the intercession of friends, removed to the jail in
Boston, where for six weeks they endured the dismal prospect
of dying together upon the scaffold.

12

But fortunately for them, and in consequence, doubtless, of the fact that English was a merchant of property, and a person of known probity, he and his unfortunate wife were admitted to bail, being allowed the privilege of the town by day, on condition of punctually returning to the prison at night, to be locked up again until the following morning. Though rendering their condition more tolerable, this did not make it the less hopeless. They were visited in their prison by some of the most eminent clergymen of the town, one of whom, the Reverend Joshua Moody, — peace to his memory ! — manifested the deepest interest in their spiritual and temporal welfare. This good man, whose sound head refused to admit the prevailing delusion, while his equally sound heart fitted him for deeds of mercy, like that upon which he was now bent, went to the prison on the day before English and his wife were to be taken back to Salem for trial, and invited them to attend at public worship in his church. They went.

When he ascended the pulpit, the clergyman announced as his text this verse, having a peculiar significance to two of his hearers: " If they persecute you in one city, flee into another ! "

In his discourse, the preacher justified, with manly courage and directness, any and every attempt to escape from the forms of justice when justice itself was being violated in them. After the service was over, the minister again visited the prisoners in their cell, and asked English pointedly whether he had detected the meaning of his sermon of the morning. English hesitating to commit himself, Mr. Moody frankly told him that his own life and that of his wife were in danger, and that he, looking this in the face, ought to provide for an escape without losing a moment. English could not believe it; it was too monstrous. " God will not suffer them to hurt me," he said in this conviction.

" What," exclaimed his wife, " do you not think that they who have suffered already were innocent ? "

" Yes."

"Why, then, may we not suffer also? Take Mr. Moody's advice; let us fly."

To make an end of this indecision, proceeding from the fear that flight would be quickly construed to mean guilt, Mr. Moody then unfolded his plan.   He told the reluctant English that everything necessary for his escape had been already provided : that the Governor, Sir William Phips, was in the secret, and countenanced it; that the jailer had his instructions to open the prison doors; and that, finally, all being in readiness, at midnight a conveyance, furnished by friends who were in the plot, would come to carry them away to a place of security. In fact every precaution that prudence could suggest or foresee, or that influence in high places could secure, had been taken by this noble and self-sacrificing Christian man in order to prevent the shedding of innocent blood.   He procured letters, under Sir William's own hand and seal, to Governor Fletcher of New York, thus providing for the fugitives, first a safeguard, and next an inviolable asylum.   Finally, he told English plainly that if he did not carry his wife off, he, Moody, would do so himself.   The affair was arranged on the spot.

At the appointed time the prison doors were unbarred, the prisoners came out, and while the solemn stillness of midnight brooded over the afflicted town, they fled from persecution in one city into another.

Governor Fletcher took the homeless wanderers into his own mansion, where he made them welcome, not as fugitives from justice, but as exiles fleeing from persecution.   They were entertained as the most honored of guests.   The next year Philip English returned home.   The storm of madness had passed by, leaving its terrible marks in many households.   His own was destined to feel its consequences in a way to turn all his joy into sorrow.   Within two years from the time she was torn from her home to answer the charge of felony, Mrs. English died of the cruel treatment she had received.   Mr. Moody's course was commended by all discerning men, as it deserved;

but he felt the angry resentment of the multitude, among whom some persons of high rank were included. In consequence of this persecution he returned to his old charge at Portsmouth, New Hampshire, the next year after his successful interposition to save Mr. and Mrs. English from the executioner's hands.

Such is the tradition long preserved in the English family. Philip English's granddaughter became Susanna Hathorne, — which was the original way of spelling the name subsequently borne by the novelist. Nathaniel Hawthorne had thus on one side for an ancestor the implacable persecutor of those to whom he was afterward to be related by intermarriage, thus furnishing the idea he has so ingeniously worked out in the "House of the Seven Gables."

Having given an extract from Hawthorne's story of "Endicott and the Red Cross," we may as well tell, with his help, the story itself.

ENDICOTT AND THE RED CROSS.

IN 1634 one of the newly arrived ships brought from England a copy of the commission granted to the two Archbishops and ten of the Council to regulate all plantations, to call in all patents, to make laws, raise tithes and portions for ministers, to remove and punish governors, and to hear and determine all causes and inflict all punishments, even to the death-penalty. This plenary power, the Colonists were advised, was levelled at them ; ships and soldiers were said to be preparing in England to bring over a royal governor and to give effect to the much-dreaded commission. A more distasteful piece of intelligence than this could hardly be imagined. It struck at once at the root of all their liberties, and it quickly aroused the spirit of resistance in full vigor. The work of erecting fortifications was hastened. A solemn consultation between the magistrates and the ministers resulted in the determination to defend themselves against these innovations by force if there was a prospect of success, or by temporizing if there were none. Only in the fourth year of its existence, the Colony now stood on the verge of open rebellion; and while thus in daily apprehension of the total subversion of the government, an act coming very little short of treasonable was performed.

CUTTING OUT THE CROSS.

At the November court complaint was made by Richard Brown, of Watertown, that the Colony flag had been defaced at Salem by cutting out part of the red cross. No action was taken at this court, but at the next, Endicott, the old governor, was called upon to answer for the defacement. The cause that he alleged for the act was that the cross was the hated emblem and banner of Popery. Opinion being divided, some upholding and others censuring, the cause was again postponed; and in the meantime the newly created military commission ordered all the ensigns to be laid aside, so that the Colony was now without any flag at all.

At the next court, which was one of election, John Haynes was chosen governor and Richard Bellingham deputy-governor. Endicott was left this time out of the number of assistants; and being again called upon to defend his mutilating the ensign, was reprimanded, and disqualified from holding office for a year. Letters disavowing the act were written to England. To allay the excitement growing out of this affair, it was seriously proposed to substitute the red and white rose for the cross in the colors. The military commission afterward, in the exercise of its powers, left out the cross in the colors borne by the Colony troops, and caused a flag having the King's arms to be raised over the castle in Boston Harbor. This leads us to observe that the fathers of the Colony were making rapid strides towards independence. They had first refused to tolerate the only form of religious worship recognized by the laws of their country, had disobeyed a royal mandate, and had at length exercised the sovereignty of an independent State by adopting a flag of their own.

SOLDIER OF 1630.

With this preamble we can take up understandingly Hawthorne's tale, and from this point it is he who speaks : —

" Such was the aspect of the times when the folds of an English banner, with the red cross in its field, were flung out over a company of Puritans. Their leader, the famous Endicott, was a man of stern and resolute countenance, the effect of which was heightened by a grizzled beard that swept the upper portion of his breastplate. . . ."

Having concluded a fiery harangue to his soldiers, in which he acquaints them with the dangers menacing the unrestrained liberty of conscience they have hitherto enjoyed, —

" Endicott gazed round at the excited countenances of the people, now full of his own spirit, and then turned suddenly to the standard-bearer, who stood close behind him.

"'Officer, lower your banner !' said he.

"The officer obeyed ; and brandishing his sword, Endicott thrust it through the cloth, and with his left hand rent the red cross completely out of the banner.   He then waved the tattered ensign above his head.

"'Sacrilegious wretch!' cried the High Churchman in the pillory, unable longer to restrain himself, 'thou hast rejected the symbol of our holy religion!'

"'Treason, treason!' roared the royalist in the stocks.   'He hath defaced the King's banner!'

"'Before God and man I will avouch the deed,' answered Endicott.   'Beat a flourish, drummer! — shout, soldiers and people! — in honor of the ensign of New England.   Neither Pope nor Tyrant hath part in it now!'

"With a cry of triumph, the people gave their sanction to one of the boldest exploits which our history records.   And forever honored be the name of Endicott!   We look back through the mist of ages, and recognize, in the rending of the red cross from New England's banner, the first omen of that deliverance which our fathers consummated, after the bones of the stern Puritan had lain more than a century in the dust."

In the King's "Missive," Whittier commemorates briefly the same incident of history.

CASSANDRA SOUTHWICK.

ANOTHER Salem legend recalls the dark day of Quaker persecution vividly before us.   It is another story of the cruelties perpetrated upon this sect, whose innovations upon the forms of religious worship established in the Puritan Colony and made part of its fundamental law, were regarded and punished as heresies threatening the stability of its institutions, — with what incredible rigor the records show.

The Quaker poet has taken this sad chapter for the theme of his poem entitled "Cassandra Southwick," and as the legitimate avenger of the cruel wrongs inflicted so long ago upon the suffering Friends, he now applies the lash unsparingly to the memory of those who acted prominent parts in commencing these barbarities.   This may be called poetic justice in its most literal sense.

We will not ask whether, in obeying the impulse to right one wrong, the poet in presenting this case has done full justice to

CONDEMNED TO BE SOLD.

the spirit of history.   His is a righteous indignation, to which every sympathetic heart quickly responds.   Nevertheless it should be said, in passing, that the sins of the rulers were those of a majority of the people, who, by first making the laws against the Quakers, and then consenting to their enforcement, — upon the maxim that a house divided against itself cannot stand, — are the really guilty objects of this posthumous arraignment. Endicott, Norton, Rawson, and the others were but the agents.

To construct his poem, to secure in advance for his theme the greatest possible sympathy, the poet has centred our attention upon a woman, — a maiden in whom faith and fortitude are strongly and beautifully developed, and who in the midst of her sufferings — for her tender back has felt the lash — confronts her persecutors with the calm resignation of a Christian martyr and the spirit of a Joan of Arc.

We cannot help it if much of the glamour thus thrown around the legendary tale should disappear in our plain, unvarnished one. But it shall speak for itself. Cassandra Southwick was the wife of Laurence Southwick, a citizen of Salem in the year 1656. They were a grave couple, advanced in years, and had three grown up children, — Provided, a daughter; and Josiah and Daniel, their sons. The whole family united with the Society of Friends, fell under suspicion, and were included in the persecution which resulted in their being driven from their homes into exile and death. The parents being banished from the Colony upon pain of death, they fled to Shelter Island, where they lived only a short time, one dying within three days' time of the other, and bequeathing the memory of their wrongs to their children.

While the aged couple and Josiah, the son, were languishing in Boston jail, Provided and Daniel being left at home, — presumably in want, since the cattle and household goods had already been distrained, in order to satisfy the fines repeatedly imposed upon them by the courts — these two, who in the narrative are called children, were also fined ten pounds for not attending public worship at Salem.

To get this money, the General Court sitting at Boston issued this order : —

"Whereas Daniel and Provided Southwick, son and daughter to Laurence Southwick, have been fined by the County Courts at Salem and Ipswich, pretending they have no estates, resolving not to work; and others likewise have been fined, and more [are] like to be fined, for siding with the Quakers, and absenting themselves from the public ordinances, — in answer to a question what course shall be taken for

the satisfaction of the fines, the Court, on perusal of the law, title
' Arrests,' resolve, that the treasurers of the several counties are, and
shall hereby be, empowered to sell the said persons to any of the
English nation at Virginia or Barbadoes."

Joseph Besse, in his account of the affair, goes on to state
that, —

"Pursuant to this order, Edward Butter, one of the treasurers, to
get something of the booty, sought out for passage to send them to
Barbadoes for sale ; but none were willing to take or carry them.
And a certain master of a ship, to put the thing off, pretended that
they would spoil all the ship's company ; to which Butter replied,
'No, you need not fear that ; for they are poor, harmless creatures,
and will not hurt anybody.'

"'Will they not so ?' replied the shipmaster ; 'and will you offer
to make slaves of such harmless creatures ?'

"Thus Butter. notwithstanding his wicked intention, when he could
get no opportunity to send them away, the winter being at hand, sent
them home again to shift for themselves."

This is the account that is followed by Whittier in "Cassandra Southwick." The parents were, as we have said, banished.
Josiah, who had been whipped from town to town at the cart's
tail, fined, imprisoned, and finally banished, went over to England, there to give testimony against his oppressors. But while
neither the Quaker maiden nor her brother was actually sold
into bondage, it was only a few months later that the former
was scourged upon the bare back and again committed to prison.

In the poet's hands these incidents are woven into a narrative of deepest pathos and fervor ; and though the coloring is
heightened, it will be observed that the incidents themselves are
nearly all true, the poet having arranged them to suit his own
fancy. The girl lies on her pallet awaiting the fulfilment of the
sentence she is to undergo on the morrow. She stands in the
market-place in the presence of a gaping crowd. She turns with
withering scorn upon the minister who is whispering counsel
or support into Endicott's ear. Her innocence, her beauty, and
her sufferings plead for her in the hearts of those who have

come to deride, perhaps to insult, her. One burst of honest wrath quickly turns the scale in her favor. No one will take her away. The iniquitous proceedings are stopped, and the Quaker maiden walks away from the spot free, as if by the intervention of a miracle.

Slow broke the gray cold morning ; again the sunshine fell,
Flecked with the shade of bar and grate within my lonely cell ;
The hoar-frost melted on the wall, and upward from the street
Came careless laugh and idle word, and tread of passing feet.

At length the heavy bolts fell back, my door was open cast,
And slowly at the sheriff's side, up the long street I passed ;
I heard the murmur round me, and felt, but dared not see,
How, from every door and window, the people gazed on me.

And there were ancient citizens, cloak-wrapped and grave and cold,
And grim and stout sea-captains with faces bronzed and old,
And on his horse, with Rawson, his cruel clerk, at hand,
Sat dark and haughty Endicott, the ruler of the land.

Then to the stout sea-captains the sheriff, turning, said, —
' Which of ye, worthy seamen, will take this Quaker maid ?
In the Isle of fair Barbadoes, or on Virginia's shore,
You may hold her at a higher price than Indian girl or Moor."

A weight seemed lifted from my heart, — a pitying friend was nigh,
I felt it in his hard, rough hand, and saw it in his eye ;
And when again the sheriff spoke, that voice, so kind to me,
Growled back its stormy answer like the roaring of the sea, —

" Pile my ship with bars of silver, — pack with coins of Spanish gold,
From keel-piece up to deck-plank, the roomage of her hold,
By the living God who made me ! — I would sooner in your bay
Sink ship and crew and cargo, than bear this child away ! "

I looked on haughty Endicott ; with weapon half-way drawn,
Swept round the throng his lion glare of bitter hate and scorn ;
Fiercely he drew his bridle-rein, and turned in silence back,
And sneering priest and baffled clerk rode murmuring in his track.

THE WITCHCRAFT TRAGEDY.

THE place where a great crime has been committed has always something strangely fascinating about it. Accursed though it may be, repulsive as its associations generally are, yet most people will go a greater distance to see the locality of a murder than they would take the trouble to do for any other purpose whatsoever. The house where a great man has been born is often quite unknown and unvisited even in its own neighborhood; the house that is associated with a murder or a homicide never is.

Charles Lamb hits the nail fairly on the head — and he is speaking not of New, but of Old, England — when he says that, —

"We are too hasty when we set down our ancestors in the gross for fools for the monstrous inconsistencies (as they seem to us) involved in their creed of witchcraft. In the relations of this visible world we find them to have been as rational and shrewd to detect an historic anomaly as ourselves. But when once the invisible world was supposed to be opened, and the lawless agency of bad spirits assumed, what measures of probability, of decency, of fitness or proportion, — of that which distinguishes the likely from the palpable absurd, — could they have to guide them in the rejection or admission of any particular testimony? That maidens pined away, wasting inwardly as their waxen images consumed before a fire; that corn was lodged and cattle lamed; that whirlwinds uptore in diabolic revelry the oaks of the forest; or that spits and kettles only danced a fearful innocent vagary about some rustic's kitchen when no wind was stirring, — were all equally probable where no law of agency was understood."

This is the judgment of a keenly analytical and thoughtful mind, expressed with the large-hearted human sympathy with which he was endowed. It deals with the universally prevalent belief in witchcraft. To reinforce this with the views of an able and discriminating jurist will not be deemed out of place here.

"We may lament, then," says Judge Story in his Centennial Address at Salem, "the errors of the times which led to these prosecutions. But surely our ancestors had no special reasons for shame in a belief which had the universal sanction of their own and all former ages; which counted in its train philosophers as well as enthusiasts; which was graced by the learning of prelates as well as the countenance of kings; which the law supported by its mandates, and the purest judges felt no compunctions in enforcing. Let Witch Hill remain forever memorable by this sad catastrophe, not to perpetuate our dishonor, but as an affecting, enduring proof of human infirmity, — a proof that perfect justice belongs to one judgment-seat only, — that which is linked to the throne of God."

What was this belief, then, which had such high moral and legal sanction? It was this, — That the Devil might and did personally appear to, enter into, and actively direct, the every-day life of men. And he did this without the intervention of any of those magical arts or conjurations such as were once thought indispensable to induce him to put in an appearance. For this there was Scripture authority, chapter and verse. He was supposed to come sometimes in one form, sometimes in another, to tempt his victims with the promise that upon their signing a contract to become his, both body and soul, they should want for nothing, and that he would undertake to revenge them upon all their enemies. The traditional witch was usually some decrepit old village crone, of a sour and malignant temper, who was as thoroughly hated as feared; but this did not exclude men from sharing in the power of becoming noted wizards, — though from the great number of women who were accused, it would appear that the Arch-Enemy usually preferred to try his arts upon the weaker and more impressible sex. The fatal compact was consummated by the victim registering his or her name in a book or upon a scroll of parchment, and with his own blood. The form of these contracts is nowhere preserved. Sometimes, as is instanced in the negotiation between Oliver Cromwell and the Devil before the Battle of Worcester, there was a good deal of haggling. The bargain being concluded, Satan delivered to his new recruit an imp or familiar spirit, which sometimes had the form of a cat, at others of a mole, of a bird, of a miller-fly, or of some other insect or animal. These were to come at call, do such mischief as they should be commanded, and at stated times be permitted to suck the wizard's blood. Feeding, suckling, or rewarding these imps was by the law of England declared FELONY.

Witches, according to popular belief, had the power to ride at will through the air on a broomstick or a spit, to attend distant meetings or sabbaths of witches; but for this purpose they must first have anointed themselves with a certain magical ointment given to them by the Fiend. This is neither more nor less than what our forefathers believed, what was solemnly incorporated into the laws of the land, and what was as solemnly preached from the pulpit. A perusal of the witchcraft examinations shows us how familiar even children of a tender age were with all the forms of this most formidable and fatal, but yet not unaccountable, superstition.

In the course of those remarkable trials at Salem, several of the accused persons, in order to save their lives, confessed to having signed their names in the Devil's book, to having been baptized by him, and to having attended midnight meetings of witches, or sacraments held upon the green near the minister's house, to which they came riding through the air. They admitted that he had sometimes appeared to them in the form of a black dog or cat, sometimes in that of a horse, and once as "a fine grave man," but generally as a black man of severe aspect. These fables show the prevalent form of the belief among the people. It was generally held to be impossible for a witch to say the Lord's Prayer correctly; and it is a matter of record that one woman, while under examination, was put to this test, when it was noticed that in one place she substituted some words of her own for those of the prayer. Such a failure of memory was considered, even by some learned judges, as a decisive proof of guilt. Even the trial of throwing a witch into the water, to see whether she would sink or swim, was once made in Connecticut.

The scene of the witchcraft outbreak of 1692 is an elevated knoll of no great extent, rising among the shaggy hills and spongy meadows that lie at some distance back from the more thickly settled part of the town of Danvers, Massachusetts, formerly Salem Village. It is indeed a quiet little neighborhood to have made so much noise in the world. Somehow, en-

THE PARSONAGE, SALEM VILLAGE.

terprise avoids it, leaving it, as we see it to-day, cold and lifeless. The first appearance of everything is so peaceful, so divested of all hurry or excitement, as to suggest an hereditary calm, — a pastoral continued from generation to generation. Then, as the purpose which has brought him hither comes into his mind, the visitor looks about him in doubt whether this can really be the locality of that fearful tragedy.

Yes, here are the identical houses that were standing when those unheard-of events took place, still solemnly commemorating them, as if doomed to stand eternally. This village street is the same

old highway through which the dreadful infection spread from
house to house unto the remote corners of the ancient shire, until,

as we read, there were forty men of Andover that
could raise the devil as well as any astrologer.
Here too is the site of the old meeting-house, in
which those amazing scenes, the witchcraft examinations, took place. A little farther on we come to
the spot of ground, as yet unbuilt upon, where the
Parsonage with the lean-to chamber stood. The
sunken outlines of the cellar are still to be seen,
and even some relics of the house itself remain
in the outbuildings attached to the Wadsworth
mansion, which overlooks the "Witch-Ground,"
and which was built in the same year that the
old Parsonage was pulled down. It was in this
"Ministry House," as it was then called, that the
circle of young girls met, whose denunciations,
equivalent to the death-warrant of the accused
person, soon overspread the land with desolation
and woe ; and it was here that the alleged
midnight convocations of witches met to celebrate
their unholy sacraments, and to renew their solemn league and covenant with Satan, in draughts
of blood, and by inscribing their names in his
fatal book.

USED BY
JACOBS WHEN
GOING TO
EXECUTION.

It makes one sick at heart to think of a child only eleven
years old, such as Abigail Williams was, taking away the
lives of men and women who had always borne unblemished
reputations among their friends and neighbors, by identifying
them as having attended these meetings, and of having hurt
this or that person. These poor creatures could scarcely understand that they were seriously accused by one so young of a
crime made capital by the law. But their doubts were soon
removed. Once they were accused, every man's hand was
against them. Children testified against their own parents,
husbands against their wives, wives against their husbands,

neighbor against neighbor. One's blood alternately boils and freezes while reading the damning evidence of the record to the fatal infatuation of the judges, to their travesty of justice, to their pitiless persecution of the prisoners at the bar, and to the over-mastering terror that silenced the voice of humanity in this stricken community. Panic reigned everywhere supreme. It is an amazing history; but, incredible as it seems, it is yet all true. Would that it were not!

The main features of these trials are so familiar to all, that it will only be necessary to refer to the fact that some hundreds of innocent persons were thrown into prison, while twenty were barbarously executed, at the instance of some young girls of the Village, who went into violent convulsions, real or pretended, as soon as they were confronted with the prisoners at the bar. The convictions were had upon " spectre " evidence, — that is to say, the strange antics of the possessed girls were considered as proof positive of the criminal power of witchcraft in the accused, — shown too in open court, — with which they stood charged. The statute assumed that this power could only proceed from a famili-arity or compact with the Evil One, and punished it with death. The evidence, however, was of two kinds. When interrogated by the magistrates, the girls first gave their evidence calmly, like ordinary witnesses to the criminal acts, and then went into their spasms, which all believed were caused by the prisoners. Their incoherent ravings and outcries were also taken as good and valid testimony, and are so recorded.

These remarkable proceedings are not, however, without a precedent. The tragical story of Urbain Grandier develops the same characteristics. His popularity as a preacher having ex-cited the envy of the monks, they instigated some nuns to play the part of persons possessed, and in their convulsions to charge Grandier with being the cause of their evil visitation. This horrible though absurd charge was sanctioned by Cardinal Richelieu on grounds of personal dislike. Grandier was tried, condemned, and burnt alive, April 18, 1634, more than half a century earlier than the proceedings occurring at Salem.

Though humanity may well revolt at the explanation, the theory of imposture, pure and simple, begun and maintained by these girls of Salem Village, is the one we turn from in dismay as a thing not indeed proved, or even admitted, but as a haunting probability that will not down at our bidding.

GILES COREY, THE WIZARD.

UNDOUBTEDLY the most dramatic incident of this carnival of death was the trial and execution of Giles Corey, who, seeing the fate of all those who had preceded him, stubbornly refused to plead; and, to vindicate the majesty of the law he had thus defied, he was condemned to the atrocious *peine forte et dure* of the Dark Ages. The incredible sentence was carried out to the letter; and this miserable prisoner, while yet a living and breathing man, was actually crushed to death under the pressure of heavy weights. This is the only instance of such a punishment being inflicted in New England. We shudder to record it.

Until the appearance of Mr. Longfellow's "New England Tragedies," there had been no serious attempt to make use of this sinister chapter for any other purpose than that of impartial history. Poets and novelists seem alike to have shunned it. The man to whom all eyes would naturally be turned, was descended from one of the most implacable of the judges, — the one, in fact, who had delivered the horrible sentence of the court in the case of Giles Corey. In the dramatic version the poet makes him say :—

> Ghosts of the dead and voices of the living
> Bear witness to your guilt, and you must die!
> It might have been an easier death ; your doom
> Will be on your own head, and not on ours.
> Twice more will you be questioned of these things,
> Twice more have room to plead or to confess.

If you are contumacious to the Court,
And if when questioned you refuse to answer,
Then by the statute you will be condemned
To the *peine forte et dure!* — to have your body
Pressed by great weights until you shall be dead !
And may the Lord have mercy on your soul!

Owing to the prisoner's indomitable attitude before his judges,
but few incidents of this extraordinary trial, or mockery of one,
remain.   The heroic figure of this old man of eighty confronting judges and accusers in stoical silence is, however, unique in
its grandeur.   From this moment he becomes their peer.   Even
the poet's art could add nothing to the simple recital of the eloquent fact.   But such an act of sublime heroism is also deeply
pathetic.   Neither the anathema of the Church, the doom pronounced upon the wife of his bosom, the solemn warnings of
his judges, thrice repeated, nor the prospect of an ignominious
death could unseal the lips of old Giles Corey, obscure husband-
man though he was.   This amazing fortitude wrung from his
enemies the title of the Man of Iron.   His was one of the last
of the murders committed in the name of the law, and with him
was thus crushed out the delusion of which he unquestionably
was the most remarkable victim.

The anonymous ballad, written in the old manner, and in an
ironical vein, perpetuates the cruel history as concisely and as
truthfully as the prose accounts do : —

Giles Corey was a Wizzard strong,
    A stubborn wretch was he ;
And fitt was he to hang on high
    Upon the Locust-tree.

So when before the magistrates
    For triall he did come,
He would no true confession make,
    But was compleatlie dumbe.

"Giles Corey," said the Magistrate,
  "What hast thou heare to pleade
To these that now accuse thy soule
  Of crimes and horrid deed ? "

Giles Corey, he said not a worde,
  No single worde spoke he.
"Giles Corey," saith the Magistrate,
  "We 'll press it out of thee."

They got them then a heavy beam,
  They laid it on his breast ;
They loaded it with heavy stones,
  And hard upon him prest.

"More weight ! " now said this wretched man ;
  "More weight ! " again he cried ;
And he did no confession make,
  But wickedly he dyed.

The tradition was long current in Salem that at stated periods
the ghost of Corey the wizard appeared on the spot where he
had suffered, as the precursor of some calamity that was impending over the community, which the apparition came to announce.
His shade, however, has long since ceased to revisit "the glimpses
of the moon," and to do duty as a bugbear to frighten unruly
children into obedience ; but the memory of this darkest deed
in New England's annals is a phantom that will not be laid.

THE BELL TAVERN MYSTERY.

THE Bell Tavern was a house for the entertainment of man
and beast situated in the town of Danvers, fronting the
highroad running through the village, and thus connecting
its movement and its events with the rest of the world. So

long ago as it was the King's own highway, this road was the great artery of New England, through which the blood of its commerce, so to speak, flowed to and from the heart of its capital, Boston. Boston Stone was then the central *milliarium* from which the diverging sections ran north and ran south into the most remote parts of the Colonies, — on the south to the Carolinas, and to the Kennebec settlements on the north. The Bell Tavern, being therefore exactly in the great current of travel as well as of events, has naturally a history of its own.

The sign of the tavern was a wooden bell, suspended to the crossbeam of a post before the door, with this couplet underneath : —

> I 'll toll you in if you have need,
> And feed you well and bid you speed.

When the reader knows that within the limits of Danvers, while it was yet a precinct of Salem, the witchcraft tragedies were enacted ; that General Israel Putnam was born here ; that on its borders is the remarkable natural curiosity known as Ship Rock ; and that it is the usual residence of the venerable poet and philanthropist, Whittier, — he will see so many reasons for spending some hours in the place, should he ever chance to be in the neighborhood. But he will no longer find the Bell Tavern there. That has disappeared, although its traditions are still most scrupulously preserved. Let us recount one of them.

The Bell was for some time the residence of Elizabeth Whitman, whose singular story, under the fictitious name of Eliza Wharton, excited, forty odd years ago, the sensibilities of thousands. In this house she died ; and such was the desire of many to obtain some memento of her, that even the stones erected over her grave were near being carried away piecemeal. When I last visited the spot where she lies, the path leading to it was, to judge from appearances, the one in the old ground oftenest traversed. This is not strange, for even in winter, after a heavy fall of snow, the path has been kept open by the feet of the morbidly curious. I expected to read upon the headstone the words, " Good people, pray for her, she died for love." But, as I have said, the stone had been carried off nearly entire. The following letter, found after her death among her effects, is, however, at once the history and the epitaph of this most brilliant and gifted, yet most unfortunate, of beings. After reading it, let him who is without sin cast the first stone upon her memory : —

" Must I die alone ? Shall I never see you more ? I know that you will come, but you will come too late. This is, I fear, my last ability. Tears fall so, I know not how to write. Why did you leave me in so much distress ? But I will not reproach you. All that was dear I left for you ; but I do not regret it. May God forgive in both what was amiss. When I go from hence, I will leave you some way to find me ; if I die, will you come and drop a tear over my grave ? "

In the month of June, 1788, a chaise in which were two persons, a man and a woman, stopped at the door of the Bell Tavern. The woman alighted and entered the house. Her companion immediately drove off, and was never again seen in the village. It may be easily guessed that the very last place for seclusion or mystery was a New England village of a hundred years ago, since the entire population regarded even the presence among them of an unknown person with suspicion ; while any attempt at mystification was in effect a spur to the curiosity of every idle gossip, far and near. In self-protection the laws of hospitality as to the stranger were reversed. To this spirit of exclusiveness we doubtless owe the national trait of inquisitiveness so often ascribed to us. Such, however, was the spirit of the laws under which these communities had grown up. It is true that the stranger was not required to show his passport ; but as he valued his own ease, on no account must he betray any reticence concerning himself or his affairs. At the entrance of each village, as one might say, an invisible but watchful sentinel cried out : " Who comes there ? " Should the stranger happen to have his secret to guard, so much the worse for him.

The unknown guest of the Bell — about whom everything — her beauty, grace of manner and address, announced her to be a person accustomed to the society of people above the ordinary condition of life — desired most of all to be unnoticed and unmolested. She desired this for peculiar reasons. Each day her life steadily darkened; every hour was bringing her nearer and nearer to the crisis of her destiny; every moment was an hour of terror and remorse. It was necessary, however, to give some account of herself, or else suspicion and calumny would soon be busy with her reputation. She there-

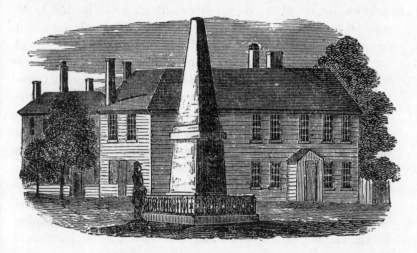

THE BELL, FROM AN OLD PRINT.

fore represented that she was married, and that her husband would soon join her. To help her story — for she, poor soul, fancied that the thin stratagem would make all seem right — she laid a letter, written and addressed by herself, upon her table, where her inquisitive neighbors would be certain to see and to read the superscription. Her days were passed at the window watching for some one who did not come. One easily imagines what her nights must have been. Once a man who went through the village was observed to stop before the tavern and attentively read the name that the " beautiful strange lady " had written on her door as a means of recognition. But when he passed on without entering the house, she was heard to exclaim, "Oh, I am undone!"

It will be supposed that the mysterious recluse of the Bell Tavern soon became the object of intense curiosity to the people of the village. They saw her sitting at her window, sometimes whiling away the heavy hours with her guitar, or else busily plying her needle "in a mournful muse." When she went out, old and young, attracted by her graceful form and presence, turned to look after her as she walked. But as the months wore on, the secret motive for her seclusion could no longer be concealed. Yet the one whose coming was the single hope left to her despairing soul abandoned her to bear all the odium of her situation alone. In this hour of bitterest trial — of two-fold desertion and danger — she found, however, one sympathizing and womanly heart courageous enough to take the friendless, forlorn Elizabeth into her own home and to nurse her tenderly. There this wretched mother gave birth to a dead infant, and there, after a short illness, she died. The letter with which this sad story is prefaced was doubtless penned upon her death-bed; yet in this hour of agony she, with rare fidelity, preserved the incognito of her heartless lover to the last; and what is rarer still, granted him, from her soul, a full and free pardon for the sacrifice of her honor and life. But this pardon should have been his perpetual remorse. These are the closing lines of some verses the poor girl destined for his eye. It will be seen that her last words were those of forgiveness and undying love : —

> O thou! for whose dear sake I bear
> A doom so dreadful, so severe,
> May happy fates thy footsteps guide,
> And o'er thy peaceful home preside.
> Nor let E——a's early tomb
> Infect thee with its baleful gloom."

An unknown hand erected a stone over her grave with this inscription : —

"This humble stone, in memory of Elizabeth Whitman, is inscribed by her weeping friends, to whom she endeared herself by uncommon tenderness and affection. Endowed with superior genius and acquirements, she was still more endeared by humility and benevolence. Let candor throw a veil over her frailties, for great was her charity to others. She sustained the last painful scene far from every friend, and exhibited an example of calm resignation. Her departure was on the 25th of July, A. D. 1788, in the 37th year of her age, and the tears of strangers watered her grave."

One would only wish to add to this : She "loved, not wisely, but too well."

Part Fifth.

MARBLEHEAD LEGENDS.

ENDICOTT'S SUN-DIAL; DESIGNS FROM OLD MONEY.

MARBLEHEAD: THE TOWN.

NEXT to Swampscott comes Marblehead. Quaintest and most dilapidated of seaports, one can hardly knock at any door without encountering a legend or a history. Indeed that idea comes uppermost on looking around you. Yet the atmosphere is not oppressive, nor are the suggestions ghostly. Far otherwise ; you are simply on the tiptoe of expectation.

Thanks to fortuitous causes, Marblehead retains more of the characteristic flavor of the past than any town in New England. And here one can revel in its memories unchecked, seeing so little to remind him of the present. Look at the great body of old houses still composing it ! There is no mistaking the era to which they belong. Once among them, one takes a long stride backward into another century, and is even doubtful if he should stop there. They are as antiquated as the garments our great-grandfathers wore, and as little in accord with modern ideas ; and yet they were very comfortable dwellings in their day, and have even now a home-like look of solid, though unpretending, thrift. They in fact indicate a republic of equality, if not one of high social or intellectual refinement. We expect to see sailors in pigtails, citizens in periwigs, and women in kerchiefs and hobnail shoes, all speaking an unintelligible jargon, and all laying violent

tongues on the King's English. We are conscious of a certain in-
congruity between ourselves and this democracy, which is not at
all disagreeable to us, nor disparaging to that.

They have covered a bare and uncouth cluster of gray ledges
with houses, and called it Marblehead. These ledges stick out
everywhere; there is not enough soil to cover them decently.
The original gullies intersecting these ledges were turned into
thoroughfares, which meander about after a most lawless and
inscrutable fashion. The principal graveyard is situated on the
top of a rocky hill, where the dead mariners might lie within
sound of the sea they loved so well. And we learn that it was
chosen because it was a "sightly place." But in general the
dead fare no better than the living, they being tucked away in
odd corners, here on a hill-top, there in a hollow, the headstones
seeming always a part of the ledges above which they rise in
straggling groups, stark, gray, and bent with age, intensifying
a thousand-fold the pervading feeling of sadness and loneliness
associated with such places.

One street carries us along with the present; the other whisks
us back into the past again. We dive into a lane, and bring up
in a blind alley without egress. Does any one know the way
here, we question? We see a crooked crack separating rows of
houses, and then read on a signboard that it is such or such a
street. In an hour we look upon the whole topography of the
place as a jest.

Now and then the mansion of some Colonial nabob — perhaps
a colonel or a magistrate — has secured for itself a little breathing space; but in general the houses crowd upon and elbow each
other in "most admired disorder." The wonder is that they
built here at all, the site was so unpromising; but the harbor was
good, there was room to dry fish, and the sailor-settlers looked
upon the sea, and not the shore, as being their home. So that
Allerton's rough fellows, who in 1633 made their rude cabins on
the harbor's edge, were not looking for farms, but for codfish.

After looking over the town a while, one comes to the conclusion that the first-comers must have tossed up coppers — always

a favorite pastime here — for the choice of building-lots, and
then have made their selection regardless of surveyor's lines.
As a consequence, Marblehead is picturesque, but bewildering.
It has a placid little harbor, indented by miniature coves, lighted
by a diminutive lighthouse, and defended by a dismantled fortress without a garrison.   Blindfold a stranger, bring him to
Marblehead, and then remove the bandage, and he would certainly exclaim, "This is in the Orkneys, or the Hebrides!"

This is what a glance reveals. We have said that nearly
every dwelling has its story.   It is probable that no other
spot of ground in the Colonies was so peculiarly adapted to
the growth of the marvellous as this.   The men, and the boys
too, as soon as they were able to handle an oar, followed the sea,
while the women did most of the shore work, taking care of
and curing the fish, as they do to-day in Newfoundland.   So
that in the fishing season the place was nearly as destitute of
men as the fabulous island that good old Peter Martyr tells about
in his wonderful "Decades."   That good and true man, the Reverend John Barnard, the patriarch and good genius of the place,
tells us that when he first went to Marblehead there was no such
thing as a proper carpenter, or mason, or tailor, or butcher in
the place ; all were fishermen.   And this was seventy or eighty
years after settlement began here.   For half a century there
was no settled minister ; and for about the same term of years
no schoolmaster.   To this day no one knows the antecedents
of these fishermen, or from whence they came.   Certain it is
that they were no part of the Puritan emigration around them ;
for all accounts agree in styling them a rude, ignorant, lawless,
and profligate set, squandering with habitual recklessness the
gains of each hazardous voyage.   Notorious pirates openly walked
the streets ; smuggling was carried on like any legitimate occupation.   In a word, a community going back to as early a day
as any here had grown up in the same way that the fishing-
stations of Newfoundland were gradually turned into permanent
settlements, having almost no law and even less religion, until a
missionary appeared in the person of the Reverend John Barnard.

The history then changes. In respect to public and private morals, Marblehead was really a little Newfoundland ; and it is more than probable, everything being considered, that its settlement may be legitimately referred to this island, — the home of a strictly seafaring and sea-subsisting people, living half of the time afloat, and half on shore.

As for the women, when we read that on a certain Sabbath-day two hostile Indians, then held as prisoners in the town, were " by the women of Marblehead, as they came out of the meeting-house," tumultuously set upon and very barbarously murdered, one easily imagines what the men were like, — and the children too, of whom it is soberly said that they were as profane as their fathers. When a stranger appeared in the streets they were in the habit of pelting him with stones. All this prepares us for the appearance of John and Mary Dimond as the legitimate outgrowth of such a place, and for those singular customs, and the still more singular speech, which two centuries could not wholly eradicate. Marblehead, it is quite clear, was neither part nor parcel of the Puritan Commonwealth in any strict sense of the term. It was and is unique.

Apropos of this state of society, although they may put the reader's credulity to a harder test than is usual, let us give one or two examples of olden superstition, in order to place him more or less in accord with the spirit of the times to which our poets and our novelists have given so much attention. It will readily be seen that there is little need to have recourse to the imagination ; truth is indeed stranger than fiction.

The belief that it is a good omen to see the new moon over one's right shoulder is still universal. Yet this is merely a relic of ancient superstition, although few, perhaps, would be willing to admit that it had any influence, either direct or indirect, upon their future welfare. But our forefathers thought otherwise. Among the early chronicles of Lynn is one giving an account of " an honest old man " who, " as it began to be darkish," went out to look for the new moon, when he espied in the west a strange black cloud, in which presently appeared a complete

man-at-arms, standing with his legs a little apart, and holding
his pike thrown across his breast in a most martial attitude.
The man then called his wife and others to behold this marvel.
After a while the man in the cloud vanished; but he was immediately succeeded by the apparition of a stately ship under full
sail, although she remained stationary in the heavens. The
black hull, the lofty stern, the brightly gleaming sails, the tapering mast, from which a long resplendent pennon streamed, were
as plainly distinguished as were those of the ships then riding in
the harbor. "This," in the words of the narrative, "was seen
for a great space, both by these and others of ye same town."

The good old English custom of saluting the new moon with
the following propitiatory address, to which the "pale goddess"
was supposed to give ear, —

> All hail to the Moon! all hail to thee !
> I prythee, good Moon, reveal to me
> This night who my husband must be, —

had its counterpart in Marblehead, where, on the nights when a
new moon was to appear, the unmarried young women would
congregate at some houses in the neighborhood for the purpose
of having a peep into futurity ; and after hanging a huge pot of
tallow on the crane over the blazing logs, would then drop, one
by one, iron hob-nails into the boiling fat, in the firm belief that
the young man who should come in while this charm was working would inevitably be the future husband of the fair one who
dropped the nails.

At other times the young woman who had a longing to pry into
the unknown would go to an upper window of the house, and
when no one saw her would throw a ball of yarn into the street,
in the belief that the lucky youth who first picked it up was the
man she would marry. All the terrors of the laws against it could
not prevent women from trying the efficacy of magical art in elucidating the, to them, most interesting of all questions. In those
"good old times" a wedding was a season of unrestrained merry-
making for a whole week together. Little ceremony was used.

Everybody who chose might attend, and when, at a late hour, the guests were ready to depart, the bride and groom being first put to bed, the entire company, regardless of the blushes or screams of the bride, marched round the nuptial couch, throwing old shoes, stockings, and other missiles of established potency in such cases, at the newly wedded couple, by way of bringing them good luck.

"Stories of phantom ships seen at sea before the loss of a vessel, of the appearance on the water of loved ones who had died at home, of footsteps and voices heard mysteriously in the still hours of the night and coming as warnings from another world, of signs and omens which foretold the approaching death of some member of the family, or prophecies whispered by the winds, that those who were away on the mighty deep would find a watery grave," were interwoven with, and allowed to have an active influence upon, the lives of these people.

Such a place would as a matter of course have its part in the "Terror" of 1692, — the fatal witchcraft delusion. The witch of Marblehead was an old crone by the name of Wilmot Redd (or Reed), but more generally known and feared as "Mammy Redd, the witch." This woman was believed to possess the power of malignant touch and sight, and she was able, so it was whispered, to cast a spell over those whom she might in her malevolence wish to injure. To some she sent sickness and death, by merely wishing that a "bloody cleaver" might be found in the cradle of their infant children. Upon others she vented her spite by visiting them with such petty annoyances as occur —

> When brass and pewter hap to stray,
> And linen slinks out of the way;
> When geese and pullen are seduced,
> And sows of sucking pigs are choused;
> When cattle feel indisposition,
> And need the opinion of physician;
> When murrain reigns in hogs or sheep,
> And chickens languish of the pip;
> When yeast and outward means do fail,
> And have no power to work on ale;
> When butter does refuse to come,
> And love proves cross and humorsome.

Among other diabolical arts, —

> Old Mammy Redd,
> Of Marblehead,
> Sweet milk could turn
> To mould in churn.

She could curdle it as it came fresh from the cow's udders, or could presently change it into "blue wool," which we take to be another name for blue mould. She was tried and convicted, chiefly on old wives' gabble, and expiated on the gallows the evil fame that she had acquired.

To this fact of history, in which the actors appear testifying under oath to their own superstitious beliefs, we may now add one of those local legends undoubtedly growing out of the frequent intercourse had with the free rovers of the main. Among these freebooters it was a law, the cruel policy of which is obvious, that every woman who might become their prisoner should suffer death. The legend is perhaps no more than the echo of one of these tragedies.

THE SHRIEKING WOMAN.

IT was said that during the latter part of the seventeenth century, a Spanish ship laden with rich merchandise was captured by pirates, who brought their prize into the Harbor of Marblehead. The crew and every person on board the ill-fated ship had been butchered in cold blood at the time of the capture, except a beautiful English lady, whom the ruffians brought on shore near what is now called Oakum Bay, and there, under cover of the night, most barbarously murdered her. The few fishermen who inhabited the place were then absent, and the women and children who remained, could do nothing to prevent the consummation of the fearful crime. The piercing screams of the victim were most appalling, and her cries of "Lord, save me! Mercy! O Lord Jesus, save me!" were distinctly heard in the silence of the night. The body was buried on the spot where the deed was perpetrated, and for over one hundred and fifty years, on each anniversary of that dreadful tragedy, the heartrending screams of the murdered woman for mercy were repeated in a voice so shrill and unearthly as to freeze the blood of those who heard them.

This legend is so firmly rooted in Marblehead, that Polyphemus himself could not tear it from the soil. Even the most intelligent people have admitted their full belief in it; and one of the most learned jurists of his time, who was native here, and to the manner born, averred that he had heard those ill-omened shrieks again and again in the still hours of the night.

To this local episode the following narrative of piracy in its palmiest days seems the appropriate pendant.

THE STRANGE ADVENTURES OF PHILIP ASHTON.

PHILIP ASHTON was a young Marblehead fisherman, who, with other townsmen of his, was, in the month of June, 1722, quietly pursuing his legitimate calling upon the fishing-grounds lying off Cape Sable. It being Friday, he and his mates hoisted sail and stood in for Port Roseway, meaning to harbor there until the Sabbath was over. When their shallop arrived, late in the afternoon, in this harbor, the fishermen saw lying peaceably among the fleet of fishing craft a strange brigantine, which they supposed

LOW'S FLAG.

to be an inward-bound West Indiaman.

But after the shallop had been at anchor two or three hours, a boat from the brigantine came alongside of her, and her men, jumping upon deck, drew from underneath their clothing the cutlasses and pistols with which they were armed, and with oaths and menaces demanded of the startled fishermen the instant surrender of themselves and their vessel. Having suspected no danger, and being thus taken unawares, these poor fishermen were unable to make the least resistance, and they could only yield themselves up in surprise and terror to their assailants. In this manner the brigantine's crew surprised twelve or thirteen more peaceable fishing-vessels that evening. The prisoners vainly asked themselves what it could all mean.

When Ashton and his comrades were taken on board the brigantine, their worst fears were more than realized upon finding themselves in the power of the red-handed pirate, Ned Low, whose name alone was a terror to all who followed the sea in honest ways, and whose ambition it was to outdo the worst cruelties of his infamous predecessors in crime.

Low presently sent for Ashton to come aft, where the young lad found himself face to face with the redoubtable rover, who, according to the pirates' custom, and in their proper dialect, asked him if he would sign their articles and go along with them as one of the band. To this Ashton returned a firm refusal; he was then without ceremony thrust down into the ship's hold.

On the ensuing Sabbath Ashton with others was again brought before the pirate chief, who this time, in a tone that struck far more terror than the pistol he held cocked in his hand, exclaimed, "Are any of you married men?" Not knowing to what this unexpected question might lead, or what trap might be set for them, the poor fellows were dumb, and they answered not a word; which so incensed the pirate, that he put his pistol to Ashton's head, crying out, "You dog, why don't you answer me?" at the same time swearing vehemently that if he did not instantly tell whether he was or was not married, he would shoot him where he stood. To save his life, Ashton, in as loud a voice as he dared to speak it, answered that he was single ; and so said the rest of his companions.

To their unspeakable dismay they learned that this answer doomed them to the fate from which they were so anxious to escape, it being one of Low's whims not to force any married man into his service. While the greater number of the captive fishermen were therefore released, Ashton was among those who were detained close prisoners on board the pirate ship.

His steady refusal to join them subjected young Ashton to the most brutal treatment at the hands of Low's miscreants, whose continued carousals, mingled with the most hideous blasphemy, converted the pirate ship into a veritable hell afloat.

Low first bent his destructive course towards Newfoundland. But here his first venture nearly proved to be his last ; for having descried a large ship lying in the Harbor of St. John's, he resolved to go in and take her, and so to furnish himself with a larger and a better ship than the one he now commanded. With this intention, after concealing the greater part of his crew below, the pirate stood boldly in towards his expected prey, meaning to run close alongside, and then to carry her by boarding, before his purpose should be suspected. But here his patron fiend served him a good turn at need. For as the buccaneer stealthily drew into the harbor, he met a fishing-boat coming out, and having hailed her, learned to his dismay that the ship he was going to take with his two or three score of cut-throats, was a large man-of-war, capable of blowing him out of the water with a single broadside.

Instead, therefore, of going into the harbor, Low made all the haste he could to put a safe distance between him and the cruiser, lest he should catch a Tartar where he had looked for an easy conquest. He now stretched away farther to the eastward, and entering Conception Bay, put into a small port called Carbonear, where he landed his men, who first sacked and then burned the place to the ground. He next made for the Grand Banks, where, after capturing and plundering seven or eight vessels, he sailed away for St. Michael's in the Azores, taking

with him one of his prizes.   When off this port Low fell in
with and made prize of a large Portuguese pink loaded with
wheat; and finding her to be a good sailer, she was manned and
turned into a piratical craft, flying the skeleton flag that Low
carried at his masthead.

To the Canaries, to the Cape de Verde Islands, to Bonavista,
the freebooter sailed on, leaving the wreck of burned and plundered ships in his track.   Then he ran down the coast of Brazil,
hoping to meet with richer prizes than any he had yet taken;
but from these shores he was driven by the fury of a gale that
nearly proved fatal to him and his fortunes.   Escaping this, the
pirate suddenly appeared in the West Indies; and after burning,
plundering, and sinking to his heart's content, he scoured the
Spanish Main for a while with variable success.

At length, after many perils encountered and escaped, Low's
two vessels entered Roatan Harbor, in the Bay of Honduras, in
order to heave down and clean their bottoms, and to get a sup-
ply of water.   Here at last came the chance which Ashton had
so ardently longed for.

Up to this time the pirates had never allowed him to land
with them.   More than one well-laid plan to escape out of their
clutches had already been thwarted in a way to crush out all
hope for the future.   But he resolutely determined to make one
more effort to gain his freedom; for besides being a lad of sense
and spirit, Ashton was young and vigorous, and ready to confront any danger, however great, that should lie in the way to
his deliverance from the pirate crew.

One morning, as Low's long-boat was passing by Ashton's
vessel, on her way to the watering-place, the lad hailed her, and
entreated to be allowed to go on shore with the men who were
taking the water-casks to be filled.   After some hesitation, the
cooper, who had charge of the boat, took him in, little imagining
that there was any danger of his running away in so desolate and
forbidding a place as this was.   Ashton jumped into the boat.

When they landed, Ashton was at first very active in helping
to get the casks out of the boat.   But by and by he gradually

strolled along the beach, picking up stones and shells, and looking sharply about him in search of a place suitable for his
purpose.

He had got a gunshot off, and had begun to edge up towards
the woods, when the cooper, espying him, called out to know
where he was going. The resolute lad shouted back the reply
that he was seeking for cocoa-nuts ; and pointing to a grove of
stately cocoa-palms growing just in front of him, moved on into
the friendly shelter of the tropical forest. As soon as he had
lost sight of his companions, he bounded away like a wounded
deer into the thick undergrowth, and he ran on until, judging
himself to have gained a safe distance, he threw himself on the
ground in the midst of a dense thicket, and awaited in breathless suspense the issue of his bold dash for liberty.

After the men had filled their casks, and were ready to go on
board, the cooper called to Ashton to come in ; but this being the
last thing this brave lad thought of doing, he made no answer,
although he plainly heard the men's voices in his snug retreat.
At last they began hallooing to him; but he was still silent.
He could hear them say, "The dog is lost in the woods, and
can't find the way out." Then, after shouting again to as little
purpose as before, to Ashton's great joy they put off for their
vessel, leaving him alone on this uninhabited island, with no
other company than his own thoughts, no clothing but a canvas
cap to cover his head, a loose tunic, and trousers to protect his
body, and nothing else besides his two hands to defend himself
from the wild beasts of prey that prowled unmolested about the
hideous thickets around him. He had jumped into the boat
just as he stood, having no time to snatch up even so indispensable a thing as a knife, or a flint and steel to kindle a
fire with. Yet he considered this condition preferable to the
company he had left.

Ashton passed the next five days in watching the pirate
vessels, fearing that Low might send a party in pursuit of him ;
but at the end of that time he saw them hoist sail and put to
sea. Not until then did he breathe freely.

In order to find out in what manner he was to live for the future, Ashton began to range the island over. He saw no evidence of any human habitation, except one walk of lime-trees nearly a mile long, with here and there some fragments of pottery strewed about the place, by which signs he guessed that he had lighted upon some long-deserted residence of the Indians. The island was mountainous, and the mountains were thickly covered with a scrubby black pine, making them almost inaccessible. The valleys abounded with fruit-trees ; but so dense was the tropical undergrowth here, that it was with great difficulty that Ashton could force his way through it, he hav-

ALONE ON THE DESERT ISLAND.

ing neither shoes nor stockings to protect his feet from the sharp thorns that pierced the flesh. There were plenty of cocoanuts to be had for the trouble of picking them up; but as Ashton had no way of breaking the thick husks, this delicious fruit was of no advantage to him. There were also many other sorts of fruits hanging most temptingly within reach of the half-starved Ashton's hand; but not knowing what they were, he dared not touch any of them until he saw the wild hogs freely feeding upon them. And some of them which were really poisonous he often handled, but luckily refrained from eating. He therefore lived for some time upon the grapes, figs, and wild beach-plums that grew abundantly everywhere about him, making such a shelter as he could from the copious night-dews that fell, by leaning some fallen branches against a tree-trunk, and then covering this rude framework with a thatch of palmetto-leaves. In time he built many of these huts in different parts of his island.

There were also upon this island, and upon the islands adjacent to it, wild deer and hogs. The woods and waters abounded too with duck, teal, curlew, pelicans, boobies, pigeons, parrots, and other birds fit to be eaten. The seas teemed with fish and the shores with tortoises. But notwithstanding his mouth often watered for a bit of them, Ashton was able to make no use whatever of all this store of beast, fish, and fowl, for want of a knife and a fire. So in the midst of plenty he was reduced even lower than the savage, — who can at least always make for himself weapons to kill and fire to dress his food.

For nine solitary months Philip Ashton lived alone on this island without seeing one human being. The parrots had not learned to talk, so that, compelled as he was to keep silence, he sometimes feared that he might lose the power of speech, or forget the sound of his own voice. To escape from the mosquitoes, black-flies, and other insect pests which made his life intolerable to him, Ashton formed the habit of swimming over a narrow channel that separated his island from one of the low-lying keys, where he mostly spent his days. In one of these journeys he narrowly escaped being devoured by a shark, which struck him just as he reached the shallow water of the shore. This key also gave him a broader and a clearer sea-view; for it may well be imagined that never during his waking hours did he intermit his weary watch for a friendly sail. Sometimes he sat with his back against a tree, and his face to the sea, for a whole day, without stirring from the spot.

Weakened by exposure and the want of proper food, unable longer to drag his torn and wounded limbs about the island, Ashton at last sickened; and as his helplessness increased, the prospect of a horrible death stared him in the face. As the days and nights wore away, he fell into a deadly stupor. In this extremity he one day espied a canoe, with one man in it, coming towards him. When he was near enough, Ashton feebly called out to him. After some hesitation the man landed. He proved to be an Englishman who, to save his life, had fled from the Spanish settlements. For three days Ashton had the unspeakable pleasure of a companion in his misery; but at the end of this brief time his solitary visitor, having left him to go upon a hunting excursion among the islands, was drowned in a squall, leaving the hermit again alone in his wretchedness and anguish of body and mind. His condition was, however, somewhat improved; for thanks to his late companion he now had a knife, a little pork, some gunpowder, and a flint, and so the means of making a fire, which was to him the greatest of luxuries.

Between two and three months after he had lost his companion, Ashton, in one of his rambles, found a small canoe stranded upon the shore. This enabled him to extend his excursions among the islands, and in this way gave promise of an escape to some of the distant settlements.

How he made a voyage to the Island of Bonacco, and while asleep was discovered and fired upon by a party of Spaniards; how he made his escape from them, finally reaching his old quarters at Roatan, — are events that we have no time to dwell upon. That he had found civilized beings more cruel than the wild beasts — for these had not harmed him — was a lesson that made him more wary about extending his explorations too far in the future.

Some time after this adventure Ashton again saw canoes approaching his place of refuge. The smoke of his fire had drawn them in towards the shore. Ashton then showed himself

on the beach. The canoes came to a standstill. Then the
parties hailed each other, and after mutual explanations, one
man ventured to come to the shore. When he saw the forlorn
and miserable object of his fear, he stood in speechless amazement; but at length the two men fell to embracing each other,
and then the stranger, taking the emaciated body of Ashton in
his arms, carried him to the canoes, where the others received
him kindly and made him welcome among them.

Ashton told them his story. The strangers then informed
him that they were from the Bay of Honduras, whence, however, they had been forced to fly, in order to escape from the
fury of the Spaniards. With them Ashton lived in comparative
ease, until his old enemies, the pirates, discovered and made a
descent upon them in their chosen retreat. Ashton's dread of
again falling into their hands may be easily conceived. He with
two or three others succeeded, however, in making good their
escape into the woods. The rest were captured and taken on
board the same vessel in which Ashton had served his appren-
ticeship as a pirate.

Two or three months more passed. Ashton with his companions had got over to the Island of Bonacco again. A gale
such as is only known in the tropic seas arose, and blew with
great violence for three days. To Ashton this proved indeed a
friendly gale, for when it had subsided he descried several vessels standing in for the island. Presently one of them anchored
near the shore, and sent in her boat for water. This vessel
proved to be a brigantine belonging to Salem, and in her Ashton
took passage for home, where he safely arrived on the 1st of
May, 1725, it then being two years and two months since he
had escaped from the pirate ship.

AGNES, THE MAID OF THE INN.

THIS pretty story, a romance of real life, makes us acquainted with two noble, but impulsive natures, whose destinies first became interwoven in a way quite the reverse of the romantic. After perusing it, as one is pretty sure to do, from beginning to end, one is very apt to think that this poor Marblehead maiden, this outcast, if you will, whose great love, finally triumphing over pride, prejudice, suffering, cruel scorn, and every other moral impediment that the world puts in the way of duty, really confers honor upon the noble knight who at last gives her his name, by awakening in him truly ennobling and elevating sentiments. In such a life as that of Agnes one cannot help seeing a design. Without her Sir Henry was a mere votary of pleasure, a man of the world. She really made a man of him at last. But to our tale.

In the summer of 1742 the course of official duty called the Collector of Boston to Marblehead. The incumbent of this office, which had been established with much opposition in the Colonial capital, and was little respected outside of it, was then Henry Frankland, of Mattersea, in Nottinghamshire, who was also connected with one of the greatest families in the North, and who was the heir presumptive to a baronetcy. This young man, who at the early age of twenty-six had come into the possession both of a fortune and of a highly lucrative and honorable appointment, was now in the pursuit of a career. With rank, wealth, and high social position as his birthright, with rare personal attractions, and with the endowments which all these had brought to his aid, Henry Frankland's future bid fair to become unusually dazzling and brilliant.

Marblehead being at this period of her history the smuggling port for Boston, it is quite probable that the Collector's visit, though referred to other causes, looked to the repression of this contraband trade, by which the King's revenues were every day defrauded, and the laws of the realm more or less openly violated.

Henry Frankland, having alighted at the Fountain Inn, found an unexpected obstacle in his path.

This was a young and remarkably beautiful girl, who was busily engaged in scrubbing the floor when he entered, and who, we are willing to affirm, found the time to dart an investigating and appreciative glance at the handsome

LOVE AT FIRST SIGHT.

young guest, to whom her own mean garb and menial occupation offered the strongest possible contrast. Struck with the rare beauty of her face and person, the young man stopped to look and to admire. His was the pride of birth and station; hers the submissive deference that the poor and lowly paid to its arrogant demands. He was booted and spurred, and wore his laced beaver; she bareheaded and barefooted, and upon her knees. He had the unmistakable air of distinction and breeding of his class; she was scrubbing the floor.

The young man called her to him, put some questions negligently, and then, pleased with her answers, dropped a piece of silver into her hand and passed on. He had seen a pretty serving-maid who told him that she was called Agnes — Agnes Surriage.

Later on, a second visit to the inn showed him the same charming picture, even to the minutest details. Agnes was still doing the drudgery of the inn without shoes or stockings to cover her little feet.

When the baronet asked why she had not bought them with the money he had given her, she naïvely answered that she had indeed done so, but that she kept them to wear in meeting. Perhaps this elegant young man had unwittingly awakened in her breast, like Eve in Adam, the knowledge that was to give a new direction to her life, — the painful discovery of a deficiency of which she had before been calmly unconscious. Perhaps something gave her the courage to measure the distance between them. We do not know. Had Agnes been plain as well as poor, he might have passed her by without noticing that her feet were bare or her dress scanty. Her beauty exacted this homage, which he would have called his condescension.

Just what was Sir Henry's first design, or what the workings of his mind, do not at this moment clearly appear; perhaps, proceeding from impulse, they were only half formed at best; but be that as it may, his growing interest in Agnes presently led him to seek an interview with her parents, who were poor and worthy people, living in the town, and to propose removing their daughter to his own home, in order — Jesuit that he was! — to give her the advantages to which her graces of mind and person, as he warmly protested, fully entitled her. The parents acceded only too readily to the seductive proposal. They could see no danger; not they! Agnes left her own humble home for that of Sir Henry; and so this girl of sixteen became the ward of this grave young gentlemen of twenty-six. But, ignorant as she was, and humble and artless, it is easy to believe that she had already taught him something he was in no haste to unlearn.

Agnes did ample justice to her guardian's high opinion of her mental qualifications. The virgin soil is deep and productive. She was taught the commoner branches, as well as the accomplishments then deemed indispensably requisite to the education of a gentlewoman moving in her adopted sphere. As her mind expanded, so, like the rose, did her beauty become more and more radiant with the consciousness of the new life opening to her. She was a being created to love and be loved. Her gratitude, her confidence, her admiration were all centred upon one object. One day she awoke to the knowledge that she was beloved, and that she loved.

By the death of his uncle, the baronetcy that was hereditary in the Yorkshire branch of the Franklands devolved upon Agnes' guardian, who, having now legitimately inherited it, publicly assumed the title.

The discovery to which we have referred had its usual consequences. Sir Henry Frankland, Baronet, could not dream of laying his noble name at the feet of a serving-maid; not he. His horror of a misalliance was even greater than his abhorrence of a different and a more equivocal connection. But he could not give her up. We will let the veil fall upon the weakness of both of these lovers. He was her idol, she his infatuation; he loved like a man, and she like a woman.

Sir Henry's conduct in openly living with his lovely ward outside of the pale of matrimony being whispered about, was an offence too flagrant for the stern morality of the city of the Puritans to endure; and its indignation was soon made manifest in a way to cut a proud and sensitive nature to the quick. Society he found has its weapons, and can use them, too, without mercy. Society could not justify his leading the girl astray; but it would have forgiven him now, had he chosen to desert her. Boston was no longer a place for Agnes or for him; so that no sooner was he established in his Eden, than an inexorable voice drove him forth. He purchased an estate and built an elegant mansion in the pleasant and secluded inland village of Hopkinton, to which he conveyed Agnes, and with her took up his residence there. While they lived here, the hospitality and luxury of the great house, and the beauty of Sir Henry's mysterious companion, were the prolific theme in all the country round. Sir Henry loved the good old English fashion, devoting himself more or less to the care and embellishment of his estate with the English gentleman's hereditary taste and method. His devotion to Agnes appears to have suffered no diminution; and when at length he was compelled at the call of urgent affairs to visit England, she accompanied him. It is said that he even had the hardihood to introduce her among his aristocratic relatives as Lady Frankland; and if he did so, Sir Henry must have grown bold indeed. But that ill-advised proceeding met with the decisive repulse it certainly deserved. Throughout all this singular history shines the one ray of hope for Agnes. Except in name, the lovers held true and unswerving faith to and in each other as fully and completely as if they had been actual man and wife.

But we must hasten on. Sir Henry's affairs calling him to Lisbon, Agnes went with him. While they were sojourning in the Portuguese capital, the dreadful earthquake of 1755 laid the city in ruins. Under these ruins sixty thousand of the miserable inhabitants were buried; the rest fled in terror. The carriage in which Sir Henry happened to be riding was crushed by falling walls, and buried underneath the rubbish. Agnes had remained behind, and to this accident she owed her escape. Running into the street at the first alarm, she indeed avoided the horrible death which had swallowed up multitudes around her; but who can tell the anguish of her soul in that moment? She was, indeed, saved; but where was her lord and protector? Frantic and despairing, but faithful to death, she followed such faint traces as in the confusion of that hour could be obtained, until chance at length led her to the spot where he lay, helpless and overwhelmed.   A fine lady would have recoiled and fainted dead away ; Agnes Surriage, again the working girl of Marble-head, instantly set to work to rescue her lover from the ruins with her own hands.   In an hour he was extricated from the rubbish.   He was still living.   She conveyed him to a place that had escaped the shock of the earthquake, where she nursed him into health and strength again.   Vanquished by this last supreme proof of her love for him, the knight gave her his hand in return for his life.   And who can doubt that with this act there came back to both that peace of mind which alone was wanting to a perfect union of two noble and loving hearts ?

We are obliged to content ourselves with the following extracts from the poem which Holmes has founded upon the story : —

A scampering at the Fountain Inn ;
    A rush of great and small ;
With hurrying servants' mingled din,
    And screaming matron's call !

Poor Agnes ! with her work half done,
    They caught her unaware,
As, humbly, like a praying nun,
    She knelt upon the stair ;

Bent o'er the steps, with lowliest mien
    She knelt, but not to pray, —
Her little hands must keep them clean,
    And wash their stains away.

A foot, an ankle, bare and white,
    Her girlish shapes betrayed, —
"Ha ! Nymphs and Graces !" spoke the Knight ;
    "Look up, my beauteous Maid ! "

She turned, — a reddening rose in bud,
    Its calyx half withdrawn ;
Her cheek on fire with damasked blood
    Of girlhood's glowing dawn !

He searched her features through and through,
    As royal lovers look
On lowly maidens when they woo
    Without the ring and book.

"Come hither, Fair one! Here, my Sweet!
    Nay, prithee, look not down!
Take this to shoe those little feet," —
    He tossed a silver crown.

A sudden paleness struck her brow, —
    A swifter flush succeeds;
It burns her cheek; it kindles now
    Beneath her golden beads.

She flitted; but the glittering eye
    Still sought the lovely face.
Who was she? What, and whence? and why
    Doomed to such menial place?

A skipper's daughter, — so they said, —
    Left orphan by the gale
That cost the fleet of Marblehead
    And Gloucester thirty sail.

SKIPPER IRESON'S RIDE.

ONE of the most spirited of Whittier's home ballads — certainly the most famous — is his "Skipper Ireson's Ride," which introduces by way of refrain the archaic Marblehead dialect that is now nearly, if not quite, extinct. Like most of this poet's characters, Skipper Ireson is a real personage, whose story, briefly told, is this : —

Late in the autumn of the year 1808 the schooner "Betsy," of Marblehead, Benjamin Ireson, master, while buffeting its way towards the home port in the teeth of a tremendous gale, fell in with a wreck drifting at the mercy of the winds and waves.

This was the schooner " Active," of Portland, that had been over-
set in the gale.   It was then midnight, with a tremendous sea
running.   The skipper of the sinking vessel hailed the "Betsy"
and asked to be taken off the wreck, from which every wave
indeed threatened to wash the distressed and exhausted crew.
To this it is said that the " Betsy's " crew — one does not like to
traduce the name by calling them sailors — strongly demurred,
alleging the danger of making the attempt in such a sea in support of their cowardly purpose to abandon the sinking craft to
her fate.   Some say that Captain Ireson was himself disposed to
act with humanity, and to lie by the wreck until daylight, but
that he was overruled by the unanimous voice of his men, who
selfishly decided not to risk their own miserable lives in order to
save others.   The " Betsy's " course was accordingly shaped for
Marblehead, where she arrived on the following Sunday.   Her
crew at once spread the news through the town of their having
fallen in with a vessel foundering in the bay, when, to their
honor, the Marblehead people immediately despatched two
vessels to her relief.   But the "Active" had then gone to the bottom of the sea, and the relieving vessels returned from a fruitless search, only to increase the resentment already felt against
Skipper Ireson, upon whom his crew had thrown all the blame
of their own dastardly conduct.   Usually dead men tell no tales;
but it so fell out that in this instance a more damning evidence
to Ireson's inhumanity appeared, as it were, from the grave
itself to confront him.   It happened that on the morning next
following the night of the " Betsy's " desertion of them, the
captain and three others were rescued from the sinking vessel.
They soon made public the story of the cruel conduct of the
" Betsy's " people ; and as ill news travels fast, it was not long
before it reached Marblehead, throwing that excitable town into a
hubbub over the aspersions thus cast upon its good name.   It
was soon determined to take exemplary vengeance upon the
offender.   One bright moonlight night Skipper Ireson heard a
knock at his door.   Upon opening it he found himself in the
nervous grasp of a band of resolute men, who silently hurried

him off into a deserted place, — with what object, his fears alone
could divine. They first securely pinioned and then besmeared
him from head to foot with a coat of tar and feathers. In the
morning the whole population of the town turned out to witness or assist in this ignominious punishment, which had been
planned by some of the bolder spirits, and silently approved by
the more timid ones. Ireson in his filthy disguise was seated in
the bottom of a dory, — instead of a cart, — and, surrounded
by a hooting rabble, the unfortunate skipper was then dragged
through the streets of the town as far as the Salem boundary-
line, where the crowd was met and stopped by the selectmen of
that town, who forbid their proceeding farther, — thus frustrating
the original purpose to drag Ireson through the streets of Salem
and of Beverly, as well as those of Marblehead. During Ireson's
rough ride, the bottom of the dory had fallen out. The mob
then procured a cart, and lifting the boat, culprit and all, upon
it, in this way Ireson was taken back to Marblehead. More
dead than alive, he was at last released from the hands of his
tormentors and allowed to go home. When he was free, Ireson
quietly said to them : " I thank you, gentlemen, for my ride ; but
you will live to regret it." And thus ended Benjamin Ireson's
shameful expiation of a shameful deed.

Using the facts as they came to him, and with the sanction of
what was in its own time very generally applauded as the
righteous judgment of the people of Marblehead, the poet has
put Ireson in a perpetual pillory, from which no sober second
thought is able to rescue him. But whether culpable or not
culpable in intention, his weakness in yielding to his dastard
crew, if in fact he did so yield, amounted to a grave fault, closely
verging upon the criminal. To-day everybody defends Ireson's
memory from the charge which was once as universally believed
to be true ; and the public verdict was, "served him right."
Unfortunately, however, for him, his exasperated townsfolk executed justice on the spot, according to their own rude notions of
it, before their wrath had had time to grow cool. But to this
fact we owe the most idiosyncratic ballad of purely home origin

in the language, although it is one for which the people of Marblehead have never forgiven the poet.

With poetic instinct Whittier seized upon the incident, using more or less freedom in presenting its dramatic side. In the versified story we are made lookers on while the strange procession, counting its

> Scores of women, old and young,
> Strong of muscle, and glib of tongue,
>
> .   .   .   .   .
>
> Wrinkled scolds, with hands on hips,
> Girls in bloom of cheek and lips,
> Wild-eyed, free-limbed, such as chase
> Bacchus round some antique vase,
> Brief of skirt, with ankles bare,
> Loose of kerchief and loose of hair,
> With conch-shells blowing and fish-horns' twang, —

goes surging on through the narrow streets, now echoing to the wild refrain, —

> "Here's Flud Oirson, for his horrd horrt,
> Torr'd an' futherr'd an' corr'd in a corrt
> By the women o' Morble'ead!"

The only liberty that the poet has taken with the story is in saying, —

> Small pity for him! — He had sailed away
> From a leaking ship, in Chaleur Bay, —
> Sailed away from a sinking wreck,
> With his own town's-people on her deck!

The disaster really happened off the Highlands of Cape Cod, and, so far as is known, there were no Marblehead people on board of the unlucky craft when she went down. But in truth such trifling departures from the literal facts are of little moment. The world long ago granted to the poets complete absolution for such venial sins as these are, seeing that since the days of Homer it has been their profession to give all possible enlargement to their subjects.

Assuming the stigma upon Ireson's memory to be an unjust one, the antidote should accompany the poison. His reputation has found a vigorous defender in the verses which follow.

A PLEA FOR FLOOD IRESON.

CHARLES T. BROOKS.

OLD Flood Ireson ! all too long
Have jeer and jibe and ribald song
Done thy memory cruel wrong.
. . . . .

Old Flood Ireson sleeps in his grave ;
Howls of a mad mob, worse than the wave,
Now no more in his ear shall rave !
. . . . .

Gone is the pack and gone the prey,
Yet old Flood Ireson's ghost to-day
Is hunted still down Time's highway.

Old wife Fame, with a fish-horn's blare
Hooting and tooting the same old air,
Drags him along the old thoroughfare.

Mocked evermore with the old refrain,
Skilfully wrought to a tuneful strain,
Jingling and jolting, he comes again

Over that road of old renown,
Fair broad avenue leading down
Through South Fields to Salem town,

Scourged and stung by the Muse's thong,
Mounted high on the car of song,
Sight that cries, O Lord ! how long

Shall Heaven look on and not take part
With the poor old man and his fluttering heart,
Tarred and feathered and carried in a cart ?

Old Flood Ireson, now when Fame
Wipes away with tears of shame
Stains from many an injured name,

Shall not, in the tuneful line,
Beams of truth and mercy shine
Through the clouds that darken thine ?

Part Sixth.

CAPE ANN LEGENDS.

CAPE ANN.

BY command of Nature, one of those iron-ribbed ridges which it astounds us to see forests growing and people living upon, detaches itself from the Essex coast, and advances steadily five leagues out into the sea. Halting there, it covers its head with a bristling array of rocky islands and jagged reefs, which, like skirmishers in the front of battle, now here, now there, announce their presence in the offing by puffs of water smoke. An incessant combat rages between these rocks and the advancing ocean. From the Highlands, at the land's end, it is possible on a clear day to make out the dim

THE MAGNOLIA.

white streak of Cape Cod stretching its emaciated arm from the south coast towards this half-extended and rock-gauntleted one from the north. Between the two capes, which really seem to belong to different zones, is the entrance to the grand basin of Massachusetts Bay, over which, in the darkness, the brilliant rays from Thacher's and Highland lighthouses cross each other like flaming sword-blades. Among the thousands that have passed in or out, one seeks in his memory for only one little bark carrying an entire nation. The "Mayflower" passed here.

The sea, we notice, welcomes the intruding headland with in-hospitable arms; but at the extreme point, where the rock is pierced and the sea flows in, there is a port of refuge that has grown to be the greatest fishing-mart in the Union. At nearly all times, without regard to season, the waters around it are covered with a flight of sails entering or leaving the principal port, reminding one of the restless sea-gulls that circle about their rocky aerie when bringing food to their young.

The muscular shoulder of the Cape is occupied by the towns of Beverly, Wenham, and Hamilton, the central portion by Manchester and Essex, and the extremity by Gloucester and Rockport. Nearly the whole interior region remains the same untamed wilderness that it was a hundred years ago; for among these rugged hills there is little land that is fit for farming, and that little is found in the hollows, or bordering upon occasional arms of the sea. There are, however, extensive and valuable forests of pine and cedar covering scattered portions with a per-ennial green. The sea having peopled it, and the land offering nothing better than stones, timber, and fuel, the fishing-villages were built close to the edge of the shore, where there were nat-ural harbors like that of Gloucester, or upon tidal creeks or inlets like those of Manchester and Annisquam. From these villages sprang a hardy race of sailors renowned in song and story. Cooper's "Captain Barnstable" comes from Chebacco, a precinct of Essex; Miss Larcom's "Skipper Ben" from Beverly. One does not think of these people as having any fixed relation with the land: they are amphibious.

Its general and apparently irreclaimable sterility drove the earliest settlers back upon the mainland. They therefore aban-doned their rude cabins and their fishing-stages at the extreme end of the Cape, and newly began at what was later on called Salem, which at first included the whole Cape. Yet notwith-standing this desertion, settlements were soon begun at Beverly and Manchester, and Gloucester was permanently re-occupied on account of the excellence and advantageous position of its har-bor. But for a time these settlements were very humble ones.

Roger Conant says that in his time Beverly was nicknamed "Beggarly." He wished to have it changed to Budleigh, from a town in Devonshire, England. Conant should find a name somewhere on Cape Ann. That would at least lead to the inquiry "Who was Conant?" He remarks that he had no hand in naming Salem, where he had built the first house. Nor was Blackstone, the first white settler of Boston, or Roger Williams, who founded Providence, more fortunate in securing posthumous remembrance.

Bayard Taylor was nevertheless extremely taken with the picturesqueness of the interior of Cape Ann, and he was a traveller who had grown something fastidious in his notions of natural scenery. He speaks of it thus, —

"A great charm of the place is the wild wooded scenery of the inland. There are many little valleys, branching and winding as if at random, where the forests of fir and pine, the great, mossy bowlders, the shade and coolness and silence, seem to transfer you at once to the heart of some mountain wilderness. The noise of the sea does not invade them ; even the salt odor of the air is smothered by the warm, resinous breath of the pines. Here you find slender brooks, pools spangled with pond-lily blossoms, and marshes all in a tangle with wild flowers. After two or three miles of such scenery there is no greater surprise than to find suddenly a blue far deeper than that of the sky between the tree trunks, and to hear the roar of the breakers a hundred feet below you."

While exploring the coast one finds it continually shifting from beaches of hard sand, strewn with a fine dark gravel, to picturesque coves bordered all around with rocks shattered into colossal fragments, and bulging out like masses that have suddenly cooled, rusted by spray, worn to glassy smoothness, yet all split and fractured and upheaved by the powerful blows dealt them by the waves. These coves make the most charming summer retreats imaginable ; and some of them, like Old Kettle Cove, — which under the name of Magnolia has a sweeter sound, — and Pigeon Cove, have turned their primitive solitudes into populousness, and their once worthless rocks into pedestals for the scores of beautiful villas that have sprung up like the work of magic upon their bald and overhanging brows.

In one place, say that you leave the road in order to walk over a smooth esplanade of sand, up whose gentle slope panting wave chases panting wave unceasingly, while the forest-trees skirting the head of the beach bend over and watch this fierce play, with all their leaves trembling. You look off over the ridged and sparkling sea-foam into the open mouth of Marble-head Harbor, whose iron headlands the distance softens to forms of wax. Two or three treeless islands, behind which a passing vessel lifts its snowy sails, are luxuriously dozing in the sun and sea. This must be the haven where the fleet of Win-throp first furled its tattered sails after a tempestuous voyage across the Atlantic of more than two months. Yes, there is Baker's Isle, and there is Little Isle, within which it anchored. Then it was here that the colonists, of whom he was the Moses, first set foot upon the soil of their Promised Land; and it was here they roamed among the rocky pastures, gathering wild strawberries and roses, examining everything with eager curi-osity, and perhaps with doubt whether it was all real, and would not vanish with the night.

From the domain of History we enter that of Poetry over the threshold of Nature.

Not many years ago, while he was the guest of the genial and gifted Fields, whose cottage is the conspicuous object on the bald brow of Thunderbolt Hill, in Manchester, Bayard Taylor was taken to visit, in his chosen and secluded retreat, the venerable poet who dated before Byron, Shelley, and Keats, and who dis-covered the genius of Bryant. The host and his guests are now dead; but the poet traveller, obeying the habit of a lifetime, jotted down some minutes of his visit, now serving to recall the man and the scene to our remembrance. He says : —

"Retracing our way a mile or so, we took a different road, and approached the coast through open, grassy fields, beyond which, on the edge of a lofty bluff, stood the gray old mansion of the venerable poet, Richard H. Dana. The place is singularly wild, lonely, and picturesque. No other dwelling is visible. A little bight of the coast thrusts out its iron headlands at a short distance on either side ; the surf thunders incessantly below ; and in front the open ocean stretches to the sky. Mr. Dana's only neighbors are the vessels that come and go at greater or less distances."

From this seclusion the Nestor of American poetry thus addresses the scene before him, in his lines to the ocean.

> Now stretch your eye off shore, o'er waters made
> To cleanse the air and bear the world's great trade,
> To rise, and wet the mountains near the sun,
> Then back into themselves in rivers run,
> Fulfilling mighty uses far and wide,
> Through earth, in air, or here, as ocean tide.
>
> Ho ! how the giant heaves himself and strains
> And flings to break his strong and viewless chains ;
> Foams in his wrath ; and at his prison doors,
> Hark ! hear him ! how he beats and tugs and roars,
> As if he would break forth again and sweep
> Each living thing within his lowest deep.
>
> .   .   .   .   .
>
> And though the land is thronged again, O sea !
> Strange sadness touches all that goes with thee.
> The small bird's plaining note, the wild, sharp call,
> Share thy own spirit : it is sadness all !
> How dark and stern upon thy waves looks down
> Yonder tall cliff — he with the iron crown.
> And see ! those sable pines along the steep
> Are come to join thy requiem, gloomy deep !
> Like stoléd monks they stand and chant the dirge
> Over the dead with thy low-beating surge.

As we approach the end of the Cape we enter a storied region. Here is the deep cleft known as Rafe's Chasm, and the tawny clump of stark ledges which the coast throws off and the sea flies incessantly at, called Norman's Woe. Then we enter the beautiful islet-studded harbor of Gloucester, and with an interest that the natural beauties of the spot enhance, we fix our eyes upon the verdurous southern shore ; for here the little colony of Roger Conant, the pioneer governor, maintained a struggling existence, until, like a garrison which can no longer hold out, it fell back to Salem, newly chose its ground, and again bravely confronted its old enemies, want and neglect. But long before him, this cape in the sea picked up many adventurous *voyageurs*, one of whom presently demands a word from us.

In the heart of the Gloucester woodlands a most interesting floral phenomenon exists. There, apparently defying nature's lines and laws, the beautiful magnolia of the South unfolds in secret its snowy flowers and exhales its spicy perfume. Another phenomenon is the beach at Manchester, whose sands emit weird musical tones when crushed by the passage of wheels through them. Still another is the enormous Moving Rock at Squam Common, — a heavy mass of granite so exactly poised that the pressure of a child's finger is sufficient to change its position.

This sterile sea-cape may also lay claim to other and more enduring associations than the memories of a summer passed among its rocky sea-nooks can afford. Beverly was the home of Robert Rantoul, whose epitaph has been written by Whittier, and of Lucy Larcom ; Hamilton that of Abigail Dodge ; Essex, of Rufus Choate ; Gloucester, of E. P. Whipple and William Winter. Manchester was Dana's by adoption, as well as the summer haunt of Holmes, James and Annie Fields, Elizabeth Phelps, and of that ancient landmark of the Boston Pulpit, the Reverend Dr. Bartol. The lamented Dr. E. H. Chapin loved his summer home at Pigeon Cove ; and it was there he sought relief from the haunting " demon of the study." This was also the favorite haunt of Bryant and of Starr King ; so that among those who were either native or who were habitually sojourners are many of the men and women most eminent in our literary annals. That fact of itself speaks volumes for the Cape.

The legends of Cape Ann are indigenous, and are mostly sea-legends, as might be expected of a seafaring and sea-subsisting population, among whom the marvellous always finds its most congenial soil. Let us add that no longer ago than last winter, in consequence of the prediction that a storm unexampled in the annals of the century was to burst forth with destructive fury over sea and land upon a given day, not a vessel of the Gloucester fishing fleet dared put to sea. Although the great "Wiggins storm" failed to make its appearance at the time predicted, the losses incurred by reason of the number of fishermen lying idly at their moorings amounted to many thousands of dollars. The first of these legends proper to be introduced — not forgetting that De Monts and Champlain had already named this peninsula the Cape of Islands — is a sort of historical complement to our description.

CAPTAIN JOHN SMITH.

THE following lines from Whittier's beautiful apostrophe to his beloved river, "The Merrimack," introducing his collection of legendary pieces, is seen to be commemorative of that prince of explorers and hero of many exploits, Captain John Smith, to whom a perverse fortune has denied any share of honor for his efforts to make New England known and appreciated in the Old World. In the belief that none of these rugged rocks had ever received other baptism than that of the waves, he first gave this promontory the name of "Tragabigzanda" for a perpetual souvenir of a fair Moslem to whom he owed a debt of love and gratitude, while for a memorial of himself he conferred that of the "Three Turks' Heads" upon the three islands, Milk, Thacher's and Straitsmouth, lying off its extreme point, and now crowning it with their triple lights.

But these names were so quickly superseded that the personal ambition of Smith has no other memorial than this : —

On yonder rocky cape, which braves
The stormy challenge of the waves,
Midst tangled vine and dwarfish wood,
The hardy Anglo-Saxon stood,
Planting upon the topmost crag
The staff of England's battle-flag ;

And, while from out its heavy fold
St. George's crimson cross unrolled,
Midst roll of drum and trumpet blare,
And weapons brandishing in air,
He gave to that lone promontory
The sweetest name in all his story ;
Of her, the flower of Islam's daughters,
Whose harems look on Stamboul's waters, —
Who, when the chance of war had bound
The Moslem chain his limbs around,
Wreathed o'er with silk that iron chain,
Soothed with her smiles his hours of pain,
And fondly to her youthful slave
A dearer gift than freedom gave.

THACHER'S ISLAND.

THACHER'S Island is one of the most important light-house stations on the whole coast of the United States. It contains about eighty acres of gravelly soil thickly strewn with coarse granite bowlders, among which the light-keeper's cows crop a scanty growth of grass. The westernmost headland, upon which are some ancient graves, said to be those of the victims of the first recorded shipwreck here, resembles Point Allerton, — it being a lofty cliff of gravel intermixed with bowlders that vary in size, from the smallest pebbles to those weighing many tons. It is continually crumbling away before the wear and tear of the southeast gales.

The light-keeper's residence is a comfortable modern brick building of two stories. There is, or rather was, at the time of the writer's visit to the island, an old stone house standing there that was reputed to be of great age. The two light-towers, built of uncut granite, are each one hundred and fifty feet high, and they are furnished with lenses in which a dozen persons might stand erect without inconvenience. The keepers have all followed the sea. Only sailors are capable of appreciating the responsibility that the station imposes. One of the keepers said to me — and habitual care is stamped upon the faces of these men — "We know how eyes may be strained in thick weather at sea to get hold of the light; and that makes us painfully anxious to keep it up to its full power, especially when frosts or sea-scud dims the lantern ; for that is the very time when minutes count for hours on board ship."

ANTHONY THACHER'S SHIPWRECK.

THE story of how Thacher's Island came by its name is one of tragical interest, and is found in a letter written by Anthony Thacher to his brother Peter, first printed in Increase Mather's " Remarkable Providences." It is also briefly related in Winthrop's " Journal," where it is entered, under the year of its occurrence, 1635, as an incident of the awful tempest that has thus become historical. The historian Hubbard, writing long after the event, says that "the like was never in this place known in the memory of man, before or since." On the land houses were overturned and unroofed, the corn was beaten down to the ground, and the harvest nearly ruined, and thousands of trees were torn up by the roots, broken in two like pipe-stems, or twisted off like withes, so that the effects of it were visible for many years afterwards. At sea its results were no less terrible, the tide rising to twenty feet on some parts of the coast, and being then kept from ebbing in its usual course by the extraordinary violence of the gale. Of the many disasters signalizing its presence, that which the letter relates is a most graphic episode. It would be an injustice to the reader not to present it in all its primitive quaintness of form and style as a specimen literary composition of the day. Here it is: —

I must turn my drowned pen and shaking hand to indite this story of such sad news as never before this happened in New England.

There was a league of perpetual friendship between my cousin Avery and myself, never to forsake each other to the death, but to be partakers of each other's misery or welfare, as also of habitation, in the same place. Now upon our arrival in New England there was an offer made unto us. My cousin Avery was invited to Marblehead to be their pastor in due time ; there being no church planted there as yet, but a town appointed to set up the trade of fishing. Because many there (the most being fishermen) were something loose and remiss in their behavior, my cousin Avery was unwilling to go thither ; and so refusing, we went to Newberry, intending there to sit down. But being solicited so often both by the men of the

THE SHIPWRECK.

place and by the magistrates, and by Mr. Cotton, and most of the ministers, who alleged what a benefit we might be to the people there, and also to the country and commonwealth, at length we embraced it, and thither consented to go. They of Marblehead forthwith sent a pinnace for us and our goods.

We embarked at Ipswich, August 11, 1635, with our families and substance, bound for Marblehead, we being in all twenty-three souls, — viz., eleven in my cousin's family, seven in mine, and one Mr. William Eliot, sometimes of New Sarum, and four mariners. The next morning, having commended ourselves to God, with cheerful hearts we hoisted sail. But the Lord suddenly turned our cheerfulness into mourning and lamentations. For on the 14th of this August, 1635, about ten at night, having a fresh gale of wind, our sails, being old and done, were split. The mariners, because that it was night, would not put to new sails, but resolved to cast anchor till the morning. But before daylight it pleased the Lord to send so mighty a storm, as the like was never known in New England since the English came, nor in the memory of any of the Indians. It was so furious, that our anchor came home. Whereupon the mariners let out more cable, which at last slipped away. Then our sailors knew not what to do ; but we were driven before the wind and waves.

My cousin and I perceived our danger, [and] solemnly recommended ourselves to God, the Lord both of earth and seas, expecting with every wave to be swallowed up and drenched in the deeps. And as my cousin, his wife, and my tender babes sat comforting and cheering one the other in the Lord against ghastly death, which every moment stared us in the face and sat triumphing upon each one's forehead, we were by the violence of the waves and fury of the winds (by the Lord's permission) lifted up upon a rock between two high rocks, yet all was one rock. But it raged with the stroke, which came into the pinnace, so as we were presently up to our middles in water, as we sat. The waves came furiously and violently over us, and against us ; but by reason of the rock's proportion could not lift us off, but beat her all to pieces. Now look with me upon our distress, and consider of my misery, who beheld the ship broken, the water in her and violently overwhelming us, my goods and provisions swimming in the seas, my friends almost drowned, and mine own poor children so untimely (if I may so term it without offence) before mine eyes drowned, and ready to be swallowed up and dashed to pieces against the rocks by the merciless waves, and myself ready to accompany them. But I must go on to an end of this woful relation.

In the same room whereas he sat, the master of the pinnace, not knowing what to do, our foremast was cut down, our mainmast broken in three pieces, the fore part of the pinnace beat away, our goods swimming about the seas, my children bewailing me, as not pitying themselves, and myself bemoaning them, poor souls, whom I had occasioned to such an end in their tender years, whenas they could scarce be sensible of death, — and so likewise my cousin, his wife, and his children ; and both of us bewailing each other in our Lord and only Saviour Jesus Christ, in whom only we had comfort and cheerfulness : insomuch that, from the greatest to the least of us, there was not one screech or outcry made ; but all, as silent sheep, were contentedly resolved to die together lovingly, as since our acquaintance we had lived together friendly.

Now as I was sitting in the cabin room door, with my body in the room, when lo! one of the sailors, by a wave being washed out of the pinnace, was gotten in again, and coming into the cabin room over my back, cried out, "We are all cast away. The Lord have mercy upon us! I have been washed overboard into the sea, and am gotten in again." His speeches made me look forth. And looking toward the sea, and seeing how we were, I turned myself to my cousin and the rest, and spake these words : "O cousin, it hath pleased God to cast us here between two rocks, the shore not far from us, for I saw the tops of trees when I looked forth." Whereupon the master of the pinnace, looking up at the scuttle-hole of the quarter-deck, went out at it ; but I never saw him afterward. Then he that had been in the sea went out again by me, and leaped overboard toward the rocks, whom afterward also I could not see.

Now none were left in the bark that I knew or saw, but my cousin, his wife and children, myself and mine, and his maidservant. But my cousin thought I would have fled from him, and said unto me : "O cousin, leave us not, let us die together ; " and reached forth his hand unto me. Then I, letting go my son Peter's hand, took him by the hand and said : "Cousin, I purpose it not. Whither shall I go? I am willing and ready here to die with you and my poor children. God be merciful to us, and receive us to himself ! " adding these words : "The Lord is able to help and deliver us." He replied, saying, " Truth, cousin ; but what his pleasure is, we know not. I fear we have been too unthankful for former deliverances. But he hath promised to deliver us from sin and condemnation, and to bring us safe to heaven through the all-sufficient satisfaction of Jesus Christ. This, therefore, we may challenge of him." To which I, replying, said, " That is all the deliverance I now desire and expect."

Which words I had no sooner spoken, but by a mighty wave I was, with the piece of the bark, washed out upon part of the rock, where the wave left me almost drowned. But recovering my feet, I saw above me on the rock my daughter Mary. To whom I had no sooner gotten, but my cousin Avery and his eldest son came to us, being all four of us washed out by one and the same wave. We went all into a small hole on the top of the rock, whence we called to those in the pinnace to come unto us, supposing we had been in more safety than they were in. My wife, seeing us there, was crept up into the scuttle of the quarter-deck, to come unto us. But presently came another wave, and dashing the pinnace all to pieces, carried my wife away in the scuttle as she was, with the greater part of the quarter-deck, unto the shore; where she was cast safely, but her legs were something bruised. And much timber of the vessel being there also cast, she was some time before she could get away, being washed by the waves. All the rest that were in the bark were drowned in the merciless seas. We four by that wave were clean swept away from off the rock also into the sea; the Lord, in one instant of time, disposing of fifteen souls of us according to his good pleasure and will.

His pleasure and wonderful great mercy to me was thus. Standing on the rock, as before you heard, with my eldest daughter, my cousin, and his eldest son, looking upon and talking to them in the bark, whenas we were by that merciless wave washed off the rock, as before you heard, God, in his mercy, caused me to fall, by the stroke of the wave, flat on my face; for my face was toward the sea. Insomuch, that as I was sliding off the rock into the sea, the Lord directed my toes into a joint in the rock's side, as also the tops of some of my fingers, with my right hand, by means whereof, the wave leaving me, I remained so hanging on the rock, only my head above the water; when on the left hand I espied a board or plank of the pinnace. And as I was reaching out my left hand to lay hold on it, by another coming over the top of the rock I was washed away from the rock, and by the violence of the waves was driven hither and thither in the seas a great while, and had many dashes against the rocks. At length, past hopes of life, and wearied in body and spirits, I even gave over to nature; and being ready to receive in the waters of death, I lifted up both my heart and hands to the God of heaven, — for note, I had my senses remaining perfect with me all the time that I was under and in water, — who at that instant lifted my head above the top of the water, that so I might breathe without any hindrance by the waters. I stood bolt upright, as if I had stood upon my feet; but I felt no bottom, nor had any footing for to stand upon but the waters.

While I was thus above the water, I saw by me a piece of the mast, as I suppose, about three foot long, which I labored to catch into my arms. But suddenly I was overwhelmed with water, and driven to and fro again, and at last I felt the ground with my right foot. When immediately, whilst I was thus grovelling on my face, I, presently recovering my feet, was in the water up to my breast, and through God's great mercy had my face unto the shore, and not to the sea. I made haste to get out, but was thrown down on my hands with the waves, and so with safety crept to the dry shore, where, blessing God, I turned about to look for my children and friends, but saw neither, nor any part of the pinnace, where I left them, as I supposed. But I saw my wife, about a butt length from me, getting herself forth from amongst the timber of the broken bark; but before I could get unto her, she was gotten to the shore. I was in the water, after I was washed from the rock, before I came to the shore, a quarter of an hour at least.

When we were come each to other, we went and sat under the bank. But fear of the seas' roaring, and our coldness, would not suffer us there to remain. But we went up into the land, and sat us down under a cedar-tree, which the wind had thrown down, where we sat about an hour, almost dead with cold. But now the storm was broken up, and the wind was calm; but the sea remained rough and fearful to us. My legs were much bruised, and so was my head. Other hurt had I none, neither had I taken in much quantity of water. But my heart would not let me sit still any longer; but I would go to see if any more were gotten to the land in safety, especially hoping to have met with some of my own poor children; but I could find none, neither dead nor yet living.

You condole with me my miseries, who now began to consider of my losses. Now came to my remembrance the time and manner how and when I last saw and left my children and friends. One was severed from me sitting on the rock at my feet, the other three in the pinnace; my little babe (ah, poor Peter!) sitting in his sister Edith's arms, who to the uttermost of her power sheltered him from the waters; my poor William standing close unto them, all three of them looking ruefully on me on the rock, their very countenances calling unto me to help them; whom I could not go unto, neither could they come at me, neither would the merciless waves afford me space or time to use any means at all, either to help them or myself. Oh, I yet see their cheeks, poor silent lambs, pleading pity and help at my hands. Then, on the other side, to consider the loss of my dear friends, with the spoiling and loss of all our goods and provisions, myself cast upon an unknown land, in a wilderness, I knew not where nor how to get thence. Then it came to my mind how I had occasioned the death of my children, who caused them to leave their native land, who might have left them there, yea, and might have sent some of them back again, and cost me nothing. These and such like thoughts do press down my heavy heart very much.

But I must let this pass, and will proceed on in the relation of God's goodness unto me in that desolate island, on which I was cast. I and my wife were almost naked, both of us, and wet and cold even unto death. I found a snapsack cast on the shore, in which I had a steel, and flint, and powder-horn. Going farther, I found a drowned goat ; then I found a hat, and my son William's coat, both which I put on. My wife found one of her petticoats, which she put on. I found also two cheeses and some butter driven ashore. Thus the Lord sent us some clothes to put on, and food to sustain our new lives, which we had lately given unto us, and means also to make fire ; for in a horn I had some gunpowder, which, to mine own, and since to other men's admiration, was dry. So taking a piece of my wife's neckcloth which I dried in the sun, I struck fire, and so dried and warmed our wet bodies ; and then skinned the goat, and having found a small brass pot, we boiled some of her. Our drink was brackish water ; bread we had none.

There we remained until the Monday following ; when, about three of the clock in the afternoon, in a boat that came that way, we went off that desolate island, which I named after my name, Thacher's Woe, and the rock, Avery his Fall, to the end that their fall and loss, and mine own, might be had in perpetual remembrance. In the isle lieth buried the body of my cousin's eldest daughter, whom I found dead on the shore. On the Tuesday following, in the afternoon, we arrived at Marblehead.

Such an event would naturally have its poetic pendant. The simple pathos of the prose narrative may now be contrasted with the chaste beauty of Whittier's " Swan Song of Parson Avery," which turns upon the popular fallacy that the swan pours forth its expiring breath in song.

THE SWAN SONG OF PARSON AVERY.

J. G. WHITTIER.

WHEN the reaper's task was ended, and the summer wearing late,
Parson Avery sailed from Newbury, with his wife and children
    eight,
Dropping down the river-harbor in the shallop "Watch and Wait."

   .   .   .   .

All day they sailed : at nightfall the pleasant land-breeze died,
The blackening sky, at midnight, its starry lights denied,
And far and low the thunder of tempest prophesied !

   .   .   .   .

All at once the great cloud parted, like a curtain drawn aside,
To let down the torch of lightning on the terror far and wide ;
And the thunder and the whirlwind together smote the tide.

There was wailing in the shallop, woman's wail and man's despair,
A crash of breaking timbers on the rocks so sharp and bare,
And, through it all, the murmur of Father Avery's prayer.

   .   .   .   .

"In this night of death I challenge the promise of thy word ! —
Let me see the great salvation of which mine ears have heard ! —
Let me pass from hence forgiven, through the grace of Christ, our
    Lord !"

   .   .   .   .

When the Christian sings his death-song, all the listening heavens
    draw near,
And the angels, leaning over the walls of crystal, hear
How the notes so faint and broken swell to music in God's ear.

The ear of God was open to his servant's last request ;
As the strong wave swept him downward the sweet hymn upward
    pressed,
And the soul of Father Avery went, singing, to its rest.

THE SPECTRE LEAGUERS.

THE fatal year 1692, in which the witchcraft terrorism so thoroughly permeated things mundane, has one ludicrous chapter to redeem it from utter fatuity.

It is gravely told in the " Magnalia Christi " of Cotton Mather, and on the authority of the Reverend John Emerson, of Gloucester, how a number of rollicking apparitions, dressed like gentlemen, in white waistcoats and breeches, kept that and the neighboring towns in a state of feverish excitement and alarm for a whole fortnight together. And neither of the reverend persons named seems to have entertained a doubt that these unaccountable molestations were caused by the Devil and his agents *in propria persona*, who took the human form for the better execution of their deep design. It is not very clear what that design was. The spectres, if such they were, — and as it would be unpardonable in us to doubt, — appear to have been a harmless sort of folk enough, for they did no injury either to the persons or the property of the inhabitants, thus laying their natural propensities under a commendable restraint. But the fact that they were spirits, and no ordinary spirits at that, being so confidently vouched for, and by such high authority on such matters as Dr. Cotton Mather, would seem to dispose of all doubt upon the subject. Should any, however, remain in the reader's mind after perusing the following account, he is reminded that what he has read is the sworn evidence of men who actually fought with, and on more than one occasion disgracefully routed and drove the invading demons before them into dark swamps and thickets. These witnesses are all persons of character and credibility. Moreover, their testimony remains unshaken by any subsequent revelations to this day. The reader may therefore depend upon the authoritative character of the narrative.

In the midsummer time, in the year 1692, of fatal memory, Ebenezer Babson, a sturdy yeoman of Cape Ann, with the rest of his family, almost every night heard noises as if some persons were walking or running hither and thither about the house. He being out late one night, when returning home saw two men come out of his own door, and then at sight of him run swiftly from the end of the house into the adjoining cornfield. Going in, he immediately questioned his family concerning these strange visitors. They promptly replied that no one at all had been there during his absence. Staggered by this denial, but being withal a very resolute, stout-hearted man, Babson seized his gun and went out in pursuit of the intruders. When he had gone a little way from the house, he saw the same men suddenly start up from behind a log and run into a swamp that was near by. He also overheard one say to the other, " The man of the house is now come, else we might have taken the house." Then he lost sight of them.

Upon this, expecting an immediate attack, the whole family rose in consternation, and went with all haste to the nearest garrison, which was only a short distance off. They had only just entered it when they heard heavy footfalls, as if a number of men were trampling on the ground around it. Then Babson again took his gun and ran out, and he again saw the two men running away down the hill into the swamp. By this time no one doubted that they were threatened with an Indian forray, that these men were the enemy's scouts, and that the danger was imminent.

The next night but one, Babson, for the third time, saw two men, who he thought looked like Frenchmen, one of them having a bright gun, such as the French Canadians used, slung on his back. Both of them started towards him at the top of their speed ; but Babson, taking to his heels, made good his escape into the garrison, and so eluded them. When he had got safely in, the noise of men moving about on the outside was again distinctly heard. Not long after these strange things had taken place, Babson, with another man, named John Brown, saw three

men (the number, like Falstaff's men in buckram, had now increased to three), whom they tried hard to get a shot at, but did
not, owing to the strangers' dodging about in so lively a manner
that they could not take aim.   For two or three nights these
men, or devils in the form of men, continued to appear in the
same mysterious way, for the purpose of drawing the Cape men
out into a wild-goose chase after them.   On July 14, Babson,
Brown, and all the garrison saw within gunshot of them half-a-
dozen men, whom they supposed to be reconnoitring, or trying

A SORTIE UPON THE DEMONS.

to decoy them into an ambush.   The brave garrison at once
sallied out in hot pursuit.   Babson, who seems to have ever
sought the forefront of battle, presently overtook two of the
skulking vagabonds, took good aim, and pulled the trigger; but
his trusty gun missed fire, and they got away and hid themselves among the bushes.   He then called out to his comrades,
who immediately answered, "Here they are! here they are!"
when Babson, running to meet them, saw three men stealing out
of the swamp side by side.   Bringing his gun to his shoulder,
with sure aim this time he fired; when all three fell as if shot.

Almost beside himself, Babson cried out to his companions that he had killed three. But when he was come nearly up to the supposed dead men, they all rose up and ran away, apparently without hurt or wound of any kind. Indeed one of them gave Babson a shot in return for his own, the bullet narrowly missing him, and burying itself in a tree, from which it was afterward dug out, and preserved as a trophy of the combat. Babson thinking this warm work, took refuge behind a tree and reloaded. Then, his comrades having joined him, they all charged together upon the spot where the fugitives lay concealed. Again the spectres started up before their eyes and ran, "every man his way." One, however, they surrounded and hemmed in, and Babson, getting a fair shot at him, saw him drop. But when search was made, the dead body had vanished. After a fruitless hunt, during which the stout-hearted Colonists heard a loud talking going on in the swamp, in some outlandish jargon they could not understand a word of, they returned, crestfallen and half dead with fatigue, to the garrison, in order to report their ill-success. But no sooner were they back there, than they saw more men skulking among the bushes, who prudently kept out of gunshot. What could it all mean?

The next morning Babson started to go over to the harbor in order to give the alarm there, for it was not doubted by any one that an attack was imminent. While on his way thither he was waylaid and fired at by the "unaccountable troublers," who, strange to say, loaded their guns with real bullets, as poor Babson was near finding out to his cost. Having procured help, the neighborhood was scoured for traces of the attacking party, two of whom were seen, but not being mortal flesh and blood, could not be harmed by lead or steel.

In the course of a few days more, two of the garrison went out upon a scout, who saw several men come out of an orchard, in which they seemed to be performing some strange incantations. They counted eleven of them. Richard Dolliver raised his gun and fired into the midst of them, where they stood the thickest; but of course without other effect than to make them scatter as before.

It now being clear that the strange visitors bore a charmed life, and that the Cape was in great peril from this diabolical invasion, the end of which no man could foresee, the aid of the surrounding towns was invoked in this truly alarming crisis. A reinforcement of sixty men from Ipswich, led by Captain Appleton, coming promptly to the rescue, gave the garrison much encouragement, beleaguered round as they were by the Powers of Darkness, against which lead and steel were of no more effect than snowballs or rushes would have been. For a fortnight they had been kept in continual alarm, night and day. The infernal visitants showed themselves first in one place and then in another, to draw out and harass them, until a foeman seemed lurking in every bush. Though repeatedly shot at, none could be killed. They threw stones, beat upon barns with clubs, and otherwise acted more in the spirit of diabolical revelry than as if actuated by any deadlier purpose. They moved about the swamps without leaving any tracks, like ordinary beings. In short, it was evident that such adversaries as these were, must be fought with other weapons besides matchlocks and broadswords; consequently a strange fear fell upon the Cape.

Finally they became still more insolently bold, and so far from showing the same cowardly disposition to take to their heels whenever they were chased, they now treated their pursuers with open contempt. For instance, seeing three of the unknown approaching him one morning, walking slowly and apparently unmindful of any danger, Babson ensconced himself behind some bushes to lie in wait for them. He held his fire until they were come within a stone's throw before he pulled the trigger. But to his unspeakable dismay his gun flashed in the pan, though he repeatedly snapped it at the phantoms, who took no other notice of him than to give him a disdainful look as they walked by. Yet he soon afterward snapped the same gun several times in succession, and it never once missed fire. The goblins had charmed it!

It being settled that these insults proceeded from spectres, and not from beings who were vulnerable to weapons of mortal make,

17

the unequal contest was abandoned.   When this was done, the demons' occupation being gone, they too disappeared.

It should be said in conclusion, and on the same authority as that to which we owe the narration, that the most conservative minds regarded these occurrences as a part of the descent from the invisible world then menacing the peace of the Colony, and threatening the churches therein with irretrievable disaster.

The poetic version of this legend opens with a glimpse of the scene that is itself worth a whole chapter of description.   We are then introduced to the Colonial garrison-house, rudely but strongly built, to protect the settlers from their savage foes, and to its valiant defenders, who with their useless arms in their hands await in dread the assault of the demons.   Mr. Whittier, be it said, is seldom happier than when dealing with the legendary lore extracted from the old chronicles.   In him the spirit of an antiquary and the feeling of the poet exist in as amiable fellowship as they did in Sir Walter Scott, who ransacked the legends of Scotland for his tales in prose or verse.

THE GARRISON OF CAPE ANN.

J. G. WHITTIER.

WHERE the sea-waves back and forward, hoarse with rolling pebbles, ran,
The garrison-house stood watching on the gray rocks of Cape Ann ;
On its windy site uplifting gabled roof and palisade,
And rough walls of unhewn timber with the moonlight overlaid.

Before the deep-mouthed chimney, dimly lit by dying brands,
Twenty soldiers sat and waited, with their muskets in their hands ;
On the rough-hewn oaken table the venison haunch was shared,
And the pewter tankard circled slowly round from beard to beard.

But their voices sank yet lower, sank to husky tones of fear,
As they spake of present tokens of the powers of evil near ;
Of a spectral host, defying stroke of steel and aim of gun ;
Never yet was ball to slay them in the mould of mortals run !

Midnight came; from out the forest moved a dusky mass that soon
Grew to warriors, plumed and painted, grimly marching in the moon.
"Ghosts or witches," said the captain, "thus I foil the Evil One!"
And he rammed a silver button, from his doublet, down his gun.

.   .   .   .   .

"God preserve us!" said the captain; "never mortal foes were there;
They have vanished with their leader, Prince and Power of the air!
Lay aside your useless weapons; skill and prowess naught avail;
They who do the Devil's service wear their master's coat of mail!"

So the night grew near to cock-crow, when again a warning call
Roused the score of weary soldiers watching round the dusky hall;
And they looked to flint and priming, and they longed for break of
     day;
But the captain closed his Bible: "Let us cease from man, and
     pray!"

To the men who went before us, all the unseen powers seemed near,
And their steadfast strength of courage struck its roots in holy fear.
Every hand forsook the musket, every head was bowed and bare,
Every stout knee pressed the flagstones, as the captain led in prayer.

Ceased thereat the mystic marching of the spectres round the wall,
But a sound abhorred, unearthly, smote the ears and hearts of all, —
Howls of rage and shrieks of anguish! Never after mortal man
Saw the ghostly leaguers marching round the blockhouse of Cape
     Ann.

———————

OLD MEG, THE WITCH.

WE can easily bring the age of credulity as far forward as
the middle of the last century, by means of a local
legend in which mediæval superstition respecting witches survives in full vigor. The test of the silver bullet recalls the
weird incantation scene in "Der Freischütz," and all the demon
lore associated with the gloomy depths of the Hartz.

There was a reputed witch by the name of Margaret Wesson, and familiarly known by the name of "Old Meg," who once resided in Gloucester. After having been for many years the object of superstitious curiosity and dread to the inhabitants of the Cape, she at length came to her end in the following strange and mysterious manner. At the time of the celebrated victorious siege of Louisburg by the Colonial troops in 1745, two soldiers of the Massachusetts line belonging to Gloucester happened to have their attention drawn to the movements of a crow that kept hovering over them. They threw stones, and then fired their muskets at it, but could neither touch nor terrify it; the bird still continued flying round them and cawing horribly in their ears. At length it occurred to one of them that it might be Old Meg. He communicated his suspicions to his comrade; and as nothing but silver was believed to have any power to injure a witch, they cut the silver buttons off from their uniform coats and discharged them at the crow. The experiment succeeded. At the first shot they broke its leg; at the second it fell dead at their feet. When they returned to Gloucester, they learned that Old Meg had broken her leg while walking by the fort in that place at the precise time when they had shot and killed the crow five hundred miles distant; after lingering for a while in great agony she died. And now comes the singular part of the story; for upon examining her fractured limb, the identical silver buttons which the soldiers had fired from their muskets under the walls of Louisburg were extracted from the flesh. The story of Old Meg was long familiarly told in Gloucester, although the credulity which once received it as solemn truth has nearly, if not quite, passed away, says the Reverend Charles W. Upham, who makes the statement so lately as 1832. It has, however, been reproduced among the sober records of fact contained in Mr. Babson's "History of Gloucester."

AN ESCAPE FROM PIRATES.

ACCORDING to the historian Thucydides, the Greeks were the first pirates. The ancient poets tell us that those who sailed along the coasts in quest of prey were everywhere accosted with the question, " whether they were pirates," not as a term of reproach, but of honor. So also the vikings of the North were little less than corsairs, whose valiant deeds of arms, and whose adventurous voyages to distant lands, celebrated in their sagas, were conceived and performed with no nobler purpose than robbery.

But the modern pirate had neither the rude sense of honor nor the chivalrous notions of warfare distinguishing his ancient prototype. He was simply a robber and a murderer, bidding all honest traders to "stand and deliver" like the aquatic highwayman that he was. Even the mildest-mannered man among them "that ever scuttled ship or cut a throat" was no more than this ; while the majority were beings fitted by nature for a career of crime, the bare recital of which makes us shudder.

During the first quarter of the eighteenth century our own seas swarmed with these freebooters, whose depredations upon our commerce are the theme of some of the most startling episodes preserved in the whole annals of piracy. Blackbeard, Low, and Phillips stand pre-eminent at the head of this black list. It is with the last that our story has to do.

In the course of his last piratical cruise, during which he swept the coast from Jamaica to Newfoundland, Phillips fell in with and captured the sloop " Dolphin," Andrew Harraden, master, belonging to Cape Ann. The " Dolphin," being a better vessel than his own, the pirate transferred his black flag to her, sending the crew away in another of his prizes. Captain Harraden was, however, detained a prisoner on board his own vessel. Two of the pirate crew, John Fillmore, of Ipswich, and Edward Cheesman were men whom Phillips had taken out of the ships that he had plundered and pressed into his service, thus making them pirates against their will. Being found useful, Cheesman had been promoted to the post of ship's carpenter shortly before the "Dolphin" was captured. Both he and Fillmore, however, were brave young fellows, and both had fully determined, come what might, to take the first opportunity that presented itself of escaping from Phillips' clutches; but the jealous watchfulness of the older pirates was such that they could get no opportunity of talking to each other about what was in their minds, except when feigning to be asleep, or when pretending to play at cards together. But by stealth they at length came to an understanding.

To Captain Harraden these two presently broached their purpose; and finding him ready and willing to strike a blow for the recovery of his vessel and his liberty, they with four confederates, who were already pledged to stand by them, fixed the day and the hour for making the hazardous attempt.

When the appointed hour of noon had arrived, Cheesman, the leader, with Fillmore and Harraden, were on deck, as also were Nut, the master of the "Dolphin," a fellow of great strength and courage, the boatswain, and some others of the pirate crew. But of all on board, Nut and the boatswain were the two whom the conspirators most feared to encounter. Cheesman, however, promised to take care of the master if the others would attend to the boatswain. No firearms were to be used. The attack was to be suddenly made, and possession of the deck to be gained, before the alarm should spread below.

Cheesman, having left his working tools on the deck, as if he were going to use them about the vessel, walked aft to begin with the master; but seeing some signs of timidity in Harraden, he came back, gave him and his mates a dram of brandy each, drinking to the boatswain and the master the toast, "To our next merry-meeting." He then took a turn up and down the deck with Nut, in order to occupy the pirate's attention, while

Fillmore, as if in sport, picked up the carpenter's axe from where it was lying, and began to twirl it around on the point.

This was the signal agreed upon. Cheesman instantly grappled with the master, and, being a man of powerful frame, after a brief struggle pitched him over the side into the sea. Fillmore, rushing upon the boatswain, with one blow of the axe laid him dead upon the deck. The noise of the scuffle brought the pirate chief on deck; but Cheesman quickly disabled him with a blow from the carpenter's mallet, which fractured his jawbone. Having armed himself with an adze, Harraden then sprang upon Phillips with his uplifted weapon; but the gunner of the pirate interposing between them, Cheesman tripped up his heels, throwing him into the arms of a confederate, who flung him overboard, after the master. Harraden then finished with Phillips.

The conspirators then jumped into the hold and fell upon the quartermaster, who was the only officer remaining alive; when a young lad on board pleaded so earnestly for his life that he was spared. The rest of the pirate crew being securely put in irons, the vessel was steered directly for Boston, where she arrived on the 3d of May, 1724, to the great joy of the people of the province. Two of the Pirates, Archer, the quartermaster, and William White, were tried, convicted, and executed. Fillmore, Cheesman, and their confederates were honorably acquitted. John Fillmore, the pirate in spite of himself, was the great-grandfather of the thirteenth President of the United States.

NORMAN'S WOE.

TOUCHING the name of the rock called Norman's Woe, little more is known than that Goodman Norman and his son were among the first to settle here; and it is therefore assumed that this headland and its outlying islet preserve a family surname at once bold and picturesque. That no record is known, to explain how the rock originally received its name, or what the catastrophe it was intended to perpetuate, is only another instance of the instability of local traditions. Many of the names now in use on Cape Ann go as far back as the first decade of the settlement. For instance, Kettle Island and Baker's Island were named before 1634. This one, like Thacher's Island, is probably commemorative of some uncommon individual experience or disaster; but whatever that may have been, its memory is probably lost beyond recovery.

NORMAN'S WOE ROCK.

Not lost its claim to a wider celebrity than some of our most famous battlefields, for it is the scene so vividly described in Longfellow's "Wreck of the 'Hesperus.'"

In his biographical sketch of the poet Longfellow, Mr. Francis H. Underwood says of this ballad that it "is deservedly admired, especially for the vigor of its descriptions. It is," he continues, "in truth a ballad such as former centuries knew, and which are seldom written now. Its free movement, directness, and pictorial power combine to make it one of the most remarkable of the author's poems."

Yet Mr. Fields, the poet's genial friend and whilom his publisher, says that the "Wreck of the 'Hesperus'" hardly caused its author an effort. The facts with regard to its composition are these: After a dreadful gale in the winter of 1839, which strewed the coast with wrecks, he had been reading the catalogue of its disasters with which the newspapers were filled. The stormy Cape had reaped its full share of this terrible harvest. Forty dead bodies, among them that of a woman lashed to a piece of wreck, had been washed up on the Gloucester shore. One of the lost vessels was named the "Hesperus," and the name of Norman's Woe now met his eye, — perhaps for the first time. The event impressed him so deeply that he determined to write a ballad upon it. Late one night as he sat by the fire smoking his pipe, the whole scene came vividly into his mind; and under the absorbing impulse of the moment, taking his pen, he wrote this most graphic of ballads. He then went to bed, but, as he tells us, not to sleep; for new thoughts were running in his head which kept him awake. He rose and added them to the first draught. At three in the morning he had finished the ballad as it stands.

Although, in point of fact, no such vessel as the "Hesperus" was wrecked on the reef of Norman's Woe, the poet's versified story is founded upon a real incident, to which the use of these names lends a terrible interest. In one sense, therefore, this ballad belongs to the legendary; but by the poet's genius it is now firmly associated with the surf-beaten rock of Cape Ann, whose name of terror, derived from some unrecorded disaster, found no reason for its being, until a few strokes of the pen gave it immortality.

From being merely the scene of a wreck, Norman's Woe has become a spot consecrated by genius. It is, therefore, no common rock, but a monument to Mr. Longfellow far more suggestive and enduring than any memorial shaft that the most reverent hands may raise over his honored dust. "The letter killeth, but the spirit giveth life."

The ballad is, as Mr. Underwood says, written in the quaint

old manner; but what is more to the purpose, it has the genuine
ring, nervous action, sonorous rhythm, and unmistakable flavor
of the sea throughout. Those stanzas descriptive of the increasing fury of the gale have never been surpassed in the language.

> Colder and louder blew the wind,
>> A gale from the Northeast,
> The snow fell hissing in the brine,
>> And the billows frothed like yeast.
>
> Down came the storm, and smote amain
>> The vessel in its strength ;
> She shuddered and paused, like a frighted steed,
>> Then leaped her cable's length.
>
> . . . . . .
>
> And fast through the midnight dark and drear,
>> Through the whistling sleet and snow,
> Like a sheeted ghost, the vessel swept
>> Towards the Reef of Norman's Woe.
>
> . . . . . .
>
> She struck where the white and fleecy waves
>> Looked soft as carded wool,
> But the cruel rocks, they gored her sides
>> Like the horns of an angry bull.
>
> Her rattling shrouds, all sheathed in ice,
>> With the masts went by the board ;
> Like a vessel of glass, she stove and sank,
>> Ho! ho! the breakers roared!
>
> At daybreak, on the bleak sea-beach,
>> A fisherman stood aghast,
> To see the form of a maiden fair,
>> Lashed close to a drifting mast.

HANNAH BINDING SHOES.

"BEVERLY FARMS, MASS., Dec. 22, 1874.

"DEAR SIR, — As to 'Hannah's' *locale*, it is hard to determine. I used to see her at all the windows in Beverly when I was a little child; but I saw her more distinctly, about twenty years ago, on the road between Beverly and Marblehead. I think she lived in the latter place quite as much as at the former. You see my home was in Beverly, and we Beverly children were rather afraid of the Marbleheaders; they had the reputation of 'rocking' their neighbors out of town. I suspect, on the whole, that 'Hannah' must have been a *tramp*, and bound shoes anywhere she put up. Mr. Wood, who painted her picture, says he was shown her house in Marblehead, and he ought to know.

"But I have honestly told you all I know about her, except as a lodger in my imagination.

"Sincerely ashamed of my ignorance, I am truly yours,

"LUCY LARCOM."

POOR lone Hannah,
Sitting at the window binding shoes!
Faded, wrinkled,
Sitting, stitching in a mournful muse.
Bright-eyed beauty once was she
When the bloom was on the tree.
Spring and winter
Hannah's at the window binding shoes.

Not a neighbor
Passing nod or answer will refuse
To her whisper:
"Is there from the fishers any news?"
Oh, her heart's adrift with one
On an endless voyage gone!
Night and morning
Hannah's at the window binding shoes.

Fair young Hannah
Ben, the sun-burnt fisher gayly wooes:
Hale and clever,
For a willing heart and hand he sues.

POOR LONE HANNAH.

May-day skies are all aglow,
And the waves are laughing so!
For her wedding,
Hannah leaves her window and her shoes.

May is passing, —
Mid the apple-boughs a pigeon cooes.
Hannah shudders,
For the wild sou'-wester mischief brews.
Round the rocks of Marblehead,
Outward bound, a schooner sped.
Silent, lonesome,
Hannah's at the window binding shoes.

'T is November:
Now no tear her wasted cheek bedews.
From Newfoundland
Not a sail returning will she lose ;
Whispering hoarsely, "Fishermen,
Have you, have you heard of Ben ?"
Old with watching,
Hannah's at the window binding shoes.

Twenty winters
Bleach and tear the rugged shore she views ;
Twenty seasons ; —
Never one has brought her any news.
Still her dim eyes silently
Chase the white sails o'er the sea.
Hopeless, faithful
Hannah's at the window binding shoes.

Part Seventh.

IPSWICH AND NEWBURY LEGENDS.

IPSWICH LEGENDS.

OLD IPSWICH is one of the most delightful corners into which the artist or the antiquary could have the good fortune to stray, for here either will find abundant occupation. Its physiognomy is old, its atmosphere drowsy, its quiet unbroken. The best residences are still the oldest ones, and among them are some very quaint specimens of the early Colonial architecture, upon which time seems to have made little impression; while here and there others stand up mere crazy hulks, so shaken and dilapidated inside and out, that every gale threatens to bring them down with a loud crash into the cellars beneath. Some of these have the reputation of being haunted houses, and are of course enveloped in mystery, — and indeed the whole atmosphere of the place is thick with legendary lore, which the old people drop their voices when they are relating.

To me now there is no more striking picture than that of some such crazy old structure, trembling, as the wind shakes it, like an old man with the palsy, its windows gaping wide, its chimney bent and tottering, the fire on its hearthstone extinguished forever, the path to it overgrown with weeds, the old well choked up with rubbish and poisonous ivy, — everything expressing irretrievable decay, — standing in the midst of a still vigorous orchard just putting forth its sweet perennial bloom, with the fresh and tender grass creeping up to the broken threshold, as if Nature claimed admittance, and would not be much longer denied. That house, you are told, was built two centuries ago. Where are the builders; and where the generations that came after them? The old well-sweep creaks mournfully in the wind, and points its bony finger to the sky. Yet here are the trees that they planted, still putting forth their buds, like mortals putting on immortality.

It is natural, I think, in such a place to try to imagine the first-comers looking about them. How did it look; what did they think? They were a mere handful, — the apostolic number, — a vanguard sent to establish a semi-military post. Upon ascending the hill above the river they found an outcropping ledge of goodly extent, forming a sort of natural platform, and upon this rock they built their church, which subsequently became so famous throughout the Colony under the successive ministrations of Ward, Rogers, Norton, and Hubbard, — all men eminent for their learning and piety. Satan himself was not able to prevail against it; for upon the smooth ledge outside is still seen the distinct print of his sable majesty's cloven foot, when he was hurled from the pinnacle to the ground for attempting to conceal himself within the sanctuary.

In another place, down by the river side, the house where Harry Main lived is pointed out to the visitor. He having thus a local habitation, the legend concerning him is no vagabond tradition. Harry Main is the Wandering Jew of Ipswich, around whom darkly hangs the shadow of an unpardonable crime and its fearful doom. It is said that he had been by turns a pirate, a smuggler, and a wrecker, who followed the wicked trade of building fires on the sands, in order to decoy vessels among the breakers, where they were wrecked, and their crews perished miserably. For these crimes, at his death he was doomed to be chained on Ipswich Bar, the scene of his former murderous exploits, and everlastingly to coil a cable of sand there. When the cable broke, his demoniacal yells of baffled rage could be heard for miles around; and when those fearful sounds announced the rising gale, mothers would clasp their babes to their breasts, while the men shook their heads and said, "Old Harry's growling again!" His name was long the bugbear used to frighten refractory children into obedience, while the rote on the bar, heard in storms, still audibly perpetuates the legend, with its roar.

The old people living on Plum Island used to say that Harry

PADLOCK AND KEY, IPSWICH JAIL.

Main's ghost troubled them by wandering about the sand-hills on stormy nights, so that they were afraid to venture out of doors after dark. Indeed the town itself, in its palmy days, was so full of ghostly legends, that certain localities supposed to be haunted, were scrupulously avoided by the timid ones, who had a mortal dread of being accosted by some vagabond spectre with its tale of horror.

Harry Main's house — for we must remember that he had

one — was ransacked, and every rod of the garden dug up for
the money that he was supposed to have buried there ; but
nothing rewarded the search.   Other places, too, have been explored with the same result, in quest of Kidd's hidden treasures.
One good man dreamed three nights in succession that vast sums
were buried in a certain hill in the town.   He could see the
very spot.   Haunted by the realism of the dream, he determined
to test the matter for himself ; and one dark night, just as midnight struck, he took his spade, his lantern, and his Bible, and
started on his weird errand.   Upon reaching the spot he recognized it as the same that he had seen in his dream.   He immediately fell to work.   After plying his spade vigorously a while,
it struck against some hard object.   He now felt sure of his
prize.   Scraping the earth away with feverish haste, he came
to a flat stone having a bar of iron laid across it.   This he
eagerly grasped with one hand, and was about to turn the stone
over with the other when he was suddenly surrounded by a troop
of cats, whose eyeballs blazed in the darkness.   The digger felt
his hair slowly rising on end.   A cold sweat stood on his brow.
Brandishing the bar aloft, he cried out, "Scat !" when these vigilant guardians of the treasure vanished in a twinkling, leaving
the crestfallen money-digger standing up to his middle in cold
water, which had poured into the hole, when he broke the spell
by speaking.   Half drowned, and wholly disgusted, he crawled
out of it.   The iron bar, however, remained tightly clutched in
his hand.   He carried it home, and I was assured that upon
going to a certain house in Ipswich I might see the identical
door-latch which a smith had made out of this bar for a souvenir
of the night's adventure.

Such are a few of the many stories which Mr. Morgan has
picturesquely grouped together in his poem entitled " Old Ipswich Town," — a charming bit of reminiscence, and charmingly
told.

OLD IPSWICH TOWN.

APPLETON MORGAN.

I LOVE to think of old Ipswich town,
  Old Ipswich town in the East countree,
Whence, on the tide, you can float down
  Through the long salt grass to the wailing sea.
Where the " Mayflower " drifted off the bar
  Sea-worn and weary, long years ago,
And dared not enter, but sailed away
Till she landed her boats in Plymouth Bay.

I love to think of old Ipswich town,
  Where Whitefield preached in the church on the hill,
Driving out the Devil till he leaped down
  From the steeple's top, where they show you still,
Imbedded deep in the solid rock,
  The indelible print of his cloven hoof,
And tell you the Devil has never shown
Face or hoof since that day in the honest town.

I love to think of old Ipswich town,
  Where they shut up the witches until the day
When they should be roasted so thoroughly brown,
  In Salem Village, twelve miles away ;
They 've moved it off for a stable now ;
  But there are the holes where the stout jail stood,
And, at night, they say that over the holes
You can see the ghost of Goody Coles.

I love to think of old Ipswich town ;
  That house to your right, a rod or more,
Where the stern old elm-trees seem to frown
  If you peer too hard through the open door,
Sheltered the regicide judges three
  When the royal sheriffs were after them,
And a queer old villager once I met,
Who says in the cellar they 're living yet.

I love to think of old Ipswich town ;
    Harry Main — you have heard the tale — lived there ;
He blasphemed God, so they put him down
    With an iron shovel, at Ipswich Bar ;
They chained him there for a thousand years,
    As the sea rolls up to shovel it back ;
So when the sea cries, the goodwives say
" Harry Main growls at his work to-day."

IPSWICH HEADS.

I love to think of old Ipswich town ;
    There 's a graveyard up on the old High street,
Where ten generations are looking down
    On the one that is toiling at their feet ;
Where the stones stand shoulder to shoulder, like troops
    Drawn up to receive a cavalry charge,
And graves have been dug in graves, till the sod
Is the mould of good men gone to God.

I love to think of old Ipswich town,
    Old Ipswich town in the East countree,
Whence, on the tide, you can float down
    Through the long salt grass to the wailing sea,
And lie all day on the glassy beach,
    And learn the lesson the green waves teach,
Till at sunset, from surf and seaweed brown,
You are pulling back to Ipswich town.

Ipswich contains many interesting memorials of its antique worthies and times. In the Old Hill burying-ground on High Street may be found incontestable proofs to the rank held by some of the founders, in the family arms that are sculptured on the ancient tombstones; but you will not find the gravestone of the Reverend William Hubbard, the historian of New England, there, because no one knows the spot where he is buried.

HEARTBREAK HILL.

TURNING away from the town through unfrequented by-lanes, all green and spotted with daisies, let us ascend Heartbreak Hill in the southeast corner. The view is certainly charming. The reader asks what we see; and, like one on a tower, we reply: In the distance, across a lonely waste of marshes, through which glistening tidal streams crawl on their bellies among reeds, and sun their glossy backs among sand-dunes, we see the bald Ipswich Hundreds, a group of smooth, gray-green, desolate-looking hills stretched along the coast. They are isolated by these marshes from the mainland, which they seem trying to rejoin. Through the openings between these hills we catch the glitter of a ragged line of sand-dunes heaped up like snow-drifts at the edge of the shore, over which rises the sea, and the harbor-bar, overspread with foam.

It being a clear day, we can see from Cape Ann as far as Cape Neddock, and all that lies or floats between; but for leagues the coast is sad and drear, and from the sand, intrenching it everywhere with a natural dyke, the eye turns gratefully upon the refreshing sea. Then, as the Maine coast sweeps gracefully round to the east, the blue domes of Agamenticus rise above it, while the long dark land-line shoots off into the ocean, diminishing gradually from the mountain, like a musical phrase whose last note we strive to catch long after it has died away.

Beneath us is a narrow valley through which a river runs with speed. The town occupies both banks, which rise into considerable eminences above it. All around are the evidences of long occupation of the land, — fields that have borne crops, and trees that have been growing for centuries; houses whose steep roofs descend almost to the ground; graveyards whose mossed stones lean this way and that with age. Finally, the traditions that we are unwilling to see expire, cast a pleasing glamour over the place, — something like the shadows which the ancient elms fling down upon the hot and dusty roads.

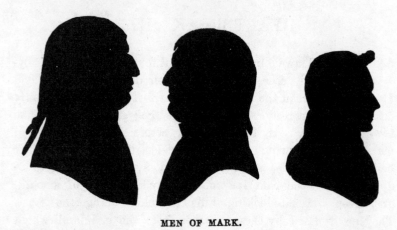

MEN OF MARK.

The river shoots through the gray arches of a picturesque stone bridge out upon the broad levels of marsh land stretching seaward. Through these it loiters quietly along down to the sea. At the town it is an eager mill-stream; at the ocean it is as calm as a mill-pond. The tide brings in a few fishing-boats, but seldom anything larger; for it is no longer an avenue of commerce, as in bygone days.

The oldest of Ipswich legends is associated with this hill, and accounts for its name; though the obscurity surrounding its origin baffles any attempt to trace it to an authentic source. The name is however found upon the earliest records of the town, and it is probably as old as the settlement, which was begun

THE MAIDEN'S WATCH.

by the whites in 1635 as a check to the expected encroachments of Cardinal Richelieu's colony, then established in Acadia. But before this, we know, from Captain Smith, that the place was the most populous Indian settlement in all Massachusetts Bay, it being the seat of a powerful sagamore, and known by its Indian name of Agawam. That a few white people were living among the Indians here previous to 1635 is evident from the tenor of one of the first recorded acts of the new Colony, dated September 7, 1630, commanding those that were planted at Agawam forthwith to come away. It is perhaps to this early time that the legend of Heartbreak Hill refers, since it is known that the Agawams were a docile and hospitable people, who welcomed the coming of the English among them with open arms; and it is also known that the place was more or less frequented by the English fishing-ships.

Briefly, the legend relates the romantic story of an Indian maiden who fell in love with a white sailor, and upon his sailing for a distant land, she used to climb this hill and pass her days sitting upon the summit watching for his return. But the months and years passed without bringing any tidings of him. He never did come back; and still the deserted one watched and waited, until she pined away, and at length died of a broken heart. There is a ledge on the summit where the Indian girl sat watching for her lover's return; and when she died, her lonely grave was made by the side of it. By others the legend is differently related. Some say that as the girl one day wended her way wearily to the top of the hill, she saw her lover's vessel making the desperate attempt to gain the port in the height of a violent gale. But it drove steadily on among the breakers, and was dashed to pieces and swallowed up before her eyes. In her poem Mrs. Thaxter adopts the former version, which, if less tragic, appeals in a more subtle way to our sympathies. In any case the hill has become a monument to faithful affection, and as such is the favorite resort of lovers in all the country round.

HEARTBREAK HILL.

CELIA THAXTER.

In Ipswich town, not far from the sea,
  Rises a hill which the people call
Heartbreak Hill, and its history
  Is an old, old legend, known to all.

· · · · ·

It was a sailor who won the heart
  Of an Indian maiden, lithe and young;
And she saw him over the sea depart,
  While sweet in her ear his promise rung;

For he cried, as he kissed her wet eyes dry,
  "I 'll come back, sweetheart; keep your faith!"
She said, "I will watch while the moons go by."
  Her love was stronger than life or death.

So this poor dusk Ariadne kept
  Her watch from the hill-top rugged and steep;
Slowly the empty moments crept
  While she studied the changing face of the deep,

Fastening her eyes upon every speck
  That crossed the ocean within her ken;
Might not her lover be walking the deck,
  Surely and swiftly returning again?

The Isles of Shoals loomed, lonely and dim,
  In the northeast distance far and gray,
And on the horizon's uttermost rim
  The low rock heap of Boone Island lay.

· · · · ·

Oh, but the weary, merciless days,
  With the sun above, with the sea afar, —
No change in her fixed and wistful gaze
  From the morning-red to the evening star!

· · · · ·

Like a slender statue carved of stone
　　She sat, with hardly motion or breath.
She wept no tears and she made no moan,
　　But her love was stronger than life or death.

He never came back!　Yet, faithful still,
　　She watched from the hill-top her life away.
And the townsfolk christened it Heartbreak Hill,
　　And it bears the name to this very day.

NEWBURYPORT LEGENDS.

LET us stroll a little about the city of Newburyport and its
　　charming environs.

Upon leaving Ipswich the landscape grows less austere.　The
flat Rowley marshes succeed the rocky pastures and tumbling
hills, with their stiffly-upright cedars and their shut-in vistas, like
a calm after a storm.　Then we glide on among haycocks, standing up out of the inflowing tide, across the beautiful and peaceful prairie of Old Newbury, and are suddenly brought up by a
ridge of high land, lifting its green wall between us and the
basin of the Merrimack.　At the right, thrust up through the
tops of the elm-trees that hide the village, like a spear tipped
with gold,

　　　　　　springs the village spire
　With the crest of its cock in the sun afire.

That is old Newbury meeting-house.　Extending now far
along the slopes of the ridge as we approach it, are the city
cemeteries, whose mingled gray and white monuments throng
the green swells, — a multitude of spectators turned into stone.
Then, cutting through the ridge, the train plunges into the
darkness of a tunnel, soon emerging again upon the farther
slope among the city streets from which the broad white sheet
of the Merrimack is seen moving steadily out to sea.　One side

of these heights then is appropriated by the living, the other by the dead.

The most remarkable and fascinating object in the landscape now is the river.

The River Merrimack, when near the end of its long course, expands into a noble basin enclosed within the sweep of picturesquely grouped and broken highlands. It is here every inch a river, broad, deep, clear, and sparkling. On one side are the

BEACON, SALISBURY POINT.

hills of Amesbury and Salisbury, on the other side the city of Newburyport rises from the curved shore to the summit of the ridge, crowned with trees and spiked with steeples.

Down below the city and toward the sea all this changes. The high shores drop into fens, marshes, and downs. A long, low island thrusts itself half across the channel and blockades it. Beyond this again the sea breaks heavily on the low bar outside, and the river disappears in a broken line of foam.

One loving and reverential hand has stamped all this region with the impress of his genius, and so has made all the world

partakers of his own feeling for the familiar scenes he describes.
Amesbury is Whittier's home, the Merrimack his unfailing
theme. Here are his surroundings : —

> Stream of my fathers ! sweetly still
> The sunset rays thy valley fill ;
> Poured slantwise down the long defile,
> Wave, wood, and spire beneath them smile.
> I see the winding Powow fold
> The green hill in its belt of gold,
> And following down its wavy line,
> Its sparkling waters blend with thine.
> There 's not a tree upon thy side,
> Nor rock which thy returning tide
> As yet hath left abrupt and stark
> Above thy evening water-mark,
>
> .   .   .   .   .
>
> But lies distinct and full in sight,
> Beneath this gush of summer light.

In the same spirit, which by a sort of poetic alchemy seems
capable of converting the waste sands of the seashore into grains
of gold, Mrs. Spofford has described the approaches to the river
through the flat lagoons that furnish a circulation to the marshes.

> We floated in the idle breeze,
>   With all our sails a-shiver :
> The shining tide came softly through,
>   And filled Plum Island River.
>
> .   .   .   .   .
>
> And clear the flood of silver swung
>   Between the brimming edges ;
> And now the depths were dark, and now
>   The boat slid o'er the sedges.
>
> And here a yellow sand-spit foamed
>   Amid the great sea-meadows ;
> And here the slumberous waters gloomed
>   Lucid in emerald shadows.
>
> .   .   .   .   .

> Around the sunny distance rose
> A blue and hazy highland,
> And winding down our winding way
> The sand-hills of Plum Island.

From the domain of poetry we pass easily into that of history. Mr. John Quincy Adams once described Siberia as being celebrated for its malefactors and malachite. Some one, in an epigrammatic vein, has summed up Newburyport as being famous for piety and privateering; and the analogy seems established when one turns to the History of Newbury written by Whittier's old schoolmaster, Joshua Coffin, and reads there that the privateersmen on putting to sea were accustomed to request the prayers of the churches for the success of the cruise, — to which petition all those having a share in the voyage responded with a hearty amen.

Newburyport, then, is a city built upon a hill. One reads its history as he walks. Like Salem, it rose and flourished through its commerce; but when that failed, the business of the place had to be recast in a wholly different mould, and its merchants became spinners and weavers, instead of shipowners and shipbuilders. It now seems trying rather awkwardly to adapt itself to the changes that the last half-century has brought about, — changes emphasized by the tenacity with which the old people cling to the traditions that are associated with its former prosperity, and gave it a prestige that mills and factories can no longer maintain.

The waterside street begins at a nest of idle shipyards, winds with the river along a line of rusty wharves, where colliers take the place of Indiamen, and ends with the antiquated suburb of Joppa, — which at least retains some of the flavor of a seaport, it having a population that gets its living by fishing, piloting, or doing such odd jobs as watermen can pick up along shore. From here the sails of a vessel that is nearing the port can be seen gliding along over the sand-drifts of Plum Island or Salisbury Beach. Joppa is crowded with houses, but it is torpid.

This long street leaves us at Oldtown, the parent settlement here, whose church spire we saw at a distance. It is narrow, irregular, and untidy; but High Street, the avenue laid out along the top of the ridge, and extending from Oldtown Green to the Chain Bridge over the Merrimack, is a thoroughfare one does not often see equalled, even if he has travelled far and seen much.

Here, upon the cool brow of the ridge, are the stately homes of the wealthy citizens; here the old merchants, who amassed fortunes in West India rum and sugar in little stuffy counting-rooms on the wharves below, lived like princes in the great roomy mansions whose windows overlooked all the town, the silvery course of the river, and the surrounding country for miles up and down. Although they are now sadly out of date, and of such size as to suggest that a blow of the hospitable knocker would fill them with echoes, there is an air of gentility and of good living about all these houses which makes us feel regret for the generation whose open-handed hospitality has passed into a tradition; while the mansions themselves, grown venerable, continue to unite two wholly dissimilar eras.

Usually there was an observatory on the roof, from which the owner could sweep the offing with his glass of a morning, and could run over in his mind the chance of a voyage long before his vessel had wallowed over the bar outside. He might then descend, take his cocked hat and cane from the hall-table, order dinner, with an extra cover for his captain, pull out his shirt-frill, and go down to his counting-house without a wrinkle on his brow or a crease in his silk stockings; everybody would know that his ship had come in. Sound in head and stomach, bluff of speech, yet with a certain homely dignity always distinguishing his class, the merchant of the olden time, undoubted autocrat to his immediate circle of dependants, was a man whose like we shall not look upon again. He left no successors.

During the two wars with England, a swarm of privateers, as well as some of the most famous vessels of the old, the invincible, navy, were launched here. In 1812 the port suffered as long and rigorous a blockade from the enemy's cruisers, as it had before been nearly paralyzed by Mr. Jefferson's embargo. Then the merchant had ruin staring him in the face whenever he levelled his glass at the two and three deckers exchanging signals in the offing, or when he paced up and down his grass-grown wharves, where his idle ships rusted; but if he did sometimes shut his glass with an angry jerk, or stamp his foot to say, between an oath and a groan, "Our masts take root, bud forth too, and beare akornes!" he was never found wanting in patriotism, nor did he show a niggardly or a craven spirit in the face of his reverses, so that the record of the Tracys, the Daltons, the Browns, is one of which their descendants are justly proud. Still, it was not thought to be a sinful thing in those days for the clergy to pray that a change of rulers might remove the embargo, or that a stiff gale of wind would raise the blockade, — the means to this end being left to the wisdom of an over-ruling Providence.

For the stranger, however, there are but two things in Newburyport for which he asks the first person he meets. One is the tomb of George Whitefield, and the other is the mansion of Lord Timothy Dexter. One is in a quiet and unpretending neighborhood; the other stands in the high places of the city. Two objects more diverse by their associations, two lives more opposite in their aspirations, it would be difficult to conceive of, yet here the memories of the two men jostle each other. Truly it is only a step from the sublime to the ridiculous.

The number of pilgrims who visit the tomb of Whitefield is very large. The great itinerant preacher is buried in a vault that is entered by a door underneath the pulpit of the Old South Presbyterian meeting-house, in Federal Street. Its slender and modest spire, with its brazen weathercock, rises above a neighborhood no longer fashionable, perhaps, but quite in keeping with its own severe simplicity. Neither belongs to the present. The house has the date 1756 over the entrance-door, and is built of wood. At the left of the pulpit, as we enter, is a marble cenotaph erected to the memory of Whitefield, one face of which

19

bears a long eulogistic inscription. Descending into the crypt, whose sepulchral darkness a lamp dimly lights, we are alone with its silent inmates. Yonder dark object presently shapes itself into a bier. We approach it. The coffin-lid is thrown open, so as to expose what is left of its tenant, — the fleshless skull and bones of George Whitefield. It is not forbidden

WHITEFIELD'S MONUMENT.

to shudder. Who, indeed, that looks can believe that "there, Whitefield, pealed thy voice"?

Owing, doubtless, to the fact that many come to gratify an idle curiosity, the trustees have closed the tomb "for a spell," as the old sexton remarked, with too evident vexation for the loss of his fees for showing it to visitors. It is a curious instance of vandalism that one of the arm-bones should have been surreptitiously taken from the coffin, and after having twice crossed the ocean, have found its way back to its original resting-place. The story goes that an ardent admirer of the eloquent preacher, who wished to obtain some relic of him, gave a commission to a friend for the purpose, and this friend, it is supposed, procured the limb through the connivance of the sexton's son. The act of desecration being, however, discovered, aroused so much indignation everywhere, that the possessor thought it best to relinquish his prize; and he accordingly intrusted it to a shipmaster, with the injunction to see it again safely placed in the vault with his own eyes, — which direction was strictly carried out. "And I," finished the sexton, "have been down in the tomb with the captain who brought that ar' bone back." But this all happened many years ago.

This neighborhood is further interesting as being the birthplace of William Lloyd Garrison, whose dwelling is the first on the left in School Street, while the next is that in which Whitefield died of an attack of asthma. The extraordinary religious awakening that followed his preaching is one of the traditions common to all our New-England seaboard towns, the houses where he stopped being always pointed out; so that everywhere Whitefield has a monument. A missionary who crossed the ocean fourteen times, an evangelist who preached more than eighteen thousand sermons, and whose audiences were so numerous that he was compelled to hold his meetings in the open air, was no ordinary man. To this exposure of himself his death is attributed. It caused a deep sensation; and so much had the public estimate of him changed, that there was even a contention for the honor of possessing his remains, which now lie in the place where he was stoned when he first attempted to preach in it. Such is the retribution that time brings. When this cowardly assault nearly struck the Bible from his hand, the man who always had an answer for everything, holding up the book, said with calm dignity, but in a voice that went through his hearers like an electric shock : " I have a warrant from God to preach : his seal is in my hand, and I stand in the King's highway."

———◆———

LORD TIMOTHY DEXTER.

TIMOTHY DEXTER was not born great, neither did he have greatness thrust upon him ; yet so effectually does he seem to have thrust his quasi-greatness upon Newburyport, that even now, after the lapse of nearly fourscore years, counting from the time when he laid his eccentricities in the dust, as all lords, sooner or later, must do, the stranger visiting Newburyport asks first to be guided to the spot where the renowned Lord Timothy lived in most unrepublican state.

Timothy Dexter was not a native of Newburyport. Malden has the honor of being his birthplace ; and the family still exists there, a branch of it having occupied one estate for more than two hundred years. Although bred to the tanner's trade, Timothy was far too shrewd to hide his talents in a vat. He saw easier avenues to wealth opening before him ; and with a forecast which would make any merchant's fortune, he bought and sold in the way of trade until he had accumulated a snug capital for future speculations.

Having "put money in his purse," Timothy Dexter became ambitious ; believing that a golden key would admit him within the circles of the aristocracy. Then, as now, Newburyport was the seat of culture, refinement, and literature ; and it was therefore to Newburyport that the titled tanner now turned his eyes. He found in its picturesque precincts two mansion houses available for his purpose, and these he purchased. He first occupied one situated on State Street ; but having soon sold this at a profit, he removed to the well-known estate situated on High Street, thenceforth making it, through an odd perversion of its real character, one of the historic mansions of Essex County.

LORD TIMOTHY DEXTER'S MANSION, NEWBURYPORT.

Vain to excess, he longed for the adulation which a certain class of people are always ready to lavish upon the possessors of great wealth.

He now began the work of renovation which transformed the sober mansion of his predecessor into a harlequinade in wood. By his directions the painters adorned the outside a brilliant white, trimmed with green. Minarets were built upon the roof, in the centre of which rose a lofty cupola surmounted by a gilded eagle with outspread wings. Standing as it did upon the crown of the hill, the house could be seen for miles around, and soon became a landmark for mariners. But the great and unique display was made in the garden fronting this house.

There then was working at his trade in the town a skilful ship-carver named Wilson, whom Dexter employed to carve from the solid wood some forty gigantic statues of the most celebrated men of the period. Gladly did the sculptor accept and execute this order, for it enabled him to lay the foundation of a small fortune, and to acquire a lasting reputation among his townsmen for his workmanship. These images were about eight feet in height. With conscientious fidelity to fact and fitness, the carved clothing was painted to resemble that worn by the real personages, — blue coats, white shirts, buff breeches, and the rest, — altogether making a display which no museum in the country could equal. Over the main entrance to the house, on a beautiful arch, stood George Washington, with John Adams, bareheaded, at his right hand; for Dexter said that no one should stand covered on the right hand of his greatest hero, General Washington. On the left was Thomas Jefferson, holding in his hand a scroll inscribed "Constitution." But my Lord Timothy, it is said, in spite of the painter's objections, insisted upon spelling the name of the Sage of Monticello, "Tomas," instead of Thomas, finally threatening to shoot the artist on the spot if he persisted in his refusal to do what was required of him.

The man who had planned and created this garden of statues was as capricious as fame itself. If he raised a statue to some favorite to-day, he reserved the right to change his name to-morrow ; and often a stroke of the painter's brush transformed statesmen into soldiers, or soldiers into civilians. General Morgan yesterday was Bonaparte to-day, to whom Dexter always paid the civility of touching his hat when he passed underneath the great Corsican's shadow. In the panels of the entablatures of each of the columns on which these images stood were the names of the characters represented. Among them were Governor John Langdon of New Hampshire, Governor Caleb Strong of Massachusetts, Rufus King, General Butler of South Carolina, General Knox, John Jay, John Hancock, William Pitt, Louis XVI., King George, Lord Nelson, and the Indian Chief, Corn Planter. There was also one allegorical figure representing Maternal Affection, and another a Travelling Preacher, besides several enormous lions occupying pedestals. Dexter himself monopolized two statues. One of these stood near the door, holding in its hand a placard, which was inscribed, " I am first in the East, the first in the West, and the Greatest Philosopher in the known world." The cost of these images, with the columns on which they were placed, is said to have been fifteen thousand dollars. This was the only way, however, in which Lord Timothy was able to bring himself into association with greatness. Society refused him recognition with the same hard obduracy that his own wooden images did, his vulgarity and ignorance being too gross even for all his gold to gild ; and so he lived only among sycophants and parasites, who cajoled and flattered him to his heart's content.

Having a house and grounds which he flattered himself would make his stuck-up neighbors split with envy, Dexter next resolved to set up an equipage fit for a lord; and one suiting his ideas of magnificence was accordingly procured. Some one having told him that the carriages of the nobility were always decorated with a coat of arms, one was composed on demand and painted on the panel. The crest may have been a dexter arm brandishing a warming-pan, with the motto, " By this I got ye."

In the matter of horses Dexter was extremely fastidious, as well as capricious. As soon as he grew tired of one color, he would sell those he had just bought at extravagant prices, and buy others. His costly carriage, drawn by beautiful cream-colored animals, became one of the sights of the day whenever the owner chose to take an airing; but to the luxury of the equipage the gaunt and mean face, half buried underneath an enormous cocked-hat, the spare figure sitting bolt upright, the hairless dog squatted beside it, offered a contrast as strikingly ridiculous as did the coach of the celebrated Tittlebat-Titmouse, and it provoked quite as much laughter when it passed through the town, the street urchins shouting ironically, " Clear the way for my lord's carriage ! "

In this coach Dexter once drove in state to the county prison at Ipswich, where he served a short sentence for firing his pistol at a countryman who stood staring at his museum of celebrities, and who did not move on when my Lord Timothy commanded him.

But this singular being did not consider his establishment as complete without the *entourage* of a nobleman in the days of chivalry. He would again revive the age of poets and troubadours. Perhaps the most unique idea of all was the engagement of a poet-laureate to write his praises and to embalm his memory in verse. There happened to be living in Newburyport one Jonathan Plummer, an eccentric pedler of fish, who had a *penchant* for extempore rhyming which with the ignorant and illiterate passed for genius. A bargain was forthwith struck with him to serve in the capacity of poet-laureate, and as such he was presently installed in Dexter's household. A handsome new livery was ordered, consisting of a fine black broadcloth coat, with stars on the collar and fringe on the skirts, shoes with large silver buckles, a cocked-hat, and a gold-headed cane. One of Plummer's poems to his patron, comprising about fifteen verses, has been preserved entire. The following is a specimen : —

Lord Dexter is a man of fame,
Most celebrated is his name,
More precious far than gold that's pure :
Lord Dexter shine forever more !

His house is white and trimmed with green ;
For many miles it may be seen ;
It shines as bright as any star ;
The fame of it has spread afar.

Lord Dexter, like King Solomon,
Hath gold and silver by the ton ;
And bells to churches he hath given,
To worship the great King of Heaven.

Not content with all this, Dexter's ambition now aimed at nothing less than literary fame ; and this was achieved at a stroke by the publication of his "Pickle for the Knowing Ones," — an autobiography which has ever since puzzled those to whom it was addressed, to decide whether the author was really more knave or fool. But as the first, and probably the last, example of the kind, the "Pickle" had immediate success, although in every way it is a most grotesque libel upon the good name of literary composition. The spelling is atrocious, and there was no attempt at punctuation ; but the author's invention supplied this defect in a second edition, by inserting a page or more of punctuation-marks at the end, with the following note : —

"Mister printer the Nowing ones complane of my book the fust edition had no stops I put in A Nuf here and they may peper and salt it as they plese."

But this odd notion hardly originated with Dexter, original as he unquestionably was, inasmuch as Tom Hood has an account in his "Reminiscences" of a literary friend who placed a number of colons, semicolons, etc., at the bottom of his communication, adding,

And these are my points that I place at the foot,
That you may put stops that I can't stop to put.

Dexter's unique speculation in warming-pans, told by himself in the "Pickle," has perhaps done more to transmit his name to posterity than anything else.   By some people the story is considered as nothing short of a pure fabrication, designed for those inquisitive people who were continually asking how Dexter made his money.   But even if the story is too good to be true, — and as a merchant his shrewdness was proverbial, — the world has accepted it upon his own testimony as the lucky blunder of fortune's favorite and fool.   The man being himself an enigma, we should say that in his case it is the improbable that is true.

WARMING-PAN.

He relates that, having dreamed three nights running that warming-pans would do well in the West Indies, he collected "no more than forty-two thousand," which were put on board nine vessels bound to different ports, and cleared him seventy-nine per cent. The story goes that one of Dexter's captains, being a shrewd fellow, took off the covers of the pans, which were then sold to the sugar-planters, all of whom were anxious to obtain them for ladles.

Dexter's speculations in whalebone and Bibles were equally comical and absurd.   Again he dreamed "that the good book was run down in this country so low as half price, and dull at that.   I had," he says, "the ready cash by wholesale.   I bought twenty-one thousand.   I put them into twenty-one vessels for the West Indies, and sent as a text that all of them must have one Bible in each family, or they would go to —— ."

Besides putting faith in dreams, Dexter believed in fortune-telling as well as fortune-making, and made many attempts to

pry into the obscurity of the future by consulting the oracle
of his neighborhood, one Madam Hooper, — a strange character,

LORD TIMOTHY DEXTER.

who, after teaching school, assumed the profession of fortune-
telling. The renowned Moll Pitcher also had Dexter for a
patron, and her influence is said to have been beneficial to him.

Another person who is said to have exerted a great influence for good over this eccentric man was a negress named Lucy Lancaster, — a female of Amazonian proportions, who is described as being possessed of unusual shrewdness and information. Her father, called Cæsar, was the son of an African king, and was brought to the country as a slave. So highly was he esteemed, that on " Nigger 'Lection Day " Lucy's father acted as generalissimo, and was entitled to have twelve footmen run by his side, while he proudly bestrode a spirited horse at the head of the sooty procession.

When the yellow fever raged in Newburyport in 1796, Lucy Lancaster proved herself indeed of royal blood. Strong and fearless, full of good works, she devoted herself day and night to the sick, principally in the families of the best people ; Dexter, among others, having need of her services, she became a firm friend and counsellor to the family. Her estimate of Dexter was much higher than the common one, and she gave him credit for more honesty of purpose than most people did. He needed some one like her to advise him, and she frequently turned his attention from mischievous pursuits by suggesting alterations and improvements to be made in his house and grounds. This woman survived Dexter nearly forty years.

One of the oddest of Dexter's freaks was his mock funeral, which was arranged by him with all the solemnity of preparation requisite for a real interment. In his garden he had caused to be built a spacious tomb, while in his house he had long kept a costly coffin made of mahogany, richly adorned.

With a curiosity perhaps unprecedented in the history of vain man, he wished to see the effect his funeral would produce. Invitations were issued, mourning apparel was prepared for his family, some one was found to officiate as minister, and the procession was duly formed, and marched to the vault in the garden. While this farce was performing, Dexter was looking from an upper window, and before the company had dispersed, he was found beating his wife for not shedding tears at his pretended demise.

Of his conjugal relations, it is reported by one who knew him

well, that, becoming dissatisfied with his wife, he made a bargain
with her to leave him, giving her a thousand, or perhaps two
thousand, dollars in exchange for his liberty.   He then advertised for another wife ; but there being no applicant, he, after
waiting some time, was glad to hire his own wife to come back
by the offer of a sum equal to that he had originally given her
to go away.

On the 26th of October, 1806, Lord Dexter died at his mansion on High Street.   His funeral was an occasion which it
would have pleased him to witness, if such sights could be permitted to vain mortals ; but as the town officers would not, for
sanitary reasons, allow his remains to be deposited in his garden
tomb, he was laid away among his fellow townsmen in the
public burying-ground near the frog-pond.

Not long after his death a gale blew down many of the
images, and the place grew dilapidated.   About the year 1846,
while it was being used as a factory boarding-house, the estate
was purchased by E. G. Kelley, of Newburyport, who possessed
wealth and taste, and he proceeded to obliterate as far as possible all traces of his predecessor's follies.   The three presidents
over the door were thrown down and demolished ; the grounds
were newly laid out ; and now nothing except the eagle on the
summit of the cupola remains to show Dexter's bizarre achievements in ornamentation, or to point a moral upon his extrava-
gances as a philosopher.

THE OLD ELM OF NEWBURY.

ON Parker Street, in Old Newbury, just out of the village,
there is still growing the gigantic elm-tree that is known
far and wide as the old elm of Newbury.   Coffin says that
it was transplanted and set out here by Richard Jaques in
1713, so that it has now been growing on this spot one hun-

dred and seventy years.   Its girth is enormous, being twenty-
four and one half feet at one foot from the ground.   Now that
the historic old elm of Boston is no more, this is undoubtedly
the largest tree of its species in New England.

Yet older than the tree are some of the houses in the neighborhood—

> Old homesteads, sacred to all that can
> Gladden or sadden the heart of man ;

and still older are the corroded stones in the village churchyard
that overlooks the broad estuary of the river, and is washed by
the pond of the floating island below it.   Legendary lore clings
around these aged houses like the mistletoe to the oak, and lends
its charm to the mystery that overshadows them.

THE OLD ELM OF NEWBURY.

In a pretty pastoral legend Miss Hannah Gould gives the origin of the old elm, and incidentally, also, an engaging picture of the farm life of those early times with which the legend itself is associated.

THE OLD ELM OF NEWBURY.

H. F. GOULD.

DID it ever come in your way to pass
The silvery pond, with its fringe of grass,
And threading the lane hard by to see
The veteran elm of Newbury ?

. . . .

Well, that old elm that is now so grand
Was once a twig in the rustic hand
Of a youthful peasant, who went one night
To visit his love by the tender light
Of the modest moon and her twinkling host ;
While the star that lighted his bosom most,
And gave to his lonely feet their speed,
Abode in a cottage beyond the mead.

. . . .

It is not recorded how long he stayed
In the cheerful house of the smiling maid.
But when he came out it was late and dark
And silent ; not even a dog would bark
To take from his feeling of loneliness,
And make the length of his way seem less.

. . . .

An elm grew close by the cottage's eaves,
So he plucked him a twig well clothed with leaves.
So, sallying forth, with the supple arm
To serve as a talisman parrying harm,
He felt that, though his heart was big,
'T was even stouter for having the twig ;
For this, he thought, would answer to switch
The horrors away, as he crossed the ditch,

The meadow and copse, wherein, perchance,
Will-o'-the-wisp might wickedly dance ;
And, wielding it, keep him from having a chill
At the menacing sound of "Whippoorwill!"
And his flesh from creeping beside the bog
At the harsh bass voice of the viewless frog ;
In short, he felt that the switch would be
Guard, plaything, business, and company.

When he got safe home, and joyfully found
He still was himself, and living, and sound,
He planted the twig by his family cot,
To stand as a monument, marking the spot
It helped him to reach ; and, what was still more,
Because it had grown by his fair one's door.

The twig took root ; and, as time flew by,
Its boughs spread wide, and its head grew high ;
While the priest's good service had long been done,
Which made the youth and the maiden one ;
And their young scions arose and played
Around the tree in its leafy shade.

THE PROPHECY OF SAMUEL SEWALL.

THIS piece, so full of the milk of human kindness, was
written to disprove the opinion advanced by the Simple
Cobbler and others, to whom it is at once a rebuke and an
answer, that it was impossible to subsist in New England by
the labor of one's hands alone. It is found in Sewall's "New
Heaven upon the New Earth." So quaintly is it expressed, that
only the original language can fitly set forth the picture of pros-
perous abundance that so gladdened the good old man's eyes
when looking down upon it from the Newbury hills. Retain-

ing this as much as possible, Mr. Whittier has phrased it in poetic form that is singularly like the prose version.

This, let us say, is the same Samuel Sewall who, as one of the witchcraft judges, gained a lasting notoriety, and whose marriage to Hannah, the daughter of Mint-master John Hull, originated the tradition that she received her own weight in silver Pine-Tree shillings as a wedding portion. The family has always held a distinguished place in the annals of Colony and State; and Sewall's remarkable "Diary," to which we have before referred, is a storehouse of information concerning the events and manners of his time. The prophecy is as follows : —

"As long as Plum Island shall faithfully keep the commanded Post, Notwithstanding the hectoring words and hard blows of the proud and boisterous ocean ; As long as any Salmon or Sturgeon shall swim in the streams of Merrimack, or any Perch or Pickeril in Crane Pond ; As long as the Sea Fowl shall know the time of their coming, and not neglect seasonably to visit the places of their acquaintance ; As long as any Cattel shall be fed with the Grass growing in the meadows which doe humbly bow themselves before Turkie Hill ; As long as any Sheep shall walk upon Old-town Hills, and shall from thence pleasantly look down upon the River Parker and the fruitful Marishes lying beneath ; As long as any free and harmless Doves shall find a White Oak or other Tree within the township to perch, or feed, or build a careless Nest upon, and shall voluntarily present themselves to perform the office of Gleaners after Barley Harvest ; As long as Nature shall not grow old and dote, but shall constantly remember to give the rows of Indian Corn their education by Pairs, — So long shall Christians be born there ; and being first made meet, shall from thence be translated to be made partakers of the Saints of Light."

PROPHECY OF SAMUEL SEWALL.

J. G. WHITTIER.

I SEE it all like a chart unrolled,
But my thoughts are full of the past and old ;
I hear the tales of my boyhood told,

And the shadows and shapes of early days
Flit dimly by in the veiling haze,
With measured movement and rhythmic chime
Weaving like shuttles my web of rhyme.
I think of the old man wise and good
Who once on yon misty hillsides stood,
(A poet who never measured rhyme,
A seer unknown to his dull-eared time,)
And, propped on his staff of age, looked down,
With his boyhood's love, on his native town,
Where, written, as if on its hills and plains,
His burden of prophecy yet remains,
For the voices of wood, and wave, and wind
To read in the ear of the musing mind: —

" As long as Plum Island, to guard the coast,
As God appointed, shall keep its post ;
As long as a salmon shall haunt the deep
Of Merrimack River, or sturgeon leap ;
As long as pickerel, swift and slim,
Or red-backed perch, in Crane Pond swim ;
As long as the annual sea-fowl know
Their time to come and their time to go ;
As long as cattle shall roam at will
The green grass meadows by Turkey Hill ;
As long as sheep shall look from the side
Of Oldtown Hill on marishes wide,
And Parker River, and salt-sea tide ;
As long as a wandering pigeon shall search
The fields below from his white-oak perch,
When the barley-harvest is ripe and shorn,
And the dry husks fall from the standing corn ;
As long as Nature shall not grow old,
Nor drop her work from her doting hold,
And her care for the Indian corn forget,
And the yellow rows in pairs to set, —
So long shall Christians here be born,
Grow up and ripen as God's sweet corn, —
By the beak of bird, by the breath of frost,
Shall never a holy ear be lost,

But, husked by Death, in the Planter's sight,
Be sown again in the fields of light ! "

The Island still is purple with plums,
Up the river the salmon comes,
The sturgeon leaps, and the wild-fowl feeds
On hillside berries and marish seeds, —
All the beautiful signs remain,
From spring-time sowing to autumn rain
The good man's vision returns again !
And let us hope, as well we can,
That the Silent Angel who garners man
May find some grain as of old he found
In the human cornfield ripe and sound,
And the Lord of the Harvest deign to own
The precious seed by the fathers sown !

THE DOUBLE–HEADED SNAKE.

ONE does not go far into the history of our legendary lore without making the discovery that Cotton Mather's study, like that of his father before him, was the congenial receptacle for everything that might happen in New England out of the common. Upon this centre the dark tales converged like a flight of bats in the night. His father had solicited the New-England ministers to contribute everything of a marvellous character that might come within their knowledge or under their observation, to the end that the mysterious workings of Providence might if possible be cleared up, and the relation to human affairs, — which it was not for a moment doubted they sustained, — be so adjusted as to point a moral or adorn a tale. To this sagacious foresight we owe that singularly interesting book, the "Remarkable Providences," of Increase Mather. To this we also owe the Double-Headed Snake of Newbury, — a reptile that would certainly have made the fortune of any itine-

rant showman of our own period, have put the four-legged girl
completely into the shade, and have caused the devil-fish of
Victor Hugo to shed tears of vexation.

The account of this wonderful snake comes in a letter from
the Reverend Christopher Toppan, minister of Newbury, addressed to Cotton Mather. Considering that it emanates from
a source so entirely respectable and trustworthy, it is to be hoped
that nobody will treat it as an idle village tale. He writes : —

"Concerning the Amphisbæna, as soon as I received your commands
I made diligent enquiry of several persons who saw it after it was
dead. . . . They directed me, for further information, . . . to the persons who saw it alive, and killed it, which were two or three lads,

YE DOUBLE—HEADED SNAKE.

about twelve or fourteen ; one of which, a pert, sensible youngster, told
me yt one of his mates, running towards him, cryed out there was a
snake with two heads running after him, upon which he run to him ;
and the snake getting into a puddle of water, he with a stick pulled
him out, after which it came toward him, and as he went backwards
and forward, so the snake would doe likewise. After a little time, the
snake, upon his striking at him, gathered up his whole body into a
sort of quoil, except *both heads*, which kept towards him, and he distinctly saw two *mouths* and two *stings* (as they are vulgarly called),
which stings or tongues it kept putting forth after the usual manner
of snakes till he killed it.

"*Postscript.* — Before ensealing I spoke with the other man who examined the Amphisbæna (and he is also a man of credit), and he assures me yt it had really two heads, one at each end, two mouths, two stings, or tongues, and so forth.

"Sir, I have nothing more to add, but that he may have a remembrance in your prayers who is,

"Sir, your most humble servant,

"CHRISTOPHER TOPPAN."

THE DOUBLE–HEADED SNAKE OF NEWBURY.

J. G. WHITTIER.

FAR away in the twilight time
Of every people, in every clime,
Dragons and griffins and monsters dire,
Born of water, and air, and fire,
Or nursed, like the Python, in the mud
And ooze of the old Deucalion flood,
Crawl and wriggle and foam with rage,
Through dusk tradition and ballad age.
So from the childhood of Newbury town
And its time of fable the tale comes down
Of a terror which haunted bush and brake,
The Amphisbæna, the Double Snake !

. . . . .

Whether he lurked in the Oldtown fen
Or the gray earth-flax of the Devil's Den,
Or swam in the wooded Artichoke,
Or coiled by the Northman's Written Rock,
Nothing on record is left to show;
Only the fact that he lived, we know,
And left the cast of a double head
In the scaly mask which he yearly shed.
For he carried a head where his tail should be,
And the two, of course, could never agree,
But wriggled about with main and might,
Now to the left and now to the right ;

Pulling and twisting this way and that,
Neither knew what the other was at.

. . . .

Far and wide the tale was told,
Like a snowball growing while it rolled.
The nurse hushed with it the baby's cry ;
And it served, in the worthy minister's eye,
To paint the primitive serpent by.
Cotton Mather came galloping down
All the way to Newbury town,
With his eyes agog and his ears set wide,
And his marvellous inkhorn at his side ;
Stirring the while in the shallow pool
Of his brains for the lore he learned at school,
To garnish the story, with here a streak
Of Latin, and there another of Greek :
And the tales he heard and the notes he took,
Behold! are they not in his Wonder-Book ?

———◇———

THOMAS MACY, THE EXILE.

THE archives of Massachusetts once more furnish the incident concerning which, as in the "King's Missive," a
letter — a mere scrap — has sufficed for the poet to construct his
legend.

Thomas Macy, yeoman, of Salisbury, in the county of Essex,
is the subject of Whittier's ballad entitled "The Exiles," which
first appeared in the "North Star," a Philadelphia annual. As it
was then published, it had two stanzas more than it now has in
the author's collected poems.

This Macy, the hero of the poem, was complained of for having given shelter to some "notorious" Quakers, or vagabonds,
as the law then termed them, in his own house. This simple
act of hospitality being in violation of the law prohibiting any
man to open his door to a Quaker, no matter how urgent soever

the call upon his humanity might be, Macy, the offending culprit, was cited forthwith to appear before the General Court at Boston to answer the complaint preferred against him.

Instead of complying with the requisition which very few would be found willing in those days to disobey, Macy wrote an humble, apologetic, and deprecatory letter to the General Court. The letter indicates a man of a very different stamp from the antique hero that the poem depicts in the act of cheating the minions of the law of their prey. From its terms we have little notion that the "Bold Macy," as he is styled there, was cast in the same stern mould that the martyrs are; but we have a very distinct one, that if not actually a craven, he believed that in his case discretion was the better part of valor. At any rate, he wisely concluded to keep out of the clutches of the law, and did so. We are sure that the reader would regard any tampering with Macy's letter as unpardonable as we do. He says : —

"This is to entreat the honored court not to be offended because of my non-appearance. It is not from any slighting the authority of this honored court, nor from feare to answer the case, but I have bin for some weeks past very ill, and am so at present, and notwithstanding my illness, yet I, desirous to appear, have done my utmost endeavour to hire a horse, but cannot procure one at present. I being at present destitute have endeavoured to purchase, but at present cannot attaine it, but I shall relate the truth of the case as my answer should be to ye honored court, and more cannot be proved, nor so much. On a rainy morning there came to my house Edward Wharton and three men more ; the said Wharton spoke to me, saying that they were traveling eastward, and desired me to direct them in the way to Hampton, and asked me how far it was to Casco bay. I never saw any of ye men afore except Wharton, neither did I require their names, or who they were, but by their carriage I thought they might be Quakers, and told them so, and therefore desired them to passe on their way, saying to them I might possibly give offence in entertaining them, and as soone as the violence of the rain ceased (for it rained very hard) they went away, and I never saw them since. The time that they stayed in the house was about three quarters of an hour, but I can safely affirme it was not an hour. They spake not many words in the time, neither was I at leisure to talke with them, for I came home wet to the skin immediately afore they came to the house, and I found my wife sick in bed. If this satisfie not the honored court, I shall subject to their sentence. I have not willingly offended. I am ready to serve and obey you in the Lord.

"Tho. Macy."

ESCAPE OF GOODMAN MACY.

Three of these men, being preachers, could look for no mercy from the Puritan authorities, who charged them with going about seducing his Majesty's good subjects to their "cursed" opinions. One of them, Edward Wharton, was an old offender. Two of them, Robinson and Stevenson, are the same persons who, a little later on, were hanged at Boston, as related in our account of Mrs. Dyer. These itinerants undoubtedly knew where to apply, and to whom. Macy knew Wharton; he was fully aware of the risk that he ran in breaking the law. But he and other Quakers of Newbury and Salisbury had already purchased the Island of Nantucket, to which it now seems probable that they intended removing out of harm's way, as that island was not within the jurisdiction of the Bay Colony.

Having thus secured an asylum in advance, and the General Court refusing to allow his explanation or accept his apology, tradition now steps in to inform us that, immediately upon learning the sentence of the Court, Macy and his wife took an open boat, put their children and their movable effects into it, and in this frail conveyance they made their way along the coast to Cape Cod, and thence to Nantucket. Edward Starbuck, of Salisbury, accompanied them. Through persecution, then, Macy became the first white inhabitant of this famed isle of the sea; and from his landing at Maddequet in the autumn of 1659 its settlement dates in history.

The ballad supposes Macy's house to be suddenly surrounded by a troop of horsemen while the proscribed Wharton is under the protection of his roof. Macy disputes with the sheriff until the minister, who is supposed to be present, urges the officer also to seize Macy, whereupon the goodman and his wife, breaking away from them, run for the river : —

> Ho! speed the Macys, neck or naught, —
>   The river-course was near: —
> The plashing on its pebbled shore
>   Was music to their ear.
>
> .   .   .   .
>
> A leap — they gain the boat — and there
>   The goodman wields his oar :
> "Ill luck betide them all," — he cried, —
>   "The laggards upon the shore."
>
> Down through the crashing underwood,
>   The burly sheriff came : —
> "Stand, goodman Macy, — yield thyself;
>   Yield in the King's own name."

"Now out upon thy hangman's face!"
    Bold Macy answered then, —
"Whip *women* on the village green,
    But meddle not with men."

          .   .   .   .

With skilful hand and wary eye
  . The harbor-bar was crossed; —
A plaything of the restless wave,
    The boat on ocean tossed.

          .   .   .   .   .

They passed the gray rocks of Cape Ann,
    And Gloucester's harbor-bar;
The watch-fire of the garrison
    Shone like a setting star.

          .   .   .   .

Far round the bleak and stormy Cape
    The vent'rous Macy passed,
And on Nantucket's naked isle,
    Drew up his boat at last.

          .   .   .   .

And yet that isle remaineth
    A refuge of the free,
As when true-hearted Macy
    Beheld it from the sea.

          .   .   .   .

God bless the sea-beat island! —
    And grant for evermore,
That charity and freedom dwell
    As now upon her shore!

------◆------

TELLING THE BEES.

RESPECTING bees, one very old superstition **among others**
is, as I can strictly affirm, still cherished, surviving, apparently, through that peculiarity of the mind which, the event being
uncertain, elects to give it the benefit of the doubt rather than to

discard it as a childish and meaningless custom. This is the common belief that bees must be made acquainted with the death of any member of the family, otherwise these intelligent little creatures will either desert the hive in a pet, or leave off working and die inside of it. The old way of doing this was for the goodwife of the house to go and hang the stand of hives with black, the usual symbol of mourning, she at the same time softly humming some doleful tune to herself. Another way was for the master

to approach the hives and rap gently upon them. When the bees' attention was thus secured, he would say in a low voice that such or such a person — mentioning the name — was dead. This pretty and touching superstition is the subject of one of Whittier's "Home Ballads."

> Here is the place ; right over the hill
>   Runs the path I took ;
> You can see the gap in the old wall still,
>   And the stepping-stones in the shallow brook.
>
> There are the beehives ranged in the sun ;
>   And down by the brink
> Of the brook are her poor flowers, weed o'errun,
>   Pansy and daffodil, rose and pink.

Before them, under the garden-wall,
   Forward and back,
Went drearily singing the chore-girl small,
   Draping each hive with a shred of black.

Trembling, I listened : the summer sun
   Had the chill of snow ;
For I knew she was telling the bees of one
   Gone on the journey we all must go !

Then I said to myself, " My Mary weeps
   For the dead to-day :
Haply her blind old grandsire sleeps
   The fret and the pain of his age away."

But her dog whined low ; on the doorway sill,
   With his cane to his chin,
The old man sat ; and the chore-girl still
   Sung to the bees stealing out and in.

    .   .   .   .   .

" Stay at home, pretty bees, fly not hence !
   Mistress Mary is dead and gone ! "

Part Eighth.

HAMPTON AND PORTSMOUTH LEGENDS.

HAMPTON LEGENDS.

THE strip of coast extending from the Merrimack to the Piscataqua is an almost unbroken line of hard sand-beach washed by the ocean. Salisbury Sands begins and Hampton and Rye continue the line that is only interrupted where some creek cuts a way through it, or some bleak foreland thrusts itself out from the shore. Salisbury has for more than a hundred years been celebrated for the annual gatherings that its citizens hold on the beach there, in imitation of the " clam feasts " of the Indians, with whom the custom originated, and who made

BOAR'S HEAD.

the occasion one of much ceremony and solemnity, inasmuch as the sea was to them a great harvest-field provided by their God of Plenty for the sustenance of his red children.

Whittier's " Tent on the Beach " was pitched at the mouth of Hampton River, at the extremity of the Salisbury Sands ; and this is also the locality of the "Wreck of Rivermouth," found in that collection, which is something in the manner of Longfellow's "Tales of a Wayside Inn," the "tent" here doing the duty of the ancient tavern there.   Both are, however, in their method, a distinct reminiscence of the "Decamerone" of Boccaccio.   But Whittier's is a voice arising from the sea, full of its charm and mystery.   Standing at his tent door, —

> Northward a green bluff broke the chain
> Of sand-hills ; southward stretched a plain
> Of salt-grass, with a river winding down,
> Sail-whitened, and beyond the steeples of the town.

That is Boar's Head ; the Merrimack, with Newburyport in the distance.

Again, the poet points us to —

> the sunny isles in view,
> East of the grisly Head of the Boar ;

and then to where —

> Agamenticus lifts its blue
> Disk of a cloud the woodlands o'er.

So we feel that the "Tent on the Beach," instead of emanating from within the narrow limits of four walls, where the doors are securely bolted and barred against the weather, is the voice of Nature herself, — of the free breeze, the billows, and the foam, which imparts the invigorating quality to these verses, and gives them a distinct and captivating out-of-door flavor.

Of his legendary stories that are associated with Hampton the poet says : —

> A simple plot is mine : legends and runes
> Of credulous days ; old fancies, that have lain
> Silent from boyhood, taking voice again,
> Warmed into life once more, even as the tunes
> That, frozen in the fabled hunting-horn,
> Thawed into sound.

Hampton, formerly the Indian Winnicumet, is an old border settlement of the Bay Colony, that was transferred, through the blundering of her agents, to New Hampshire when the long dispute about the boundary between the two governments was finally settled. The singular and apparently eccentric course of this line, resembling a Virginia fence, is not due to chance, but to the crookedness of Colonial politics. While this controversy was pending, the legislative bodies of both governments once held a session at Hampton Falls, — which course, it was thought, by bringing the rival interests together, might end the dispute, but did not. Whereupon some poetaster of the period gave the following rhymed version of the "pomp and circumstance" attending the entry of the Massachusetts dignitaries into the humble frontier village. He says : —

> Dear Paddy, you ne'er did behold such a sight
> As yesterday morning was seen before night.
> You in all your born days saw, nor I did n't neither,
> So many fine horses and men ride together.
> At the head the lower house trotted two in a row,
> Then all the higher house pranced after the low ;
> Then the Governor's coach galloped on like the wind,
> And the last that came foremost were troopers behind.
> But I fear it means no good to your neck nor mine,
> For they say 't is to fix a right place for the line.

As soon as you have crossed this line, the people, pointing toward their mountains, will tell you that there is no air like New-Hampshire air. As soon as you shall have passed beyond this boundary you no longer breathe the atmosphere of the old Puritan life, but one emanating from a different and antagonistic source, — into which, nevertheless, the more vigorous currents originating on the other side of the border constantly infused themselves and kept it pure.

The most interesting thing about Hampton, apart from its legends, is the singular promontory of Boar's Head, which is one of the noted resorts of the New-England coast, and one of the earliest to be visited for health or pleasure.

Boar's Head is indeed a puzzle. It is a heap of drift gently ascending from the marshes to the crumbling brow of a lofty headland, against which, far below you, the sea dashes wildly. The bowlders sticking in its sides look as if they might have been shot there in the days when stones supplied the want of cannon-balls; for we look around without seeing anything to account for their presence. It is wind-swept and treeless. A few dwarf junipers and some clumps of bushes cling mournfully to its sides, which they are unable to ascend. A low reef stretching out towards the southeast, resembling the broken vertebræ of some fabled sea-monster, shows in what direction the grand old headland has most suffered from the unremitting work of demolition carried on by the waves, which pour and break like an avalanche over the blackened bowlders, and fly hissing into the air like the dust rising from its ruins. As if to confirm this theory, nothing grows on the southeast point, while on the northeast grasses flourish and daisies nod to the cool sea-breeze. We say again, Boar's Head is a puzzle.

It is indeed an inspiring sight to see the surf breaking on each side of you in a continuous line of foam from the mouth of the Merrimack to Little Boar's Head, and then, turning towards the offing, see the dark cluster of the Isles of Shoals lying low on the still more extended expanse of the ocean.

JONATHAN MOULTON AND THE DEVIL.

(From "The Heart of the White Mountains.")

THE legendary hero of Hampton is General Jonathan Moulton. He is no fictitious personage, but one of veritable flesh and blood, who, having acquired considerable celebrity in the old wars, lives on through the medium of a local legend.

The General, says the legend, encountered a far more notable adversary than Abenaki warriors or conjurers, among whom he

Jonathan Moulton and ye ✶ Devil

had lived, and whom it was the passion of his life to exterminate.

In an evil hour his yearning to amass wealth suddenly led him to declare that he would sell his soul for the possession of unbounded riches. Think of the Devil, and he is at your elbow. The fatal declaration was no sooner made — the General was sitting alone by his fireside — than a shower of sparks came down the chimney, out of which stepped a man dressed from top to toe in black velvet. The astonished Moulton noticed that the stranger's ruffles were not even smutted.

"Your servant, General!" quoth the stranger, suavely. "But let us make haste, if you please, for I am expected at the Governor's in a quarter of an hour," he added, picking up a live coal with his thumb and forefinger, and consulting his watch with it.

The General's wits began to desert him. Portsmouth was five leagues — long ones at that — from Hampton House, and his strange visitor talked, with the utmost unconcern, of getting there in fifteen minutes! His astonishment caused him to stammer out, —

"Then you must be the — "

"Tush! what signifies a name?" interrupted the stranger, with a deprecating wave of the hand. "Come, do we understand each other? Is it a bargain, or not?"

At the talismanic word "bargain" the General pricked up his ears. He had often been heard to say that neither man nor devil could get the better of him in a trade. He took out his jack-knife and began to whittle. The Devil took out his, and began to pare his nails.

"But what proof have I that you can perform what you promise?" demanded Moulton, pursing up his mouth and contracting his bushy eyebrows, like a man who is not to be taken in by mere appearances.

The fiend ran his fingers carelessly through his peruke, when a shower of golden guineas fell to the floor and rolled to the four corners of the room. The General quickly stooped to pick up one; but no sooner had his fingers closed upon it, than he dropped it with a yell.   It was red-hot!

The Devil chuckled; "Try again," he said.   But Moulton shook his head and retreated a step.

"Don't be afraid."

Moulton cautiously touched a coin; it was cool.   He weighed it in his hand, and rung it on the table; it was full weight and true ring.   Then he went down on his hands and knees, and began to gather up the guineas with feverish haste.

"Are you satisfied?" demanded Satan.

"Completely, your Majesty."

"Then to business.   By the way, have you anything to drink in the house?"

"There is some Old Jamaica in the cupboard."

"Excellent!   I am as thirsty as a Puritan on election-day," said the Devil, seating himself at the table, and negligently flinging his mantle back over his shoulder, so as to show the jewelled clasps of his doublet.

Moulton brought a decanter and a couple of glasses from the cupboard, filled one, and passed it to his infernal guest, who tasted it, and smacked his lips with the air of a connoisseur. Moulton watched every gesture.   "Does your Excellency not find it to your taste?" he ventured to ask; having the secret idea that he might get the Devil drunk, and so outwit him.

"H'm, I have drunk worse.   But let me show you how to make a salamander," replied Satan, touching the lighted end of the taper to the liquor, which instantly burst into a spectral blue flame.   The fiend then raised the tankard to the height of his eye, glanced approvingly at the blaze, — which to Moulton's disordered intellect resembled an adder's forked and agile tongue, — nodded, and said, patronizingly, "To our better acquaintance!"   He then quaffed the contents at a single gulp.

Moulton shuddered; this was not the way he had been used to seeing healths drunk.   He pretended, however, to drink, for fear of giving offence; but somehow the liquor choked him. The demon set down the tankard, and observed, in a matter-of-fact way that put his listener in a cold sweat : "Now that you are convinced I am able to make you the richest man in all the province, listen ! Have I your ear ? It is well! In consideration of your agreement, duly signed and sealed, to deliver your soul " — here he drew a parchment from his breast — "I engage, on my part, on the first day of every month, to fill your boots with golden elephants, like these before you. But mark me well," said Satan, holding up a forefinger glittering with diamonds, "if you try to play me any trick, you will repent it ! I know you, Jonathan Moulton, and shall keep my eye upon you; so beware ! "

Moulton flinched a little at this plain speech; but a thought seemed to strike him, and he brightened up. Satan opened the scroll, smoothed out the creases, dipped a pen in the inkhorn at his girdle, and pointing to a blank space, said, laconically, "Sign ! "

Moulton hesitated.

"If you are afraid," sneered Satan, "why put me to all this trouble ?" and he began to put the gold in his pocket.

His victim seized the pen; but his hand shook so that he could not write. He gulped down a mouthful of rum, stole a look at his infernal guest, who nodded his head by way of encouragement, and a second time approached his pen to the paper. The struggle was soon over. The unhappy Moulton wrote his name at the bottom of the fatal list, which he was astonished to see numbered some of the highest personages in the province. "I shall at least be in good company," he muttered.

"Good !" said Satan, rising and putting the scroll carefully away within his breast. "Rely on me, General, and be sure you keep faith. Remember !" So saying, the demon waved his hand, flung his mantle about him, and vanished up the chimney.

Satan performed his part of the contract to the letter. On the first day of every month the boots, which were hung on the crane in the fireplace the night before, were found in the morning stuffed full of guineas. It is true that Moulton had ransacked the village for the largest pair to be found, and had finally secured a brace of trooper's jack-boots, which came nearly up to the wearer's thigh; but the contract merely expressed boots, and the Devil does not stand upon trifles.

Moulton rolled in wealth ; everything prospered. His neighbors regarded him first with envy, then with aversion, at last with fear.   Not a few affirmed that he had entered into a league with the Evil One.   Others shook their heads, saying, "What does it signify?— that man would outwit the Devil himself."

But one morning, when the fiend came as usual to fill the boots, what was his astonishment to find that he could not fill them.   He poured in the guineas, but it was like pouring water into a rat-hole.   The more he put in, the more the quantity seemed to diminish.   In vain he persisted ; the boots could not be filled.

The Devil scratched his ear.   "I must look into this," he reflected.   No sooner said, than he attempted to descend ; but in doing so he found his progress suddenly stopped.   A good reason.   The chimney was choked up with guineas !   Foaming with rage, the demon tore the boots from the crane.   The crafty General had cut off the soles, leaving only the legs for the Devil to fill.   The chamber was knee-deep with gold.

The Devil gave a horrible grin, and disappeared.   The same night Hampton House was burned to the ground, the General only escaping in his shirt.   He had been dreaming he was dead and in hell.   His precious guineas were secreted in the wainscot, the ceiling, and other hiding-places known only to himself.   He blasphemed, wept, and tore his hair.   Suddenly he grew calm.   After all, the loss was not irreparable, he reflected.   Gold would melt, it is true ; but he would find it all, — of course he would, — at daybreak, run into a solid lump in the cellar, — every guinea.   That is true of ordinary gold.

The General worked with the energy of despair, clearing away the rubbish.   He refused all offers of assistance ; he dared not accept them.   But the gold had vanished.   Whether it was really consumed, or had passed again into the massy entrails of the earth, will never be known. It is only certain that every vestige of it had disappeared.

When the General died and was buried, strange rumors began to circulate. To quiet them, the grave was opened; but when the lid was removed from the coffin, it was found to be empty.

Another legend runs to the effect that upon the death of his wife under — as evil report would have it — very suspicious circumstances, the General paid his court to a young woman who had been the companion of his deceased spouse. They were married. In the middle of the night the young bride awoke with a start. She felt an invisible hand trying to take off from her finger the wedding-ring that had once belonged to the dead and buried Mrs. Moulton. Shrieking with fright, she jumped out of bed, thus awaking her husband, who tried in vain to calm her fears. Candles were lighted and search made for the ring; but as it could never be found again, the ghostly visitor was supposed to have carried it away with her. This story is the same that is told by Whittier in the "New Wife and the Old."

GOODY COLE.

GOODWIFE Eunice Cole, the witch of Hampton, was for a quarter of a century or more the terror of the people of that town, who believed her to have sold herself body and soul to the Devil. Whom we hate we also fear. The bare mention of her name would, it is said, hush crying children into silence, or hurry truant boys to school. Although she was repeatedly thrown into prison, she was yet unaccountably suffered to continue to live the life of an outcast, until death finally freed the community from their fears. In 1680 she was brought before the Quarter Sessions to answer to the charge of being a witch; and though there was "noe full proof" that she was a witch, yet for the satisfaction of the Court, which "vehemently suspects her so to be," and probably too of the people, Major Waldron, the presiding magistrate, ordered her to be imprisoned, with " a lock kept on her leg," at the pleasure of the Court. As she was first prosecuted as early as 1656, she must have been a very old woman when this harsh sentence was pronounced. For some years — how many it is not known — Goody Cole lived alone in a hovel which stood a little way back from the spot where the Academy now stands ; and in this wretched hut, without a friend to soothe her last moments, she miserably died. Several days elapsed before her death became known ; and even then, such was the fear her supposed powers had inspired, that it required a great deal of courage on the part of the inhabitants to force an entrance into her cabin, where she lay dead. When this had been done, the body was dragged outside, a hole hastily dug, into which it was tumbled, and then — conformably with current superstition — a stake was driven through it, in order to exorcise the baleful influence she was supposed to have possessed.

The ballad supposes her to have cast the spell of her malevolence over a merry company of villagers who sailed out of the river for a day of pleasure, — soon to be turned into mourning by the drowning of the whole party, the storm in which they perished being raised by Goody Cole.

THE WRECK OF RIVERMOUTH.

J. G. WHITTIER.

Once, in the old Colonial days,
  Two hundred years ago and more,
A boat sailed down through the winding ways
  Of Hampton River to that low shore,
Full of a goodly company
Sailing out on the summer sea,
Veering to catch the land-breeze light,
With the Boar to left and the Rocks to right.

.   .   .   .

"Fie on the witch!" cried a merry girl,
  As they rounded the point where Goody Cole
Sat by her door with her wheel atwirl,
  A bent and blear-eyed poor old soul.
"Oho!" she muttered, "ye're brave to-day!
But I hear the little waves laugh and say,
'The broth will be cold that waits at home;
For it's one to go, but another to come!'"

"She's cursed," said the skipper; "speak her fair:
  I'm scary always to see her shake
Her wicked head, with its wild gray hair,
  And nose like a hawk, and eyes like a snake."
But merrily still, with laugh and shout,
From Hampton River the boat sailed out,
Till the huts and the flakes on Star seemed nigh,
And they lost the scent of the pines of Rye.

They dropped their lines in the lazy tide,
  Drawing up haddock and mottled cod;
They saw not the Shadow that walked beside,
  They heard not the feet with silence shod.
But thicker and thicker a hot mist grew,
Shot by the lightnings through and through;
And muffled growls, like the growl of a beast,
Ran along the sky from west to east.

.   .   .   .   .

The skipper hauled at the heavy sail:
  "God be our help!" he only cried,
As the roaring gale, like the stroke of a flail,
  Smote the boat on its starboard side.
The Shoalsmen looked, but saw alone
Dark films of rain-cloud slantwise blown,
Wild rocks lit up by the lightning's glare,
The strife and torment of sea and air.

Goody Cole looked out from her door:
  The Isles of Shoals were drowned and gone,
Scarcely she saw the Head of the Boar
  Toss the foam from tusks of stone.

She clasped her hands with a grip of pain,
The tear on her cheek was not of rain :
" They are lost," she muttered, " boat and crew!
Lord, forgive me ! my words were true ! "

Suddenly seaward swept the squall ;
    The low sun smote through cloudy rack ;
The Shoals stood clear in the light, and all
    The trend of the coast lay hard and black.
But far and wide as eye could reach,
No life was seen upon wave or beach ;
The boat that went out at morning never
Sailed back again into Hampton River.

PORTSMOUTH LEGENDS.

THE early voyagers soon discovered the Piscataqua River,
and they quickly perceived its advantages as a harbor.
There was Agamenticus for a landmark, and there was a swift-
flowing tide, which the natives told them was never frozen.
There were spacious basins, deep and sheltered, in which a navy
might ride securely ; and there were also high and gently sloping banks, over which the swaying pines looked down upon their
own dark shadows in the eddying stream below. The river was
found to conduct into a fertile and heavily-timbered region, of
which it was the natural outlet. The shores were seen to afford
admirable sites for the settlement that one and the other were
destined to support.

This was accordingly begun in 1623, under the direction and
by the authority of Gorges and Mason, in whom the successful
experiment of the Plymouth Pilgrims had inspired new hopes of
turning their royal grants to account.

The promoters of the settlement were Churchmen, who had
little sympathy with Puritan ideas, and none at all with its

scheme of government; and as some of those who had found the rule of these ideas too hard for their stomachs had removed into New Hampshire, a prejudice grew up between the two communities, which for the rest, afford to the student of history an example of two diverse systems growing up side by side. Wheelwright and his friends were of the latter class. Time, mutual interest, and the rapid ascendency obtained by the sister colony, with other considerations, finally closed the breach.

The system of Gorges and Mason, to establish a colony of tenants having only leaseholds subject to quit-rents, which they should govern by their agents, worked only eventual evil to themselves. It was an attempt to graft the landed system of Old upon New England by the side of the freehold plan of the thrifty and sagacious Massachusetts patentees; and it was a disastrous failure. Finding that they were growing poor, while the Puritan freeholders were growing rich, the people threw off their yoke, and sought a union with Massachusetts.

Still, the old leaven of prejudice survived in the descendants of the original inhabitants, who loved royalty and its forms, adhered to the Mother-Church and its traditions, and felt no sympathy whatever for the austere manners, the rigid economy, or the quasi-ecclesiastical government of their more powerful neighbors. These people gave tone to the principal settlement; and since there was no aristocracy of blood, one of wealth rose and flourished in its stead.

As the capital, the chief town, and the only seaport of the province, Portsmouth long enjoyed a peculiar distinction. It remained the political centre until the seat of government was transferred, early in the present century, to the interior of the State. Inevitable changes turned commerce into other channels. Its commercial importance waned, progress was arrested, and the place came to a standstill; and it is to-day more remarkable for what it has been than for what it is.

Therefore Portsmouth has the stamp of a coin of fifty years ago. It is of the true weight and ring, but the date and the legend are old. The best houses are still the oldest; and those

of the Wentworths, the Langdons, and the Sherburnes, rival
the traditional splendors of the Colonial mansions of the Puritan
capital in spaciousness, richness of decoration, and that rare
combination of simplicity and elegance which lifted the Colonial
magnate above the heads of his own generation, and has made
his housekeeping the admiration of ours. It is among these old
houses that we must look for our legendary lore.

The West of England seaports are known to have furnished
a great proportion of the original settlers in New England; and
certainly no class were more susceptible to the influence of
superstition than these sea-faring or sea-subsisting people. Upon
the folk-lore of home was now grafted that of the Indian; whilst
over this again hovered the mystery of an unexplored country,
— in itself a keen spur to the appetite that grows with what
it feeds upon. The region round about Portsmouth, Newcastle,
Kittery, York, and the Isles of Shoals, is therefore prolific in
legends of a homely and primitive kind; one of which we are
about to relate.

THE STONE–THROWING DEVIL.

UNDER the title of "Lithobolia," the story of the Stone-
Throwing Devil was printed in London in the year 1698.
It purports to be the narrative of an eye-witness, and is signed
with the initials "R. C." This tract, consisting of a few leaves
only, is now extremely rare; but a synopsis of its contents
may be found in the "Wonderful Providences" of Increase
Mather.

George Walton was an inhabitant of Portsmouth in the year
1682. He had incurred the bitter enmity of an old woman of
the neighborhood by taking from her a strip of land to which
she laid claim; and it is the opinion of the writers whom we
have quoted that she, being a witch, was at the bottom of all
the mischief that subsequently drove Walton's family to the

brink of despair. This beldam had in fact told Walton that he should never peacefully enjoy the land he had wrested from her.

One still Sabbath night in June all at once a shower of stones rattled against the sides and roof of Walton's house. It came as fiercely and as unexpectedly as a summer hailstorm. As soon as it had ceased, the startled inmates, who were in bed, hurried on their clothes and sallied out to see if they could discover the perpetrators of this outrage upon the peace and quiet of the family. It was ten o'clock, and a bright moonlight night. They found the gate taken off the hinges and carried to a distance from the house, but could neither see nor hear anything of the stone-throwers.

While thus engaged, a second volley of stones whistled about their heads, which drove them, much terrified by its suddenness and fury, back to the shelter of the house. They first went into the porch; but the stones reaching them here, they were quickly pelted out of this into an inner chamber, where, having bolted and barred all the doors, they awaited in no calm frame of mind the next demonstration of their assailants. Some had been struck and hurt, and all were in consternation. But to the dismay of these poor people, this proved no secure refuge; for the stone battery opened again presently, filling the room itself with flying missiles, which crashed through the casements, scattering the glass in every direction, came down the chimney, bounding and rebounding along the floor like spent cannonballs, while the inmates looked on in helpless amazement at what threatened to demolish the house over their heads. This bombardment continued, with occasional intermission, for four hours.

While it was going on, Walton was walking the floor of his chamber in great disorder of mind, when a sledge-hammer cast with vindictive force thumped heavily along the floor overhead, and, narrowly missing him, fell at his feet, making a great dent in the oaken floor; at the same time the candles were swept off the table, leaving him in total darkness.

All this, it is true, might have been the work of evil-minded persons; but certain things hardly consistent with this theory convinced the family beyond any reasonable doubt that the stones which bruised and terrified them were hurled by demon hands. In the first place, some of the stones which were picked up were found to be hot, as if they had just been taken out of the fire. In the second, notwithstanding several of them were marked, counted, and laid upon a table, these same stones would afterward be found flying around the room again as soon as the person's back was turned who had put them there. In the third, upon examination, the leaden cross-bars of the casements were found to be bent outwardly, and not inwardly, showing conclusively that the stones came from within, and not from without. Finally, to settle the matter, some of the maidens belonging to the household were frightened out of their wits upon seeing a hand thrust out of a window, or the apparition of a hand, — there being, to their certain knowledge, no one in the room where it came from.

This was not all. After Walton had gone to bed, though not to sleep, a heavy stone came crashing through his chamber-door. He got up, secured the unwelcome intruder, and locked it in his own chamber; but it was taken out by invisible hands, and carried with a great noise into the next room. This was followed by a brickbat. The spit flew up the chimney, and came down again, without any visible agency. This carnival continued from day to day with an occasional respite. Wherever the master of the house showed himself, in the barn, the field, or elsewhere, by day or by night, he was sure to receive a volley. No one who witnessed them doubted for a moment that all these acts proceeded from the malevolence of the aforesaid witch; and an attempt was accordingly made to brew a powerful witch-broth in the house, to exorcise her. But for some reason or other its charm failed to work; and so the spell remained hanging over the afflicted family.

Some of the pranks of the demon quite outdo the feats of Harlequin in the Christmas pantomimes. Walton had a guest staying with him, who became the faithful recorder of what happened while the storm of stones rained down upon the doomed dwelling. In order to soothe and tranquillize his mind, he took up a musical instrument and began to play; when "a good big stone" rolled in to join in the dance, while the player looked on in amazement. Among other tricks performed by the mischievous demon who had taken up its unwelcome residence among the family, was that of taking a cheese from the press and crumbling it over the floor; then the iron used in the press was found driven into the wall, and a kettle hung upon it. Several cocks of hay that had been mowed near the house were adroitly hung upon trees near by; while the mischievous goblin, twisting bunches of hay into wisps, stuck them up all about the house kitchen, — "cum multis aliis."

The relater of all these unaccountable doings indeed admits that certain sceptical persons persisted in believing that any or all of them might have been the work of human beings; but as every one credits what he wishes to credit, so this ancient writer appears to mention the fact only with the view of exposing its absurdity. Our own purpose is, not to decide between two opinions, but to declare that people in general considered George Walton to be a victim of supernatural visitation, or, in other words, bewitched; and to show that the temper of his day was such, that any occurrence out of the common was sure to be considered according to its character, either as emanating from heaven or from the bottomless pit. There were no such things as accidents; everything had some design.

LADY WENTWORTH.

A ROMANCE OF REAL LIFE.

GOVERNOR BENNING WENTWORTH, a man of "family," in the language of his day, the owner of large estates too, and likewise endowed with a sufficiently exalted idea of his own importance, social, political, and hereditary, had nevertheless matrimonial idiosyncrasies wholly at odds with the traditions and the susceptibilities of his class. We do not clearly know whether he was really superior to their demands, or altogether indifferent upon the subject; but we do know that had he been other than he was, there would have been no groundwork for our story.

This royal Governor lived in his fine mansion at Little Harbor, which, out of deference, probably, to his Excellency's convenience, to say nothing of his dinners, became also a sort of official residence, where he received visits of ceremony, punctually drank the King's health, and presided over the sittings of his Majesty's Council for the province. All this, it may be assumed, added a good deal to his sense of personal dignity, and not a little to his vanity, besides exerting a certain influence upon provincial politics, by establishing a coterie, of which he was the head, with its headquarters under his own roof. — And this roof, by the way, might tell a good many queer stories. But we have no time to dwell upon these phases of the mixed political and social life of Governor Wentworth's day. The old fellow liked display. He had his personal guard, he had his stud, and it was his ambition to have the best wine-cellar of any of his Majesty's subjects in the province; therefore his personal surroundings did no discredit to the commission with which his sovereign's favor had honored him. His house contained half a hundred apartments, all of which were probably in use when the Honorable Council met, at the Governor's bidding, to make a levy of troops for Louisburg, or upon other matters of public concern. Business being over, the company repaired to the billiard-room or the card-rooms, to the stables or to the river, for relaxation, — the oldsters to kill time, the youngsters to kill the ladies.

> It was a pleasant mansion, an abode
> Near and yet hidden from the great high-road,
> Sequestered among trees, a noble pile,
> Baronial and colonial in its style;
> Gables and dormer-windows everywhere,
> And stacks of chimneys rising high in air.
>
> .   .   .   .   .
>
> Within, unwonted splendors met the eye,
> Panels, and floors of oak, and tapestry;
> Carved chimney-pieces, where on brazen dogs
> Revelled and roared the Christmas fires of logs.

But this brave establishment lacked one thing to render it complete, — it needed a mistress. The Governor had been left widowed and childless in his old age to sustain the cares of office and the management of his extensive household alone. He determined to marry again.

The world, had it been consulted in the matter, might have imposed upon him a bride of mature years and experience; above all, one taken from his own rank, or at least having a pedigree. But the Governor was not yet too old to be insensible to the charms of youth and beauty; and he proceeded to snap his fat fingers in the face of society by proposing marriage to a young woman of the town of Portsmouth, who possessed all the personal graces that were requisite in his eyes to make her Lady Wentworth. The lady, however, saw nothing but a gouty old man, — who might, it was true, soon leave her a widow; but this was not the life that she looked forward to. She having moreover formed another attachment in her own sphere of life, rejected the Governor, for whom she cared not a button, in favor of a young mechanic whom she dearly loved. This double

wound to his love and vanity the old Governor determined
signally to avenge; and to this end he wickedly caused the
bridegroom to be kidnapped by a press-gang and carried off
to sea.

The Governor's second matrimonial venture was more fortunate. This time his eyes fell upon Martha Hilton, a saucy, red-
lipped gypsy of the town, who is first introduced to us while
she is carrying a pail of water — probably fresh-drawn from the
town pump yonder — along the street. Her feet are bare, her
dress scarcely covers her decently; yet for all that she belongs
to one of the oldest families in the province. But she is charming, even in these mean habiliments.

> It was a pretty picture, full of grace, —
> The slender form, the delicate, thin face ;
> The swaying motion, as she hurried by ;
> The shining feet, the laughter in her eye.

The sight of the girl in this plight so incenses the sharp-
tongued landlady of the Earl of Halifax inn, that she exclaims
from her doorway, "You Pat ! you Pat ! how dare you go looking so ? You ought to be ashamed to be seen in the street !"

The warm blood comes into the maiden's cheeks at this sharp
reproof. She gives her head a toss, and haughtily says : "No
matter how I look, I shall ride in my chariot yet, ma'am !" and
passes on, leaving Mistress Stavers nailed to her doorstep at
such unheard-of presumption in a half-dressed slip of a girl,
who is carrying water through the public street. Ride in her
chariot, indeed !

Like Cinderella, Martha Hilton next makes her appearance in
the kitchen of the Governor's mansion at Little Harbor. But
she is not to stay here. One day the Governor gives a splendid
banquet. The company is assembled, —

> He had invited all his friends and peers, —
> The Pepperels, the Langdons, and the Lears,
> The Sparhawks, the Penhallows, and the rest ;
> For why repeat the name of every guest ?

"I SHALL RIDE IN MY CHARIOT YET, MA'AM."

and among the red coats of the quality is the black one of the
Reverend Arthur Brown, rector of the Episcopal church, —

> With smiling face
> He sat beside the Governor and said grace.

The dinner is served; the wine circulates freely round the
board; and the guests, having dined well, have reached the moment of supreme content following, when the Governor whis-
pers something to a servant, who bows and goes out. Presently
there is a little bustle at the door, and then Martha Hilton,
blushing like fire, walks into the room and takes her stand in
front of the fireplace.

> Can this be Martha Hilton? It must be!
> Yes, Martha Hilton, and no other she!
> Dowered with the beauty of her twenty years,
> How ladylike, how queenlike, she appears!

She is now richly dressed; and would hardly be recognized as the
same person whom we saw in the street not long ago. Conversation ceases; all the guests look up to admire the beautiful woman.

The Governor rises from his chair, goes over to where Martha
is struggling to maintain her self-possession, and then, addressing himself to the clergyman, while all the guests stare, he says:
"Mr. Brown, I wish you to marry me."

"To whom?" asks the bewildered rector.

"To this lady," replies the Governor, taking Martha's hand in
his.

As the dumfounded rector remained speechless, the irascible
old Governor became imperative.

"Sir," he said, "as the Governor of his Majesty's province of
New Hampshire, I command you to marry me."

The ceremony was then performed; the maiden of twenty
became the bride of the gouty old man of sixty; and thus her
saucy answer came true.

Mr. Longfellow's poem, founded upon this romance of real
life, is also

> A pretty picture, full of grace, —

in which the social distinctions of Governor Wentworth's day are emphasized, in order to show how easily Love laughs at them and at all those safeguards behind which society intrenches itself against a misalliance.   But here a maiden of twenty marries a man old enough to be her grandfather.   Is it for love?   He marries his lovely dependant because he is lonesome.

Part Ninth.

YORK, ISLES-OF-SHOALS, AND BOON-ISLAND LEGENDS.

ISLES–OF–SHOALS LEGENDS.

THREE leagues off the coast of New Hampshire, huddled together in a group, the Isles of Shoals rise out of the gray line of old ocean like mountain peaks above a cloud; and, as if disinherited by Nature, nothing grows upon them except a little grass, a few hardy shrubs, and the yellow lichens that spot the gaunt rocks like the scales of a leper. One solitary lighthouse lifts its warning finger upon the outermost rock, but, like a monument to the many wrecks that have happened there, this only signals a rock of danger, and not a haven of safety for distressed mariners.

Treeless, unblessed by the evidences of cultivation or thrift, with no other sound than that of the sea breaking heavily against them, and no other sign of life than the surf whitening their sides of granite and flint, a more lonely scene can hardly be imagined. Upon landing and looking about him in silent wonder, one is more and more impressed with the idea that the sea has bared these imperishable rocks by its subsidence, and that he is standing on the summit of a submerged mountain, emerging from the ocean like one risen from the dead.

> A heap of bare and splintery crags
>   Tumbled about by lightning and frost,
> With rifts and chasms and storm-beat jags
>   That wait and growl for a ship to be lost ;
> No island, but rather the skeleton
> Of a wrecked and vengeance-smitten one.

· · · · · · ·

Away northeast is Boon-Island Light ;
   You might mistake it for a ship,
Only it stands too plumb upright,
   And, like the others, does not slip
Behind the sea's unsteady brink.
   .   .   .   .   .   .

On the mainland you see a misty camp
   Of mountains pitched tumultuously :
That one looming so long and large
   Is Saddleback ; and that point you see
Over yon low and rounded marge,
Like the boss of a sleeping giant's targe
   Laid over his heart, is Ossipee :
That shadow there may be Kearsarge.

There can be little room for doubt that these islands were, from a very early time, the resort of occasional fishing ships, as they subsequently became the haunt of smugglers and outlaws, — I mean pirates. The cluster enclosed a tolerable harbor, were uninhabited, were convenient to the fishing-grounds, and they afforded excellent facilities for curing fish. In later times their isolated position rendered them a secure refuge for the lawless rovers who infested our coasts, and who could snap their fingers at the Colonial authorities while refitting their ships, disposing of their ill-gotten booty, or indulging in their habitual carousals on shore. From these conditions came at length a puny settlement, equally without law, morals, or religion. Such was its reputation, that a Colonial order prohibited women from living on any one of the islands.

A legend is of course associated with the record declaring these islands to have been the resort of freebooters. Kidd is supposed to have buried immense treasure here ; and as if to confirm the story, the ghost of one of his men, who was slain for its protection, was always firmly believed by the fishermen to haunt Appledore. At one time nothing would have induced the inhabitant of another island to land upon this after nightfall, although there was much search made for the treasure that the spectre was supposed to guard. One islander, indeed, had really encountered the grisly shade while making its solitary round, and he described it as shedding a dimly luminous and unearthly appearance, like that of a glow-worm, as it walked, and as having a face pale and very dreadful to look upon.

For a time, while the fishery flourished, the islands enjoyed a kind of prosperity; but those clergymen who, like the Reverend John Tucke, went into a voluntary exile here, to become fishers of men, might truly be said to have cast their lines in stony places. Yet with unabated zeal the good Father Tucke persevered in the effort to reform the morals of his charge, to watch over their spiritual welfare, and to bring them into something like accord with the idea of a civilized community, until they carried him from the little church on the ledge down into the hollow, and there laid him away to his rest.

Sometimes the minister would see his entire congregation rush out of the meeting-house in the middle of the sermon because, it being a good lookout, some of the men had caught sight of a school of mackerel in the offing. Sometimes, when to make his image more impressively real he used sea terms to describe the condition of the unregenerate sinners before him, and put the question bluntly, "What, my friends, would you do in such a case?" some rough sea-dog would retort, "Square away and scud for Squam!" — that being their customary refuge when overtaken at sea by a northeaster. Both Mather and Hubbard give numerous instances of the "memorable providences" overtaking these dissolute and godless fishermen in the midst of their carousals. Let us now give one illustrating the efficacy of prayer.

In his "Magnalia Christi" Mather relates this incident: — A child of one Arnold lay sick, — so nearly dead that it was judged to be really dead. Mr. Brock (the minister), perceiving some life in it, goes to prayer; and in his prayer was this expression: "Lord, wilt thou not grant some sign, before we leave prayer, that thou wilt spare and heal this child? We cannot leave thee till we have it." The child sneezed immediately.

On account of the isolation which left them to the mercy of

the enemy's cruisers, the islands were nearly depopulated during the time of the Revolution. After this the few inhabitants who remained lived in a deplorable condition of ignorance and vice. Some of them lost their ages for want of a record. The town organization was abandoned, and the settlement at Star Island relapsed into its old half-barbarous way of life. Men and women lived openly together without the form of marriage. Finally some of the more depraved pulled down and burned the old meeting-house, which had so long been a prominent landmark for seamen; and the parsonage might have shared a similar fate, had it not, like the ark, been launched and floated over to the mainland out of harm's way.

But enough of this rude chronicle. Emerging from the shadow into the sun, the islands became in time noted for their healthfulness; and presently, when the light-keeper, who had hitherto lived here like a hermit, took courage and established a boarding-house on Appledore, they drew a constantly increasing number of visitors, who affirmed the Isles of Shoals to be the most idiosyncratic watering-place in the Union. Since then they have been celebrated in song and story. Every nook and alcove has been ransacked to procure materials for history, legend, or romance; and finally little or nothing except the ancient tombstones, the little Gosport church, and some rude walls, declare the presence here of a different generation, who were rocked in the cradle of the deep, and who now slumber in its embrace.

ON STAR ISLAND.

SARAH O. JEWETT.

HIGH on the lichened ledges, like
　　A lonely sea-fowl on its perch
Blown by the cold sea-winds, it stands,
　·　Old Gosport's quaint forsaken church.

No sign is left of all the town
　　Except a few forgotten graves;

But to and fro the white sails go
   Slowly across the glittering waves ;

And summer idlers stray about
   With curious questions of the lost
And vanished village, and its men,
   Whose boats by these same waves were tossed.

.   .   .   .

Their eyes on week-days sought the church, —
   Their surest landmark, and the guide
That led them in from far at sea,
   Until they anchored safe beside

The harbor wall that braved the storm
   With its resistless strength of stone.
Those busy fishers all are gone :
   The church is standing here alone.

But still I hear their voices strange,
   And still I see the people go
Over the ledges to their homes, —
   The bent old women's footsteps slow ;

The faithful parson stop to give
   Some timely word to one astray ;
The little children hurrying on
   Together, chattering of their play.

I know the blue sea covered some ;
   And others in the rocky ground
Found narrow lodgings for their bones —
   God grant their rest is sweet and sound !

I saw the worn rope idle hang
   Beside me in the belfry brown ;
I gave the bell a solemn toll —
   I rang the knell for Gosport town.

A LEGEND OF BLACKBEARD.

THE various legends relative to the corsairs, and the secreting of their ill-gotten gains among these rocks, would of themselves occupy a long chapter; and the recital of the fearful sights and sounds which have confronted such as were hardy enough to seek for hidden treasure, would satisfy the most inveterate marvelmonger in the land.

Among others to whom it is said these islands were known was the celebrated Captain Teach, or Blackbeard, as he was often called. He is supposed to have buried immense treasure here, some of which has been dug up and appropriated by the islanders. On one of his cruises, while lying off the Scottish coast waiting for a rich trader, he was boarded by a stranger, who came off in a small boat from the shore. The new-comer demanded to be led before the pirate chief, in whose cabin he remained some time shut up. At length Teach appeared on deck with the stranger, whom he introduced to the crew as a comrade. The vessel they were expecting soon came in sight; and after a bloody conflict she became the prize of Blackbeard. It was determined by the corsair to man and arm the captured vessel. The unknown had fought with undaunted bravery during the battle, and to him was given the command of the prize.

The stranger Scot was not long in gaining the bad eminence of being as good a pirate as his renowned commander. His crew thought him invincible, and followed wherever he led. At last, after his appetite for wealth had been satisfied by the rich booty of the Southern seas, he arrived on the coast of his native land. His boat was manned, and landed him on the beach near an humble dwelling, whence he soon returned, bearing in his arms the lifeless form of a woman.

The pirate ship immediately set sail for America; and in due time dropped her anchor in the road of the Isles of Shoals.

Here the crew passed their time in secreting their riches and in carousal. The commander's portion was buried on an island

CAPTAIN TEACH, OR BLACKBEARD.

apart from the rest. He roamed over the isles with his beautiful companion, forgetful, it would seem, of his fearful trade, until one morning a sail was discovered standing in for the islands.

All was now activity on board the pirate; but before getting under way the outlaw carried the maiden to the island where he had buried his treasure, and then made her take a fearful oath to guard the spot from mortals until his return, were it till Doomsday. He then put to sea.

The strange sail proved to be a warlike vessel in search of the freebooter. A long and desperate battle ensued, in which the King's cruiser at last silenced her adversary's guns. The vessels were grappled for a last struggle, when a terrific explosion strewed the sea with the fragments of both. Stung to madness by defeat, and knowing that if taken alive the gibbet awaited him, the rover had fired the magazine, involving friend and foe in a common fate.

A few mangled wretches succeeded in reaching the islands, only to perish miserably, one by one, from cold and hunger. The pirate's mistress remained true to her oath to the last, or until she also succumbed to want and exposure. By report, she has been seen more than once on White Island, — a tall, shapely figure, wrapped in a long sea-cloak, her head and neck uncovered except by a profusion of golden hair. Her face is described as exquisitely rounded, but pale and still as marble. She takes her stand on the verge of a low projecting point, gazing fixedly out upon the ocean in an attitude of intense expectation. A former race of fishermen avouched that her ghost was doomed to haunt those rocks until the last trump shall sound, and that the ancient graves to be found on the islands were tenanted by Blackbeard's men.

THE SPANISH WRECK.

WO betide any ship that was driven among these islands before the lighthouse warned the mariner how to steer clear of them! Engulfed in pitch darkness, the doomed vessel bore steadily down upon an unseen danger, whose first warning was the shock that snapped her masts asunder like dry twigs, and that crushed in her stout timbers like egg-shells. The waves and the rocks then finished their work of destruction. Such a scene of horror, with its dismal sequel of suffering and death, enacting while the islanders lay fast asleep in their beds, is that of the unknown Spanish wreck.

This wreck took place on Smutty-Nose Island in January, 1813, according to the Gosport records, which give the ill-fated vessel's name as the "Sagunto." Fourteen rude graves count the number of bodies that were recovered, and buried in a little plot together. "There is no inscription on the rude bowlders at the head and foot of these graves. A few more years, and all trace of them will be obliterated."

Although the ship "Sagunto" was not stranded here, as the record incorrectly states, the wreck of a large vessel either Spanish or Portuguese, with every soul on board, remains a terrible fact, only too well attested by these graves. The "Sagunto," it is known, after a stormy voyage, made her port in safety. But the horror of the event is deepened by that word "unknown." The name of the ship, who were her captain and crew, are all swallowed up at the same instant of time.

It was in the height of a blinding snow-storm and a gale that strewed the coast from Hatteras to the Penobscot with wrecks, that a ship built of cedar and mahogany was thrown upon these rocks. Not a living soul was left to tell the tale of that bitter January night. The ill-fated craft was richly laden, for boxes of raisins and almonds from Malaga drifted on shore the next morning. No clew to the ship or crew was found, except a silver watch, with the letters "P. S." engraved upon the seals, and some letters which came on shore with the wreckage. The watch had stopped at exactly four o'clock, while those on the island ticked on.

One account says that part of the crew were thrown upon the rocks more dead than alive, and that, seeing a light shining through the storm, some of them crawled toward it; but they were too far spent to reach the kindly shelter it announced.

"The roaring of the storm bore away their faint cries of distress; the old man slept on quietly, with his family about him, — sheltered, safe, — while, a stone's throw from his door, these sailors strove to reach that friendly light. Two of them gained the stone wall in front of the house; but their ebbing strength would not allow them to climb over." Their stiffened bodies, half buried in the falling snow, were found hanging over it in the morning.

This is the story of this little clump of graves, and of the wreck that is to this day unknown. Mrs. Celia Thaxter tells it in verse with much feeling; for to her such scenes are not unfamiliar, nor are the dangers of these inhospitable isles things of the imagination.

THE SPANIARDS' GRAVES AT THE ISLES OF SHOALS.

CELIA THAXTER.

> O SAILORS, did sweet eyes look after you,
>   The day you sailed away from sunny Spain? —
> Bright eyes that followed fading ship and crew,
>   Melting in tender rain?
>
> Did no one dream of that drear night to be,
>   Wild with the wind, fierce with the stinging snow,
> When, on yon granite point that frets the sea,
>   The ship met her death-blow?
>
> Fifty long years ago these sailors died:
>   None know how many sleep beneath the waves;
> Fourteen gray headstones, rising side by side,
>   Point out their nameless graves, —
>
> Lonely, unknown, deserted, but for me
>   And the wild birds that flit with mournful cry,
> And sadder winds, and voices of the sea
>   That moans perpetually.

.   .   .   .   .

O Spanish women, over the far seas,
   Could I but show you where your dead repose!
Could I send tidings on this northern breeze,
   That strong and steady blows!

Dear dark-eyed sisters, you remember yet
   These you have lost; but you can never know
One stands at their bleak graves whose eyes are wet
   With thinking of your wo!

BOON   ISLAND.

EVEN the Isles of Shoals have their outlying picket.   The
solitary gray shaft of Boon-Island Lighthouse, shooting
high up out of the sea, is by day a conspicuous object anywhere
between York River and Cape Neddock; and by night its light
is a star shining brightly amid the waste of waters.   This island,
with its outlying ledges, long had the worst reputation among
sailors of any that endanger the navigation of our eastern coasts, —
until the erection of a lighthouse here in 1811, upon the larger
rock, robbed the place of some of its terrors.   Its name goes
back as far as 1630, thus disposing of the local traditions associating it with the wreck of the "Nottingham Galley," which
occurred nearly a century later.

As the seas in great storms break completely over it, driving
the inmates to the upper story of the shaft, one is lost in wonder to think that this barren rock, scarcely elevated above the
waves, was for nearly a month, and in the heart of winter, the
melancholy refuge of a shipwrecked crew, whose strength daily
wasted away while they were in full sight of the friendly shore
they could not reach.

The following is all that can be learned concerning the incident commemorated in Mrs. Thaxter's verses: "Long ago, when
lighthouses were not so well manned as now, 'two lovers, lately

wed,' went out to keep the light on this perilous reef. In a great storm in the beginning of winter the husband suddenly died; and the bereaved wife kept the light burning three nights, till the storm lulled, and then left it unkindled as a signal of distress. There was no human creature on the rock except themselves."

THE WATCH OF BOON ISLAND.

CELIA THAXTER.

THEY crossed the lonely and lamenting sea;
　　Its moaning seemed but singing. "Wilt thou dare,"
He asked her, "brave the loneliness with me?"
　　"What loneliness," she said, "if thou art there?"

Afar and cold on the horizon's rim
　　Loomed the tall lighthouse, like a ghostly sign;
They sighed not as the shore behind grew dim, —
　　A rose of joy they bore across the brine.

They gained the barren rock, and made their home
　　Among the wild waves and the sea-birds wild.
The wintry winds blew fierce across the foam;
　　But in each other's eyes they looked and smiled.

Aloft the lighthouse sent its warnings wide,
　　Fed by their faithful hands; and ships in sight
With joy beheld it; and on land men cried,
　　"Look, clear and steady burns Boon Island Light!"

　　.　　.　　.　　.　　.　　.　　.

Death found them; turned his face and passed her by,
　　But laid a finger on her lover's lips;
And there was silence. Then the storm ran high,
　　And tossed and troubled sore the distant ships.

Nay, who shall speak the terrors of the night,
　　The speechless sorrow, the supreme despair?
Still like a ghost she trimmed the waning light,
　　Dragging her slow weight up the winding stair.

　　.　　.　　.　　.　　.　　.

Three times the night, too terrible to bear,
  Descended, shrouded in the storm.   At last
The sun rose clear and still on her despair,
  And all her striving to the winds she cast,

And bowed her head, and let the light die out,
  For the wide sea lay calm as her dead love.
When evening fell, from the far land, in doubt,
  Vainly to find that faithful star men strove.

.   .   .   .

Out from the coast toward her high tower they sailed;
  They found her watching, silent, by her dead, —
A shadowy woman, who nor wept nor wailed,
  But answered what they spake, till all was said.

THE GRAVE OF CHAMPERNOWNE.

O N Gerrish's Island, at the mouth of the Piscataqua River,
   there is a rude heap of stones marking, according to tradition, the last resting-place of Francis Champernowne, a former
owner and resident of this island.   Tradition further says he
forbid that any monument should be raised to his memory,
although he was of gentle blood, a nephew of the famous Sir
Ferdinando Gorges, and a man of much personal worth and distinction.   (See " Nooks and Corners of the New England Coast,"
p. 149, and notes.)

THOMAS DE CAMBERNON for Hastings' field
  Left Normandy ; his tower saw him no more !
And no crusader's warhorse, plumed and steeled,
  Paws the grass now at Modbury's blazoned door ;
No lettered marble nor ancestral shield, —
  Where all the Atlantic shakes the lonesome shore,
Lies ours forgotten : only cobble-stones
To tell us where are Champernowne's poor bones.

JOHN ELWYN.

YORK, MAINE.

AGAMENTICUS.

ANONYMOUS.

WHERE rises grand, majestic, tall,
As in a dream, the towering wall
 That scorns the restless, surging tide,
Once spanned the mart and street and mall,
 And arched the trees on every side
 Of this great city, once in pride.
For hither came a knightly train
 From o'er the sea with gorgeous court ;
  The mayors, gowned in robes of state,
Held brilliant tourney on the plain,
 And massive ships within the port
  Discharged their load of richest freight.
Then when at night, the sun gone down
 Behind the western hill and tree,
The bowls were filled, — this toast they crown,
 " Long live the City by the Sea ! "

Now sailless drift the lonely seas,
No shallops load at wharves or quays,
 But hulks are strewn along the shore, —
Gaunt skeletons indeed are these
 That lie enchanted by the roar
 Of ocean wave and sighing trees !
Oh, tell me where the pompous squires,
 The chant at eve, the matin prayers,
  The knights in armor for the fray ?
The mayors, where, and courtly sires,
 The eager traders with their wares, —
  How went these people hence away ?
And when the evening sun sinks down,
 Weird voices come from hill and tree,
Yet tell no tales, — this toast they crown,
 " Long live the Spectre by the Sea ! "

SAINT ASPENQUID OF AGAMENTICUS.

MOUNT Agamenticus, the locality of the following legend, is the commanding landmark for sixty miles up and down the neighboring coast. The name has the true martial ring in it. This mountain rears its giant back on the border of Maine, almost at the edge of the sea, into which, indeed, it seems advancing. Its form is at once graceful, robust, and imposing. Nature posted it here. It gives a character to the whole region that surrounds it, over which it stands guard. Nature endowed it with a purpose. It meets the mariner's eye far out to sea, and tells him how to steer safely into his destined port.

In his "Pictures from Appledore," the poet Lowell makes this reference to the sailor's mountain : —

> He glowers there to the north of us
> Wrapt in his mantle of blue haze,
> Unconvertibly savage, and scorns to take
> The white man's baptism on his ways.
> Him first on shore the coaster divines
> Through the early gray, and sees him shake
> The morning mist from his scalp-lock of pines :
> Him first the skipper makes out in the west,
> Ere the earliest sunstreak shoots tremulous,
> Plashing with orange the palpitant lines
> Of mutable billow, crest after crest,
> And murmurs *Agamaticus !*
> As if it were the name of a saint.

The name is in fact a legacy of the Indians who dwelt at its foot, and who always invested the mountain with a sacred character. From this circumstance comes the Indian legend of Saint Aspenquid, whom some writers have identified with the patriarch Passaconaway, the hero of so many wonderful exploits in healing and in necromancy.

According to the little we are able to recover concerning him, Saint Aspenquid was born in 1588, and was nearly one hundred years old when he died. He was converted to Christianity — possibly by the French Jesuits — and baptized by this name when he was about forty years old; and he at once set about his long and active ministration among the people of his own race, to whom he became a tutelary saint and prophet. For forty years he is said to have wandered from east to west and from north to south, preaching the gospel to sixty-six different nations, healing the sick, and performing those miracles which raised him in the estimation of his own people to the character of a prophet appointed by Heaven, and in that of the whites to a being endowed with supernatural powers. These wanderings had carried him from the shores of the Atlantic to the Californian Sea. Grown venerable in his good work, warned that he must soon be gathered to his fathers, the saint at last came home to die among his own people. Having called all the sachems of the different tribes together to attend his solemn funeral obsequies, they carried the body of their patriarch to the summit of Mount Agamenticus. Previous to performing the rite of sepulture, and agreeable to the custom held sacred by these people, the hunters of each tribe spread themselves throughout the forests. A great number of wild beasts were slaughtered as a sacrifice to the manes of the departed saint. Tradition affirms that on that day were slain and offered up between six and seven thousand wild animals, — from the bear, the buffalo, and the moose, down to the porcupine, the woodchuck, and the weasel.

SAINT ASPENQUID.

JOHN ALBEE.

THE Indian hero, sorcerer, and saint,
Known in the land as Passaconaway,
And after called the good Saint Aspenquid,
Returning, travel worn and spent with age
From vain attempt to reconcile his race

With ours, sent messengers throughout the East
To summon all the blood-bound tribes to him ;
For that upon the ancient meeting-place,
The sacred mountain Agamenticus,
When next the moon should show a new-bent bow,
He there would celebrate his funeral feast
With sacrifices due and farewell talk.
The dusky people heard and they obeyed ;
For known was Aspenquid in all the camps, —
Known was his name where unknown was his face ;
His conjuries, his valor, and his wit
The trackless forests traversed many a year,
And made his name a word of omen there.
Then gathered they from all the hither land
Of wide St. Lawrence and the northern lakes,
The warriors of the great Algonkin race

      .   .   .   .   .

The feast was ended : bird and beast were slain
(Three thousand, so the ancient annals say) ;
The dance was danced ; and every rite performed ;
And gathered round the summit of the mount
The stately, silent sachems stood intent
On Aspenquid.   He over all was tall
And straight as ash, though ripe with ninety years.
He rose majestic on the sovereign top
Of his own land, and in that solemn hour
He seemed to tower above his wonted height
As towers in midmost air the stricken bird.
His locks were thin, but raven black and long ;
Nor yet his eyes had lost their splendid dark,
But glowed deep set beneath a low, broad brow.
Unpinched by age, his face was firm, and bronzed
Like leaves that hang all winter on the oak.

      .   .   .   .   .

" Warriors and braves, come nearer to your chief !
My eyes, that once could brook the midday sun,
And see the eagle ere myself was seen,
Are dimmed with age ; and but a pace beyond
A misty light seems settled over all.

Come nearer, braves, that I may feast my eyes
On your young limbs, on what myself once was !

.   .   .   .   .

My race decays, and I have lived too long ;
My limbs with ninety weary winters' strife
Are spent ; my fathers call me unto them.
I go to comfort their impatient shades,
And respite find for all my own mischance.
And here once more on Agamenticus,
My old ancestral powwow's sacred seat,
That saw the waters burn and trees to dance,
And winter's withered leaves grow green again,
And in dead serpent's skin the living coil,
While they themselves would change themselves to flame ;
And where not less did I myself conjure
The mighty magic of my fathers' rites
Against my foe, — yet all without effect ;
The spirits also flee where white men come.
I turn to join my kindred sagamores,
And fly before the doom I could not change.

.   .   .   .   .

Light not the fires of vengeance in your hearts,
For sure the flame will turn against yourselves,
And you will perish utterly from earth.
Nor yet submit too meekly, but maintain
The valorous name once ours in happy days.
Be prudent, wise, and always slow to strike.
Fall back ; seek other shores and hunting-grounds, —
I cannot bear you perish utterly !
Though, looking through the melancholy years,
I see the end, but turn my face away,
So heavy are my eyes with unshed tears ;
And yours too I would turn, warriors and braves !
And mind not my prophetic vision much, —
Th' unhappy gift of him who lives too long ;
But mind the counsel many years have taught,
The last I give : remember it, and live ! "

Part Tenth.

OLD–COLONY LEGENDS.

HANGING BY PROXY.

IN his "New English Canaan," first published at London in
1632, Thomas Morton, the dispossessed and exiled planter
of Mount Wollaston, *alias* Merry Mount, relates the droll
doings "Of a Parliament held at Wessaguscus." Wessaguscus
is now Weymouth, Mass. It was first settled by a trading company sent out by Thomas Weston, — a London merchant with whom the Plymouth Pilgrims had had some
dealings, but whose present enterprise they regarded with no
particular favor. This Morton is a character about which there
are at least two opinions : the one generally received being that
he was a lawless, dissolute, reckless, and able scamp, who led
a vagabond life among vagabond followers ; whence Hubbard
styles him "lord of misrule." There is no question that the
Pilgrims looked upon him as a dangerous neighbor, or that
he regarded them with unconcealed aversion and disdain. So
far as he was anything, he was a Churchman ; while they were
out-and-out Separatists. He used the Book of Common Prayer ;
they abhorred and rejected it. He calls them ironically the
"Brethren ;" they term him "pettifogger" and "atheist."
Such opposite views in morals and government were not long
coming into collision.

Morton was, however, a man of education and ability, — which
by no means proves that he was not all the Pilgrims allege him

to have been, — an unprincipled adventurer. Taking his "New English Canaan" as the index of his character, one reads at every few lines some evidence of his strong predilection for a life of indolence and pleasure. His idea was to establish an Arcadia, with the natives as his vassals. He restored the Old-English holiday customs, which the Puritans considered idolatrous, and which they had prohibited among themselves. He rechristened his plantation of Mount Wollaston by the name of Merry Mount, with the old May-Day ceremonies of wine, wassail, and the dance around the May-pole, to celebrate the change. He composed riddles in verse addressed to his followers that show an equal familiarity with classical lore and with the debased manners of the court wits and rhymesters of the day. He furnished the Indians with firearms to hunt for him, which they soon learned to use against their masters. Taking the alarm, the outraged Pilgrims seized and shipped Morton a prisoner to England, without law or other warrant than the "higher law" that might makes right ; and it was while smarting under the sense of injury that Morton wrote this most entertaining account of his personal adventures in the New English Canaan.

This brings us back to Morton's story of how justice was administered at that early day in New England, notably at the plantation of Wessaguscus. It is no fault of Morton that the tale has grown since leaving his capable hands. But to him belongs the honor of having first set it down in black and white. He says : —

"Master Weston's plantation being settled at Wessaguscus, his servants, or many of them, being lazy persons that would use no endeavor to take the benefit of the country, some of them fell sick and died.

"One among the rest, an able-bodied man that ranged the forest to see what it would afford him, stumbled by accident on an Indian granary, concealed, as the custom was with those people, underground ; and from it he took a capful of corn, and then went his way. The Indian owner, finding by the footprint that the thief was an Englishman, came and made his complaint at the plantation.

"The chief commander of the company immediately called together a parliament of all those who were not sick, to hear and determine the cause of complaint. And wisely now," continues Morton, with playful irony, "they should consult upon this huge complaint, that a knife or a string of beads would well enough have disposed of, Edward Johnson being made a special judge of this business. The fact was there in repetition, construction made that it was a felony, and by the laws of England punished with death ; and this in execution must be put for an example, and likewise to appease the savage ; when straightway one arose, moved as it were with some compassion, and said he could not well gainsay the former sentence, yet he had conceived within the compass of his brain an Embrion (an unborn child) that was of special consequence to be delivered and cherished. He said that it would most aptly serve to pacify the savage's complaint, and save the life of one that might (if need should be) stand them in some good stead, being young and strong, fit for resistance against an enemy, which might come unexpected for anything they knew.

"This oration was liked by every one ; and the orator was entreated to show how this end might be reached. He went on : —

"Says he, 'You all agree that one must die, and one shall die. This young man's clothes we will take off, and put upon one that is old and impotent, — a sickly person that cannot escape death ; such is the disease on him confirmed, that die he must : put the young man's clothes on this man, and let the sick person be hanged in the other's stead.' 'Amen,' says one ; and so say many more.

"And this had like to have proved their final sentence, and being there confirmed by Act of Parliament to after-ages for a precedent, but that one with a ravenous voice began to croak and bellow for revenge, and put by that conclusive motion, alleging that such deceits might be a means hereafter to exasperate the minds of the complaining savages, and that by his death the savages should see their zeal to do justice ; and therefore he should die. This was concluded. Yet, nevertheless, a scruple was made ; now to countermand this act did represent itself unto their minds, which was how they should do to get the man's good-will. This was indeed a special obstacle, for without (that they all agreed) it would be dangerous for any man to attempt the execution of it, lest mischief should befall them, every man. He was a person, that in his wrath did seem to be a second Samson, able to beat out their brains with the jawbone of an ass. Therefore they called the man, and by persuasion got him fast bound in jest, and then hanged him up hard by in good earnest, who with a weapon, and at liberty, would have put all these wise judges of this parliament to a pitiful *non plus* (as it hath been credibly reported), and made the chief judge of them all buckle to him."

This is Morton's own narration. The actual culprit, he declares, was really hanged, in spite of the ingenious proposal to hang up another man in his stead, which at first had tickled the fancy of the parliament. As if to corroborate the story, Bradford tells us that these Wessaguscus planters were fain to hang one of their men whom they could not reclaim from stealing, in order to give the Indians content.

Morton's story is generally admitted to be the foundation for Butler's mirth-provoking one in "Hudibras," which appeared thirty years later, to delight the world with its incomparable drollery and satire. The satirist, whom nothing escaped, there puts it into the mouth of Ralpho, who is endeavoring in a most Jesuitical way to clear away his master's scruples in regard to the flagellation he had promised to undergo for his lady's sake, but was disposed to avoid. The squire artfully debates the point of honor involved : —

> Though nice and dark the point appear,
> Quoth Ralph, it may hold up and clear.
> That sinners may supply the place
> Of suffering saints, is a plain case.
> Justice gives sentence many times
> On one man for another's crimes.
> Our brethren of New England use
> Choice malefactors to excuse,
> And hang the guiltless in their stead,
> Of whom the churches have less need.
> As lately 't happened ; in a town
> There liv'd a cobbler, and but one
> That out of doctrine could cut use,
> And mend men's lives as well as shoes.

This precious brother having slain,
In time of peace, an Indian,
Not out of malice, but mere zeal,
Because he was an infidel,
The mighty Tottipottimoy
Sent to our elders an envoy,
Complaining sorely of the breach
Of league, held forth by brother Patch,
Against the articles in force
Between both churches, his and ours.
But they maturely having weigh'd
They had no more but him o' th' trade,
A man that serv'd them in a double
Capacity to teach and cobble,
Resolv'd to spare him ; yet to do
The Indian Hoghan Moghan too
Impartial justice, in his stead did
Hang an old weaver that was bedrid.

In the author's notes to the early editions of "Hudibras" the story is asserted to be true.   Hubbard repeats it with the qualification that the hanging was only pretended, although he had seen the extract we have given from Bradford; and he had also read and enjoyed the manner "with which the merry gentleman that wrote 'Hudibras' did in his poetical fancy make so much sport."

That in one form or another the story now became current as true, is no longer a matter of doubt.   We next discover it in a different dress, related with much gusto by Governor Dudley to Captain Uring, and printed at length in the latter's "Voyages." It will be seen that the anecdote has lost nothing by passing from mouth to mouth.   This is Governor Dudley's version : —

"One day, while a carpenter was cutting down a tree, and a crowd of Indians stood around, watching every blow with the greatest attention, the tree fell on one of them who did not get out of the way, killing him on the spot.   The other Indians set up a great howling over the dead body, while the frightened carpenter ran and hid himself to escape their vengeance ; for they foolishly thought him to blame for the death of their companion. The English tried to persuade them that the carpenter was not at fault; but nothing short of his death would pacify them. They demanded that he should be given up to them for execution. Seeing them thus enraged, and fearing that they might fall upon and destroy them, the English finally promised to hang the unlucky carpenter themselves. The Indians were told to come the next morning, and they would see him hanging from a particular tree. But the carpenter being a young and lusty fellow, and very useful, they concluded they could not spare him; and there being in the fort an old bedridden weaver who had not long to live, he was taken out to the tree and quietly hanged in the room of the carpenter, to the entire satisfaction of the Indians, who did not detect the cheat, and who became good friends again.

THE OLD OAKEN BUCKET.

THE touch of nature to which all yield, has no higher exemplification than in those simple ballads of home and its associations that have made the names of Payne and Woodworth immortal. One does not care to analyze his sensations; he forgets the homely phrase; he feels, and is deeply affected by the awakening of those memories which carry him back to the days of his happy and innocent childhood; he is a child again. This secret, yet powerful chord was struck by Samuel Woodworth in his "Old Oaken Bucket;" and it has not yet ceased to vibrate a tender harmony whenever that masterpiece of human emotion is spoken or sung.

Dear old "Goldy" has well expressed that inextinguishable yearning for the spot of ground we call "home" in these touching lines: —

> In all my wanderings round this world of care,
> In all my griefs, — and God has given my share, —
> I still had hopes, my long vexations past,
> Here to return, and die at home at last.

What are those endearing scenes which in the "Old Oaken Bucket" find their counterpart in the memory of thousands?

The town of Scituate, Massachusetts, one of the most ancient of the Old Colony, joins Cohasset on the south. Its history is memorable and interesting. The people come of a hardy and determined ancestry, who fought for every inch of ground that their descendants now hold. To this fact may perhaps be referred the strength of those associations, clinging like ivy around some of the most notable of the ancient homesteads. To borrow from Mr. Nason: "The scene so vividly described in Mr. Woodworth's charming lyric is a little valley through which Herring Brook pursues its devious way to meet the tidal waters of North River. The view of it from Coleman Heights, with its neat cottages, its maple-groves and apple-orchards, is remarkably beautiful. The 'wide-spreading pond,' the 'mill,' the 'dairy-house,' the 'rock where the cataract fell,' and even the 'old well,' if not the 'moss-covered bucket' itself, may still be seen just as the poet described them."

Among these scenes Samuel Woodworth, the people's poet, was born and reared. Although the house is no longer there, many pilgrims stop at its modern successor in order to slake their thirst at the waters, the recollection of which gave the poet such exquisite pleasure in after years. One would still have the surroundings unchanged, — the cot where he dwelt, the ponderous well-sweep, creaking with age, that his youthful hands tugged feebly at; and, finally, the mossy bucket overflowing with crystal nectar fresh from the cool depths below. But since changes will come to transform the picture, the susceptible visitor must be content to quaff a draught of purest water to the memory of one of the kindliest poets that our New England soil has produced.

To this rapid sketch of the scene we may now add the history of the popular ballad, "The Old Oaken Bucket." The circumstances under which it was composed and written — and they embody a moral as well as consecrate a memory — are said to be as follows : —

THE OLD OAKEN BUCKET.

Samuel Woodworth was a printer, who had served his appren-ticeship under the veteran Major Russell, of "The Columbian Centinel," a journal which was in its day the leading Federalist organ of New England. He had inherited the wandering propen-sity of his class ; yielding to which he in due time removed first to Hartford, and then to New York, where, after an unsuccessful career as a publisher, he became associated with Morris as one of the founders of "The Mirror." It was while he was living in New York, and after many vicissitudes had tempered the enthusiasm of his youth, that, in company with some brother printers, he one day dropped in at a well-known establishment, then kept by Mallory, to take a social glass with them. The cognac was pronounced excellent. After tasting it, Woodworth set his glass down on the table, and smacking his lips, declared emphatically that Mallory's *eau de vie* was superior to anything that he had ever tasted.

"There you are mistaken," said one of his comrades quietly ; then adding, "there certainly was one thing that far surpassed this in the way of drinking, as you, too, will readily acknowledge when you hear it."

"Indeed ; and pray what was that ?" Woodworth asked, with apparent incredulity that anything could surpass the liquor then before him.

"The draught of pure and sparkling spring water that we used to get from the old oaken bucket that hung in the well, after our return from the labors of the field on a sultry summer's day."

No one spoke ; all were busy with their own thoughts.

A tear-drop glistened for a moment in Woodworth's eye. "True, true," he exclaimed ; and soon after quitted the place. With a heart overflowing with the recollections that this chance allusion in a bar-room had inspired, the scene of his happier childhood life rushed upon him in a flood of feeling. He hastened back to the office in which he then worked, seized a pen, and in half an hour had written the popular ballad which follows. Wood-worth died in 1842, at the age of fifty-seven. His reputation rests upon this one stroke of genius. He never wrote anything better than this beautiful lyric, which is capable of hushing the most boisterous assemblies into silence, — such is the homage that all instinctively pay to the purest and holiest of human associations.

THE OLD OAKEN BUCKET.

SAMUEL WOODWORTH.

How dear to this heart are the scenes of my childhood,
    When fond Recollection presents them to view!
The orchard, the meadow, the deep-tangled wildwood,
    And every loved spot which my infancy knew, —
The wide-spreading pond, and the mill which stood by it,
    The bridge, and the rock where the cataract fell ;
The cot of my father, the dairy-house nigh it,
    And e'en the rude bucket which hung in the well, —
The old oaken bucket, the iron-bound bucket,
The moss-covered bucket which hung in the well.

That moss-covered vessel I hail as a treasure ;
    For often, at noon, when returned from the field,
I found it the source of an exquisite pleasure, —
    The purest and sweetest that nature can yield.
How ardent I seized it, with hands that were glowing !
    And quick to the white-pebbled bottom it fell ;
Then soon, with the emblem of truth overflowing,
    And dripping with coolness, it rose from the well, —
The old oaken bucket, the iron-bound bucket,
The moss-covered bucket, arose from the well.

How sweet from the green mossy brim to receive it,
    As, poised on the curb, it inclined to my lips !
Not a full blushing goblet could tempt me to leave it,
    Though filled with the nectar that Jupiter sips.
And now, far removed from the loved situation,
    The tear of Regret will intrusively swell,
As Fancy reverts to my father's plantation,
    And sighs for the bucket which hangs in the well, —
The old oaken bucket, the iron-bound bucket,
The moss-covered bucket which hangs in the well.

DESTRUCTION OF MINOT'S LIGHT.

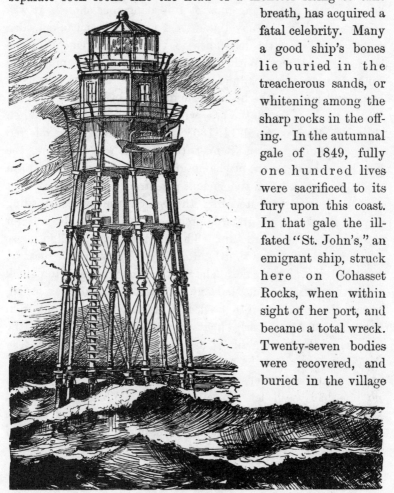

THE dangerous reef stretching far out into the sea from Cohasset, so shaggy with kelp and rockweed that each separate rock looks like the head of a monster rising to take breath, has acquired a fatal celebrity. Many a good ship's bones lie buried in the treacherous sands, or whitening among the sharp rocks in the offing. In the autumnal gale of 1849, fully one hundred lives were sacrificed to its fury upon this coast. In that gale the ill-fated "St. John's," an emigrant ship, struck here on Cohasset Rocks, when within sight of her port, and became a total wreck. Twenty-seven bodies were recovered, and buried in the village

THE FIRST MINOT'S LIGHTHOUSE.

graveyard. Those who have visited the Minot's Lighthouse only on a summer's day can faintly imagine the fury of a wintry storm, or the power with which the seas then dash themselves high over the lantern of the tower. The place had long been one of terror to mariners, when, aroused by the long catalogue of disasters signalling it, the Government in 1849 began the erection of a lighthouse on Minot's Rock, known to be one of the most dangerous of this dangerous shore. It was constructed upon the novel, and as it proved the mistaken, idea of opposing as little resistance to the free movement of the waves as possible. With this view ponderous iron piles were sunk deep in the rock, and upon them was built the keeper's house and lantern, the floor of the dwelling being thus elevated fully forty feet above the seas which rolled beneath it. When the great storm of April 14, 1851, to which people long referred with a shudder, began, Bennet, the keeper, was on shore, the lighthouse being then in charge of two assistants. The storm steadily increased to a tremendous gale from the northeast, that continued with unabated fury throughout the two succeeding days. By this time grave apprehensions began to be felt for the security of the structure. The last time that the lighthouse was seen standing was shortly after three o'clock on Wednesday, the third day of the gale. The weather then became too thick to distinguish it; but the lantern was not lighted, as usual, during that night, or if lighted, it could not be made out from the shore. At an early hour on the following morning the keeper, while making his round, found fragments of the residence strewed along the beach. The lighthouse with all it contained had been swept away during that night of fear, and no one had been left to tell the tale. When the gale had spent itself, the great waves were seen tossing in mad glee on the spot where it had stood : the beautiful aërial tower had disappeared.

MINOT'S LEDGE, MASS.

BY FITZ-JAMES O'BRIEN.

LIKE spectral hounds across the sky,
The white clouds scud before the storm ;
And naked in the howling night
The red-eyed lighthouse lifts its form.
The waves with slippery fingers clutch
The massive tower, and climb and fall,
And, muttering, growl with baffled rage
Their curses on the sturdy wall.

Up in the lonely tower he sits,
The keeper of the crimson light ;
Silent and awestruck does he hear
The imprecations of the night ;
The white spray beats against the panes
Like some wet ghost that down the air
Is hunted by a troop of fiends,
And seeks a shelter anywhere.

He prays aloud, the lonely man,
For every soul that night at sea,
But more than all for that brave boy
Who used to gayly climb his knee, —
Young Charlie, with his chestnut hair
And hazel eye and laughing lip.
" May Heaven look down," the old man cries,
" Upon my son, and on his ship ! "

While thus with pious heart he prays,
Far in the distance sounds a boom :
He pauses ; and again there rings
That sullen thunder through the room.
A ship upon the shoals to-night !
She cannot hold for one half hour ;
But clear the ropes and grappling-hooks,
And trust in the Almighty Power !

On the drenched gallery he stands,
Striving to pierce the solid night :
Across the sea the red eye throws
A steady crimson wake of light ;
And, where it falls upon the waves,
He sees a human head float by,
With long drenched curls of chestnut hair,
And wild, but fearless hazel eye.

Out with the hooks !   One mighty fling !
Adown the wind the long rope curls.
Oh ! will it catch ?   Ah, dread suspense,
While the wild ocean wilder whirls !
A steady pull ; it tightens now :
Oh ! his old heart will burst with joy,
As on the slippery rocks he pulls
The breathing body of his boy.

Still sweep the spectres through the sky ;
Still scud the clouds before the storm ;
Still naked in the howling night
The red-eyed lighthouse lifts its form.
Without, the world is wild with rage ;
Unkennelled demons are abroad :
But with the father and the son
Within, there is the peace of God.

LEGENDS OF PLYMOUTH ROCK.

NO good American would willingly die without having seen
Plymouth Rock.

There is no certain record of a day upon which all of the
" Mayflower's " company disembarked ; but those having the best
right to do it fixed the date as the 22d of December, 1620.

Justly regarded as the most important one in American history, the event has been celebrated by some of the most spirited

poems in the language ; and to those who love the old songs —
and who does not ? — the stanzas of Felicia Hemans, Pierpont,
Sigourney, Sprague, and Percival, retain all the freshness and
inspiration of their childhood's days.

The honor of having first touched the shore on the ever-
memorable day is shared by two claimants. Both are supported

MARY CHILTON'S LEAP.

by family tradition. That giving it to John Alden was handed
down through successive generations, until it was printed in his
collection of Epitaphs, by the Reverend Timothy Alden, D.D.,
a lineal descendant of John, and thus obtained a permanent
record.

The second claimant is Mary Chilton, a maiden who subsequently became the wife of John Winslow of Plymouth, and the mother of a large family inheriting the most distinguished traits of the Pilgrims, with an honorable name. The husband of Mary Chilton removed after a time from the Old Colony to Boston, where the family tomb, with its arms, may be seen in King's Chapel Yard.

It is a somewhat curious fact that a precisely similar tradition exists with respect to the landing at Boston, which runs to the effect that, being then a romping girl, Anne Pollard declared that she would be the first person to jump on shore, and was as good as her word as soon as the boat's keel grounded upon the beach.

But whoever may be entitled to the preference, — and that question will probably remain unsettled, — the simple act surrounds the statuesque figure of the eager youth or maiden with a glamour rendering it the foremost and striking object of the historical picture. There is still another point of view. A youth in the full vigor of manhood, whose posterity should inherit the virgin land, sets his nervous foot upon the cornerstone of a nation, and makes it an historic spot. A young girl in the first bloom of womanhood, the type of a coming maternity, boldly crosses the threshold of a wilderness which her children's children shall possess and inhabit, and transforms it into an Eden. Surely John Alden should have married Mary Chilton on the spot.

MARY CHILTON.

GEORGE BANCROFT GRIFFITH.

FAIR beams that kiss the sparkling bay,
　　Rest warmest o'er her tranquil sleep,
Sweet exile ! love enticed away, —
　　The first on Plymouth Rock to leap !
Among the timid flock she stood,
　　Rare figure, near the " Mayflower's " prow,
With heart of Christian fortitude,
　　And light heroic on her brow!

O ye who round King's Chapel stray,
    Forget the turmoil of the street ;
Though loftier names are round her, lay
    A wreath of flowers at Mary's feet !
Though gallant Winslows slumber here,
    E'en worthy Lady Andros too,
Her memory is still as dear,
    And poets' praise to Mary due.

ANCIENT STONE, BURIAL HILL.

But besides being the renowned stepping-stone of history,
Forefathers' Rock has exerted in the course of time upon the
minds of men who stood in the presence of grave events, a
secret, a talismanic influence. In the antique days of chivalry
men seldom set out upon any doubtful or hazardous adventure

without first visiting some holy shrine, and imploring the aid or protection of their patron saint. In these later times men have repaired for inspiration to this rock as they would to a shrine, and they have not been ashamed to confess that they found it a Living Rock, nerving them to patriotic effort, or moving them to inspired utterances in behalf of mankind.

When in 1774 all the land was in a flame, the spirit of the Old Colony having risen to fever heat, it was determined

MONUMENT OVER FOREFATHERS' ROCK, PLYMOUTH.

newly to consecrate the rock to the divine spirit of Liberty. On the appointed day all the roads leading into Plymouth were thronged. Four thousand freemen had assembled within the town by noonday on the 5th of October. They were met to pledge themselves to each other against the oppression of the mother country. All were animated by the consciousness of acting in a rightful cause that moved them as one man; all were burning with patriotic zeal. They first required all the Tory partisans of the Crown to make a public recantation. This being done, they proceeded to the spot where their ancestors had landed, with the purpose of removing Forefathers' Rock to the public square in the centre of the village. But while it was being raised from its primitive bed, and as if to oppose the act of desecration, the rock suddenly split in two.

This accident, which to many seemed a warning, so dashed the spirit of the actors, that the proceedings were near coming to an abrupt end; but some quick-witted spectator having declared it to presage the violent sundering of the empire in twain, it was accepted as a good omen, the upper half was drawn in triumph to the open space in front of the meeting-house, and there deposited, at the foot of the liberty-pole, from which a flag bearing the legend, "Liberty or Death," was flung to the breeze. And thus the rock was made to play an active part in the great controversy.

This is the portion of Forefathers' Rock that so many thousand curious pilgrims have seen lying on the grass plat in front of Pilgrim Hall; while a monument, built in the form of a shrine, enclosed, at the edge of the beach, the original spot whence it was taken, the lower fragment of the rock, and the bones that a pious care had recovered from the earliest burial-place of the Pilgrims, hard by on Cole Hill. In 1881, after a separation of one hundred and six years, the upper half was replaced upon the lower. What God has joined together let no man put asunder!

THE COURTSHIP OF MYLES STANDISH.

OF all our New-England legends, one of the most popular, as well as one of the most picturesque, is the story of the courtship of Myles Standish, which is the subject of Longfellow's poem of that name.

The action centres in three persons. First there is the martial figure of the redoubted captain of Plymouth, the rude but tried soldier, the man of manly virtues, with all a soldier's contempt for courtly graces, the owner of a noble name which he had made more illustrious by his deeds, — brusque, quick-tempered, brave to rashness, but wearing the heart of a lion in his little, undersized body, though his head might sometimes be hot and unsteady in council, — in short, a man to be admired, feared, trusted, but not, alas! always loved, nor born to woo. Such was Myles Standish, the Captain of Plymouth. Though disinherited by fraud, and self-exiled, this soldier of fortune yet possessed a title to distinction that elevates him upon a pedestal above the sober and industrious artisans with whom he had loyally cast his lot, although it is doubtful if he belonged to their communion.

To this hard Puritan soldier, whose wife had died during the

STANDISH HOUSE, DUXBURY.

first dreadful winter of their pilgrimage, enters the stripling John Alden, who is asserted to be the same person that first leaped upon the world-renowned Rock when these exiles landed from the "Mayflower" on that December day. He was only twenty-two; but in the eyes of two persons, at least, this constituted no defect. These persons were Priscilla Mullins, the Puritan maiden, and Myles Standish. One looked upon the youth with a smile; the other with a sigh. Family tradition makes this youth one of Standish's household; for in this patriarchal community, over which the spirit of economy ruled supreme, the unmarried members were sagaciously joined with some family, both for the sake of unity and for the equal distribution of work and goods. This constituted one large family divided into many. In some sense, therefore, Myles Standish was the guardian and protector of Alden, whom he is said to have loved as his own son.

The third person, completing the group, is Priscilla, the daughter of William Mullins, one of the original Pilgrim band, who had died within two months after the landing, leaving her fatherless. There was only one Priscilla, and there were two lovers.

Rose Standish, the first wife, having died, as we have said, the Captain finding his loneliness insupportable, the lovely Priscilla found favor in his eyes, and he therefore determined to install her as the mistress of his heart and household. But this lion in love, who had so often faced death without flinching, wanting courage to lay both at a simple maiden's feet in his own person, made choice of John Alden, of all others, as his envoy in this delicate negotiation. He unfolded his purpose, and gave his hopes into Alden's keeping. How much this disclosure may have troubled the youth, being himself a victim to the fair Priscilla's charms, yet bound in honor and gratitude to his patron, the Captain, is easily imagined. He had been asked to go and declare another man's passion to the object of his own heart's desire, — to woo her for another! How bitterly he must have bewailed the weakness that had prevented his speaking to her sooner, and had now thrust him into this awkward dilemma!

Loyal still to his friend and patron, though pursued all the way by these regrets, he took the well-known path to Priscilla's house, steeling himself for the coming interview. Being welcomed, but ill at ease, he first asked permission to urge the Captain's suit. The damsel was then called into the room, when the young man rose and delivered his errand, — at once his renunciation and his despair. Knowing as we do his feelings, we may pardon his confusion, as doubtless the keen-eyed Priscilla did, and we may excuse the way in which he stammered through his speech, every syllable of which must have blistered his tongue in giving it utterance.

We are no true interpreter if the young man's mental and moral perplexity is not the key to the blushing Priscilla's answer, which, like a ray of sunshine piercing through a wintry cloud, instantly breaking through all restraint, turned the formality and false sentiment that Alden had fortified himself with, incontinently out of doors.

With a beating heart Priscilla listened to his plea for another. He, poor wretch! could not disguise his real feelings from her, worn as they were upon his sleeve; and nobly did she come to the rescue. What a world of archness, of tender chiding, and of the love which is so pure that it knows no shame, is here revealed!

"Prithee, John, why don't you speak for yourself?"

The tradition says that John left the house without speaking, but that the look he gave Priscilla spoke for him. We can see his dark figure striding homeward through the Plymouth woods, and we can guess something of the frame of mind in which the young man contemplated his approaching interview with the wrathful little Captain. It is indeed said — and here family tradition takes an issue with the poet — that Myles Standish never forgave his ambassador to the court of Hymen for thus supplanting him; but it is certain that the maiden herself poured balm into the wounded spirit of the youth, by giving her hand where she had already given her heart. And from these twain come all of the name of Alden in the Union.

So through the Plymouth woods John Alden went on his errand;
Crossing the brook at the ford, where it brawled over pebble and
    shallow,
Gathering still, as he went, the May-flowers blooming around him,
Fragrant, filling the air with a strange and wonderful sweetness,
Children lost in the woods, and covered with leaves in their slumber.
"Puritan flowers," he said, "and the type of Puritan maidens,

"PRITHEE, JOHN, WHY DON'T YOU SPEAK FOR YOURSELF?"

Modest and simple and sweet, the very type of Priscilla !
So I will take them to her ; to Priscilla the May-flower of Plymouth,
Modest and simple and sweet, as a parting gift will I take them ;
Breathing their silent farewells, as they fade and wither and perish,
Soon to be thrown away, as is the heart of the giver."

. . . .

Then, as he opened the door, he beheld the form of the maiden
Seated beside her wheel, and the carded wool like a snow-drift
Piled at her knee, her white hands feeding the ravenous spindle,
While with her foot on the treadle she guided the wheel in its motion.
Open wide on her lap lay the well-worn psalm-book of Ainsworth,
Printed in Amsterdam, the words and the music together,
Rough-hewn, angular notes, like stones in the wall of a churchyard,
Darkened and overhung by the running vine of the verses.

. . . .

So he entered the house : and the hum of the wheel and the singing
Suddenly ceased ; for Priscilla, aroused by his step on the threshold,
Rose as he entered, and gave him her hand, in signal of welcome,
Saying, "I knew it was you, when I heard your step in the passage ;
For I was thinking of you, as I sat there singing and spinning."

. . . .

Thus he delivered his message, the dexterous writer of letters, —
Did not embellish the theme, nor array it in beautiful phrases,
But came straight to the point, and blurted it out like a school-boy ;
Even the Captain himself could hardly have said it more bluntly.
Mute with amazement and sorrow, Priscilla the Puritan maiden
Looked into Alden's face, her eyes dilated with wonder,
Feeling his words like a blow, that stunned her and rendered her
    speechless ;
Till at length she exclaimed, interrupting the ominous silence :
" If the great Captain of Plymouth is so very eager to wed me,
Why does he not come himself, and take the trouble to woo me ?
If I am not worth the wooing, I surely am not worth the winning !"

. . . .

Still John Alden went on, unheeding the words of Priscilla,
Urging the suit of his friend, explaining, persuading, expanding.

. . . .

Though he was rough, he was kindly ; she knew how during the
    winter

He had attended the sick, with a hand as gentle as woman's ;
Somewhat hasty and hot, he could not deny it, and headstrong,
Stern as a soldier might be, but hearty, and placable always,
Not to be laughed at and scorned, because he was little of stature ;
For he was great of heart, magnanimous, courtly, courageous ;
Any woman in Plymouth, nay, any woman in England,
Might be happy and proud to be called the wife of Miles Standish !

But as he warmed and glowed, in his simple and eloquent language,
Quite forgetful of self, and full of the praise of his rival,
Archly the maiden smiled, and, with eyes overrunning with laughter,
Said, in a tremulous voice, "Why don't you speak for yourself,
    John ?"

THE PILGRIM FATHERS.

OUR fathers crossed the ocean's wave
    To seek this shore ;
They left behind the coward slave
To welter in his living grave.
With hearts unbent and spirits brave,
    They sternly bore
Such toils as meaner souls had quelled ;
But souls like these such toils impelled
    To soar.

PERCIVAL.

THE Pilgrim spirit has not fled :
    It walks in noon's broad light ;
And it watches the bed of the glorious dead,
    With the holy stars, by night.
It watches the bed of the brave who have bled,
    And shall guard this ice-bound shore,
Till the waves of the Bay where the "Mayflower" lay
    Shall foam and freeze no more.

PIERPONT.

Ay, call it holy ground,
   The soil where first they trod ;
They have left unstained what there they found, —
   Freedom to worship God !

                   HEMANS.

And never may they rest unsung,
While Liberty can find a tongue !
Twine, Gratitude, a wreath for them
More deathless than the diadem,
   Who to life's noblest end
Gave up life's noblest powers,
   And bade the legacy descend
Down, down to us and ours.

                   SPRAGUE.

Part Eleventh.

RHODE-ISLAND LEGENDS.

THE SKELETON IN ARMOR.

LONGFELLOW'S ballad of "The Skeleton in Armor" is the legitimate product of one of those obscure traditions which, through frequent repetition, acquire all the consistency of authentic facts; yet, like other illusions, disappear as soon as the light is turned on them. In this case the Scandinavian tradition recounts the adventurous voyages of the two Norse corsairs, Leif and Thorwald, to the New World as early as A. D. 1000. They are said to have sailed from Iceland, and to have passed a winter in New England.

The terms of these sagas are so ambiguous, even should they be accounted true relations, as to render any serious attempt to trace the voyages they narrate, with the purpose of fitting them to our own coasts or harbors, a lost labor. That Danish antiquaries would be deeply interested in establishing the validity of the claim on the part of their countrymen to a discovery preceding by nearly five centuries that of Columbus, was only natural; for should they succeed it would prove the most brilliant jewel in the crown of their nation. The relations themselves, however, amounted to little; and without stronger evidence the reputable historian would probably content himself merely with mentioning them. He would certainly hesitate long, and examine critically, before installing the vague and the veritable side by side.

Should he positively declare America to have been discovered by the Northmen in the year 1000, he must first withdraw the assertion made in favor of the illustrious Genoese to a discovery in 1492.

Several things contributed to produce in the public mind an effect favorable to the Scandinavian claim. The most important

OLD WINDMILL, NEWPORT.

of these were the alleged evidences then existing of an occupation of the country by the Norse voyagers in question. Let us run over them.

There was, and still is, at Newport, in Rhode Island, an old windmill of peculiar, and for New England unique, construction, which Time has left a picturesque ruin. The main structure, being of stone, presents the appearance of a round tower

thirty feet high, supported by massive stone columns, also round ;
for the woodwork having fallen away, nothing but the bare walls
remain to identify its original form or purpose. It stands on the
heights overlooking the harbor ; and until Time's changes hid it
from view, was always a conspicuous object when the city was
approached from the sea. This structure had been so long un-
used, that little importance need be attached to the fact that the
purpose for which it was originally built had gradually died out
of the memory of the oldest inhabitant. The natural growth
of the town was certain in time to bring this result about. Its
proper functions then having so long ceased, no one regarded it
except with a feeble curiosity, nor was there even a local tradition concerning it. For a century and a half it had stood on
the same spot without a question arising as to its origin ; it
was completely ignored. But at length some one discovered a
resemblance to Scandinavian architecture. The Danish *savans*
at once claimed the windmill as the work of their countrymen
centuries before the arrival of the English.

There was also on the shore of Taunton River, — a tidal
stream that flows into Narragansett Bay, and might therefore
be easily ascended by an exploring vessel, — a moderately large
bowlder, one face of which, being smooth, was completely covered
with mysterious hieroglyphics which no one had been able to
decipher. The strange characters had originally been deeply
cut into the perpendicular face toward the channel; but in the
course of years, and owing to the rock itself being partly submerged at high tide, the continual abrasion of water and ice has
nearly obliterated them ; so that it is now scarcely possible to
identify these marks as the work of human hands. The bowlder
received the name of Dighton Rock because the shore where it lay
imbedded was within the limits of the town of Dighton. Here
now was a veritable relic of antiquity. Unlike the windmill,
this had always been the subject of eager curiosity and discussion, — so much so, that copies of the inscription had been
transmitted by Cotton Mather to the learned societies of London
as a worthy and valuable contribution to the purposes and aims

of archæological research ; while the windmill, notwithstanding its alleged peculiarity of construction, and the clear presumption that it must have been a most poignant spur to curiosity, as proving the residence here of Europeans so long ago, was not thought to be worthy of a single word, and no one of the thousands to whom it was a familiar object so much as hinted that it had any title to such consideration. The sculptured rock remained, however, an unsolved enigma. A vague local tradition only rendered it all the more perplexing. It is true that many who were acquainted with their rude commemorative drawings, which those of the rock greatly resembled, believed that the Indians had at some time cut the unknown characters. This very natural solution of the mystery became the subject of controversy. The Danish antiquaries, better instructed, immediately declared Dighton Rock to be the imperishable record of the adventurous voyages of their countrymen.

Still another thing, most opportunely occurring, by investing it with the glamour of romance, secured for the new theory a certain amount of sympathy, — thus giving it a strength of a wholly different kind in the popular mind. Hitherto the new idea had taken less with the general public than with scholars ; the materials were now found for a veritable *coup de théâtre.*

There was exhumed at Fall River the skeleton of a man whose breast — whether for ornament or defence is uncertain — was protected by an oval plate of brass, and on whose fleshless thighs still loosely hung a belt of curious workmanship, made of hollow tubes of brass much corroded, and fitted together in the manner of the bandoliers worn when firearms were in their infancy. There were also found lying near the skeleton some arrow-heads made of the same metal. It is true that the body had been buried in a sitting posture, with its arms and ornaments, agreeable to the funeral customs of the Indians of this coast. It is also true that from the voyages of the Cabots down to the coming in of the English settlers here, the possession of copper ornaments, and even weapons of war, by the Indians, was a fact constantly repeated. Even the chains and collars, one of which was worn by the skeleton, had been exactly and minutely described in some of the Relations printed by Hakluyt. But the sagas had said that Thorwald, the Norse rover-chief, was slain in an encounter with the natives, and had been hastily interred near the spot where he fell. The breastplate and arrows were said to be identical with those in use among the Scandinavians of this ancient period. To the silent evidence of the mill and to the testimony of the rock was now joined that of a supposed Norse warrior in his armor. The Danish scholars unhesitatingly adopted the skeleton.

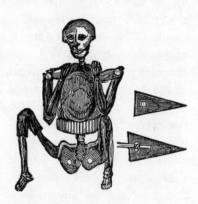

THE SKELETON IN ARMOR.

The case as it now stood may be briefly summed up thus. A building said to be of a construction similar to the most ancient ones in the Scandinavian peninsula, — in fact not dating later than the twelfth century, — certainly unlike anything of British architecture, had been found; a rock inscribed with Runic characters, — for the Danish scholars claimed to decipher portions of its inscription, — had been discovered; a skeleton wearing armor of the kind used by Norse warriors had been disinterred, — and these things existed within such neighborhood to each other as to constitute a chain of evidence strong in itself, strengthened by probability, and further supported by the very general feeling in its favor, that they were the work or the remains of the adventurous sea-rovers of the North. To such an array, presented with such authority and with so much confidence, it is no wonder that the sceptical at first hardly knew what to answer.

But each and every one of these pieces of evidence has been fully disproved. It has been shown that the Newport Mill was of a similar build to those erected in some parts of England, —

notably like one at Chesterton. The settlers, therefore, built after
known British models. The attempt to convert the characters
of Dighton Rock into Runic, or even into an intelligible historic
record of any kind, signally failed to convince either learned
or unlearned. And lastly, the metal found upon the skeleton
turned out to be different from that used for warlike purposes
by the ancient Scandinavians. To this the direct evidence that
a windmill was erected on the very spot where the ruin now
stands; that Governor Arnold mentions it in his will; that the
way leading to it is still called Mill Street; and that it was
commonly known as a windmill and nothing else, — would seem
finally to dispose of what was left of the Northmen's antique
tower, and to leave it the simple and striking memorial of the
forefathers that it undoubtedly is. This whole controversy may
be said signally to demonstrate the ease with which any historical fact may be perverted or unsettled.

In a note to his "Skeleton in Armor," Mr. Longfellow says
that he considers the tradition sufficiently established for the
purpose of a ballad. *Voilà tout!* But he very naïvely adds
what few will now be found willing to dispute, that, "doubtless
many an honest citizen of Newport, who has passed his days
within sight of the round tower, will be ready to exclaim, with
Sancho: 'God bless me! did I not warn you to have a care what
you were doing, for that it was nothing but a windmill; and nobody could mistake it but one who had the like in his head.'"

In the ballad the Viking's ghost is supposed to appear to the
poet, and is exhorted to tell him his story. One instinctively
recalls Hamlet's midnight colloquy on the platform of the castle
at Elsinore: —

> Speak! speak! thou fearful guest!
> Who, with thy hollow breast
> Still in rude armor drest,
>   Comest to daunt me!
> Wrapt not in Eastern balms,
> But with thy fleshless palms
> Stretched, as if asking alms,
>   Why dost thou haunt me?

And the grisly corse replies : —

> I was a Viking old !
> My deeds, though manifold,
> No Skald in song has told,
>   No Saga taught thee !
> Take heed, that in thy verse
> Thou dost the tale rehearse,
> Else dread a dead man's curse ;
>   For this I sought thee.

The weird tale proceeds without further regard to the legend as it is told in the sagas. The rude corsair wins the love of a gentle maiden, — a prince's child, — somewhat in the manner of Othello, by telling her the story of his deeds : —

> Once as I told in glee
> Tales of the stormy sea,
> Soft eyes did gaze on me,
>   Burning yet tender ;
> And as the white stars shine
> On the dark Norway pine,
> On that dark heart of mine
>   Fell their full splendor.

Then the Viking, having persuaded the old Hildebrand's daughter to fly with him, is hotly pursued by the incensed father " with seventy horsemen." He puts to sea in his vessel, and is followed by Hildebrand in another, when the catastrophe that makes him an outcast occurs : —

> And as to catch the gale
> Round veered the flapping sail,
> Death ! was the helmsman's hail,
>   Death without quarter !
> Mid-ships with iron keel
> Struck we her ribs of steel ;
> Down her black hulk did reel
>   Through the black water !

After this the outlaw who has carried off the daughter, and has slain the father before her eyes, steers into the open and unknown sea. The stanza introducing the round tower is as follows : —

> Three weeks we westward bore ;
> And when the storm was o'er,
> Cloud-like, we saw the shore
>   Stretching to leeward ;
> There for my lady's bower
> Built I the lofty tower
> Which, to this very hour,
>   Stands looking seaward.

Here the hawk and the dove dwelt until a child was born to them ; but the maiden sickened ; and at length, as the ballad tells us, —

> Death closed her mild blue eyes :
> Under that tower she lies ;
> Ne'er shall the sun arise
>   On such another !

In despair, the Viking puts on his armor and falls upon his spear, — the poet thus accounting for the skeleton in armor by a stroke of genius, as he does for the tower by a touch of humanity ; so that it is not strange to find people saying they would rather believe in the legend than not.

But Mr. Longfellow was not the first poet to discover the capabilities of the old mill for a poem. The poet Brainard makes it the subject of an Indian tradition to the effect that its perishing walls were typical of the gradual disappearance of the Red Man in the home of his fathers, and that its final fall would signalize the total extinction of his race. His is the earliest poetical use of the tower that the writer has seen.

THE NEWPORT TOWER.

J. G. BRAINARD.

THERE is a rude old monument,
Half masonry, half ruin, bent
With sagging weight, as if it meant
    To warn one of mischance ;
And an old Indian may be seen
Musing in sadness on the scene,
And casting on it many a keen
    And many a thoughtful glance.

When lightly sweeps the evening tide
Old Narragansett's shore beside,
And the canoes in safety ride
    Upon the lovely bay, —
I 've seen him gaze on that old tower,
At evening's calm and pensive hour ;
And when the night began to lower,
    Scarce tear himself away.

   .   .   .   .   .

But once he turned with furious look,
While high his clenchèd hand he shook,
And from his brow his dark eye took
    A reddening glow of madness ;
Yet when I told him why I came,
His wild and bloodshot eye grew tame,
And bitter thoughts passed o'er its flame
    That changed its rage to sadness.

"You watch my step, and ask me why
This ruin fills my straining eye.
Stranger, there is a prophecy
    Which you may lightly heed :
Stay its fulfilment if you can :
I heard it of a gray-haired man ;
And thus the threatening story ran, —
    A boding tale indeed.

" *He* said that when this massy wall
Down to its very base should fall,
And not one stone among it all
   Be left upon another,
Then should the Indian race and kind
Disperse like the returnless wind,
And no red man be left to find
   One he could call a brother.

" Now yon old tower is falling fast :
Kindred and friends away are passed ;
Oh ! that my father's soul may cast
   Upon my grave its shade,
When some good Christian man shall place
O'er me, the last of all my race,
The last old stone that falls, to grace
   The spot where I am laid ! "

Mrs. Sigourney, following Longfellow, has also addressed some characteristic lines to its gray walls in a half serious, half playful vein. She, too, believed it to be a veritable relic of the Northmen. But the poets, it should be said, are much too susceptible to the charm of romance to be intrusted with making history.

THE NEWPORT TOWER.

MRS. L. H. SIGOURNEY.

Dark, lonely Tower, amid yon Eden-isle,
Which, as a gem, fair Narragansett wears
Upon her heaving breast, thou lift'st thy head,
A mystery and paradox, to mock
The curious throng.
           Say, reared the plundering hand
Of the fierce buccaneer thy massy walls,
A treasure-fortress for his blood-stained gold ?
Or wrought the beings of an earlier race
To form thy circle, while in wonder gazed
The painted Indian ?

We see thou art
A right substantial, well-preserved old tower, —
Let that suffice us.
        Some there are who say
Thou wert an *ancient windmill.*
             Be it so !
Our Pilgrim-sires must have been much in love
With extra labor, thus to gather stones,
And patient rear thy Scandinavian arch,
And build thine ample chamber, and uplift
Thy shapely column, for the gadding winds
To play vagaries with.
          In those hard times
I trow King Philip gave them other work
Than to deck dancing-halls, and lure the blasts
From old Eolus' cave.
         Had'st thou the power,
I think thou'dst laugh right heartily to see
The worthy farmers, with their sacks of corn,
Mistaking thy profession, as of old
Don Quixote did mistake thine ancestor, —
If haply such progenitor thou hadst.

BLOCK ISLAND.

THE introduction to Dana's celebrated narrative poem, "The Buccaneer," is a beautiful piece of descriptive writing, that stands out in strong relief against the dark legend upon which it casts a solitary ray of sunshine.

THE ISLAND.

THE island lies nine leagues away.
    Along its solitary shore,
Of craggy rock and sandy bay,
    No sound but ocean's roar,
Save where the bold, wild sea-bird makes her home,
Her shrill cry coming through the sparkling foam.

But when the light winds lie at rest,
　　And on the glassy, heaving sea,
The black duck, with her glossy breast,
　　Sits swinging silently,
How beautiful!　No ripples break the reach,
And silvery waves go noiseless up the beach.

And inland rests the green, warm dell;
　　The brook comes tinkling down its side;
From out the trees the Sabbath bell
　　Rings cheerful, far and wide,
Mingling its sounds with bleatings of the flocks
That feed about the vale amongst the rocks.

Nor holy bell nor pastoral bleat
　　In former days within the vale;
Flapped in the bay the pirate's sheet;
　　Curses were on the gale;
Rich goods lay on the sand, and murdered men:
Pirate and wrecker kept their revels then.

The island merits a further word of description. It is a bank of clay, treeless and wind-swept, eight miles long, rising out of the ocean between Montauk and Gay Head, and lying nearest to Point Judith, on the Rhode-Island shore, from which it is about five miles distant. Planted, as it is, right athwart the highway of a vast and increasing commerce, it is a veritable stumbling-block in the way of the anxious navigator. In clear weather its brilliant light cheers the grateful mariner on his voyage with its signal of "All's well, and a fine night!" till it sinks or fades from his view.

We know that a tribe of the once powerful and warlike Narragansetts possessed and inhabited this sea-girt isle, to which their fathers gave the euphonious name of Manisses. But powerful and warlike as they were, they were also a race of plunderers, having the lawless traits common to islanders everywhere; so that, as early as the infancy of the white settlements in Massachusetts Bay, their thieving propensities brought down upon them the vengeance of the whites, who made an armed descent upon the island with the sanguinary purpose of exterminating every warrior upon it. Before the wars, of which this is a mere episode, were over, the island passed forever from the ownership of these Indians, who had fled from it in terror, into that of their enemies, — first taking a civilized name from the Dutch sailor

ANCIENT WINDMILL.

Adrian Block, and subsequently that of New Shoreham, which the township still retains.

Then began the gradual peopling of the island under the rule of a new race, and a development, sometimes checked by the wars, but tending slowly toward an improved condition. It being first available for pasturage, the islanders were mostly farmers, who raised cattle, sheep, and poultry, which they exported to the mainland. Tillage gradually superseded this. The farms are still productive, and the inhabitants, contrary to the general belief, get their living chiefly by the soil.

Those who were not farmers were fishermen. The seas around the island teemed with the cod, the mackerel, and the blue fish, besides other valuable species, — thus furnishing subsistence to another class, who toiled with net and line, and who built their rude cabins and flakes by the shore. But the island having no good harbor, fishing and trading went on by boats in the old primitive way.

Somehow, the reputation of the island was never good. Sailors always shook their heads when they spoke of Block Island. A bad lee shore, a place of no good hap for the unlucky mariner who might be driven upon it, were prevailing notions, — and firmly rooted ones, — which dark hints, and still darker traditions, concerning shipwrecked crews and valuable cargoes, give a certain color and consistency. "I would rather be wrecked anywhere than upon Block Island," became a common and significant saying in the forecastle or the midnight watch, when the dark mass of the island heaved in sight. But all this refers to long ago ; for though there are still wreckers, — and they are universally held by sailors to be but one remove from pirates, — their work now proceeds with some regard for the saving of life and the lawful claims of the owners. In " the good old times " the wreckers stripped a ship, and divided her cargo upon the principle that to the finders belongs the spoil. " Everything is fish," said they, "that comes to our net."

Like all islanders, these people were generally hardy, sober, and industrious. But a difference is to be observed between the farmers and the fishermen, — a name often synonymous with that of wreckers or smugglers. So isolated were they from the rest of the world, that the intermarriage of those more or less related by blood was a thing of common occurrence. The result was naturally unfavorable to the physical condition of the islanders. Indeed, one instance is mentioned of a woman who left three deaf-and-dumb sons at her death.

Dana's " Buccaneers " and Whittier's " Palatine " are the

legitimate outcome of a state of things which so naturally affords materials for romance ; and both are also the outgrowth of a singular legend, whose very obscurity lends it a weird fascination.

Some time during the last century — even the year is uncertain — an emigrant ship bound for Philadelphia came upon the American coast, only to be driven off to sea again by stress of weather. The emigrants were substantial and thrifty Dutch people of the better class, who had brought all their property along with them to their new home, whither many of their countrymen had preceded them. Some of them are even alleged to have been wealthy. It was in the dark and dreary season of midwinter, when the voyage, already long, was thus disastrously lengthened. With the coast in sight, but unable to gain her port, the ship, buffeting the frozen seas, was driven northward far out of her course ; while scenes were being enacted on board, the bare thought of which makes the blood run cold. The captain had died, or had been murdered, at sea, before the vessel came in sight of the land. All discipline was at an end ; and the ship's crew then began a system of cold-blooded robbery, to which the act of boldly hoisting the black flag and of cutting the throats of their miserable victims would have been mercy indeed. The wretches armed themselves ; and having taken possession of the water and provisions, with a refined cruelty demanded from the famishing emigrants twenty guilders for a cup of water, and fifty rix-dollars for a biscuit. To save their lives the poor passengers were obliged to beggar themselves. Those who could not or would not comply with the atrocious demand were allowed to starve, and their emaciated bodies were coolly thrown into the sea. The ship soon became a floating hell. Having plundered their victims of everything that they possessed of value, the inhuman crew finally took to the boats ; and deserting the stricken ship, they left her to the mercy of the winds and waves. With no one left on board to navigate her, the doomed ship drifted on. Days of despair were succeeded by nights of horror. She was now a madhouse, tenanted only by maniacs or the unburied corpses of those who had died from famine or disease.

One calm Sabbath morning the "Palatine" struck on the northernmost reef of Block Island. But her voyage was not to end here. The wreckers manned their boats and humanely rescued all those who had survived starvation, except one woman, who had gone stark mad, and who now refused to leave the wreck.

The ship, having only touched the reef, floated off again with the rising tide; and the wreckers, who surrounded the grimy hulk like vultures the carcass of a noble stag, now making their boats fast to it, towed her into a neighboring cove, in order that they might dismantle her at their leisure. But before this could be done a gale sprang up; when the wreckers, seeing that the ship, in spite of their efforts, would be blown off to sea, set her on fire; and she was soon in flames.

Enveloped in fire from truck to deck, the "Palatine" drove out into the thickening darkness of a stormy sea, — an object of dread even to those who had so recklessly applied the torch. But this feeling was turned to deeper horror when the frenzied shrieks borne to their ears from the burning ship told the lookers-on that a human being was perishing miserably in the flames before their eyes.

These appalling sounds were supposed to proceed from the maniac woman, who had been forgotten in the excitement of the moment. The "Palatine" drifted away, and burned to the water's edge. And so ends the dismal tale of the actual ship.

But it is now averred that on that very night twelvemonth, the anniversary of the same storm, the islanders were affrighted by the startling and sublime spectacle of a ship on fire in the offing, which, as the gale rose, drifted before it, and gradually faded from their sight, exactly as the ill-fated "Palatine" had done. Year after year the same strange sight continued to keep the fate of the "Palatine" fresh in the memory of every man, woman, and child upon the island. Hundreds had seen it; and all were fully convinced that this annual visitation was a portent of disaster to them and theirs. Some of the better-informed were, it is true, inclined to class the phantasm of the burning ship with atmospheric phenomena ; but the islanders only shrugged their shoulders as they pointed to the unerring certainty with which it reappeared, the faithfulness with which every detail of the conflagration repeated itself, and the mysterious way in which the vessel first came on shore.

THE BUCCANEER.

DANA'S tragic story of the "Buccaneer" would hardly be recognized for the same that we have related, were not its leading incidents firmly associated with Block Island. He makes Lee, the "buccaneer" of the poem, native here. Lee is a man fitted by nature for leadership in a career of crime, — a monster from whom we turn in abhorrence, and for whose evil destiny even the poet's art can hardly make us feel one touch of compassion. The grandeur of the design of the poem is in fact marred by the hideousness of the central figure. Lee is a wretch without one redeeming trait, — he is simply a cut-throat.

The poem opens with Lee's ship lying in a port of Spain. He has grown weary of the life of a peaceful trader, and has resolved to turn pirate. While the vessel is being refitted for sea a Spanish lady seeks a passage in her to America. Her husband has fallen in the wars, and she is scarcely wedded before she is a widow and an exile from her native land. Lee receives her with well-affected sympathy, and tenders her a passage in his ship. The bereaved lady unsuspectingly puts herself, her attendants, and all that she possesses in the corsair's power. Her rich jewels and her gold inflame the rapacity of Lee, — who, however, is crafty enough to bide his time. The Señora has a strange attachment for a favorite milk-white Arabian horse : this too is brought on board, and then the ship sets sail. She is no sooner out of sight of land, than the crew, at a signal from Lee, stab the lady's servants in their sleep. They then, with a deadlier purpose, break into her cabin : —

> A crash!   They force the door ; and then
>   One long, long, shrill, and piercing scream
> Comes thrilling 'bove the growl of men !
>   'T is hers ! O God, redeem
> From worse than death thy suffering, helpless child !
> That dreadful shriek again, — sharp, sharp and wild !
>
> It ceased : with speed o' th' lightning's flash
>   A loose-robed form, with streaming hair,
> Shoots by ; a leap, — a quick, short splash !
>   'T is gone ! and nothing there !
> The waves have swept away the bubbling tide, —
> Bright-crested waves, how calmly on they ride !

With a brutal jest on his lips, Lee then orders the horse to be thrown alive into the sea ; the men obey.

> Such sound to mortal ear ne'er came
>   As rang far o'er the waters wide ;
> It shook with fear the stoutest frame, —
>   The horse is on the tide !
> As the waves leave, or lift him up, his cry
> Comes lower now, and now is near and high.

The ill-fated lady's gold is then divided ; but a quarrel springing up over it, Lee stabs one of his men to the heart.   When the ship is near the land, she is abandoned and set on fire.   Lee with his cut-throats gains the shores of Block Island.   They drown remorse in drink, and silence suspicion by scattering their ill-gotten gold right and left.   At length the night of their horrid anniversary comes round.   The buccaneers are celebrating it by a carousal, when a sudden glare, lighting up the sea, brings the orgy to a pause.

> Not bigger than a star it seems ;
>   And now 't is like the bloody moon ;
> And now it shoots in hairy streams !
>   It moves ! — 't will reach us soon !
> A ship ! and all on fire ! — hull, yard, and mast !
> Her sails are sheets of flame ! — she 's nearing fast !

And what comes up above the wave
   So ghastly white ?   A spectral head !
A horse's head ! (May Heaven save
   Those looking on the dead, —
The waking dead !)   There on the sea he stands, —
The Spectre Horse !   He moves !   He gains the sands !

The spectre horse gallops like the wind up to the door-stone, and stands with his burning eyes fixed on Lee.   A power he cannot resist compels the villain to mount the dreadful steed,

LEE ON THE SPECTRE HORSE.

which instantly dashes off with his rider to the highest cliff of the island, from which Lee sees not only the ship on fire, but beholds in the depths it lights the bodies of those whom he had slain.   At dawn the spectre vanishes, leaving him rooted to the spot.   Lee's doom has begun ; thenceforth he is accursed.   All shun him, all turn from him with fear and loathing ; for all have seen the spectre ship. Weary of life, yet afraid to die, the outcast wanders about the shores of the island, — a broken, hopeless wreck of his former self.

> They ask him why he wanders so,
>   From day to day, the uneven strand.
> "I wish — I wish that I might go!
>   But I would go by land!
> And there's no way that I can find; I've tried
> All day and night!" He seaward looked and sighed.

At last the fatal summons comes. The fireship again bears down upon the island. Again the unearthly messenger, the spectre horse, strides over the waves. The pirate pleads for mercy; but his hour is come.

> He's on the beach, but stops not there;
>   He's on the sea, — that dreadful horse!
> Lee flings and writhes in wild despair.
>   In vain! The Spirit Corse
> Holds him by fearful spell; he cannot leap:
> Within that horrid light he rides the deep.

> It lights the sea around their track, —
>   The curling comb and steel-dark wave;
> And there sits Lee the Spectre's back, —
>   Gone! gone! and none to save!
> They're seen no more; the night has shut them in!
> May Heaven have pity on thee, man of sin!

THE PALATINE.

J. G. WHITTIER.

OLD wives spinning their webs of tow,
Or rocking weirdly to and fro
In and out of the peat's dull glow,

And old men mending their nets of twine,
Talk together of dream and sign,
Talk of the lost ship " Palatine," —

The ship that, a hundred years before,
Freighted deep with its goodly store,
In the gales of the equinox went ashore.

.　　.　　.　　.　　.　　.

Down swooped the wreckers, like birds of prey
Tearing the heart of the ship away,
And the dead had never a word to say.

And then, with ghastly shimmer and shine
Over the rocks and the seething brine,
They burned the wreck of the " Palatine."

In their cruel hearts, as they homeward sped,
" The sea and the rocks are dumb," they said :
" There 'll be no reckoning with the dead."

But the year went round, and when once more
Along their foam-white curves of shore
They heard the line-storm rave and roar,

Behold ! again, with shimmer and shine,
Over the rocks and the seething brine,
The flaming wreck of the " Palatine ! "

So, haply in fitter words than these,
Mending their nets on their patient knees,
They tell the legend of Manisees.

THE LAST OF THE WAMPANOAGS.

THE beautiful eminence of Mount Hope was the ancient seat of Philip, the great sachem of the Wampanoags. When his reverses had left him only a handful of followers Philip took the sublime resolution of returning to his mountain home and dying like a chief of royal blood, with his arms in his hands. Mount Hope was quickly surrounded by his enemies; and here the dreaded warrior fell, shot through the heart by a renegade of his own race.

When here King Philip stood,
  Or rested in the niche we call his throne,
He looked o'er hill and vale and swelling flood,
  Which once were all his own.
Before the white man's footstep, day by day,
  As the sea-tides encroach upon the sand,
He saw his proud possessions melt away,
  And found himself a king without a land.
    Constrained by unknown laws,
    Judged guilty without cause,
    Maddened by treachery,
  What wonder that his tortured spirit rose
    And turned upon his foes,
And told his wrongs in words that still we see
Recorded on the page of history.

Part Twelfth.

CONNECTICUT LEGENDS.

THE PHANTOM SHIP.

THIS marvel comes to us in a letter written at New Haven, where it happened, to Cotton Mather, and printed in his "Magnalia Christi." As Wagner has confirmed to our own age the immortality of the Flying Dutchman, so have Mather and Longfellow decreed that of this wondrous sea-legend. There is no power in science to eradicate either of them. One would not have his illusions rudely dispelled by going behind the scenes while "Der fliegende Holländer" is being performed; and he does not ask if under such or such atmospheric conditions a mirage may not have deceived the good people of New Haven in the year A. D. 1647.

In that year a Rhode-Island-built ship of about one hundred and fifty tons' burden, carrying a valuable cargo, besides "a far more rich treasure of passengers," put to sea from New Haven. Among those who sailed in her were five or six of the most eminent persons in that colony. The ship was new, but so "walty," that Lamberton, her master, often said that she would prove the grave of passengers and crew. It was in the heart of winter; the harbor was frozen over, and a way was cut through the ice, through which the ship slowly passed on her voyage, while the Reverend Mr. Davenport, besides many other friends who witnessed her departure, accompanied her with their prayers and tears until she was lost to view.

An ill-omened gloom overspread the scene, to which the prayer of the pastor lent an emphasis of its own. They who were departing heard these solemn words of invocation, wafted like a prayer for the dead to their ears : "Lord, if it be thy pleasure to bury these our friends in the bottom of the sea, take them ; they are thine : save them !"

When, in the following spring, the ships arriving from England brought no tidings either of ship or company, "New Haven's heart began to fail her." This, says the narrative, "put the godly people upon much prayer, both public and private, that the Lord would — if it was his pleasure — let them hear what he had done with their dear friends, and prepare them with a suitable submission to his holy will."

One afternoon in June a great thunderstorm arose out of the northwest. After it had spent itself, — after this grand overture had ceased, — the black clouds rolled away in the distance, and the skies again became serene and bright. All at once, about an hour before sunset, the people saw a large ship, with all her sails spread and her colors flying, coming gallantly up from the harbor's mouth. But such a ship as that had never before been seen ; for notwithstanding the wind was blowing dead against her from the land, she moved steadily on against it as if her sails were filled with a fresh and favorable gale. The people looked on in wonder and in awe. The strange vessel seemed floating in air ; there was no ripple at her bow, nor on her deck any of the bustle denoting preparation to anchor. All those who had assembled to witness the strange sight gazed in stupefaction. The children clapped their hands and cried out, "There 's a brave ship !" while up the harbor she sailed, stemming wind and tide, and every moment looming larger and more distinct.

At length, crowding up as far as there is depth of water sufficient for such a vessel, — in fact so near to the spectators that the figure of a man standing on her poop, with a naked sword, which

THE PHANTOM SHIP.

he pointed seaward, was
distinctly seen, — sud-
denly and noiselessly, as
if struck by a squall, her
main-top seemed blown
away, and, falling in a
wreck, hung entangled in
the shrouds; then her
mizzen-top, and then all
her masts, spars, and
sails blew away from her
decks, and vanished like

thistledown, leaving only a dismantled hulk floating in the quiet haven. As if yielding now to an invisible but resistless force, this too began to career dangerously more and more, until it went down before the eyes of the beholders in a mist-like cloud, which after a little time melted away, leaving the space lately occupied by the Phantom Ship, as everywhere else, clear and unobstructed.

The wonder-struck lookers-on, while this weird counterfeit of a wreck at sea was enacting before their eyes, could so far distinguish the peculiar form and rigging of the Spectre Ship as to be able to say that " This was the very mould of our ship, and thus was her tragic end." The learned and devout Mr. Davenport also declared publicly, " That God had condescended, for the quieting of their afflicted spirits, this extraordinary account of his sovereign disposal of those for whom so many fervent prayers were made continually."

Mr. Bryant, writing to the poet Dana in 1824, says that he had formed the idea of constructing a narrative poem on this subject; but upon finding that the legend had already been made use of by Irving, he abandoned the purpose, which Longfellow subsequently carried out, with dramatic effect, as follows : —

> A ship sailed from New Haven ;
> And the keen and frosty airs,
> That filled her sails at parting,
> Were heavy with good men's prayers.
>
> .   .   .   .   .
>
> But Master Lamberton muttered,
> And under his breath said he,
> " This ship is so crank and walty,
> I fear our grave she will be ! "
>
> .   .   .   .
>
> And at last their prayers were answered : —
> It was in the month of June,
> An hour before the sunset
> Of a windy afternoon,

When, steadily steering landward,
    A ship was seen below,
And they knew it was Lamberton, Master,
    Who sailed so long ago.

On she came, with a cloud of canvas,
    Right against the wind that blew,
Until the eye could distinguish
    The faces of the crew.

Then fell her straining topmasts,
    Hanging tangled in the shrouds,
And her sails were loosened and lifted,
    And blown away like clouds.

And the masts, with all their rigging,
    Fell slowly, one by one,
And the hulk dilated and vanished,
    As a sea-mist in the sun !

And the people who saw this marvel
    Each said unto his friend,
That this was the mould of their vessel,
    And thus her tragic end.

THE CHARTER OAK.

WERE an American schoolboy to be asked to name the most celebrated tree of history, he would undoubtedly mention the Charter Oak. Other trees are locally famous; but this tree may be said to have a national reputation.

It is now not quite thirty years since the sturdy oak itself went down before one of those terrific storms that it had for centuries refused to budge an inch to; but so firmly had it become rooted in the event of history which first drew conspicuous attention to it, that this will be as soon forgotten as the oak will. Nothing illustrates like this the strength of old associations, or more clearly expresses that demand of the human mind for something that may establish a relation with the invisible through the visible. The Charter Oak is no more. Yet it is still the tree that commemorates to most minds the preservation of the Colonial Charter, more distinctly than the event itself does the tree ; for it is undoubtedly true that when we cast our eyes over the field of history we instinctively seek out those objects that rise above the common level, like steeples above a city. One sees there the Charter Oak ; the chapter of history then swiftly unfolds itself.

The fall of this mighty monarch of the ancient forests occurred in the year 1856. It was announced throughout the Union as a public calamity ; and in Hartford, where the Charter Oak had almost become an object of veneration, the intelligence created a feeling of loss to the glory of the city which nothing in the way of monuments could make good. The smallest pieces of the tree were eagerly secured by relic-hunters, and they are still carefully treasured up, in order to perpetuate, in the thousand forms into which a piece of wood may be turned, the memory of the brave old oak from which Hartford derived its familiar sobriquet of the Charter-Oak City, of which her citizens are justly proud.

The Charter Oak stood on the slope of Wyllys's Hill, in the city of Hartford ; and it had stood on the same spot for centuries. No man knew its exact age ; but there is little doubt that it was an object of veneration to the Indians long before the discovery of America by Columbus. Tradition says that when the white people began to build here at Hartford, Mr. Samuel Wyllys, who was one of these pioneers, was busy clearing the forest away around his homestead, and he had marked this tree for destruction with the rest ; but the savages who dwelt in the neighborhood so earnestly begged that it might be spared, because its first putting forth its leaves had been a sign to them from immemorial time when to plant their corn, that at their request the oak was left standing.

Some idea of the great age of this historic tree may, however, be formed by considering its dimensions. Thirty odd years before it fell to the ground, a wreck, it measured thirty-six feet in circumference at the base. The famous hiding-place in its trunk had then nearly closed up, although the old people could remember when it would easily admit a child into the hollow cavity of the tree. The same generation believed this to be a sign that it had fulfilled its mission. When Mr. Lossing visited

THE CHARTER OAK.

it in 1848 he found the trunk then having a girth of twenty-five feet around it at one foot from the ground ; and the opening at the bottom was then a narrow crevice only large enough for a person's hand to go in.

This oak appeared to have lost its upper trunk during some battle with lightning or gale, so that many others of its species of more recent growth surpassed it in height ; but the accident had also enormously strengthened the lower trunk, and extended the spread and thickness of the limbs, which continued to flaunt defiance in the face of the elements that were surely destroying them piecemeal. In time the tree had recovered its old symmetry of form, while its foliage was still remarkably rich and exuberant. Year by year it became more and more closely imprisoned within the walls of the growing city, until it stood a solitary, though not unregarded, survivor of its race and time.

There is another relic intimately associated with the Charter Oak for which the people of Connecticut have a great regard. Hanging up in the office of the Secretary of State, in the State Capitol, in a frame made of the Charter Oak, is the venerable original charter of the Colony, bearing not only the autograph, but the portrait of King Charles II. It is the genuine world-renowned document whose mysterious disappearance one evening, about two centuries ago, caused such a hubbub to be raised throughout the Colonies; and it is, therefore, of all the historical treasures of the State the most valued.

The story of how the Colonial charter was saved from the clutches of Sir Edmund Andros is a stirring episode of those stirring times, when Tyranny, boldly unmasking, began openly to threaten New England with the loss of all her time-honored franchises. In contempt of their chartered rights, King James II. had appointed Sir Edmund governor over all the New-England Colonies. Neither the wishes, the interests, nor the happiness of the people were to be for a moment considered. It was to be a rule of iron, and a man of iron was chosen for it. The first step was to seize and declare void the old charters. Massachusetts had already been dispossessed of hers; everything there was in confusion. It was now the turn of the other colonies. With this object Sir Edmund despatched to the Connecticut authorities an order demanding in good set terms the surrender of their charter; for even the arbitrary James would have it appear that he paid some respect to the majesty of the law by observing its forms; and the charter, being a royal grant of power, could not be ignored. The people of Connecticut considered this an act of usurpation, and their representatives naturally hesitated. But the charter not being forthcoming on his demand, Sir Edmund determined to let the good people of Connecticut know with whom they had to deal. He was a man of action; and he quickly put himself at the head of his soldiers, and went to fetch the instrument at the point of the sword. Never before had a body of royal troops trodden the soil of the Land of Steady Habits. Now, their errand was to sow the seeds of rebellion and disloyalty. The Governor, nursing his wrath all the way, arrived at Hartford in no gentle frame of mind; and going at once to the House where the Colonial Assembly was sitting, he strode into the chamber and imperiously demanded, in the King's name, the immediate delivery to him of the charter, at the same time declaring the old government to be dissolved and its proceedings unlawful. The representatives of the people saw the structure that their fathers had raised falling in ruins around them. There stood the dictator. Open resistance would be treason. But certain of the members had resolved that he should never have the charter, cost what it might. Wishing to gain time, the Assembly fell into debate over the matter, while the King's viceroy haughtily awaited its determination without leaving the chamber. The countenances of all present were anxious and pre-occupied. The debate grew warm, and Sir Edmund impatient. It became so dark that candles were lighted. The charter was then brought in and laid upon the table in full view of every one present. A hush fell upon the Assembly, every man of whom knew that the crisis had been reached. By this time the house was surrounded by the populace, in whom the feeling of resistance only wanted a spark to set it in a flame. But a better way had been found. All at once the lights in the chamber were extinguished; and when they were officiously relighted, the precious instrument was gone! The faces of that body of men when this fact dawned upon them must have been a study.

The tradition is — for of course no official record could be made of such an act of treason — that when the candles were put out, the box containing the royal patent was snatched from

the table, hurried out of the chamber, and thrust into the
hollow of the tree that has ever since borne the name of the
Charter Oak.   This daring act was performed by Captain Jeremiah Wadsworth; and it subsequently saved Connecticut from
having imposed upon her the same humiliating terms that
were granted under favor of King William to the old Mother-
Colony.

   But notwithstanding his main purpose had thus been
thwarted, Sir Edmund took upon him on the spot the reins
of government, by a formal declaration which is entered upon
the record, closing with the ominous word "finis." So the
people of Connecticut had after all to submit, until the Revolution in England tumbled King James's rotten throne about
his ears, and in its turn wrote "finis" at the end of his
fatal dynasty in characters large enough to convey their warning to his successors, — "Resistance to tyranny is obedience
to God."

THE CHARTER OAK AT HARTFORD.

L. H. SIGOURNEY.

Once there came, in days of yore,
A minion from the mother shore,
With men-at-arms and flashing eye
Of predetermined tyranny.
High words he spake, and stretched his hand,
Young Freedom's charter to demand.

But lo! it vanished from his sight,
And sudden darkness fell like night,
While, baffled still, in wrath and pain,
He, groping, sought the prize in vain ;
For a brave hand, in trust to me,
Had given that germ of liberty ;
And like our relative of old
Who clasped his arms, serenely bold,

Around the endangered prince who fled
The scaffold where his father bled,
I hid it, safe from storm and blast,
Until the days of dread were past ;
And then my faithful breast restored
The treasure to its rightful lord.

For this do pilgrims seek my side,
And artists sketch my varying pride ;
And far away o'er ocean's brine,
An acorn or a leaf of mine,
I hear, are stored as relics rich
In antiquarian's classic niche.

THE PLACE OF NOISES.

WE take the following weird tale partly from the historian
Trumbull, and partly from the poet Brainard.   History
and romance are thus amicably blended, — each elucidating
according to its own spirit the singular phenomenon which
so long disturbed the good people of East Haddam.

"The Indian name of the town was Machemoodus, which in
English is *the place of noises*, — a name given with the utmost pro-
priety to the place.   The accounts given of the noises and quakings
there are very remarkable.   Were it not that the people are accustomed to them, they would occasion great alarm.   The Reverend Mr.
Hosmer, in a letter to Mr. Prince, of Boston, written August 13th,
1729, gives this account of them : 'As to the earthquakes, I have
something considerable and awful to tell you.   Earthquakes have
been here (and nowhere but in this precinct, as can be discerned, —
that is, they seem to have their centre, rise, and origin among us),
as has been observed for more than thirty years.   I have been informed that in this place, before the English settlements, there were
great numbers of Indian inhabitants, and that it was a place of extraordinary *Indian pawaws*, — or, in short, that it was a place where

the Indians drove a prodigious trade at worshipping the devil. Also
I was informed that, many years past, an old Indian was asked
what was the reason of the noises in this place. To which he replied, that the Indian's God was very angry because Englishmen's
God was come here. Now whether there be anything diabolical in
these things, I know not ; but this I know, that God Almighty is
to be seen and trembled at in what has been often heard among us.
Whether it be fire or air distressed in the subterraneous caverns of
the earth, cannot be known, — for there is no eruption, no explosion
perceptible, — but by sounds and tremors, which sometimes are very
fearful and dreadful. I have myself heard eight or ten sounds successively, and imitating small arms, in the space of five minutes.
I have, I suppose, heard several hundreds of them within twenty
years ; some more, some less terrible. Sometimes we have heard
them almost every day; and great numbers of them in the space of
a year. Oftentimes I have observed them to be coming down from
the north, imitating slow thunder; until the sound came near or right
under, and then there seemed to be a breaking like the noise of a
cannon-shot or severe thunder, which shakes the houses and all that
is in them. They have in a manner ceased since the great earthquake. As I remember, there have been but two heard since that
time, and those but moderate.' "

The poetic version of the story is introduced by the following
account in prose, for the truth of which the poet vouches. We
will only add to it the statement that the carbuncle was highly
prized by our ancestors for its supposed power to protect the
wearer from the danger of infection ; but it was only to be found
in inaccessible places, like the bowels of the earth or unviolated
mountain peaks.

"A traveller who accidentally passed through East Haddam
made several inquiries as to the *Moodus noises* that are peculiar to
that part of the country. Many particulars were related to him of
their severity and effects, and of the means that had been taken to
ascertain their cause and prevent their recurrence. He was told
that the simple and terrified inhabitants, in the early settlement of
the town, applied to a book-learned and erudite man from England,
by the name of Doctor Steele, who undertook by magic to allay
their terrors ; and for this purpose took the sole charge of a black-

smith's shop, in which he worked by night, and from which he excluded all admission, tightly stopping and darkening the place, to prevent any prying curiosity from interfering with his occult operations. He, however, so far explained the cause of these noises as to say that they were owing to a carbuncle which must have grown to a great size in the bowels of the rocks, and that if it could be removed, the noises would cease until another should grow in its place. The noises ceased; the doctor departed, and has never been heard of since. It was supposed that he took the carbuncle with him. Thus far was authentic. A little girl who had anxiously noticed the course of the traveller's inquiries sung for his further edification the following ballad."

MATCHIT MOODUS.

J. G. BRAINARD.

SEE you upon the lonely moor
   A crazy building rise?
No hand dares venture to open the door;
No footstep treads its dangerous floor;
   No eye in its secrets pries.

Now why is each crevice stopped so tight?
   Say why the bolted door?
Why glimmers at midnight the forge's light?
All day is the anvil at rest; but at night
   The flames of the furnace roar.

Is it to arm the horse's heel
   That the midnight anvil rings?
Is it to mould the ploughshare's steel,
Or is it to guard the wagon's wheel,
   That the smith's sledge-hammer swings?

The iron is bent, and the crucible stands
   With alchemy boiling up;
Its contents were mixed by unknown hands,
And no mortal fire e'er kindled the brands
   That heated that cornered cup.

O'er Moodus River a light has glanced,
　　On Moodus Hills it shone ;
On the granite rocks the rays have danced,
And upward those creeping lights advanced,
　　Till they met on the highest stone.

Oh, that is the very wizard place,
　　And now is the wizard hour,
By the light that was conjured up to trace,
Ere the star that falls can run its race,
　　The seat of the earthquake's power.

By that unearthly light I see
　　A figure strange alone ;
With magic circlet on his knee,
And decked with Satan's symbols, he
　　Seeks for the hidden stone.

Now upward goes that gray old man,
　　With mattock, bar, and spade :
The summit is gained, and the toil begun,
And deep by the rock where the wild lights run,
　　The magic trench is made.

Loud and yet louder was the groan
　　That sounded wide and far ;
And deep and hollow was the moan
That rolled around the bedded stone
　　Where the workman plied his bar.

Then upward streamed the brilliant's light, —
　　It streamed o'er crag and stone ;
Dim looked the stars and the moon that night ;
But when morning came in her glory bright,
　　The man and the jewel were gone.

But wo to the bark in which he flew
　　From Moodus' rocky shore ;
Wo to the captain, and wo to the crew
That ever the breath of life they drew
　　When that dreadful freight they bore.

　　　　·　　　　·　　　　·　　　　·

The carbuncle lies in the deep, deep sea,
  Beneath the mighty wave ;
But the light shines upward so gloriously
That the sailor looks pale, and forgets his glee,
  When he crosses the wizard's grave.

THE SPANISH GALLEON.

"IT is a fact," writes the poet Brainard, "that two men from Vermont are now (July 11th, 1827) working by the side of one of the wharves in New London, for buried money, by the advice and recommendation of an old woman of that State, who assured them that she could distinctly see a box of dollars packed edgewise. The locality was pointed out to an inch ; and her only way of discovering the treasure was by looking through a stone, — which to ordinary optics was hardly translucent. For the story of the Spanish galleon that left so much bullion in and about New London, see Trumbull's 'History of Connecticut;' and for Kidd, inquire of the oldest lady you can find."

The story related by Trumbull is this : —

"About this time [1753] an unhappy event took place, dishonorable to the Colony, injurious to foreigners, and which occasioned a great and general uneasiness, and many unfriendly suspicions and imputations with respect to some of the principal characters in the Colony. A Spanish ship, coming into the port of New London in distress, ran upon a reef of rocks, and so damaged the vessel that it was necessary to unlade her and put her freight into stores at New London. The cargo was delivered into the custody of Joseph Hill, Esq., collector of the port of New London. The supercargo was Don Joseph Miguel de St. Juan. That he might sail with his cargo early in the spring, he obtained a ship of about two hundred tons, and was ready to sail in April. But when he had shipped part of his cargo, other parts of it were withholden from him or lost, and could not by any means of his be recovered. As he could obtain no relief, and was determined not to sail without the recovery of his cargo or some indemnification for the loss of it, he waited until October, and then preferred a memorial to the Assembly, representing his arrival in the snow 'St. Joseph and

OLD WAREHOUSES, NEW LONDON.

St. Helena' from Havana, bound to Cadiz, at the port of New London; and that he had stored his cargo there, in the custody of Joseph Hill, Esq., the collector; and that when he had procured a vessel in April, and required his cargo, that it might be reshipped, a considerable part of it had been withholden, lost, and embezzled; and praying for relief, or that he might reland that part of his cargo which remained, and secure it at their expense; and also that his men might be discharged.

"The Assembly, after hearing and deliberating on the memorial, resolved, That whatever losses he had sustained, it was
either by means to them unknown, or which they were by no
means able to prevent. . . . It was declared, That the requests
of the petitioner were unreasonable, and therefore could not be

ANCIENT MILL, NEW LONDON.

granted; but that as protection and assistance were due to a
foreigner cast among them, the Assembly did advise the Governor to grant all due protection and relief to the said Don Miguel,
according to the laws of trade, nature, and nations. The Governor was also desired and empowered, in case the said Joseph
Miguel should desire it, to direct a full search after any part
of his cargo which might have been embezzled or lost, and to

28

take all such reasonable measures therein as should be necessary to do justice in said case.

"Before the meeting of the freemen in April, it was generally known that the Spaniards had been robbed, or at least that an important part of a rich and very valuable cargo had been stolen, embezzled, or by some means lost or kept back from the owners; and it occasioned a great ferment through the Colony. It was imagined that it might involve the Colony in great difficulties; that it might be obliged to indemnify the owners, and that it would bring a heavy debt upon it; or that it might effect a rupture, and hostilities between the two nations. Others were moved with a sense of honor, sympathy, and justice. They were ashamed and grieved that, when foreigners in distress had cast themselves upon not only a civilized, but Christian people, they had been plundered as though they had fallen among heathens, thieves, and robbers. All the feelings of covetousness, honor, sympathy, and justice, were touched. Great blame was imputed to some of the principal characters in the Colony, especially to Governor Wolcott. It was imagined by many that he had not taken such care and adopted such measures to secure the property of those foreigners, and to save them harmless, as he ought to have done. Whether there was any just foundation for faulting him or not, it so disaffected the freemen that, notwithstanding his former popularity, he lost their suffrages, and Thomas Fitch, Esq., was chosen governor in his place. Mr. Hill did not escape a share of blame, among others. How such a quantity of stores of various kinds should be lost or embezzled without his knowledge or privity, and that no thorough search should be made for them in so many months, is very unaccountable. But where the fault lay, or what became of the lost goods, never came to public view. Nor does it appear that the Colony was ever put to any extraordinary expense or trouble on that account. The war was now commencing, and private concerns were neglected and forgotten, while national interests of greater moment and more general concern engrossed the public mind both in Europe and America."

THE MONEY-DIGGERS.

J. G. BRAINARD.

THUS saith the Book : " Permit no witch to live ! "
Hence Massachusetts hath expelled the race ;
Connecticut, where swap and dicker thrive,
Allowed not to their foot a resting-place.
With more of hardihood and less of grace,
Vermont receives the sisters gray and lean,
Allows each witch her airy broomstick race,
O'er mighty rocks and mountains dark with green,
Where tempests wake their voice, and torrents roar between.

And one there was among that wicked crew
To whom the enemy a pebble gave,
Through which, at long-off distance, she might view
All treasures of the fathomable wave ;
And where the Thames' bright billows gently lave
The grass-grown piles that flank the ruined wharf,
She sent *them* forth, those two adventurers brave,
Where greasy citizens their beverage quaff,
Jeering at enterprise, aye ready with a laugh.

They came, those straight-haired, honest-meaning men,
Nor question asked they, nor reply did make,
Albeit their locks were lifted like as when
Young Hamlet saw his father ; and the shake
Of knocking knees, and jaws that seemed to break,
Told a wild tale of undertaking bold,
While as the oyster-tongs the chiels did take,
Dim grew the sight, and every blood-drop cold,
As knights in scarce romant sung by the bards of old.

For not in daylight were their rites performed ;
When nightcapped heads were on their pillow laid,
Sleep-freed from biting care, by thought unharmed,
Snoring e'er word was spoke or prayer was said, —

'T was then the mattock and the busy spade,
The pump, the bucket, and the windlass-rope,
In busy silence plied the mystic trade,
While Resolution, beckoned on by Hope,
Did sweat and agonize the sought-for chest to ope.

Beneath the wave the iron chest is hot,
Deep growls are heard, and reddening eyes are seen ;
Yet of the black dog she had told them not,
Nor of the gray wild geese with eyes of green,
That screamed and yelled and hovered close between
The buried gold and the rapacious hand.
Here should she be, though mountains intervene,
To scatter, with her crooked witch-hazel wand,
The wave-born sprites that keep their treasure from the land.

She cannot, may not come.   The rotten wharf
Of mouldering planks and rusty spikes is there ;
And he who owned a quarter or an half
Is disappointed ; and the witch is, — where ?
Vermont still harbors her.   Go, seek her there,
The grandam of Joe Strickland ; find her nest
Where summer icicles and snowballs are,
Where black swans paddle and where petrels rest !
Symmes be your trusty guide, and Robert Kidd your guest !

———————◆———————

THE NORWICH ELMS.

L. H. SIGOURNEY.

I DO remember me
  Of two old Elm-Trees' shade,
With mosses sprinkled at their feet,
  Where my young childhood played ;

While the rocks above their head
    Frowned out so stern and gray,
And the little crystal streamlets
    Went leaping on their way.

There, side by side, they lifted
    Their intertwining crown,
And through their broad embracing arms
    The queenly Moon looked down ;
And methought, as there I lingered,
    A musing child alone,
She fain my secret heart would read
    From her bright silver throne.

I do remember me
    Of all their wealth of leaves,
When Summer in her radiant loom
    The burning solstice weaves ;
And how, with firm endurance,
    They braved an adverse sky,
Like Belisarius doomed to meet
    His country's wintry eye.

I 've roamed through varied regions,
    Where stranger-streamlets run ;
And where the proud magnolia flaunts
    Beneath a Southern sun ;
And where the sparse and stunted pine
    Puts forth its sombre form, —
A vassal to the Arctic cloud
    And to the tyrant storm ;

And where the pure unruffled lakes
    In placid wavelets roll,
Or where sublime Niagara shakes
    The wonder-stricken soul ;
I 've seen the temple's sculptured pile,
    The pencil's glorious art, —
Yet still those old green trees I wore
    Depicted on my heart.

Years fled : my native vale I sought,
   Where those tall Elm-Trees wave ;
But many a column of its trust
   Lay broken in the grave.
The ancient and the white-haired men,
   Whose wisdom was its stay,
For them I asked ; and Echo's voice
   Made answer, " Where are they ? "

I sought the thrifty matron
   Whose busy wheel was heard
When the early beams of morning
   Awoke the chirping bird :
Strange faces from her window looked,
   Strange voices filled her cot ;
And 'neath the very vine she trained,
   Her memory is forgot.

I left a youthful mother,
   Her children round her knee :
These babes had risen into men,
   And coldly looked on me ;
But she, with all her bloom and grace,
   Did in the churchyard lie,
While still those changeless Elms upbore
   Their kingly canopy.

Though we, who 'neath their lofty screen
   Pursued our childish play,
May show amid our sunny locks
   Some lurking tints of gray,
And though the village of our love
   Doth many a change betide,
Still do these sacred Elm-Trees stand
   In all their strength and pride.

Part Thirteenth.

NANTUCKET AND OTHER LEGENDS.

NANTUCKET LEGENDS.

THE islands of Nantucket, Martha's Vineyard, and of the Elizabeth group all possess more or less legendary lore of the kind that surrounds them with a peculiar fascination. One by one these islands have emerged from the sea into the light of history, and have taken a place upon the map. Little by little and with caution were their inhospitable coasts and foaming reefs explored by the early navigators, and step by step did Christian missionaries approach the fierce islanders who inhabited them in happy ignorance that any other world than the neighboring mainland existed.

In the order of chronology it is the Elizabeth Islands that should be the first mentioned, since it was there that the bold attempt to found in New England a colony of Europeans was made. One cannot forbear a smile at its futility. Vaguely conceived, not half matured, and feebly executed, it was abandoned, as so many enterprises of "great pith and moment" have been, in the very hour that should most fully test the mettle of those who were conducting it ; and it is now memorable only because it was the first serious endeavor to naturalize Englishmen upon the soil. Yet although these men left only a perishable footprint behind them, they did bestow enduring names upon the various capes and headlands that successively rose out of the sea to greet them. So far as is known, however, not one is a memento of themselves; nevertheless it is these names thrown at random in passing which has rendered the voyage of Captain Bartholomew Gosnold a fact worth preserving; otherwise it is a cipher.

In the whole company who set

BASS ROCKS.

GAY HEAD.

CUTTYHUNK.

sail with him from Falmouth there were only thirty-two persons; of whom but twelve, the Apostolic number, purposed remaining in the country as actual settlers. It would be difficult to conceive of an empire with its millions dating its origin from this handful, had they been the fortunate ones to leave us the duty of inscribing their names at the head of the illustrious roll of founders; but their personality having no greater substance than their enterprise, they, with the exception of a few whose names the care of Hakluyt has preserved, have all vanished.

From Falmouth, then, on the 25th of March, 1602, the "Concord" put to sea. On the 14th of May, the day being Friday, — mark that, ye superstitious mariners! — Gosnold had in view the lumpy coast of New England, stretching from Agamenticus to Cape Ann; and presently, to the great wonder of all on board — for these English could not believe that any had preceded them here, — they fell in with a Basque shallop, manned by eight tawny, black-haired natives, who could speak a few English words intelligibly, and could name Placentia, in Newfoundland. It seemed that these savages had communicated with the French there. This encounter could not but cheapen Gosnold's estimate of himself as a discoverer in unknown seas, — for that *rôle* he was fully a century too late. But having thus got hold of the land, Gosnold now put his helm to starboard, and steering southward into the Bay, and keeping good watch, found himself brought to by the bended forearm of the great sandspit to which he gave the name of Cape Cod. He continued cautiously working his way along the south coast, shortening sail at night, until he was again embayed within the chain of islands extending between Buzzard's Bay and the open sea, — a broken, but still magnificent barrier. One of these he called Martha's Vineyard, thinking so little of the matter that he left nothing to satisfy the curiosity of another age respecting the person he had meant to honor, either in token of remembrance, or perhaps as a *gage d'amour*. The knowledge, therefore, died with the giver; and so Martha's Vineyard remains a monument with an incomplete inscription which nobody is able to complete.

Eleven days after sighting the coast the adventurers landed upon Cuttyhunk Island, to which Gosnold gave the name of Elizabeth, the Queen, — a name that has since been applied to the whole group. They decided to make this island their residence.

Having great fear of the savages, Gosnold's men set to work building a fort, in which they dwelt until they had procured a cargo of sassafras for their ship, when they hurriedly decamped and set sail for England; but upon the grand scheme of colonization of which this was to be the entering wedge, this voyage had no further result than to act as a spur to the lords-proprietors, who impoverished themselves in fruitless efforts, until the year 1620 of happy memory showed them what might be done without other resources than courage, persistency, and a firm reliance on the assistance of Heaven.

Gosnold also saw and named the remarkable promontory of Gay Head, — probably so called from its brilliant and variegated coloring when the sun shone full upon it. The structure of this lofty headland bears upon it certain evidences of its volcanic origin. Four or five craters are more or less distinctly traced. The most ancient of these, long since overgrown with grass, and called the Devil's Den, measures twenty rods across at the top, fourteen at the bottom, and is one hundred and thirty feet deep at the sides, except upon the one next the sea, which is open. The most fantastic stories continued to pass current respecting this wizard spot until the beginning of the present century; for here, as fame reports, was one of the residences of Maushope, the Indian giant, the tutelary genius of all the tribes inhabiting these islands, as well as the adjacent mainland of Cape Cod. Like Fingal, Maushope was in the habit of wading across the Sound when the humor took possession of him. Here he broiled the whale on coals made from the largest trees, which he pulled up by the roots. After separating No-man's Land from Gay Head, metamorphosing his children into fishes, and throwing his wife on Seconnet Point, where she now lies, a misshapen rock, he broke up housekeeping and left for parts unknown.

The fishermen used to say that it was a common thing to see a light upon Gay Head in the night-time, and it was handed down as a matter undisputed among them that the whalemen were in the habit of guiding themselves at night by the lights that were seen glancing upon Gay Head. When they appeared flickering in the darkness the sailors would say, "Old Maushope is at it again!" But the beacon-lights were held to be friendly ones; for, like the stars, they showed the belated mariner what course to steer. The sea has encroached greatly upon the clay cliffs in the course of centuries. The harmless descendants of the warlike race still inhabit the place; but the light of a powerful Fresnel shining from a massive tower has superseded the midnight orgies of the wandering Maushope.

Like the Eastern wizards, Maushope was capable of raising mists whenever he wished; but that his was wholly an original method will appear from the following traditional account of the discovery of Nantucket, which is presented *verbatim*.

"In former times, a great many moons ago, a bird, extraordinary for its size, used often to visit the south shore of Cape Cod and carry from thence in its talons a vast number of small children. Maushope, who was an Indian giant, as fame reports, resided in these parts. Enraged at the havoc among the children, he on a certain time waded into the sea in pursuit of the bird, till he had crossed the Sound and reached Nantucket. Before Maushope forded the Sound the island was unknown to the red men. Maushope found the bones of the children in a heap under a large tree. He then, wishing to smoke a pipe, ransacked the island for tobacco; but finding none, he filled his pipe with poke,—a weed which the Indians sometimes used as a substitute. Ever since the above memorable events fogs have been frequent at Nantucket and on the Cape. In allusion to this tradition, when the aborigines observed a fog rising, they would say, 'There comes old Maushope's smoke!' This tradition has been related in another way: that an eagle having seized and carried off a papoose, the parents followed him in their canoe till they came to Nantucket, where they found the bones of their child dropped by the eagle. There is another Indian tradition, that Nantucket was formed by Maushope by emptying the ashes from his pipe after he had done smoking. The two tribes on the island were hostile to each other. Tradition has preserved a pleasing instance of the power of love. The western tribe having determined to surprise and attack the eastern tribe, a young man of the former, whose mistress belonged to the latter, being anxious for her safety, as soon as he was concealed by the shades of night, ran to the beach, flew along the shore below the limit of high water, saw his mistress a moment, gave the alarm, and returned by the same route before daybreak ; the rising tide washed away the traces of his feet. The next morning he accompanied the other warriors of the tribe to the attack : the enemy was found prepared, and no impression could be made on them. He remained undetected till, several years after, peace being restored between the two tribes, and the young man having married the girl, the truth came to light."

We have elsewhere related the circumstance that led to the settlement of Nantucket by the whites. The Quaker element long continued to be the dominant one in the social life of the island, as well as of its religion and government. Here, free from persecution, these much-abused followers of George Fox were supposed to have found their Arcadia. They established a patriarchal government. Instead of laws, they had usages which were obeyed as laws. It was nearly the happy ideal condition, where men live without quarrels, without crime, and without the enforcement of law. They were husbandmen and shepherds. They fished, planted, and traded in peace. Although some of them amassed wealth, everything about them continued to wear the appearance of a primitive economy ; they lived on independently and prosperously. But notwithstanding a natural predilection for the land — and we can hardly think of Quakers as making good sailors — there was the sea continually calling, continually asserting itself, at their doors. By a transition as curious as it is absolute, these peaceful shepherds became the most noted sailors of our continent and the most renowned whalemen of the world. With this change the native Indians doubtless had much to do ; for in their primitive way they too were expert in taking those monsters of the deep. The Nantucket whale-fishery began in the waters immediately surrounding the island, and in boats. The whaleman finished his career amid the Arctic ice, where he quietly made for himself a route long before Governments entered into the disastrous contest with King Frost in which so many valuable lives have been lost. Had there been certain indications that whales were to be

found at the Pole, the Nantucket whalemen would have discovered it.

The sea-annals of Nantucket are consequently very numerous; and as they chiefly relate to stubborn conflicts with whales,
they are very interesting. But as we now get our oil upon the
land, the industry which brought Nantucket into world-wide
notice has no longer any existence there. There is, however,
a museum, in which are preserved many evidences to the fact,
in the same manner that Salem preserves the memorials of her
departed East-Indian trade. Alas! one cannot but regret these
changes. The whale-fishery gave to the nation a race of intrepid sailors, who might have become at need her defenders:
the petroleum discovery has given us some millionnaires.

It is well known that sailors are able to discover their where-
abouts, even in thick weather, by making an examination of
the soundings that the lead has brought up from the bottom.
Nantucket skippers, it would seem from the following ballad, are
able to go even farther than this, and to tell with their eyes shut
in what neighborhood they are: —

THE ALARMED SKIPPER.

JAMES T. FIELDS.

MANY a long, long year ago,
  Nantucket skippers had a plan
Of finding out, though "lying low,"
  How near New York their schooners ran.

They greased the lead before it fell,
  And then, by sounding through the night,
Knowing the soil that stuck, so well,
  They always guessed their reckoning right.

A skipper gray, whose eyes were dim,
  Could tell, by *tasting*, just the spot;
And so below he'd "dowse the glim," —
  After, of course, his "something hot."

Snug in his berth, at eight o'clock,
   This ancient skipper might be found.
No matter how his craft would rock,
   He slept ; for skippers' naps are sound!

The watch on deck would now and then
   Run down and wake him, with the lead ;
He 'd up and taste, and tell the men
   How many miles they went ahead.

One night 't was Jotham Marden's watch,
   A curious wag, — the pedler's son ;
And so he mused (the wanton wretch!) :
   " To-night I 'll have a grain of fun!

" We 're all a set of stupid fools
   To think the skipper knows by *tasting*
What ground he 's on, — Nantucket schools
   Don't teach such stuff, with all their basting!"

And so he took the well-greased lead
   And rubbed it o'er a box of earth
That stood on deck, — a parsnip-bed ;
   And then he sought the skipper's berth.

" Where are we now, sir ?   Please to taste."
   The skipper yawned, put out his tongue ;
Then oped his eyes in wondrous haste,
   And then upon the floor he sprung!

The skipper stormed and tore his hair,
   Thrust on his boots, and roared to **Marden :**
" *Nantucket 's sunk, and here we are*
   Right over old Marm Hackett's garden ! "

THE UNKNOWN CHAMPION.

WHEN Charles I. was about to lay his royal head upon the block, he took his St. George from his neck and handed it to Bishop Juxon, saying as he did so, "Remember!" This was the last word uttered by the royal martyr; for a moment later the axe fell. According to Hume, after the execution was over, the Council of State called Juxon before them, and demanded to know what this command of the King signified. Juxon replied that on the day before his death the King had expressly recommended to him to convey to his son, should that son ever ascend the throne, his wish that his murderers might be pardoned; and that it was his own promise, then given, that the King had recalled when handing him his St. George, — destined to be placed in his son's hands. The following story is an example of the memory of kings and of the filial obedience of Charles II.

We now enter upon one of those romantic episodes belonging to the heroic age of our history and embodying its true spirit.

The history of the tradition is briefly this. It originated in the family of Governor Leverett, who ruled over the destinies of the Bay Colony during its desperate struggle with King Philip, and it has first a permanent record in the pages of Hutchinson, who had in his possession, when he wrote, the original manuscript diary and many other of the private papers belonging to the fugitive regicide, Colonel William Goffe, the hero of the traditional story.

There are, it is true, some zealous antiquaries who do not hesitate to characterize the story as a romance pure and simple; but as they have only succeeded at the most in involving it in doubt, a tradition possessing sufficient vitality to live unchallenged for so long a period as a hundred and fifty years may well be entitled to have the benefit of that doubt. Truth above all things; but before treating one of our most valued traditions as an impostor, conclusive evidence to the imposition becomes a logical necessity to the framers of the indictment. They certainly ought not to come into court without a clear case.

Adhuc sub judice lis est. Without joining in the discussion here, let us perform a more gracious duty, and tell the story as it was always told and believed before its credibility was called in question.

In the month of October, 1664, feeling no longer safe in their retreat at New Haven, Goffe and Whalley fled up the valley to Hadley, which was then one of the remote frontier plantations. Every precaution was taken to render the journey a profound secret. Upon arriving there they were hospitably received, given shelter, and carefully guarded from all intrusion upon their privacy by the minister of the place, the Reverend John Russell, — whose house thenceforth became their abode for fifteen or sixteen years, until death released one of them forever from the enmity of men and kings. Only a few, whose fidelity could be depended upon, were admitted into the secret; and for greater security it was given out that the regicides had fled to New York, with the purpose of again crossing the seas and taking refuge in Holland.

Behold these two outcasts, behind whom "stalked the headsman," finally immured within the four walls of an humble frontier dwelling, like men who have forever taken leave of the world and its concerns, but whom the world still vindictively pursues. The same ruthless spirit of revenge that had violated the senseless bodies of Cromwell and Ireton was now abroad in New England; and her people, willing though they might be, dared not openly resist the hard logic of events. That spirit was the vengeance of a king; that logic, the restoration of Charles Stuart to the throne.

Eleven years had rolled over the heads of the exiles. One by one their hopes had fallen to the ground and withered away. Whalley had become decrepit; Goffe indeed retained some of the old fire he had shown when, at the head of Cromwell's Ironsides, he charged at Dunbar, and turned the doubtful issue of that glorious day. This brings us to the year 1675.

The year 1675 ushered in the gigantic struggle with Philip, the great Narragansett chieftain. Never before had such a storm of war assailed poor New England. Calamity followed calamity. An adversary who concentrated in his own athletic person all the hatred, the subtlety, the thirst for vengeance of his race, suddenly rose, the majestic and fateful figure of the hour. Philip, King of Pokanoket, had proclaimed war, — war in its most terrible aspect, — war to the knife. Philip the leader had aroused his people from their deadly lethargy of forty years to make one last, one supreme effort. It was now a struggle for life or death, and as such had to be met.

The menaced Colonies hastened to put forth their utmost efforts in order to meet the emergency, whose gravity increased every hour. A general insurrection of all the tribes was Philip's hope and New England's fear. John Leverett, a soldier of Cromwell, was then at the head of affairs; and he, rising to the crisis, now showed all the energy that might be expected from a scholar who had served his apprenticeship under so able a master. But at first the scale of victory inclined heavily in Philip's favor. Instead of combats we read only of massacres; instead of victories, the record shows disaster upon disaster.

Driven at length from his own stronghold, Philip, at the head of a small band of his warriors, retired into the heart of the Nipmuck Country, which then extended, a wilderness of swamps, thickets, and mountain-defiles, between the seaboard settlements and those lying in the lovely Connecticut Valley. A single road traversed it. A solitary outpost, around which a feeble settlement had grown up, was planted in the midst of this solitude; this was Brookfield.

The sanguinary struggle was here renewed; and here some of the best blood in the Colony was uselessly shed. Upon this isolated post Philip's confederates, the crafty Nipmucks, fell with fury. Soon after this they were joined by Philip in person. He now aimed at nothing less than the total destruction of the isolated valley-settlements. The Colonial forces that had been sent for the relief of Brookfield, after suffering severely in several bloody encounters, succeeded in driving the exasperated enemy back upon the Connecticut settlements, which thus speedily became the battle-ground of the combatants. Here, alas! the bones of many a stout soldier moulder in unknown graves.

There were several tribes living at peace with the whites in this valley whom the news of Philip's successes now threw into a fever of excitement; his agents did the rest. These tribes had received his wampum, and were secretly sharpening their hatchets. The white people, taking the alarm, and being more-over warned of what they might presently expect from such dangerous neighbors, attempted to disarm them; but the attempt resulted in these Indians going over to Philip in a body. They were pursued, overtaken, and brought to bay near Sugar-Loaf Mountain, in Deerfield; but they succeeded after a sharp fight in making good their retreat. This occurred on the 25th of August.

On the 27th the English were defeated at Northfield, and fled in confusion back as far as Hadley before they rallied again. On the 1st day of September the enemy made a bold onslaught upon Deerfield, and nearly destroyed the whole settlement. Thus for a whole week the inhabitants of this part of the valley had been constantly harried and beset. With the enemy always at their doors; with the war-whoop sounding hourly in their ears; with the hurrying to and fro of armed men and of fugitives, — one does not ask whether the inhabitants were in a state of perpetual alarm.

Such was the condition of the little community, among whom the regicides lay concealed, on the 1st of September, 1675. Their lives were now doubly threatened.

We will now let an eminent historian and novelist take up the narrative. The dramatic power of the simple incident needed no attempt at embellishment, and none is made.

In Sir Walter Scott's "Peveril of the Peak" Bridgenorth relates this story : —

"I was by chance at a small village in the woods more than thirty miles from Boston, and in a situation exceedingly lonely, and surrounded by thickets. Nevertheless there was no idea of any danger from the Indians at that time ; for men trusted in the protection of a considerable body of troops who had taken the field for the protection of the frontiers, and who lay, or were supposed to lie, betwixt the hamlet and the enemy's country. But they had to do with a foe whom the Devil himself had inspired with cunning and cruelty. It

GOFFE RALLYING THE SETTLERS.

was on a Sabbath morning, when we had assembled to take sweet counsel in the Lord's house. . . . An excellent worthy, who now sleeps in the Lord, Nehemiah Solsgrace, had just begun to wrestle in prayer, when a woman with disordered looks and dishevelled hair entered our chapel in a distracted manner, screaming incessantly, 'The Indians! The Indians!' In that land no man dare separate himself from his means of defence; and whether in the city or in the field, in the ploughed land or in the forest, men keep beside them their weapons, as did the Jews at the rebuilding of the Temple. So we sallied forth with our guns and pikes, and heard the war-whoop

of these incarnate devils, already in possession of a part of the town.
. . . In fine, there was much damage done ; and although our arrival
and entrance into combat did in some sort put them back, yet, being
surprised and confused, and having no appointed leader of our band,
the devilish enemy shot hard at us, and had some advantage. . . . In
this state of confusion, and while we were about to adopt the desperate project of evacuating the village, and, placing the women and
children in the centre, of attempting a retreat to the nearest settlement, it pleased Heaven to send us unexpected assistance. A tall
man, of reverend appearance, whom no one of us had ever seen before, suddenly was in the midst of us as we hastily agitated the resolution of retreating. His garments were of the skin of the elk, and
he wore sword and carried gun : I never saw anything more august
than his features, overshadowed by locks of gray hair, which mingled
with a long beard of the same color. ' Men and brethren,' he said, in a
voice like that which turns back the flight, ' why sink your hearts ?
and why are you thus disquieted ? Fear ye that the God we serve will
give ye up to yonder heathen dogs ? Follow me ; and ye shall see
that this day there is a captain in Israel!' He uttered a few brief
but distinct orders, in the tone of one who was accustomed to command; and such was the influence of his appearance, his mien, his
language, and his presence of mind, that he was implicitly obeyed by
men who had never seen him until that moment. We were hastily
divided by his orders into two bodies, — one of which maintained the
defence of the village with more courage than ever, convinced that
the unknown was sent by God to our rescue. At his command they
assumed the best and most sheltered positions for exchanging their
deadly fire with the Indians ; while under cover of the smoke the
stranger sallied from the town at the head of the other division of
the New-England men, and fetching a circuit, attacked the red
warriors in the rear. The surprise, as is usual among Indians, had
complete effect ; for they doubted not that they were assailed in their
turn, and placed betwixt two hostile parties by the return of a
detachment from the provincial army. The heathens fled in confusion, abandoning the half-won village, and leaving behind them such
a number of their warriors that the tribe hath never recovered their
loss. Never shall I forget the figure of our venerable leader, when
our men, and not they only, but the women and children of the village, rescued from the tomahawk and scalping-knife, stood crowded
around him, yet scarce venturing to approach his person, and more

minded, perhaps, to worship him as a descended angel than to thank him as a fellow-mortal. ' Not unto me be the glory,' he said ; ' I am but an implement frail as yourselves in the hand of Him who is strong to deliver. Bring me a cup of water, that I may allay my parched thirst ere I essay the task of offering thanks where they are most due.' Sinking on his knees, and signing us to obey him, he poured forth a strong and energetic thanksgiving for the turning back of the battle, which, pronounced with a voice loud and clear as a war-trumpet, thrilled through the joints and marrow of the hearers. . . . He was silent : and for a brief space we remained with our faces bent to the earth, no man daring to lift his head. At length we looked up ; but our deliverer was no longer amongst us, nor was he ever again seen in the land which he had rescued."

To this faithful rendering of the tradition from the matchless pen of the Wizard of the North is pendant Southey's unfinished poem of "Oliver Newman," — a work intended to realize this author's long-meditated purpose of writing an Anglo-American epic. The story of Goffe's appearance among the panic-stricken settlers at Hadley so strongly impressed him, that he determined to make it the main incident of an historical poem, which, unfortunately for the world, never advanced beyond the first stages of development. The characters are introduced, and the action begins, — when the curtain falls, leaving us, indeed, with the programme in our hands, in the form of notes, but with the sense of irreparable loss to us and to our historic annals. As if to compel the admiration due to genius, Southey makes one of the despised sect of Quakers his hero, who, from a double sense of duty and filial love, has crossed the ocean in search of his proscribed and fugitive parent.

This remarkable tradition did not escape the quick recognition of our own master of romance. It is accordingly the subject of one of Hawthorne's earliest tales, entitled "The Gray Champion." It is true that the action is transferred to Boston, that the time is brought forward ten years, and that the author seeks to produce a moral rather than a physical effect in his climax. But the incident is still the same. The Gray Champion who suddenly confronts Sir Edmund Andros and his retinue in the streets of Boston and bids them "stand," is no other than the fugitive regicide; and his purpose is still to exalt the spirit of the people by the timely display of the superiority of moral over mere physical power on the side of the rightful cause. Such is the tradition.

Dr. Dwight relates that Mr. Russell's house had been pulled down some years previous to his visit to the spot in 1796, but

GRAVES OF THE REGICIDES, NEW HAVEN.

that Mr. Gaylord, the owner of the estate, gave him the following fact concerning it. When the workmen were demolishing the building they discovered, just outside the cellar wall, a crypt built of solid masonry and covered with hewn flagstones. Within this tomb were found the bones of Whalley. After Whalley's death Goffe quitted Hadley, living sometimes in one place and sometimes in another, under various disguises and aliases that have given rise to other legendary tales concerning him or the places that became his asylum.

By a hyperbole, exaggerated perhaps, but still pardonable in a people who traced everything in man or nature to the active intervention of the Most High, the unknown savior of Hadley was long spoken of as an angel sent for their deliverance. His sudden appearance among them, his strange garb and speech, the dignity and authority of his manner, and finally his unaccountable disappearance in the moment of victory, may well have exalted him in their minds to a supernatural being. King Charles would have decapitated the regicide; our antiquaries would decapitate both angel and legend with as little remorse. As the custodian of each, we say, in the language of the royal martyr when upon the scaffold, "Do not touch the axe."

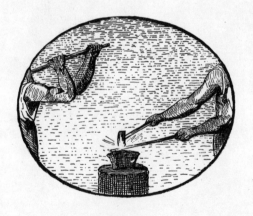

INDEX.

ADAMS, Samuel, 84.
Agamenticus, Mount, 331.
Agassiz, Louis, 155.
Alden, John, 379.
Alden, Rev. Timothy, 379.
Andros, Lady, 382; Sir Edmund, 424.
Anville, Duc d', 71.
Arnold, Governor Benedict, 398.
Ashton, Philip, 212.
Avery, Joseph, 245; Avery's Fall, 250.

BABSON, Ebenezer, 254.
Barnard, Rev. John, 207.
Bellingham, Richard, 33, 51.
Besse, Joseph, 186.
Blackbeard, 66, 350.
Blackstone, William, 6, 10.
Boar's Head, 322.
Boston, ideal description of, 3–6; in 1634, 14; in 1770, 99.
Bradford, William, 368.
Brainard, J. G., 427, 431, 435.
Bray, John, 119.
Brewster, Margaret, 57.
Brock, Rev. John, 347.
Brown, Rev. Arthur, 341.
Butter, Edward, 186.

CALEF, Robert, 60.
Cape Ann, description of, 237.
Champernowne, Francis, 357.
Charter Oak, The, 421.
Cheesman, Edward, 262.
Chilton, Mary, 380.
Clifton, Hope, 40.
Coddington, William, 16, 20, 21.
Coffin, Joshua, 287.
Cole, Eunice, 328.
Conant, Roger, 167.
Coolidge, Cornelius, 153.
Corey, Giles, 194.
Cotton, Rev. John, 13.

DANA, R. H., 240, 403.
Davenport, Rev. John, 417.

Davis, Nicholas, 40.
Dawes, William, 84.
Dexter, Timothy, 292.
Dighton Rock, 395.
Dimond, John, 144.
Double-headed Snake, 307.
Dudley, Thomas, 137.
Dungeon Rock, 134.
Dyer, Mary, 36.

EGG ROCK, 148, 161.
Eliot, John, 20, 123.
Eliot, William, 246.
Eliot Oak, 121.
Endicott, John, 41, 44, 51, 170, 180.
English, Philip, 176.

FAMILIST Controversy; see Anne Hutchinson.
Fields, James T., 240, 265, 447.
Fillmore, John, 261.
Fitch, Thomas, 434.
Frankland, Sir Charles H., 221.
Franklin, Benjamin, 66.

GAGE, General Thomas, 81.
Gallup, John, 67.
Garrison, William Lloyd, 138.
Goffe, Colonel William, 449.
Goldsmith, Ralph, 49.
Gorges, Robert, 153; Ferdinando, 331.
Gosnold, Bartholomew, 442, 443, 444.
Gould, Hannah, 303.
Great Elm of Boston, 35, 69, 105.
Green Dragon, 81.

HAMPTON, N.H., 319.
Hancock, John, 84.
Harraden, Andrew, 261.
Hawthorne, Nathaniel, 163, 169, 172.
Heartbreak Hill, 279.
Hibbins, Ann, 28.
Hibbins, William, 30.
High Rock, 141.
Hill, Joseph, 431.

Hilton, Martha, 339.
Hollingsworth, William, 176; Susanna, 176.
Holmes, O. W.; see "Contents."
Hooper, Madam, 299.
House of Seven Gables, 173, 174.
Hubbard, William, 245, 369.
Hutchinson, Anne, 11.
Hutchinson, William, 12, 14, 15.
Hutchinson, Thomas, 18.

IPSWICH, Mass., description of, 273.
Ireson, Benjamin, 227.

JAQUES, Richard, 301.
Josselyn, John, 158.

KELLEY, E. G., 301.
Kidd, Captain Robert, 346.

LAMB, Charles, 188.
Larcom, Lucy, 242, 267.
Leverett, Governor John, 449, 450.
Lewis, Alonzo, 132, 144.
Longfellow, H. W., 151, 155. See "Contents."
Louisburg, C.B., 71, 259.
Low, Edward, 213.
Lynn, Mass., description of, 137.

MACY, Thomas, 310.
Main, Harry, 274.
Marble, Hiram, 135.
Marblehead, description of, 205.
Martin, Michael, 119.
Mason, Captain John, 331.
Mather, Cotton, 61, 395, 417.
Mather, Increase, 64, 245, 307.
Maushope, 444, 445.
Moody, Rev. Joshua, 178.
Morton, Thomas, 128, 365.
Motley, J. L., 152.
Moulton, Jonathan, 322.
Mullins, Priscilla, 385.
Mullins, William, 385.

NAHANT, description of, 148.
Nason, Elias, 371.
Newbury, Mass., 284.
Newburyport, description of, 284.
Newport Mill, The, 394.
Nix's Mate, 66.
Norman's Woe, 263.
Noyes, Rev. Nicholas, 174.

OLD ELM of Newbury, 301.
Omens, 208, 209.

PASSACONAWAY, 129, 359.
Perkins, Thomas H., 153.

Philip, King, 414, 451.
Phips, Sir William, 179.
Piracy, 132, 211, 212, 261.
Pitcher, Mary, 137. See Dimond.
Pitcher, Robert, 144.
Plum Island, 286.
Plummer, Jonathan, 296.
Pollard, Anne, 380.
Poquanum, 153.
Prescott, W. H., 152, 155.
Prince, Rev. Thomas, 75.

QUAKERS, 46, 56, 184, 310. See Brewster; Dyer; King's Missive; Macy, etc.

RAINSBOROUGH, William, 22–27.
Redd (or Read) Wilmot, 210.
Revere, Paul, 78.
Robinson, William, 40, 312.
Roxbury Pudding-stone, 111.
Rule, Margaret, 62.
Russell, Benjamin, 373; Rev. William, 450.

SAINT ASPENQUID, 360.
Salem, description of, 167.
Salem Village, 191.
Scarlet Letter, 171, 172.
Scott, Sir Walter, 453.
Sea-serpent, 156.
Sewall, Samuel, 57, 304.
Shattuck, Samuel, 49, 50, 51.
Shawmut; see Boston.
Shirley, William, 73.
Sigourney, L. H.; see "Contents."
Skeleton in Armor, 397.
Smith, Captain John, 153, 243.
Southey, Robert, 455.
Southwick, Cassandra, 184; Daniel, 185; Josiah, 185; Laurence, 185; Provided, 185.
Spofford, Harriet P., 286.
Standish, Myles, 383.
Stevenson, Marmaduke, 40, 312.
Story, Joseph, 189.
Story, W. W., 168.
Surriage, Agnes, 223.
Swampscott, 162.

TAYLOR, Bayard, 239.
Thacher, Anthony, 245.
Thacher's Island, 244.
Thaxter, Celia, 355.
Toppan, Rev. Christopher, 308.
Trimountain; see Boston.
Trumbull, Benjamin, 427, 431.
Tucke, Rev. John, 347.
Tudor, Frederick, 153.

UNDERWOOD, Francis H., 264.
Upham, Rev. Charles W., 260.
Uring, Captain Nathaniel, 369.

VANE, Sir Henry, 15, 18.
Veale, Thomas, 134.

WABAN, 121.
Wadsworth, Captain Jeremiah, 426.
Waldron, Richard, 329.
Walford, Thomas, 6.
Walton, George, 333.
Wardwell, Lydia, 56.
Washington, George, 117.
Washington Elm, 115.
Wentworth, Benning, 337.
Wesson, Margaret, 260.
Weston, Thomas, 365.
Whalley, Colonel Edward, 450.

Wharton, Edward, 311.
Wheelwright, Rev. John, 13, 18.
Whitefield, Rev. George, 289.
Whitman, Elizabeth, 196.
Whittier, J. G., 138, 145, 286. See "Contents."
Willis, N. P., 148.
Wilson, Deborah, 56.
Winnepurkit, 128.
Winslow, John, 380.
Winthrop, John, 17–21, 240.
Witchcraft, 169, 170, 188, 210, 253, 259. See Calef; Corey; Hibbins.
Wolcott, Governor Roger, 434.
Woodbridge, Benjamin, 69.
Woodworth, Samuel, 370.
Worthylake, George, 66.
Wyllys, Samuel, 422.
Wyllys Hill, 422.

University Press: John Wilson & Son, Cambridge.